PRAGMATICS

Routledge Applied Linguistics is a series of comprehensive textbooks, providing students and researchers with the support they need for advanced study in the core areas of English language and applied linguistics.

Each book in the series guides readers through three main sections, enabling them to explore and develop major themes within the discipline.

- Section A, Introduction, establishes the key terms and concepts and extends readers' techniques of analysis through practical application.
- Section B, Extension, brings together influential articles, sets them in context and discusses their contribution to the field.
- Section C, Exploration, builds on knowledge gained in the first two sections, setting thoughtful tasks around further illustrative material. This enables readers to engage more actively with the subject matter and encourages them to develop their own research responses.

Throughout the book, topics are revisited, extended, interwoven and deconstructed, with the reader's understanding strengthened by tasks and follow-up questions.

Pragmatics:

- Provides a broad view of pragmatics from a range of perspectives, gathering readings from key names in the discipline, including Geoffrey Leech, Michael McCarthy, Thomas Kohnen, Joan Manes and Nessa Wolfson
- Covers a wide variety of topics, including speech acts, pragmatic markers, implicature, research methods in pragmatics, facework and politeness, and prosody
- Examines the social and cultural contexts in which pragmatics occurs, such as in cross-cultural pragmatics (silence, indirectness, forms of address, cultural scripts) and pragmatics and power (the courtroom, police interaction, political interviews and doctor-patient communication)
- Uses a wide range of corpora to provide both illustrative examples and exploratory tasks
- Is supported by a companion website at www.routledge.com/cw/archer featuring extra activities and additional data for analysis, guidance on undertaking corpus analysis and research, including how to create your own corpus with CMC, and suggestions for further reading.

Written by experienced teachers and researchers in the field, *Pragmatics* provides an essential resource for students and researchers of applied linguistics.

Dawn Archer is Professor of Pragmatics and Corpus Linguistics at the University of Central Lancashire, UK. **Karin Aijmer** is Emeritus Professor of English at the University of Gothenburg, Sweden. **Anne Wichmann** is Emeritus Professor of Speech and Language at the University of Central Lancashire, UK.

'Pragmatics is a field of linguistics that has developed and diversified so immensely over the past thirty years, that it can easily make the student feel confused as well as fascinated. *Pragmatics: An advanced resource book for students* is an excellent answer to this problem – a rich tapestry of discussion, textual materials, and thought-provoking tasks, rendering pragmatic concepts and methods accessible both to the beginner and the advanced student. It is highly readable yet deeply informative, containing discussion of a wealth of stimulating and well-chosen textual examples. It introduces a wide range of approaches and key contributions to pragmatics with admirable clarity and even-handedness. It will undoubtedly prove a resource of lasting value and can be unreservedly recommended.'
Geoffrey Leech, *University of Lancaster, UK*

'This is an unusually rich textbook, which provides a wealth of resources for the study of the vast field of pragmatics. It includes some of the classics in the field as well as recent cutting-edge research in the various new subfields of pragmatics, such as politeness research, cross-cultural and intercultural research, and the pragmatics of prosody and non-verbal communication, and it accompanies these with student-friendly introductions and contextualizations as well as eminently doable exercises and research projects.'
Andreas H. Jucker, *University of Zurich, Switzerland*

'If a colleague, still active in teaching would ask me, as an emeritus, what I most regretted to have missed in my long teaching career, a serious candidate for an answer would be: Not to have had access to this eminent, and indeed practical, new textbook of pragmatics . . . the clear exposition, combined with a very practical approach . . . the clear and comprehensive, yet succinct coverage of many difficult subjects . . . and its up-to-date coverage make this an ideal acquisition . . . as a textbook for university courses at the senior undergraduate or early graduate level.'
Jacob L. Mey, *University of Southern Denmark*

'This book covers a wide range of topics, including the history and development of pragmatics, from issues which interested the speech act philosophers to an empirical area of study – how language is used in communication – with data from large corpora and experimental methods. The authors have managed to achieve a pedagogic structure of the book which makes it an ideal student text.'
Jan Svartvik, *Lund University, Sweden*

ROUTLEDGE APPLIED LINGUISTICS

SERIES EDITORS

Christopher N. Candlin is Senior Research Professor in the Department of Linguistics at Macquarie University, Australia. At Macquarie, he has been Chair of the Department of Linguistics; established and was Executive Director of the National Centre for English Language Teaching & Research and was the founding Director of the Centre for Language in Social Life . He has written or edited over 150 publications in the fields of language education, discourse analysis and professional communication and co-edits the *Journal of Applied Linguistics and Professional Practice*. From 1996 to 2002 he was President for two terms of the International Association of Applied Linguistics (AILA). He has acted as a consultant and as external faculty assessor in over 30 universities worldwide.

Ronald Carter is Professor of Modern English Language in the School of English Studies at the University of Nottingham. He has published extensively in the fields of applied linguistics, literary studies and language in education. He has given consultancies in the fields of applied linguistics and English language education, mainly in conjunction with The British Council, in over thirty countries worldwide and has been a regular linguistic adviser to UK government organisations. He is a fellow of the British Academy of Social Sciences and has been a recent chair of the British Association for Applied Linguistics (BAAL).

TITLES IN THE SERIES

Translation: An advanced resource book
Basil Hatim and Jeremy Munday

Grammar and Context: An advanced resource book
Ann Hewings and Martin Hewings

Second Language Acquisition: An advanced resource book
Kees de Bot, Wander Lowie and Marjolijn Verspoor

Corpus-Based Language Studies: An advanced resource book
Anthony McEnery, Richard Xiao and Yukio Tono

Language and Gender: An advanced resource book
Jane Sunderland

English for Academic Purposes: An advanced resource book
Ken Hyland

Language Testing and Assessment: An advanced resource book
Glenn Fulcher and Fred Davidson

Bilingualism: An advanced resource book
Ng Bee Chin and Gillian Wigglesworth

Literacy: An advanced resource book
Brian V. Street and Adam Lefstein

Language and Interaction: An advanced resource book
Richard F. Young

Intercultural Communication: An advanced resource book for students, Second Edition
Adrian Holliday, Martin Hyde and John Kullman

Research Methods for Applied Language Studies
Keith Richards, Steven J. Ross and Paul Seedhouse

Pragmatics

An advanced resource book for students

Dawn Archer, Karin Aijmer and Anne Wichmann

Routledge
Taylor & Francis Group

LONDON AND NEW YORK

First published 2012
by Routledge
2 Park Square, Milton Park, Abingdon, Oxon OX14 4RN

Simultaneously published in the USA and Canada
by Routledge
711 Third Avenue, New York, NY 10017

Routledge is an imprint of the Taylor & Francis Group, an informa business

British Library Cataloguing in Publication Data
A catalogue record for this book is available from the British Library

Library of Congress Cataloging in Publication Data
Archer, Dawn.
Pragmatics : an advanced resource book for students / Dawn Elizabeth Archer,
Karin Aijmer, Anne Wichmann.
p. cm. – (Routledge applied linguistics)
1. Pragmatics. 2. Linguistics. I. Aijmer, Karin. II. Wichmann, Anne, 1946– III. Title.
P99.4.P72A73 2012
401'.45–dc23
2011042494

ISBN: 978-0-415-49786-2 (hbk)
ISBN: 978-0-415-49787-9 (pbk)

Typeset in Akzidenz, Minion and Novarese
by Keystroke, Station Road, Codsall, Wolverhampton

Printed and bound in Great Britain by
TJ International Ltd, Padstow, Cornwall

Contents

Contents

Contents

Contents cross-referenced

Series editors' preface

The Routledge Applied Linguistics series provides a comprehensive guide to a number of key areas in the field of applied linguistics. Applied Linguistics is a rich, vibrant, diverse and essentially interdisciplinary field. It is now more important than ever that books in the field provide up-to-date maps of what is an ever-changing territory.

The books in this series are designed to give key insights into core areas of Applied Linguistics. The design of the books ensures, through key readings, that the history and development of a subject is recognized while, through key questions and tasks, integrating understandings of the topics, concepts and practices that make up its essentially interdisciplinary fabric. The pedagogic structure of each book ensures that readers are given opportunities to think, discuss, engage in tasks, draw on their own experience, reflect, research and to read and critically reread key documents.

Each book has three main sections, each made up of approximately ten units:

A: An **Introduction** section in which the key terms and concepts which map the field of the subject are introduced, including introductory activities and reflective tasks, designed to establish key understandings, terminology, techniques of analysis and the skills appropriate to the theme and the discipline.

B: An **Extension** section in which selected core readings are introduced (usually edited from the original) from existing key books and articles, together with annotations and commentary, where appropriate. Each reading is introduced, annotated and commented on in the context of the whole book, and research or follow-up questions and tasks are added to enable fuller understanding of both theory and practice. In some cases, readings are short and synoptic and incorporated within a more general exposition.

C: An **Exploration** section in which further samples and illustrative materials are provided with an emphasis, where appropriate, on more open-ended, student-centred activities and tasks, designed to support readers and users in undertaking their own locally relevant research projects. Tasks are designed for work in groups or for individuals working on their own. They can be readily included in award courses in Applied Linguistics, or as topics for personal study and research.

The target audience for the series is upper undergraduates and postgraduates on language, applied linguistics and communication studies programmes as well as teachers and researchers in professional development and distance learning programmes. High-quality applied research resources are also much needed for teachers of EFL/ESL and foreign language students at higher education colleges and universities worldwide. The books in the Routledge Applied Linguistics series are aimed at the individual reader, the student in a group and at teachers building courses and seminar programmes.

We hope that the books in this series meet these needs and continue to provide support over many years.

THE EDITORS

Professor Christopher N. Candlin and Professor Ronald Carter are the series editors. Both have extensive experience of publishing titles in the fields relevant to this series. Between them they have written and edited over one hundred books and two hundred academic papers in the broad field of applied linguistics. Chris Candlin was president of AILA (International Association of Applied Linguistics) from 1996 to 2002 and Ron Carter was Chair of BAAL (British Association for Applied Linguistics) from 2003 to 2006.

Professor Christopher N. Candlin
Senior Research Professor
Department of Linguistics
Division of Linguistics and Psychology
Macquarie University
Sydney NSW 2109
Australia

Professor Ronald Carter
School of English Studies
University of Nottingham
Nottingham NG7 2RD
UK

and

Professor of Applied Linguistics
Faculty of Education & Language Studies
The Open University
Walton Hall
Milton Keynes MK7 6AA
UK

Acknowledgements

The authors are extremely grateful to the many colleagues and, most importantly, the students past and present who have inspired our presentation of the topics in this advanced textbook. We hope that they are pleased with the result – and that our readers find this book stimulating and challenging in equal measure.

Several people deserve a special mention. The general editors of the volume, Ron Carter and Chris Candlin, provided us with extremely useful feedback on an earlier draft. The Routledge team, Isabelle Cheng, Nadia Seemungal and Louisa Semlyen, have been hugely supportive throughout the whole process. We are grateful to Nicole Dehé and Kevin Watson for providing the Praat pictures, to Traci Walker for the transcription sample in Unit A2.4, to Christian Jones for advice on pragmatics in EFL, and to Nicole Richter for discussion of non-verbal communication. Finally, we would like to thank our families for their support during the writing process.

6. Verlag Walter De Gruyter GmbH & Co. for permission to reprint extracts from Joan Manes and Nessa Wolfson 1981 'The compliment formula', in Coulmas, F. (ed.) *Conversational routine. Explorations in standardized communication situations and prepatterned speech.* The Hague: Mouton. Pp. 115–132. Selected pages 116–19.

7. Reprinted from *Journal of Pragmatics*, Vol. 41, edition number 8, Andreas Jucker 2009. 'Speech act research between armchair, field and laboratory. The case of compliments', pp. 1621–2. Copyright 2009 with permission from Elsevier.

8. Oxford University Press for permission to reprint Eisenstein, M. and J. Bodman. 1993. 'Expressing gratitude in American English', in Kasper, G. and S. Blum-Kulka (eds) *Interlanguage Pragmatics.* Oxford: Oxford University Press, pp. 65–8.

9. Penguin Group UK for kind permission to reprint 574 words from *Semantics* by Geoffrey Leech (Penguin Books, 1974, 1981). Copyright Geoffrey Leech, 1974, 1981.

10. Wilson (2010) 'Relevance Theory' section, pp. 393–7, extracts from *The Routledge pragmatics encyclopedia*, edited by Louise Cummings. Copyright © 2010 Routledge. Reproduced by permission of Taylor & Francis Books UK.

11. Reproduced by permission Oxford University Press. From OAL: *English Conversation* by Amy Tsui © Oxford University Press 1994. Pp. 30–5.

12. University of Chicago Press for permission to reprint Michael Stubbs. 1983. *Discourse analysis: the sociolinguistic analysis of natural language.* Oxford: Blackwell, selected pages: pp. 184–6 with omissions.

13. Taylor and Francis Ltd for permission to reprint Michael McCarthy. 2003. 'Talking back: "small" interactional response tokens in everyday conversation', in *Research on language and social interaction*, pp. 46–50. Reprinted by permission of the publisher (Taylor & Francis Ltd, http://www.tandf.co.uk/journals).

14. John Benjamins Publishing Co. for permission to reprint extracts from Giuliana Diani. 2004. 'The discourse functions of "I don't know" in English conversation', in Aijmer, K. and A.-B. Stenström (eds) *Discourse patterns in spoken and written corpora.* Benjamins. Pp. 161–3.

15. Verlag Walter De Gruyter GmbH & Co. for permission to reprint extracts from Guilquin, G. 2008. 'Hesitation markers among EFL learners: pragmatic deficiency or difference?', in J. Romero-Trillo (ed.) *Pragmatics and corpus linguistics.* Berlin: Mouton de Gruyter. Selected pages: pp. 128–30, 141–2, 142–3.

16. Continuum for permission to reprint Christoph Rühlemann. 2007. *Conversation in context: A corpus-driven approach.* London: Continuum. Pp. 143–7. By kind permission of Continuum International Publishing Group.

17. Verlag Walter De Gruyter GmbH & Co. for permission to reprint extracts from O'Driscoll. 2007. 'Brown and Levinson's face – how it can and can't help us to understand interaction across cultures'. *Intercultural Pragmatics* 4-4 (2007), pp. 473–7.

18. Cambridge University Press and the author for permission to reprint Watts, R. 2003. *Politeness.* Cambridge University Press. Extracts totalling 389 words

within pp. 257–9 © Richard J. Watts, 2003, published by Cambridge University Press, reproduced with permission.

19. Reprinted from *Journal of Pragmatics*, Vol. 35, edition number 10/11, Culpeper, J., D. Bousfield and A. Wichmann. 2003. 'Impoliteness revisited: with special reference to dynamic and prosodic aspects', pp. 1545–79. Copyright 2003 with permission from Elsevier. Pp. 1562–8 (edited).

20. Verlag Walter de Gruyter for permission to print extracts (pp. 53–4, 56–7 with omissions) from Mennen, I. 2007 'Phonological and phonetic influences in non-native intonation', in J. Trouvain and U. Gut (eds) *Non-native prosody: phonetic description and teaching practices* (2007), pp. 53–76.

21. Reprinted from *Journal of Pragmatics*, Vol. 36, edition 9, Wichmann, A. 2004. 'The intonation of please-requests: a corpus based study', pp. 1543–5. Copyright 2004 with permission from Elsevier.

22. Cambridge University Press and the author for permission to reprint Carlos Gussenhoven. 2004. *The phonology of tone and intonation.* Cambridge University Press. Section on the 'frequency code' pp. 80–2. © 2004 Carlos Gussenhoven, published by Cambridge University Press, reproduced with permission.

23. Verlag Walter De Gruyter GmbH & Co. for permission to reprint extracts from Wierzbicka. 2003. *Cross-cultural pragmatics.* Berlin: Mouton de Gruyter, pp. 88–9, 92–93.

24. Equinox Publishing Ltd for permission to reprint Jenny Thomas. 1983. 'Cross-cultural pragmatic failure'. *Applied Linguistics* 4: 102, 103, 106–8. Copyright © Equinox Publishing Ltd, 1983.

25. Routledge for permission to reprint Argyle. 1988. *Bodily communication,* second edition, London: Routledge, pp. 57–60, with omissions. © 1988 Routledge. Reproduced by permission of Taylor & Francis Books UK.

26. Culpeper. 2010. Overview of 'Historical pragmatics', pp. 190–2 with omissions from *The Routledge pragmatics encyclopedia,* edited by Louise Cummings. Copyright © 2010 Routledge. Reproduced by permission of Taylor & Francis Books UK.

27. Editions Rodopi B.V. for permission to reprint extracts from Thomas Kohnen. 2009. 'Historical corpus pragmatics: focus on speech acts and texts', in *Corpora: pragmatics and discourse.* Papers from the 29th International Conference on English Language Research on Computerized Corpora, ed. by Andreas H. Jucker, Daniel Schreier and Marianne Hundt. Amsterdam: Rodopi. Pp. 19–20.

28. John Benjamins Publishing Co. for permission to reprint extracts from Taavitsainen and Jucker. 2008. '"Methinks you seem more beautiful than ever". Compliments and gender in the history of English', in *Speech acts in the history of English.* Benjamins. Pp. 208–11.

29. Van Dijk, Teun. 'Discourse, context and cognition'. *Discourse Studies* 8(1). Sage publishers, pp. 159, 165, 166–8 with omissions. Copyright © 2006 by Sage. Reprinted by Permission of SAGE.

30. Reprinted from *Journal of Pragmatics*, Vol. 23, edition number 2, Harris, Sandra. 1995. 'Pragmatics and power', pp. 119, 122–4. Copyright 1995 with permission from Elsevier.

31. Sage for permission to reprint extracts from Haworth, Kate. 2006. 'The dynamics of power and resistance in police interview discourse'. *Discourse & Society*, Vol. 17(6), pp. 744, 745, 746–7, 754, 755 with omissions. Copyright © 2006 by Sage. Reprinted by Permission of SAGE.

DISCLAIMER

How to use this book

Pragmatics is a rapidly developing field. From its beginnings in ordinary language philosophy with a focus on 'how to do things with words', pragmatics has grown into a full-blown theory of communication and language use.

Whilst a pragmatics-based perspective could be said to be pervading linguistics and communication studies more generally, 'pragmatics' as a term remains an elusive notion. In this book we have tried to do justice to the origins of the discipline, to its cross-fertilization with other disciplines such as sociolinguistics, psycholinguistics and discourse analysis and to more recent developments. Hence, in addition to covering the origins of pragmatics and the essential concepts in pragmatics, the present volume also describes some of the newer areas in pragmatics. These include historical pragmatics, critical pragmatics, cross-cultural pragmatics and the contribution of prosody and non-verbal communication to pragmatic meaning.

We also include an overview of the methodological approaches to pragmatics. Pragmatics has become an empirical area of study, and we discuss what constitutes empirical evidence. In particular, pragmatics research has become characterized by the use of corpora and more experimental methods. Large corpora can provide the data for studying how pragmatic phenomena such as speech acts or pragmatic markers are used in a variety of social activities and by different speakers. Corpus data provides illustration for many of the points we make, and is also the basis of some of the exploratory tasks that are proposed in the third section of the book.

The book has three sections

- Section A Introduction: contains twelve chapters which address the origins, essential concepts and applications of pragmatics. These chapters, some of which contain brief exercises to guide your understanding, can stand alone as an overview of the current extent of the field of pragmatics.
- Section B Extensions: the twelve chapters provide extracts from published books or articles that relate to each topic in Section A. Each reading is followed by tasks that help you to understand and to critically evaluate what you have read. In addition we suggest a number of other publications that will help you to understand the topic, and explain how they are relevant.
- Section C Exploration: contains nine chapters, each of which addresses one or more of the topics presented systematically in Sections A and B. They contain

questions, activities and small research projects. These chapters are designed first to help you understand first hand some of the problems that arise in empirical work: what sounds so simple in a published article is often much more difficult to achieve in practice. Second, and most importantly, these projects should help you apply your understanding of pragmatics to your own context and culture, whether English is your first language or a language you are in the process of learning. In many cases we provide corpus data for you to work on, or links to corpora that you can explore yourself, but you are also encouraged to gather your own data, in situations determined by yourself.

There are a number of ways of working with this book. As we said above, Section A can stand alone as an overview of the field, but it is best read in conjunction with the respective units of Section B, which introduce you to some of the original research on which our overview is based. Before embarking on any of the research projects in Section C, it is crucial to understand something of the methodologies used in pragmatics, and for this reason we recommend that Unit C1 should be addressed before any of the others. Whatever order you choose, however, there are extensive cross-references that should help you find your way around the book.

SECTION A
Introduction

Unit A1
The origins of pragmatics

Pragmatics, according to Robin Lakoff (1993: 367), is concerned with 'the interesting stuff about language'. And indeed there is a lot of 'interesting stuff' out there in the real world which needs to be explained. How is it that what we say is not always what we mean? And how is it that we are nonetheless understood? How is language used to manipulate, challenge or change ideas? How can it be used to exert power in a social context? Linguistic pragmatics has opened up a large area of research and given us tools to explain why we say what we do. However, there is little consensus about the definition of pragmatics, how pragmatics should be delimited from semantics and grammar, the scope of a discipline of linguistic pragmatics and the terminology we need to describe pragmatic phenomena (e.g. terms such as inference, illocutionary force, presupposition). In this introduction we will give a preview of the pragmatic issues dealt with in the rest of the book. We will discuss what we mean by pragmatics in this work and why we believe it is such an attractive and innovative area of linguistic research.

A1.1 DEFINITION AND DELIMITATION OF PRAGMATICS

The word 'pragmatics' was a newcomer on the scene when it was introduced into linguistics in the 1980s but had been used before that to refer to one of the branches of inquiry in the philosopher Charles Morris' (1938) tripartite division of semiotics (the theory of signs) into syntax, semantics and pragmatics. Syntax described the combinatory possibility of signs; semantics the relationship between signs and their denotata; while pragmatics referred to the relationship between signs and their interpreters. Morris' semiotic theory gives a broad definition of pragmatics which is not only limited to linguistic signs. The definition of pragmatics as the relationship between signs and their users is open to several interpretations when it is used in linguistics. The term pragmatics as used by Morris has therefore been redefined in different ways to suit the goals of a discipline, 'linguistic pragmatics'.

In one sense of the term, pragmatics now refers to a special perspective on different aspects of linguistic communication (including phonetics, lexicology, syntax and semantics). This usage of the term linguistic pragmatics (characterized by Mey 2001 as the Continental view) is well described in the following quotation:

> Linguistic pragmatics . . . can be said to characterize a new way of looking
> at things linguistic [i.e. a 'perspective'] rather than marking off clear bound-
> aries to other disciplines.
>
> (Haberland and Mey 1977: 5, quoted from Mey 2001: 9)

The perspective view of pragmatics does not delimit pragmatics from other
components of linguistic theory such as syntax or semantics, but it does show
how pragmatics differs from related disciplines involved in research on language
use:

> . . . some major questions remain: how to delimit pragmatics vis-à-vis
> syntax and semantics (let alone phonology)? What is the role of pragmatics
> in the so-called 'hyphenated areas' of research (psycho-, neuro-, socio-,
> ethno-, . . . etc. linguistics)?
>
> (Mey 2001: 5)

In the Anglo-American tradition the term pragmatics is distinguished from
semantics (i.e. meaning is approached from a point of view which regards semantics
and pragmatics as complementary perspectives). Semantics in the narrow sense is
concerned with the kind of meaning which belongs in truth-conditional semantics,
and pragmatics with other types of meaning (e.g. the type of inferences we can make
from what is said) (see Unit A5). However, the boundary between semantics and
pragmatics may well be fuzzy since lexical elements are constantly drawn into the
pragmatic sphere by means of changes associated with grammaticalization and
particularly 'pragmaticalization' (see Unit A3).

Pragmatics is a fast-growing discipline characterized by a large output of research.
There are many reasons for this. One explanation is that an increasing number of
phenomena are now seen to depend on context for their interpretation and should
be analysed in pragmatics. These include pragmatic markers such as *well, anyhow*
and related phenomena such as interjections or vocatives. Notions such as presupposition are problematic to analyse in semantics and need a pragmatic solution.
Besides linguistic features there are prosodic phenomena such as stress and
intonation which can be related to the function of an utterance or to features of the
context such as speaker attitudes or power relations (Unit A12).

A second contributing factor to the expansion of pragmatics as a discipline is the
realization that we need a broad theory of human communication going beyond
what is treated in semantics, which can explain how human beings use language to
express what they mean on different levels. As Levinson (1983: 38) has noted:

> . . . there is a very substantial gap between current linguistic theories of
> language and accounts of linguistic communication . . . For it is becoming
> increasingly clear that a semantic theory alone can give us only a propor-
> tion, and perhaps only a small if essential proportion, of a general account
> of language understanding.

Despite the clear need/motivation for such an approach, there are a number of problems for a pragmatic theory of communication or language use. How do we define context? How do we define 'pragmatic meaning' and how is it distinguished from other types of meaning? What principles are needed to explain how we can read new things into what is said? How is pragmatics delimited (if at all) from other disciplines studying language usage? How is it related to the analysis of discourse (conversation), for example? Should pragmatics be defined in a broad sense as a cognitive theory of communication or as 'pragmatics only' (explaining what people mean by what they are saying)? Cognitive approaches have been influential in areas such as cognitive psychology, artificial intelligence and the neurosciences. Cognitive issues are also the basis for the approach to pragmatics represented in Relevance Theory (often known as RT) (Sperber and Wilson 1995). The focus in Relevance Theory is on the human cognitive ability to interpret what is said by means of inferencing, and a general communicative principle guaranteeing that the hearer arrives at the most appropriate interpretation with a minimum of cognitive efforts.

A1.2 PRAGMATICS AND THE RELATIONSHIP TO OTHER DISCIPLINES

Philosophers interested in language are concerned with the truth of sentences. When the Oxford philosopher Austin questioned the long-established 'truth' that all (declarative) sentences had to be either true or false and changed the perspective to asking 'how we do things with words' this had far-reaching consequences not only for philosophy but concurrently for linguistics. From the idea of 'doing things with words' came the notion of a 'speech act', which will be discussed in a separate chapter in this book (Unit A4). Despite recent criticisms of its applicability, philosophical speech act theory remains important to our understanding of the development of pragmatics:

> . . . even if historically, the discovery of speech acts has been instrumental
> in paving the way toward a better understanding of our use of language,
> the actual input of speech act theory to the analysis of 'real' language use
> has not always been impressive.
>
> (Mey 2001: 189)

Recently, pragmatic research has taken a different turn. There is now little discussion of the issues which interested the speech act philosophers (such as felicity conditions, speech act classification, etc.). Rather, speech acts tend to be analysed from the perspective of 'real language use', for example, in terms of their structuring role of building up dialogic units or speech events (see Unit A6). Pragmatics has also become more oriented to societal issues, and hence is increasingly being drawn upon when exploring the connections between language, ideology and power (see Unit A12).

Pragmatics is analysed differently depending on the researcher's perspective and aims. The social aspects of language use were neglected for a long time perhaps because of the philosophical bias of the foundations of pragmatics. Leech (1983) introduced a useful distinction between sociopragmatics and pragmalinguistics, where pragmalinguistics is the study of pragmatics focusing on the linguistic resources used for a particular function, while sociopragmatics is the 'sociological interface of pragmatics'. It deals, for instance, with the influence of sociolinguistic variables, such as the speaker's age, gender, etc., on their use of language. The result is a 'rapprochement' between pragmatics and other disciplines such as sociolinguistics.

★ Task A1.2

➤ Sociolinguistic variables such as gender and age have an effect on a speaker's use of language. For example, despite the folk-linguistic belief that women swear less than men, Jennifer Coates claims that both 'women and men swear more in the company of their own sex' (2004: 97). What other social variables might affect a speaker's use of language such as swearing?

Pragmatics can also be studied in a way that draws on cognitive science (see above), computational linguistics and other disciplines. In this sense pragmatics is – and always has been – interdisciplinary:

> Linguistic pragmatics . . . is at the intersection of a number of fields within and outside of cognitive science: not only linguistics, cognitive psychology, cultural anthropology, and philosophy (logic, semantics, action theory) but also sociology (interpersonal dynamics and social convention) and rhetoric contribute to its domain.
>
> (Green 1996: 1–2, quoted from Cummings 2005: 1)

Fields such as philosophy but also the ethnography of speaking, conversation analysis and contemporary linguistic anthropology (Gumperz, Ochs) have, for instance, been central to the growth of pragmatics as a discipline. Pragmatics also has applications within a number of areas resulting in new 'types of pragmatics' such as clinical pragmatics, developmental pragmatics, discourse pragmatics, etc.

A1.3 SPEAKER MEANING AND SENTENCE MEANING

We have already suggested that meaning is used differently in semantics than in pragmatics. Semanticists are mainly interested in the type of meaning which involves the truth-conditional content of utterances. In pragmatics, meaning includes the inferences which can be drawn from the structural or literal meaning. For example, 'It's hot in here' can be a statement of fact, but it can also constitute an indirect request (for a window to be opened). The two types of meaning can be talked about as sentence meaning (or literal meaning) on the one hand and speaker meaning on the other (if we take the hearer's perspective we can also refer to utterance meaning).

The meaning communicated by the utterance may also convey something about the speaker's attitudes, social roles, the type of situation, attitudes, etc. How much of this meaning is 'pragmatic' (and hence can be studied as part of a pragmatic approach) is still a matter of some debate (as we will discuss in Units A3 and A12).

A1.4 CONTEXT AND FUNCTION

The study of the use of language can be approached in different ways. One starting point is to focus on the different functions that utterances can have. Halliday (1970, 1973), for instance, has suggested that we need to distinguish between an ideational, textual and interpersonal function. The ideational function describes language as a way of experiencing and interpreting the world. This function is intrinsic to grammar. The two latter functions on the other hand are closely associated with how language is used. The interpersonal function is associated with language as an expression of attitudes and an influence on the attitudes of the hearer. The textual function is defined as the function of language in constructing a text.

Pragmatics has opened our eyes to the fact that we need a rich description of the context in order to understand what is said. For example, how we use language to mean different things can depend on whether we have a chat with a friend or engage in a job interview or take part in a debate. Context has been studied in many disciplines but there is little consensus about the features which are needed to describe how it is used in the production and interpretation of utterances. The linguistic context is limited to what is grammatically expressed in the utterance and cannot explain linguistic phenomena, which can only be understood with reference to the speaker or hearer. We therefore need a broader definition of context which goes beyond the linguistic context (or cotext) and includes the speaker, the hearer and other situational variables which are relevant for the interpretation of the utterances. In the social sciences one finds a number of descriptions of the dimensions of the socio-cultural situation. According to Ochs (1996: 410; emphasis in original), for example:

> . . . 'situation' is usually broadly conceived and includes socio-cultural dimensions a member activates to be part of the situation at hand such as the *temporal and spatial locus* of the communicative situation, the *social identities* of participants, the *social acts* and *activities* taking place, and participants' *affective and epistemic stance.*

Typical examples might be the social activity (such as a debate or classroom lesson), the social role or identity of the speaker (as a judge or a teacher), mental elements such as beliefs or affects which can be reflected in the speaker's involvement in the message communicated. The challenge for the pragmatician is to discover which features are mobilized by the speaker in the production process in actual language use (and which the hearer recovers in order to interpret the utterance).

Task A1.4

➤ Language is used differently in the classroom from ordinary conversation. For example, it is often thought that only the teacher is allowed to ask questions. Is this true in your experience? Is there a difference between the kinds of questions that teachers ask and those that students ask? How might we account for this difference – what role might power, age or status play?

In the theory referred to as Conversation Analysis (often known as CA) people's use of language is explored without any previous assumptions of what the context is. What Conversation Analysis considers to be context is strictly that of co-text, i.e. the analyst does not to go beyond the speech event and its sequential environment to describe the context. Unlike other ideas discussed above which assume a rich description of the context, 'CA is a minimalist approach, which allows only so much hypothesizing as is strictly required to explain the phenomena at hand' (Mey 2001: 135). Conversation Analysis (to be discussed in Unit A6) shows how the context needed to interpret what is said is created by the interactants themselves in the course of the sequential development of the discourse, for example. In the inter-actional perspective we can study how the speaker's utterance is affected by the preceding discourse and by the beliefs and assumptions which are the result of what has taken place earlier in the communication. In a Critical Discourse Analysis (CDA) approach, on the other hand, the societal aspects of the (institutional) context are important. These include any relevant cultural, historical or political conditions.

A1.5 PRAGMATIC THEORIES

There is a tension between socio-cultural and cognitive approaches to pragmatics reflecting the fact that communication can be studied from different perspectives. The cognitive approach which has received most attention is Relevance Theory. Relevance Theory was launched as a pragmatic theory 'rethinking Grice' (Sperber and Wilson 1995). There is now a strong Relevance Theory movement sometimes referred to as the London School of Pragmatics (Mey 2001: 83). In Relevance Theory, the interpretation of the utterances is achieved by balancing the mental effort of processing what is said with processing it in the most economic (and optimally relevant) way (see Unit A5).

Relevance Theory has been criticized as being abstract and removed from how 'real people' use language to communicate. Although it can successfully explain the speakers' cognitive abilities to interpret utterances, it explains the role of culture and society in communication only indirectly in the form of speakers' assumptions and cultural beliefs (but see Unit A12).

In a social or sociopragmatic perspective on the other hand there is more focus on how people use language in conversation, debates, courtroom examinations, and how they use languages for their social goals. However, we do not have to choose between pragmatic theories. Both the sociopragmatic and the cognitive or relevance-theoretic approach are needed to analyse the complexities of communication and have resulted in fresh insights about how meaning is produced and understood in context.

A1.6 PRAGMATICS AND METHODOLOGY

We are open to different methodological approaches. For example, pragmatic research can be carried out by using 'laboratory' methods or field methods using the researcher's own ethnographic data (Clark and Bangerter 2004). This has been common especially in speech act studies where the use of questionnaires makes it possible to control the influence of contextual factors in the study of requests and apologies across different cultures (see Unit A10). However, throughout the book we will show how data from electronic spoken corpora can bring new insights about pragmatic issues by providing detailed information about the context (who the speakers and hearers are, their relationship, the social setting, topic, etc.).

A1.7 CHALLENGES FOR THE FUTURE

The field of pragmatics is characterized both by a lively discussion of theoretical issues and a broadening of the field to new applications and new areas of research. The number of applications is numerous and only a few can be discussed in this work. For example, pragmatics has been applied to societal issues such as power structure and class, and Unit A12 on Pragmatics and Power examines these issues, in a way that compares CDA studies with pragmatics-based studies of institutional interaction. We also pick up on applied pragmatics. For example, we explore how researchers have sought to apply/test pragmatic theory and pragmatic notions as part of an experimental approach (see Unit C3). Pragmatics also has important applications in the area of second or foreign language learning. The branch of interlanguage pragmatics studies how learners use speech acts or pragmatic markers on the basis of corpora consisting of learner language and makes quantitative and qualitative comparisons with native speakers. 'Pragmatics' as a term has not made its way into school books. However, the pragmatic perspective is visible in the teaching of language functions and communication skills and in the Council of Europe's description of learning objectives needed to assure learners' communicative ability and in most modern language teaching materials.

We can expect to see more cross-fertilization between pragmatics and other branches of linguistics. The interest in the social and cultural context and the revival of interest in the Whorfian ideas about the relationship between language forms and patterns of thinking in linguistic anthropology are close to the concerns of pragmatics. Variational pragmatics (Schneider and Barron 2008; Barron and Schneider 2009) is a new area of study with roots in dialectology which studies speech acts and other pragmatic phenomena especially in regional social varieties of languages.

Another developing area of interest is the relationship between pragmatics, gesture and prosody (see Unit A9). Last but not least, the availability of large electronic corpora of spoken and written language has provided new methods of analysis for pragmaticians. For example, large corpora with parallel texts from different languages mean that we can now study the minutiae of language use; and hence test current ideas regarding language universals (or the lack thereof). Globalization and internationalization of society also create a demand for more cross-linguistic studies with applications in areas such as translation studies.

Summary and looking ahead

In this introductory chapter, a large number of topics have been introduced which will be expanded on in the following units. We have discussed different definitions of pragmatics focusing on the distinction between the perspective view of pragmatics and a broader view of pragmatics, including its societal aspects and applications in different areas. In Unit B1 we include excerpts which also discuss the emergence of pragmatics. In the first extract, Nerlich draws attention to the development of pragmatics from its semiotic roots. It is shown that in addition to the British 'philosophical school' there is also a German and a French tradition in pragmatics. In the second extract Leech describes the emergence of a linguistic pragmatic discipline as a shift which co-occurred with the undermining of generative theory as a paradigm for studying pragmatic phenomena.

As will become clear as you work through the coming units, pragmatics is a rapidly expanding discipline that includes the study of many different phenomena which depend on 'the context' for their interpretation. These phenomena include pragmatic markers (Unit A7) and also presupposition and implicature (Unit A5). This broadening of the discipline, in turn, has raised questions about what we mean by context. Context, in the Conversation Analytic tradition, often equates to co-text, for example (see Unit A6). This approach can be contrasted with the rich interpretation of context in sociolinguistics. We have also suggested that there is no single pragmatic theory. Relevance Theory has focused on the role of conversational principles for inferencing and utterance interpretation (see Unit A5). However, it is criticized by some for being too abstract in comparison with social theories of communication. Much of our introductory discussion has dealt with pragmatics in general. It is useful to go beyond 'general pragmatics' and distinguish between sociopragmatics and pragmalinguistics. This distinction constitutes a watershed between studies focusing on sociopragmatic beliefs and communicative misunderstandings, and pragmatic studies dealing with linguistic phenomena which can only be explained by bringing in pragmatic notions.

Unit A2
Research methods in pragmatics

As you read this unit, you will become familiar with the different methodologies available to those who study pragmatics and also the practical limitations of engaging in research into pragmatics. Even before we begin our studies, however, we must first consider what it is that we want to research, and why we want to research it. This, in turn, raises additional questions. These include where to find our evidence: should we use existing data, for example, or collect our own data; and, if the latter, what should we do about the 'observer's paradox'? Let us begin by considering the observer's paradox in more detail.

A2.1 DATA COLLECTION AND THE OBSERVER'S PARADOX

Pragmatics is the study of how language is used to express meaning in context. Although introspection is still commonly used in other areas of linguistics and some parts of pragmatics, observational studies – i.e. noting what people actually say and write in real life – are most common in pragmatics. Observational studies are not as easy to undertake as we might imagine, however. Indeed, it has been shown that, when people know they are being observed, they change their behaviour. We are therefore faced with a paradox:

> ... the aim of linguistic research in the community must be to find out how people talk when they are not being systematically observed; yet we can only obtain this data by systematic observation.
>
> (Labov 1970: 32)

This paradox is at the heart of difficulties in obtaining data for pragmatic research in an ethical and legitimate way, without fearing that the interaction that has been observed has been influenced in some way by the observational situation. The problem depends to some extent on the kind of data being collected: to overhear someone in a public place and note down what they say is not unethical providing that the source remains anonymous. Researchers today, however, are increasingly recording their data. Although recording spoken language does not eliminate the observer's paradox, there are ways in which we can minimize its effect. We know, for example, that participants tend to become less aware of the recording process as time passes, and it is therefore sensible to focus our analysis on the later parts of recordings. We also know that people can be distracted if they are emotionally involved in the talk: if they are retelling frightening or amusing events, for example, they are much less likely to think about the recording equipment.

Even when we use broadcast speech as data we must be aware that participants are to some extent 'performing' for an audience. This may affect certain aspects of talk – there may be self-censoring in the use of taboo language, for example – but it is unlikely to affect all aspects of their talk. Hence, the value of such data will depend very much on the goal of one's research. With this 'observer's paradox' in mind, we will now examine the kinds of data that are commonly investigated in pragmatics.

A2.2 DATA TYPES

The kind of data used for most pragmatic research (excluding that derived from introspection) consists of collections of written and spoken language. Some of this data is described as 'authentic': this means that it would have occurred anyway without the intervention of the researcher. Data can also be deliberately elicited by the researcher, by setting up conversations or speaking tasks for the purpose of analysis, for example. In essence, then, elicited data is 'brought into being for research purposes' whilst authentic data 'is motivated and structured by participants' without the involvement of the researcher (Kasper 2000: 317). In the following sub-sections, we discuss the main differences between authentic and elicited data, and provide you with examples of studies which have drawn on different data types.

A2.2.1 Authentic data – written

Authentic written data includes a large variety of published texts, from instructions given with medicines through posters to government leaflets – and even university mission statements. Newspaper articles have proven to be a particularly popular (authentic) dataset. Van Dijk (1992a) and Baker *et al.* (2008), for example, represent two of many news-related studies which explore the 'hidden agenda' in the discourse around ethnic minority groups and racism in Britain.

Baker *et al.*'s study, in particular, is typical of many studies based on collections of written texts: the authors compiled a corpus containing articles taken from twelve national and three regional newspapers, as well as their Sunday editions, between 1996 and 2005. Because the corpus is electronic in format, the authors also make use of computerized text analysis tools to investigate their data. Two tools often used by Baker and others are WordSmith Tools and the UCREL Semantic Annotation System (USAS). These particular tools enable researchers to undertake systematic searches of certain words/phrases. For example, they can look at how these words/ phrases are used in context, via concordances, and hence determine instances of hidden association or 'semantic prosody' (i.e. how apparently neutral terms come to be perceived with positive or negative associations). In Unit C9, we give you an opportunity to undertake your own newspaper studies using an existing corpus of newspaper front pages, LexisNexis and/or other sources.

A2.2.2 Authentic data – spoken

A2.2.2.1 Field notes

Unlike writing, speech is ephemeral, and the challenge to the researcher is how to capture something that by its nature is not permanent. One way of doing this is to observe and to take field notes. Many researchers in pragmatics are persistent 'eavesdroppers' in their everyday lives. Jenny Thomas' (1995) book contains very many examples that she overheard – on the bus, in the university corridor or in friends' houses. These examples usually serve to illustrate well-known phenomena rather than serving as data for research. Nevertheless, some casual observations can reveal language use that is surprising, and hence become the start of a wider project. For example, a chance overhearing of a train passenger's response to an announce-ment led to an extensive study of the prosody of emphatic requests (Wichmann 2005). Some field notes – such as those Labov made when studying rhoticity in American speech – are gathered with a particular phenomenon in mind. When such studies are based on a large amount of data – say, a substantial number of apologies or requests – researchers often enlist the help of assistants or students in collecting them (see Units A4 and A10). The advantage of such field notes is that the subjects are not aware of being observed. The disadvantage is that we cannot check the accuracy of the observation, as would be possible if the speech was recorded.

A2.2.2.2 Broadcast data

Radio and television broadcasts provide researchers with a huge amount of spoken data. Some broadcasts are scripted, of course, but it is possible to collect unscripted data in this way too. Culpeper (1996, 2010) and Bousfield (2008), for example, have drawn on television 'docusoaps' such as *Soldiers To Be, Soldier Girl, Clampers, Boiling Point*, etc., to study impoliteness. Such data needs to be used sensitively, of course, as it has been heavily edited by others for entertainment purposes. In addition, we need to consider what impact the observer's paradox may be having: we do not know whether people are behaving exactly as they would if they were not being recorded. The positive features of such data include it being in the public domain, meaning that no permissions are required to use it. It is also considered to be 'authentic', in the sense that it was not produced for the benefit of the researcher.

Fictional programmes offer researchers another useful form of broadcast data. Although artificially constructed, TV sitcoms such as *Friends* have not been brought into being for research purposes either (cf. Kasper 2000: 317). It's worth noting, however, that some of the disfluency features that we commonly associate with speech will not be present in television dialogue. It is therefore worth checking with a source like Quaglio (2009) before beginning any studies that make use of *Friends* and similar sitcoms (Quaglio compares dialogues from *Friends* with natural conversation).

A2.2.2.3 Recording

The problems associated with recording authentic conversation have already been mentioned, as have some of the ways of minimizing the effect of the observer's paradox (see above). There are other challenges to be faced too. Natural data is generally recorded in its natural habitat (as opposed to a sound-proofed laboratory, for example). However, natural habitats can be noisy. Background noise can include the sounds of plates, knives and forks during a dinner conversation, other people's conversations in public places, and interruptions such as telephones ringing. In addition, people tend to move about and their voices are not always picked up by microphones. All this can pose a serious challenge to transcribers, who are often forced to add '[*unintelligible*]' in various places in their transcription. It poses an even greater challenge to anyone wishing to make a study of prosody. Most work on prosody nowadays exploits a mixture of auditory and instrumental analysis. Special software can display pitch patterns on the computer screen, and allow close analysis of pauses, for example. But – unlike a human listener – a computer cannot differentiate between the human voice and clattering plates. Hence, we always have to be prepared to compromise – for high-quality recordings mean unnatural situations. To make the best use of language produced in an everyday situation, it is often necessary to rely in places solely on auditory analysis, in other words what the researcher can identify by close (and often repeated) listening. But this means that the transcription itself, not only of what was said but how it was said, can be a crucial source of information. We will look closely at the transcription process in Unit A2.4.

A2.2.3 The hybridity issue

Some texts are hybrid, i.e. display both written and spoken language features. This is true for spoken language that is scripted, such as stories read aloud, lectures or speeches. As we highlight in Unit A2.2.2.2 above, we can also have the opposite: a written text that represents spoken language – these include play/TV scripts and courtroom trial transcripts. Let us focus, for a moment, on trial transcripts. These are a particularly interesting text-type because the transcript represents speech that actually occurred but which is unlikely to be *truly* verbatim (see Unit A2.4). For the study of present day spoken language, it is better (for this reason) to study recordings of what was actually said (whenever possible). However, when we are trying to find out how people spoke in the past – centuries before tape recording was a possibility – trial transcripts often provide one of the best means of re-enacting what was said and how it was said. We return to this issue in Unit A11.

A2.2.4 Elicited data

It is important to say at the outset that elicited data is not ideal, mainly because people do not necessarily know what they would actually say or do in a real situation. What they think they would say is not necessarily what they would really say. This does not mean that informants are not telling the truth, but simply that native speakers do not usually think about how they express thanks, or apologize, or make requests; they simply know that they do these things. Nevertheless, elicited data can be a useful guide to the range of resources available to speakers, and can provide the starting point for systematic study of naturally occurring data.

A2.2.4.1 Discourse completion tasks

A common way of eliciting pragmatic information such as the formulation of speech acts (thanking, apologizing, etc.) is the discourse completion task (DCT). These sometimes involve giving a written description of a communicative situation to the subject and asking them to write what they would say in that situation. An oral DCT, in contrast, requires subjects to listen to a recorded description of a situation and then say aloud what they would say in that situation. We explore DCTs in more detail in the first reading in Unit B2.

A2.2.4.2 Role-play (and role-enactment)

The kinds of judgement/self-assessment tasks highlighted above can also be based on role-play or role-enactment. Role-play involves 'pretending to react as if one were someone else in a different situation'. Role-enactment involves 'performing a role that is part of one's normal life or personality' (McDonough 1981: 80). Typically, A and B are provided with different descriptions of the same situation and asked to play a particular role in that situation or to respond as themselves. Kasper (2000: 323) provides the following example:

> A. You are going to move into a new apartment on Saturday. It is Thursday today, and you have just received a call from a friend of yours who was supposed to help you move house, saying that he is unable to help you move after all. You don't have a car or a driver's licence, so you depend on the help of somebody who does. You decide to ask B, your next-door neighbour. The two of you are friends, and you have helped each other out before. You go to see B.

> B. It is Thursday. You have just made arrangements with some friends to spend the weekend in the country. You and your friends are planning to go in your car, leaving Saturday morning and coming back Sunday night. You are at home, watching TV, when the door rings. You can see through the peephole that it is your friend and neighbour, A.

Role-play has been used with some success to study conflict discourse (Brenneis and Lein 1977; Lein and Brenneis 1978). In these particular studies, the researchers asked children to role-play an argument ('whose ball is it?', 'who is the strongest?'). The benefit of this approach is that it allows conflict discourse to be readily available and on a topic that we can specify at a moment's notice. Indeed, the children are thought to have become quite absorbed in their roles and to have generated spontaneous and lengthy disputes (which were tape recorded and transcribed). On the other hand, ethical questions are raised by activities that induce negative emotions, including conflict, in young subjects.

A2.3 EVIDENCE IN PRAGMATIC RESEARCH

Acquiring data is but a first step in any pragmatic investigation. The next step involves analysing the data. If we are interested in speech acts such as requests and apologies, for example, we are likely to make use of four types of evidence: perlocutionary effect (i.e. subsequent events that happen after or because of a given utterance (U) or utterance sequence); subsequent discourse triggered by U; explicit comment by the speaker; and/or explicit comment by another participant (see Thomas 1995 for details).

Ethnographers sometimes use a further source of evidence in the analysis of meaning – they take their analysis back to the participants and ask for their judgement on the analysis. Instead of presenting the researcher's own interpretation, it is also possible simply to replay a recording of a conversation to the participants, and allow them to comment, retrospectively, on what they thought was happening. Deborah Tannen calls this technique 'playback' (Tannen 1984). A Japanese researcher (Yohena 2003) used 'playback' when studying married couples' use of ellipsis (unfinished sentences). According to Tannen (1984), ellipsis contributes to a feeling of rapport between participants, but when Yohena played the recordings back to her subjects some months later she found that, far from creating rapport, it was a source of great irritation, especially for the men.

We can also glean evidence from the context, of course. Some of our assumptions about what is polite or impolite in a particular set of data will be guided by our knowledge of who is speaking to whom, where and in what capacity, for example (see Unit A8). We may also be guided by our knowledge of a political and/or historical context. This is particularly important when evaluating the hidden agenda in a political text, which may subtly appeal to readers' or hearers' past experiences and prejudices: this is something we return to in Unit A12. This type of evidence comes (in part) from outside the text, from our knowledge of society. Naturally, this is problematic when we are analysing data from a culture that is not our own, something that ethnographers are particularly concerned with (cf. Scollon and Scollon 2001). We explore cross-cultural pragmatics in detail in Unit A10.

Depending on their (sub-)discipline, some researchers will value certain kinds of evidence above others. Those working within the Conversation Analysis framework, for example, consider the subsequent response of participants in a conversation to be the only valid evidence, anything else being a post hoc imposition of the researcher's perspective (see Unit A6). However, for those who study the underlying ideological messages to be found in (political) texts, it is not easy to establish what the subsequent response may be. For this reason, researchers interested in the connections between language, power and ideology will focus on the text, its social and historical context and its potential meanings, in addition to its reception.

Even those who regard participant response as the only valid evidence for how utterances are understood do not necessarily explain how these meanings are inferred, in other words, what the mental processes are that lead participants to one particular inference rather than another. This cognitive aspect of meaning processing is the focus of Relevance Theory, which claims that hearers infer the meaning that requires the least 'mental effort' (see Unit A5). In order to find evidence for this kind of claim we need to 'see inside people's minds'. A possible clue to such hidden processes is the speed at which interlocutors respond to different tasks. The need to gather such evidence has generated a new area of research known as experimental pragmatics, involving carefully designed experiments in which, as in the natural sciences, variables are carefully controlled and measurements taken. We give you an opportunity to replicate different experimental studies in Unit C3.

A2.4 TRANSCRIBING SPOKEN LANGUAGE

If you decide to make an electronic recording of your data, you have the option of transcribing it. Transcribing spontaneous speech is not as simple as it sounds, however. Consider the following examples, from Clark and Fox Tree (2002: 73–4), both of which 'say' the same thing:

Well, Mallet said he felt it would be a good thing if Oscar went

Well, . I mean this . uh Mallet said Mallet was uh said something about uh you know he felt it would be a good thing if u:h . if Oscar went

Some professional transcribers, such as those who transcribe for the courts or parliament, will 'filter out' repetitions and filled pauses (*um, uh*), because their task is to make a record of *what* was said rather than *how* it was said. However, pragmaticians usually want to preserve some evidence of both what was said and how it was said, so they will record (some) disfluency features. We present here a few examples of the different transcription methods currently used within linguistics and comment on them.

International Corpus of (British) English (ICE-GB)

> but that was a bad ball from uh Michalichenko <,,> who now plays his football in Italy of course for Sampdoria who've just won the Italian league championship with a win three nil win over Lecce on <,> Sunday <ICE-GB:S2A-001 #42:1:A>
>
> *This is a broad orthographic transcription without punctuation and with pauses marked (<,> short and <,,> long). Repetitions and disfluencies are also included (although not in this extract).*

London-Lund Corpus (LLC)

> A> ^n\o# ^n\o# you ^look on the b/\ack# . [ə:m . ðhə] if ^you 'look . (. coughs)
>
> B> the the ^{thr\ee} :little :br\/own# . [ðh] the ^scr\/ew things# .
>
> A> ^no n\o# [ə: i ə ə:m] if ^you 'just '((turn)) ^you ^which 'clock do you m\ean# the *e^l\ectric 'one#*
>
> B> *the e^l\ectric#* .^y/eah#
>
> A> ^w\ell# you ^look you ^unh/ook it#
>
> Key to prosodic symbols (not all represented in the example):
>
> | | |
> |---|---|
> | # | tone unit boundary |
> | { } | subordinate tone unit |
> | ^ | onset |
> | ' " | degrees of stress |
> | \ | fall |
> | / | rise |
> | \/ | fall-rise |
> | (( )) | incomprehensible speech |
> | . - — | pauses of different length |
> | _ : ! | degrees of booster |
>
> *The transcription system used here is based on Crystal (1969) and includes a large number of prosodic features. The text is organized into tone units or 'chunks' of different length carrying the nucleus, i.e. the most prominent syllable. The other prosodic features which have been identified are onset (the first prominent syllable of the tone unit), pitch direction (e.g. falls, rises, levels, fall-rises, etc.), boosters (relative pitch levels) short and long pauses and stress. In addition, the transcription indicates simultaneous speech. In the example above 'the electric' is uttered simultaneously by speaker A and B (shown by the asterisk). A number of disfluencies have been marked such as repetition (the the) and filled pauses (ə:m). Also transcribed are contextual comments such as 'coughs' and unclear elements. Elements within double parentheses (( )) are unclear. For more information on the corpus see Svartvik (1990).*

Modified Jefferson-type CA (by courtesy of Traci Walker)

B: what'd he say
A: (m but) he sent you a le:tter too
   >yeah< he's lookin' forward to it
   (.)
A: he'[s got eighteen days t]otal
B: [well I am]
   (0.6)
B: huh
   (.)
A: he's only got eighteen days total
   but
B: yeah
   (0.7)
B: does he play mostly soprano or
   what
A: he plays everything he plays alto

This kind of transcription shows pause length in seconds; it also indicates where turns overlap, and noises such as intakes of breath (.hh). The aberrant spelling used in early Jefferson transcriptions (to represent pronunciation variation) has been avoided here. In many cases the pronunciation was predictable (e.g. 'fuh' instead of 'for' in order to show the vowel reduction) and in any case, the wide availability of speech software makes it possible to attend in great detail to phonetic realization where it is important.

Praat

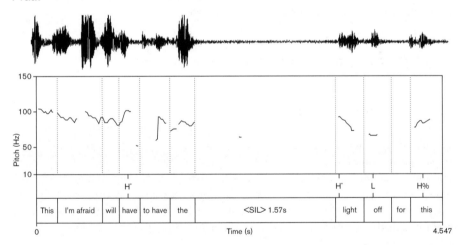

The Praat system is a good example of how transcriptions can be time-aligned with the original sound (and in some cases vision), using annotation 'tiers' (Boersma 2001): for example, one tier can be used for an orthographic representation, another for detailed phonetic or phonemic annotation and pauses, others for the annotation of non-speech sounds such as laughter, coughing, or for prosodic annotation (stressed syllables, intonation patterns, etc.). This kind of annotation process allows the user to transcribe at different levels of detail, or even to add certain details at a later date, depending on what is of interest to the analyst. In the above example, two of the annotation tiers have been used: one for a broad orthographic transcription, with the words or phrases being marked off in relation to where they occur in the pitch contour; the other is for prosodic information including which syllables are accented (marked by *) (for more about prosodic transcription see Unit A9). In this way, each word or string is clearly aligned with the sound file, and phonetic realization can be studied without difficulty.

As the four examples make clear, there are various ways in which spoken language can be 'captured', ranging from a narrow phonetic and prosodic transcription to a broad orthographic transcription, which represents what was said in normal spelling. Regardless of the method used, it is important to remember that a transcription is not the primary data. Rather, it constitutes a partial representation of the speech event in question. This means that you may need to be prepared to adapt or to add to the transcripts you use depending on your research needs.

A2.5 CORPUS PRAGMATICS: COMBINING QUANTITATIVE AND QUALITATIVE ANALYSES

Traditionally, much of pragmatic research has been qualitative in orientation. However, the increasing availability of electronic corpora has led to a growing interest in quantitative investigations, and has made it possible to study patterns of language use on a much larger scale than hitherto.

A2.5.1 Searching a corpus for pragmatic phenomena

One method of extracting pragmatic phenomena from corpora involves searching for words or phrases that are likely to be associated with pragmatic meanings (e.g. *sorry* for apologies, *thanks/thank you* for thanking, *please* for requesting), and then to study their functions and contexts of use, as well as to compare the frequencies of particular forms and functions. In Unit B11, we provide a reading by Taavitsainen and Jucker (2008b), which has used *beautiful, (really) nice, (really) great, lovely, well done, like/love your, what a, you look/'re looking* to search for compliments in historical texts. As we highlight in our discussions in Unit A11, however, we cannot assume that the forms used today (and their meanings) were used in exactly the same way by our ancestors.

Modern studies which adopt a similar approach to Taavitsainen and Jucker (2008b) include Aijmer (1996) and Wichmann (2004, 2005). Aijmer has studied the linguistic realizations of various speech acts, such as requests, thanks and apologies in the LLC. Wichmann has searched for occurrences of *please* in the ICE-GB in order to study the prosody of polite requests. Although these studies provide valuable insights, there are obvious weaknesses in their methodology. For example, Wichmann was only able to retrieve requests containing *please*, not all cases of request. To extend such a search one could look for occurrences of *could you*, as in *Could you give me a hand?*, or *do you mind*, as in *Do you mind parking your car over there?* You will be given an opportunity to elicit possible strings as a means of searching for different speech acts in Unit B11.3.

A2.5.2 Using POS and syntactic annotation to investigate pragmatic phenomena

The most popular form of linguistic annotation (to date) is part-of-speech (often abbreviated to POS), followed by syntactic parsing. Although not designed with pragmatic phenomena in mind, POS and parsing schemes can be used successfully to explore such phenomena. For example, syntactic annotation forms the basis for studies of expressions such as *I think, I believe, I suppose* in ICE-GB (Dehé and Wichmann 2010a, b). Many of these are tagged as comment clauses (CC) in ICE-GB, and searching for these generates a large number of cases, including *guess, assume, reckon, understand*, in addition to *think, believe* and *suppose*. A similar use of POS tagging combined with lexical searches enabled typical compliment formulae to be searched for by Jucker *et al.* (2008). A search for *What a [adjective] [noun]* was able to find *What a lovely dress, What a brilliant idea*, etc. As a next step, Jucker and colleagues had to check their results by exploring each, in context, to determine whether they did actually function as compliments. This means that pragmatic studies which rely on corpus evidence are by necessity qualitative as well as quantitative in focus.

A2.5.3 Pragmatic annotation

The benefits of annotating corpora are obvious: it allows researchers to access specific phenomena quickly and easily. But annotation – especially pragmatic anno- tation – brings with it its own problems. The first problem is how to delimit fragments of the text: it can, for example, prove to be extremely difficult when we're dealing with transcribed speech to decide what constitutes an utterance – or even a complete turn at speaking. Indeed, some of these decisions can only be made by listening to the original tapes, because the necessary information is actually in the prosody and not in the words themselves. The second problem is to find a means of ensuring the accuracy – or the applicability, at least – of any pragmatic labels we may use. For example, most pragmatic annotation schemes currently focus on speech acts (and hence add speech act labels to their data) or focus on 'moves' (and hence identify whether an utterance works as initiation, response or feedback, for example). Once the tags have been added, the usual quantitative searches are pos- sible. However, it's important to remember that the interpretive process is itself a qualitative one, and one moreover that is coloured by the annotators' theoretical perspective. Archer (2005) and Culpeper and Archer (2008) are amongst several researchers who therefore make explicit how their categories have been derived and then applied. They also advocate the use of 'indeterminate' categories when dealing with speech acts, in particular, as utterances can be fuzzy in respect to their force or, indeed, have multiple forces.

The purpose of an annotation scheme is to tag phenomena so that they can be automatically retrieved by others. Therefore, annotators will most often assign a primary (and, where relevant, an additional) force. We provide an example of Archer's (2005) annotation scheme below, which captures an exchange between a male prosecution lawyer, identified as 's4tfranc001', and a male witness, identified as 's4tfranc003':

> <u stfunc="fol-ini" force="m" force1="c" force2="q" q="iqp" qtype="y" qform="is" speaker="s" spid="s4tfranc001" spsex="m" sprole1="v" spstatus="1" spage="9" addressee="s" adid="s4tfranc003" adsex="m" adrole1="w" adstatus="4" adage="x">Look upon this Book; Is this the Book?</u>

As Archer identifies something akin to discourse moves or dialogue acts in addition to speech act labels (see Unit A6 for more details of this approach), we can work out that the lawyer's question to the witness is a 'follow-up' utterance as opposed to an opening question. We also know, based on the annotation, that the lawyer's utterance functioned as both a command (force1="c") and a question (force2="q"), which, in this case, had a clarificationary aim (q="iqp"). The above example also makes use of a second annotation scheme, developed by Archer and Culpeper (2003), which captures sociopragmatic information about the speaker and the addressee at the level of the utterance (i.e. their gender, status, age and role). This type of scheme is extremely useful when we want to link pragmatic phenomena to the user (i.e. who is saying what, to whom and in what capacity).

As Archer's scheme was applied to historical trial data, she was not able to make use of prosodic features. All of the anotation also had to be applied manually, and hence was extremely time consuming. Shriberg *et al.* (1998), in contrast, were able to use prosodic features to automatically identify a set of 'acts' including backchannels, agreements, two kinds of statement (description and opinion) and four kinds of question (yes/no, wh-, declarative, open). Attempts at automation are generally carried out with the aim of developing more reliable speech recognition for use in human–machine interaction, and less out of interest in the way humans interact with each other. When the aim is the latter (i.e. the study of human–human interaction), pragmatic annotation schemes tend to be manually applied (and, on occasion, applied semi-automatically). Once applied, manual and (semi-)automatic schemes provide users with access to useful information at a touch of a button – and make possible systematic studies that have previously been impossible within pragmatics.

Summary and looking ahead

In this section we have described the methods and the kinds of data that are used in the study of pragmatic meaning. We have discussed in some detail the issues involved in transcribing speech and the degree to which a transcription can capture the original speech event. Since many recent studies in pragmatics are making use of large electronic corpora as a source of data, we have presented some of the kinds of corpora available and the means to analyse them. Pragmatics has focused mainly on meaning from the point of view of the speaker, but increasingly researchers are interested in how hearers interpret what they hear (see Unit A5). In Unit B2 you will find a critical discussion of data elicitation techniques, and also an account of some experiments designed to explore how far speakers design their contributions for the benefit of hearers. The final reading addresses methodological issues in historical pragmatics.

Unit A3
The semantic–pragmatic interface

Semantics and pragmatics are related and complementary fields of study. Both concern the transmission of meaning through language. The difference between them relates to *usage*: pragmatics is concerned with meaning described in relation to speakers and hearers, or speakers/writers and their audiences, in a given context; semantics, with meaning that is independent of any particular usage (Saeed 1997: 18). As will become clear in this section, some linguistic phenomena – reference, deixis and presupposition – appear to share both semantic and pragmatic characteristics. Before we explore these linguistic phenomena let's first consider the *meaning* of 'meaning' from both a semantic and pragmatic perspective.

A3.1 THE *MEANING* OF MEANING IN PRAGMATICS

Semantic interpretation is strictly linguistic, that is, it is all about:

> . . . applying the tacit theory that speaker-hearers are said to possess, and that formal semantics tries to make explicit . . . [as a means of] deductively establish[ing] the truth conditions of any sentence of the language. To do so, it is argued, one does not need to take the speaker's beliefs and intentions into account: one has simply to apply the rules.
>
> (Recanati 2004: 450)

Hence, *Where did you get that dress?* is a question relating to location (i.e. where the dress came from). For pragmaticians, in contrast, a speaker's beliefs and intentions are crucial to interpretation. Typical questions they might ask, then, is what the speaker was doing (i.e. *meant* in an intentional sense), when s/he said *Where did you get that dress?*, and what the hearer inferred, based on what she knew about the speaker and the context of utterance. They might point out, for example, that – in the context of a conversation between partners – the utterance actually implicated something negative about the dress. However, because this is not stated explicitly (as part of what is said), the original speaker, if challenged with *Why what's wrong with it?*, can always claim that they meant 'nothing' by it beyond its literal meaning, hence providing themselves with some plausible deniablity (cf. Leech 1983).

A focus on truth conditions means that some propositions – take, for example, those found within 'An invisible car came out of nowhere, hit our car and vanished' (adapted from Thomas 1995: 30) – are considered to be illogical, and thus non-interpretable. But such propositions are far from meaningless when we consider the speaker's motivation for uttering such a statement. By way of illustration, if we were to tell you that 'An invisible car came out of nowhere, hit our car and vanished', we wouldn't mean for you to take us literally – after all, how can something that is already invisible vanish! Instead, we'd want you to infer that we had been in a vehicular accident, which (we believed) we had not caused; that we had failed to see the other car until (or very near to) the actual point of impact; and that the driver of that car had then fled the scene of the accident.

Pragmatics, then, moves us away from abstract meaning towards utterance meaning and (from the latter through to) speaker meaning. In other words, the main focus is not to determine literal meaning via the rules of language but to get to the speaker's intent in uttering X in context C – whilst also determining the hearer(s)'s (and, if relevant, others') (mis)interpretation of that intent.

Task A3.1

➤ The following quotation comes from Lewis Carroll's *Through the Looking-Glass* (1871). Humpty Dumpty is discussing what words 'mean' with Alice:

> 'I don't know what you mean by "glory",' Alice said.
>
> Humpty Dumpty smiled contemptuously. 'Of course you don't – till I tell you. I meant "there's a nice knock-down argument for you!"'
>
> 'But "glory" doesn't mean "a nice knock-down argument",' Alice objected.
>
> 'When *I* use a word,' Humpty Dumpty said, in rather a scornful tone, 'it means just what I choose it to mean – neither more nor less.'
>
> 'The question is,' said Alice, 'whether you *can* make words mean so many different things.'
>
> 'The question is,' said Humpty Dumpty, 'which is to me master – that's all.'

➤ Is Humpty Dumpty right?

A3.2 REFERENCE

Within formal semantics, meaning is strongly associated with reference, by which is meant the relations which hold between linguistic expressions (such as noun phrases) and what they stand for in the world. Hence, a semanticist might seek to demonstrate the links between 'British Prime Minister' and 'leader of the government in the UK'. This said, we cannot apply the appropriate word-to-worlds relation without also considering its usage in real time (Recanati 2004: 443). When we refer to the British Prime Minister, for example, we have David Cameron in mind (given we are writing in 2012). But other authors may wish their readers to bring to mind one of a number of men – or even Mrs Thatcher, who was the British PM from 1979 to 1990. Such examples nicely illustrate the overlapping nature of semantics and pragmatics: such that we cannot understand meaning without considering use; yet, we must equally acknowledge that some meanings are conventional, and hence remain constant across various contexts. We turn our attention now to one of 'the most obvious and direct linguistic reflection[s] of the relationship between language and context', that of deixis (Marmaridou 2010: 101).

A3.3 DEIXIS

Originating from the Greek word for pointing or indicating, deixis encodes/grammaticalizes features of the speech event such as the (role/status of the) participants, the activities being talked about or referred to and the spatio-temporal context (Lyons 1977: 37; Levinson 1983: 54). Categories therefore include:

Person deixis:	e.g. 'I'll see **you** there'
Social deixis:	e.g. 'Nice to meet you, **Professor Aijmer**'
Place (spatial) deixis:	e.g. 'I'm not **here** right now' (phone message)
Emphatic deixis:	e.g. 'I hate **those** curtains'
Time (temporal) deixis:	e.g. 'She's coming to visit us **soon**'
Discoursal deixis:	e.g. '**Besides**, she's a very good driver'

Person deixis encodes the speakers (e.g. *I*, *we*) and addressees (e.g. *you*) within a speech event. Indeed, *I* indicates the deictic centre – or *origo* – of utterances containing such first person pronouns. Hence, when the speaker says, 'I'll see you there', we understand the place deitic *there* to signal somewhere away from the speaker (and also the hearer(s), in this case; if the latter were already there, the speaker is more likely to say 'I'll see you soon'). In contrast to *there*, the place deictic *here* usually denotes a space/place close to the speaker. Notice, however, that the speaker must have been present at the time of uttering 'I'm not here right now' for their phone message (see above): what this particular utterance seeks to do, then, is switch the deictic centre of the speaker so that it addresses a future state where s/he won't be available to answer the phone.

Another type of place deixis – shown separately above – is that of emphatic deixis (Lyons 1977). This equates to a marked use of demonstratives like *that* and *those*, which serve to highlight the speaker's psychological (as opposed to physical) 'distance' from a given entity (in our case, curtains). Their effect is much more noticeable when you compare them with the use of *this* and *these*, which tend to signal the speaker's psychological closeness to the entity, situation or place (cf. 'I like these curtains'). *This/that* and *these/those* can also signal the speaker's attempt to identify with (or distance) themselves from 'the attitude or viewpoint of the addressee' (ibid.: 677); something to which we return in the next section.

Social deixis encodes the social identities of and/or relationships between speakers, addressees and others. We can thus talk about two types of social deixis: absolute and relational. Absolute expressions – such as the gender referents Miss/Ms/Mrs and Mr – are fixed across contexts. Relational expressions such as honorifics and kinship terms, in contrast, are determined by speaker and referent, speaker and addresee or speaker and bystander (Levinson 1983: 90). By way of illustration, when one person greets another there are an array of possible referents they might use, depending on who H is and also the (in)formality of the context of utterance. In our example, 'Nice to meet you Professor Aijmer', the speaker has opted to empha-size H's (high) occupational status. But such a greeting is not a 'must' when greeting academic professors; if H were a close friend, a more informal greeting would be much more appropriate – unless, that is, the formality of the situation dictated otherwise.

Time or temporal deictic terms are understood relative to the speaker's utterance time. They can look backwards, as in *yesterday*, fix upon the present, as in *now*, or look forward to the future, as in the example, 'She's coming to visit us soon.' Some temporal deictic terms – e.g. 'She's coming to visit July 2013' – serve as absolute time indicators. Typically, however, time deixis is grammaticalized in English via: adverbs such as *now* and *then*; demonstrative expressions such as *this Monday/year* and *that summer*; adjectival phrases such as *last Tuesday/month* and *next year*; and verbs of motion such as *the past month*, *the coming year*, *the following Monday*. 'Time metaphors' which are understood spatially point, in turn, to the close links between time and space deixis (Marmaridou 2000: 102).

Discoursal deictic terms are similar to temporal deictic terms, in that they point to parts of a text or discourse which occurred prior to or occur following the speaker's current utterance. In our example, *besides* points to some preceding discourse (relating to who might drive). It's worth noting that discoursal deictic reference can be anaphoric, cataphoric and exophoric. As such, it is closely linked to text cohesion. For example, Marmaridou (ibid.) provides the example of 'Her mother walked in. This woman was the tallest female I had ever seen', where *this woman* is used anaphorically to refer to *her mother*, rather than deictically pointing to the woman. As Marmaridou (ibid.) also points out, specific expressions can sometimes have both a deictic and non-deictic function in the same utterance. Consider *here* in the utterance, 'I'm at UCLAN. I've been working here since 2005': *here* can be said to be working deictically if the speaker is at her place of work when making the utterance; yet, *here* also works anaphorically, by relating back to *the university*.

Expressions which are not normally associated with indexicality (because their semantic value/meaning is fixed) can be used deictically in some contexts. Consider, for example, the utterance, 'It's Alfie's bedtime.' If said with the force of a directive to a child by their caregiver, the third person reference becomes deictic (as it acts like the pronoun *your*). The property of indexicality, then, 'is not exhausted by the study of inherently indexical expressions. For just about any referring expression can be used deictically' (Levinson 2004: 101).

A3.3.1 Deixis and attitudinal orientation: some case studies

Several authors have focused on the way(s) in which speakers engage in deictic practice as a means of positioning themselves and others attitudinally. For example, Glover (2000) has shown that the participants involved in a 70-minute planning meeting used proximal and distal deixis in different but specific ways when seeking to negotiate the location of an access road which linked the developer's site with land owned by a hospital trust. *This*, *these* and *here* tended to reflect a negotiable orientation, that is, they referred to objects of reference which were recognized as problematic or as yet unresolved by the participants. *That*, *those* and *there*, in contrast, were used to encode the objects of reference which had been (or were assumed to have been) agreed. The following extract (adapted from ibid.: 919–20) captures a brief interaction between the senior planner (P) and the developer's Director (D):

P: [. . .] we are a little unclear and this may now have been resolved with the hospital trust as to where the access should be – we we felt it should just come straight through at *this point*

D: [. . .] before we submitted the bid and certainly after we'd seen yourselves [. . .] I went to see the uh the agents acting on behalf of the hospital trust with *these points* of access

P: yea

D: and they eventually came back and said that they were happy with a point *there* and a point even below this one because there's a cottage down from there um Rose cottage [. . .]

P: yeah that's right

Notice that the access issue is introduced by P in a way that signals it is as yet unresolved (i.e. *this point*). D's *these points* reflects P's *this point*, but D then switches to distals to indicate that the developers and the hospital agents had, in fact, now agreed some of the points of contention to which P was alluding. A comment using proximal deixis, made later by P, suggests that, for him, the access issue remained unresolved, however (see, e.g., his reiteration of *this point*) (adapted from ibid.: 920–1):

P: right (1.0) but they didn't you didn't discuss any al-alternatives with them they jus said they were they were you know satisfied with those – I mean the reason I ask that is that the brief saw access umm I think jus coming through at *this point*

Attitudinal deixis can also have power implications. This is particularly obvious in a courtroom context. Consider, for example, the following extract (adapted from Harris 1994: 161) taken from a magistrate's interaction with a defendant who had not paid his maintenance payments:

> Don't you think that it's up to you to use some of *that* fourteen pounds [defendant's unemployment benefit as a maintenance payment] rather than everybody else sitting in *this* court – and everybody else in the country

Notice how the magistrate uses *that* to refer to the defendant's unemployment benefit and *this* to refer to the court, which cumulatively have the effect of distancing the magistrate and, by extension, those present in court (and one could argue society in general) from the defendant's 'inappropriate' behaviour. This emphatic stance adds saliency to the ideological meaning underpinning the magistrate's rhetorical question – that defendants should pay their fines, not society in general – and in so doing indirectly points to the reason we have a legal system: to protect society. We can also see the link between an implicit ideological proposition and attitudinal or emphatic deixis in the following extract (adapted from Thornborrow 2002: 99, taken from a BBC Radio show, aired in 1995, which sought public opinion in respect to whether council housing should be funded by the taxpayer):

Caller: people have been coming into these flats um single people (1.0) uh with no priorities (0.7) an' they've been getting ground floor flats
Host: so you think people are jumping the queue
Caller: they are definitely jumping the queue [. . .]

Notice that the caller indicates their (psychological) closeness to the flats using the proximal marker *these*. But the implicit assumption of their utterance – that some people are unfairly appropriating council housing – is only made explicit when they confirm the caller's reformulation. The same technique of recycling a(n implicit) proposition was used by the host in another phone conversation. In this case, the reformulation allowed the caller to make explicit that council housing provides a much-needed safety net (adapted from ibid.):

Host: [. . .] d'you think it's ethically right that taxpayers should be expected to find you a home for the rest of your life
Caller: [. . .] yes=
Host: =it is right=
Caller: =it is right [. . .] it is the safety net that is there and I would like to see it continue to be there

We discuss the relationship between pragmatics and power in more detail in Unit A12.

A3.4 PRESUPPOSITION

Presuppositions are propositions whose truth is taken for granted as opposed to being explicitly stated. Consider 'When did you stop beating your wife?', for example. The wh-question presupposes that the target of the question is married to someone he (or she, in countries which allow same-sex marriages) has beaten at some point in the past. Compare this wh-question with the yes/no question, 'Do you beat your wife?', or the statement, 'I think he beats his wife', which presuppose 'X is married' but do not presuppose 'X beats his wife' (even though we could argue that the *think*-statement implies the speaker *believes* the proposition to be a possibility). We'll return to this characteristic of presuppositions in Unit A3.4.1. A second characteristic of presuppositions is that they remain *constant under negation*. For example, the utterances 'My husband is at home' and 'My husband is not at home' share the same proposition: *I have a husband.* A third characteristic of presuppositions is that they are defeasible (i.e. can be cancelled) in certain contexts. Compare, for example:

> John didn't manage to pass the exam >> *he tried to pass the exam*
> John didn't manage to pass the exam. In fact, he didn't even try

Presuppositions are typically generated by lexical items or linguistic constructions. These items and constructions are called presupposition triggers (Levinson 1983: 184), and include:

- definite descriptions ('**John** didn't manage to pass the exam' assumes that *John exists*);
- factive verbs ('John **knows** that Mary passed the exam' assumes that *Mary passed*);
- change-of-state verbs ('Mary has **stopped** revising' assumes that *Mary has revised previously*);
- implicative verbs ('John **didn't manage** to pass the exam' assumes *John tried to pass*);
- temporal clauses ('John consoled himself in the pub, **after** he failed the exam' assumes that *John failed the exam*);
- cleft sentence ('**It wasn't** Mary who got drunk' assumes *someone other than Mary got drunk*);
- comparatives ('Mary is **better at** revising than John' assumes *both Mary and John revised*);
- counterfactual conditionals ('**If** John were better at revising, he would have passed the exam' assumes *John isn't good at revising*).

Using the above examples, we can identify different types of presupposition (adapted from Yule 2006: 30):

Type	Presupposition	Example
Existential	>> X exits	'The X' (generally a definite noun phrase)
Factive	>> I left	'I **regret** leaving' (+ factive verbs such as **sorry/glad**)
Non-factive	>> He wasn't happy	'He **pretended** to be happy' (+ other non-factive verbs)
Lexical	>> He tried to escape	'He **managed** to escape' (+ implicative verbs such as **struggle**: see also the change-of-state verbs, **stop**, **begin**, **enter**, **come**, **go**, and the iteratives, **again**, **returned**, **repeat**)
Structural	>> The car ran the red light	'How fast was the car going **when** it ran the red light?'
Counter-factual	>> The class is not my responsibility	'**If** this was my class, that wouldn't happen'

A3.4.1 Presuppositions and our knowledge of the world

An overtly pragmatic feature of presuppositions is their dependency on our knowledge of how the world works. For example, the meaning of *resign* prevents our presupposing Mary got a promotion when told *Mary resigned before she got a promotion.* But a similar utterance – *Mary trained before she got a promotion* – does presuppose a promotion on Mary's part. This is because the temporal clause *before* . . . is consistent with our background knowledge in this case (that training precedes/can lead to promotion).

Presuppositions are also blocked when they are inconsistent with conversational implicatures (see Unit A5). Consider *If Mary has lied, John will be upset,* for example, which – thanks to the if-clause structure – implicates that Mary may not have lied (although the *possibility* that she has remains strong).

A third way in which presuppositions are blocked has to do with the linguistic context. *I don't know that Mary passed the exam* will not give rise to the proposition that *Mary passed the exam,* for example, because (without additional evidence) the speaker's denial of the necessary knowledge effectively serves to override what we would otherwise presuppose.

> This peculiarity in the use of *know* as a trigger cannot be accounted for in truth conditional semantic terms, since it does not relate to the truth conditions of the containing sentence. Rather, it relates to the commonly held general assumption that, when speakers do not know something, they cannot be taken to verify its truth.
>
> (Marmaridou 2010: 350)

As the following example reveals, a presupposition can be triggered by the first part of an utterance and then blocked by the second part: *Mary doesn't regret failing the exam . . . because, in fact, she passed.* In this case, our understanding of *passed* effectively blocks the presupposition normally triggered by (*doesn't*) *regret.*

A3.5 GRICE'S ENDURING INFLUENCE

Semantic underdetermination constitutes one of the first ideas put forward to account for linguistic features which – like reference, deixis and presuppositions – transcend the semantics-pragmatics interface. Discussed in some detail in the Unit B3.2 reading, the basic premise of the notion of semantic underdetermination is that pragmatic inference can contribute to – by pragmatically enriching – truth conditional representation. This idea has led, in turn, to a focus on delimiting *what is said* in an utterance and the *implicatures* of that utterance; that is, any wider meaning the speaker intended to convey which is above the words uttered (and thus not dependent on truth conditions).

Such a focus highlights the important influence of H. Paul Grice and other members of the Ordinary Language Philosophers, a group championed by John Austin. The group advocated that we seek to understand the semantics of actual language use and not merely the semantics of idealized, formal languages. Grice, in particular, sought to reconcile the differences between ordinary language philosophy and idealized language philosophy (as posited by Frege and Russell) by proposing a distinction that we are very familiar with today: that semantics should be regarded as a theory of linguistic meaning and pragmatics, as the study of language use. The importance of this distinction? It allowed 'idealized and ordinary language philosophy to coexist' (Wharton 2010: 182).

Grice's (1989: 40) thesis in regard to semantic underdetermination was that 'what words mean is a matter of what people mean by them', that is, speaker intent. He also suggested a means by which we might explain these additional propositions without resorting to truth conditions (as we would when dealing with what is said). For example, when dealing with conversational implicatures, Grice (1975) suggested that we assume that participants will (in general) be obeying a cooperative principle and its attendant conversational maxims (Quality, Quantity, Relation and Manner). It is when these maxims are flouted that conversational implicatures are generated. However, because of the assumption of cooperation, hearers will look for a meaning beyond the words uttered. As Unit A5 highlights, such *conversational implicatures* are context-based and, hence, are distinct from *conventional implicatures*, which tend to be generated by words whose meaning is fixed over many contexts. *But,* for example, carries a conventional implicature that there is some sort of contrast between the contents of the two assertions it conjoins. Hence *but* in *She's a pensioner but she's very active* conventionally implicates that pensioners are not usually active.

Other researchers have picked up on the explicit/implicit distinction, but have sought to explain it in a different way to Grice. Carston (1998) has suggested that pragmatic enrichment stops as soon as optimal relevance is reached, for example.

Optimal relevance is a relevance-theoretic assumption that any ostensive stimulus will be relevant enough to be worth the hearer(s)'s/audience's attention and hence will repay their cognitive efforts (we discuss optimal relevance in relation to Relevance Theory in Unit A5). Under this type of approach, implicatures have their own, independent logical forms and function as separate premises in reasoning. Consider the following example, given initially by Searle (1978) and discussed in detail by Taylor (2010): 'Smith weighs 80kg.' As Taylor points out, this utterance would express different propositions in the following contexts:

(1) Smith, who has been dieting for the last eight weeks, steps on the scale naked one morning before breakfast and it registers 80kg.
(2) Smith is wearing a heavy overcoat and carrying a briefcase full of books. He is about to step on an elevator with a capacity of no more than an extra 80kg.

(1) would communicate a proposition about the weight of Smith's naked body, whilst (2) would communicate a proposition about the combined weight of Smith, his briefcase and clothes. We'd know which meaning to assign because of our understanding of the different contexts of utterance. What we would not need to do, then, is 'first directly cognize the minimal proposition about the weight of Smith's body and then indirectly cognize the enriched proposition about the combined weight of Smith's body, briefcase and overcoat' (ibid.: 78).

As well as debating ways by which to capture the difference between what is said and what is implicated, researchers have begun to debate what might be *implicit* in what is said. Bach (1994: 267) provides the example of a mother telling her son (who's cut his finger) 'You're not going to die', with the implicit intention of communicating to him that he *won't die from this particular cut*. The mother's *impliciture*, then, is distinct from the implicature generated by 'You're not going to die'; that the son should stop whinging about the cut. Jaszczolt (2010: 40) also provides the example of a semantically complete utterance, 'Bill is not good enough', which implicitly signals what he's not good enough for (e.g. the King's College choir). Implicitures, then, constitute incomplete propositions which need to be completed, or full propositions which fall short of what the speaker intends to mean and thus need to be expanded (i.e. enriched pragmatically). Hence, when we hear an utterance such as 'I have nothing to wear', we understand it to mean 'I have nothing *[appropriate/suitable]* to wear *[for X event]*.' This type of meaning is meant to constitute a middle ground between what is said and what is implicated according to researchers such as Bach, as it goes beyond what is said and yet is truth-conditionally relevant (cf. implicatures, which – as we'll discuss in Unit A5 – constitute additional propositions which are external to what is said).

Relevance theorists have put forward a similar concept to impliciture – that of *explicature*. Explicatures constitute 'a development of a logical form encoded by U' (Sperber and Wilson 1995: 182). Carston (2010: 158) offers the following example, where (3) equates to the original exchange between Alex and Brit, and (4) equates to Brit's pragmatically enriched meaning:

(3)   Alex: How was the party? Did it go well?
      Brit: There wasn't enough drink and everyone left early.
(4)   There wasn't enough *alcoholic* drink *to satisfy the people at [the party]*
      and so everyone *who came to [the party]* left *[the party]* early.

Relevance theorists suggest explicatures work in one of two ways: 'saturation' or 'free enrichment'. Saturation involves finding the intended content (or 'value') for some linguistically indicated variable or slot. Free enrichment, in contrast, involves the *pragmatic* enrichment of the decoded linguistic meaning in the absence of any indication (overt or covert) within the linguistic form. Brit's comment above – 'There wasn't enough drink *and* everyone left early' – provides us with an example of such pragmatic enrichment.

Although semanticists readily accept the notion of saturation, they find the notion of 'free enrichment' more difficult, not least because it 'intrudes' on the truth-conditional context (the 'semantics', as they construe it) of an utterance (ibid.: 161) – and in a way that Grice's distinction between semantics and pragmatics didn't (see above). There is also disagreement amongst pragmaticians in regard to what might constitute free enrichment and what might constitute conversational implicature – such that some Neo-Gricean pragmaticians would want to explain Brit's comment (above) as an example of conversational implicature (as opposed to being something which is implicit in what is said). Hence, Alex would infer *alcoholic drink* because of his culturally determined party 'script', and would use that same script to make sense of the guests leaving early. We'll return to the issue of how to account for the cause-consequence of *and*-conjunctions after our first reading in Unit B3.

Summary
and looking
ahead
In this unit, we've explored the relationship between semantics and pragmatics, and also discussed how these two linguistic disciplines approach 'meaning' differently. We've done so, primarily, by focusing on linguistic phenomena – reference, deixis and presupposition – which transcend the semantics-pragmatics interface. In Unit B3, we give you access to three readings which explore the semantics-pragmatics interface: the first offers a general overview, the second and third deal specifically with presupposition and deixis (and come to slightly different conclusions in regard to whether they believe them to constitute a pragmatic phenomenon only or a pragmatic and semantic phenomenon!). A key issue to have emerged in this unit is the enduring influence of H. Paul Grice within pragmatics (see Unit A3.5). We continue our discussion of Grice in Unit A5, and also outline how researchers (like Horn, Leech, Levinson and Sperber and Wilson) have developed his ideas. Some of these researchers – in particular, Dan Sperber – are part of a group of (mainly British and European) researchers who have used traditional psycholinguistic method-ologies to investigate (issues relating to) the semantics-pragmatics interface. You will learn about some of their 'experimental pragmatics' studies in Unit C3, and also be encouraged to undertake similar studies of your own.

Unit A4
Speech acts: doing things with words

As pragmatics owes much to philosophical speech act theory, we start this chapter with a description of how philosophers became interested in language as action, and how speech acts have become one of the cornerstones in pragmatics. As this unit will show, there are various ways of capturing how we 'do things' with words, some of which draw on corpus linguistic techniques. We begin by tracing the philosophical origins of speech act theory and how it becomes part of linguistic pragmatics (Units A4.1–A4.3). Unit A4.4 deals with direct and indirect speech acts and Unit A4.5 with more or less routinized speech acts.

A4.1 AUSTIN'S PERFORMATIVES

The interest in speech acts can be traced back to the idea that we use language not only to describe phenomena in the real world but also to 'do things'. The founding father of philosophical speech act theory is the philosopher John L. Austin. In a lecture delivered at Harvard in 1955, later published as the monograph *How to do things with words* (1962), he argued against the current philosophical creed that meanings could only be assigned to sentences on the basis of their correspondence with truth, and showed that there are many different things we do with language. For example, the sentence 'I [hereby] bet you £5 it will rain' does not describe an event but constitutes a bet. Austin referred to such sentences as *performatives* and distinguished them from constative sentences such as 'It is raining', which can be true or false. Performatives have certain linguistic characteristics such as the possibility to insert *hereby* before the verb and the use of the present tense form of the verb associated with the action.

The 'hereby' test spotting the performative

*I [hereby] like apples
I [hereby] apologize
I [hereby] name this ship Queen Elizabeth II
I [hereby] bet you £5 it will rain

Only in the three last sentences above can *hereby* can be inserted. Pragmatically, these utterances perform the actions of apologizing, naming a ship and betting respectively. *I hereby like apples*, in contrast, does not constitute a performative utterance. Compare *I like apples* which describes or 'constates' something.

It is important that certain conditions are fulfilled for performative utterances to be successful ('felicity conditions'). Such felicity conditions are (adapted from ibid.: 14–15):

- There must be a conventional procedure having a conventional effect
- The circumstances and persons must be appropriate
- The procedure must be executed (i) correctly and (ii) completely
- Often . . . the persons must have the requisite thoughts, feelings and intentions and if consequent conduct is specified, then the relevant parties must do it.

As Levinson (1983: 230) suggests, some performatives 'are . . . rather special sorts of ceremony'. Ceremonial performatives are associated with specific (felicity) conventions associated with an institution such as the courtroom or the church. They must also be uttered by a person with the authority to do so, and in the manner prescribed by the institution:

- 'I sentence you to 10 years' imprisonment' (as uttered by the judge in the courtroom addressed to a person found guilty of a crime).
- 'I pronounce you husband and wife' (as uttered by a registrar or priest to a woman and man in a church or registry office in the presence of witnesses).

The above examples are 'infelicitous' if the circumstances and persons are not appropriate. This doesn't cover all types of performatives, however. Consider apologies, for example, a class of performatives which Austin described as behabitives (see Unit A4.2.1). Here, the emphasis is on the speaker having the requisite thoughts, feelings and intentions. An example of a violation of this condition is if the speaker says 'I apologize' without feeling sorry. Such violations result in abuses with the consequence that an apology still takes place but 'unhappily'.

A4.1.1 Explicit and implicit performatives

The examples referred to so far contain explicit pointers to the performative (I pronounce you, I sentence you . . .) but in some cases such pointers are missing. We therefore make a distinction between explicit performatives and implicit performatives:

- 'I promise to cook you a meal' (explicit performative)
- 'I'll cook you a meal' (implicit performative)
- 'I request you to do as I told you' (explicit performative)
- 'Do what I told you' (implicit performative)

The explicit performative is used to avoid misunderstanding or to emphasize the speaker's authority and power. It is generally present in the more ceremonial cases, but less often in casual conversation. Sometimes this leads to misunderstanding in the conversation, and a hearer might have to ask 'Is that an order?' 'Is that a promise?' or 'Is that a threat or a promise?'

A4.1.2 A full-blown theory of action

Having introduced the distinction between performative and constative, Austin abandoned it in a later lecture in order to argue for a new framework for the study of language based on the notion of speech act. In this lecture he showed that all utterances including constatives (statements) could be seen as 'doing things' just like performatives. The result is a full-blown theory of language as action. A distinction is made between three types of act performed by an utterance:

- a locutionary act referring to the actual words uttered
- an illocutionary act referring to what is performed in saying something. Apologizing, thanking and requesting are examples of illocutionary acts (acts with a certain illocutionary force)
- a perlocutionary act is the result of taking the hearer's perspective. However, some researchers distinguish between the *intended* perlocutionary act and the *actual* perlocutionary force or effect. That is, the act is seen as having certain effects on the actions, thoughts and beliefs of hearers which may or may not be intended. Thus what the speaker says can be taken as a threat even if it is intended as something else. 'Hands up' is an illocutionary act from the speaker's perspective (an order) but can be interpreted by the hearer as a threat (see also Units A8 and A11). Some intended acts can only be regarded as felicitous if the actual perlocutionary effect matches the intended perlocutionary act. An insult will only be an insult if the hearer hears it as such (see also Units A8 and A11). More problematic is the case of the apology: as it may be sincerely intended, but not accepted. In which case, has an apology been made or not?

Utterances, then, can be shown to have both illocutionary force (and perlocutionary effects) in addition to their propositional content (the meaning as locutionary acts). In the sentence *I apologize* the illocutionary force is for instance that of an apology. What distinguishes an apology from a statement can now be described in terms of differences in illocutionary force. The 'performative' verb is said to serve as an illocutionary force indicating device (IFID) together with other devices such as word order, stress, intonation contour, punctuation, the mood of the verb (Searle 1969: 30).

A4.2 SEARLE'S THEORY OF SPEECH ACTS

The philosopher John Searle continued the work initiated by Austin (see, e.g., Searle 1969). Searle emphasized that 'speaking a language is engaging in a rule-governed form of behaviour' (ibid.: 16) and proposed a number of 'felicity conditions' (different from Austin's) for a handful of illustrative examples of speech acts. Below we illustrate Searle's analysis for thanking (a speech act which is easy to recognize because of the presence of the verb *thank you (for something)* which serves as an illocutionary force-indicating device).

Propositional content condition (restrictions on the content of the sentence): past act A done by H (the hearer)

Preparatory condition: A benefits S (the speaker) and S believes A benefits S

Sincerity condition (beliefs, feelings and intentions of the speaker): S feels grateful or appreciative for A

Essential condition: counts as an expression of gratitude or appreciation
(Adapted from ibid.: 67)

The conditions proposed by Searle are not linguistic rules in the usual, normative sense and they are not of equal importance. The sincerity condition has to do with the speaker's psychological state. The preparatory content condition specifies that there must be something to be grateful for (the act benefits the speaker). Furthermore the object of thanking must refer to an act done by the hearer in the past (propositional content condition). The essential condition makes explicit the connection between saying 'thank you' and performing an act of thanking (*thank you* 'counts as' an act of thanking).

However, there are problems with some of the conditions. For example, the propositional content condition that the act must have taken place is not fulfilled when someone is thanked for not smoking. Moreover, you could thank someone for what is just a promise, offer or invitation. For example, I could thank my neighbour for promising to water my plants while I'm away on holiday. The sincerity condition does not handle cases of thanking where the speaker does not feel grateful. These include cases where *thank you* is used to receive a ticket from the bus conductor. Finally, Searle does not mention the response to thanking although the response could be regarded as a part of thanking.

There seems to be no end to what we can do with language: we complain, we ask for advice, we make offers, ask other people to do things, etc. How many ways of using language are there? Searle only provided a few examples of 'recognition criteria' for speech acts. If we go beyond the paradigm examples additional distinctions need to be made. Consider for instance the problems in describing the differences between speech acts which seem to share the same pragmatic space (i.e. recommending, suggesting and giving advice). Instead of trying to distinguish between speech acts on the basis of speech act verbs we need to look for a typology of speech acts.

A4.2.1 A typology of speech acts

Searle (1976) suggested a number of dimensions of variation making it possible to classify speech acts into broader categories referring to a number of basic things we can do with language. The dimensions are based on their fit with the world, psychological state and above all the purpose of the illocution (illocutionary point). The five categories are representatives (or assertives), commissives, directives, expressives and declarations:

■ Representatives (or assertives). These are illustrated by speech acts expressing the speaker's belief that something is true. They show 'word-to-world' fit, i.e. in using a representative the speaker makes a belief fit an already existing state of affairs in the world. Examples of speech acts are stating, suggesting, boasting, complaining, claiming, concluding, deducing.

■ Commissives. By using a commissive the speaker commits him/herself to do some future act. Commisives show 'world-to-word' fit, i.e. the speaker undertakes to make the world fit the words. Examples of speech acts are promises, pledges, vows.

■ Directives are speech acts whereby the speaker attempts to get the hearer to do something. Directives show 'word-to-world' fit, i.e. the hearer is supposed to carry out an action. Examples are: 'Will you help me?', 'I want you to help me.' Directive speech acts are used for functions such as asking, ordering, commanding, requesting, begging, pleading, praying, entreating, inviting, permitting, advising.

■ Expressives are illustrated by speech acts where the speaker expresses a psychological state towards the hearer. Thanking presupposes, for example, that the speaker 'feels grateful'; apologies, that the speaker is sorry. Some examples are thanking, congratulating, apologizing, condoling, deploring, welcoming.

■ Declarations, i.e. 'declare the verdict that' something is the case (e.g. acquit, disqualify). Declarations change the world by uttering something. Notice that the speech acts in this category are institutionalized, i.e. their success depends on the speaker being sanctioned by the social community. Here belong, for example, judges sentencing offenders, priests baptizing a child, etc.

The five classes have parallels in Austin's 'five very general classes' of illocutionary verbs (1962: 151):

■ Verdictives (cf. Searle's declarations) – 'declare a verdict'. Typical examples given by Austin are estimating, reckoning or appraising.

■ Exercitives (cf. Searle's directives) – 'the exercising of authority, rights or influencing' (e.g. appointing, voting, ordering, advising, warning).

■ Commissives (= Searle's commissives).

■ Behabitives (cf. Searle's expressives) – 'reactions to events or behaviours'. Typical examples include apologizing, congratulating.

■ Expositives (cf. Searle's assertives) – 'expanding of views'. Typical examples given by Austin are 'I reply', 'I argue', 'I concede', etc.

The definitions proposed in speech act theory are based on isolated examples and define an ideal or prototypical use of the speech act. When we try to analyse speech acts in authentic texts they have fuzzy boundaries and often seem to overlap with other speech acts. An utterance such as *the window is open* can be used as a statement or a request (to close the window) or be deliberatively ambiguous between the two interpretations. We can draw parallels with more recent speech act classifications which recognize the fuzziness of speech acts. Jucker and Taavitsainen (2000) discuss the problem of defining speech acts which overlap in some of their functions. They suggest, for example, that insults and compliments are related and can be distinguished by dimensions such as evaluation, in what they refer to as a multidimensional 'pragmatic space'. Speech acts can be more or less prototypical and more or less creative (see Unit A11.4). This can be illustrated with 'thanking'. Thanking can be performative ('I thank you') or descriptive (truth conditional) ('I am grateful'). It can be a sincere act of gratitude or a conventionalized gesture only. Moreover, there are degrees of conventionalization. In order to thank someone speakers can use a conventionalized pattern ('thank you') but they can also be more or less creative in the sense that they use a pattern which is not or only partly conventionalized ('that is nice'). In some of its uses, thanking comes close to apologizing. A past act (on the part of the hearer) may be differently interpreted and result either in the speaker thanking the hearer or apologizing because it places him or her in a position of debt to the hearer. As a result we find apologetic thanks: 'I'm so grateful – how can I ever repay you.'

A4.3 CRITICIZING SPEECH ACT THEORY

According to Levinson (1983) 'there has been a tendency to approach speech act theory as a dead body rather than use its insights'. However, speech acts are still a major topic in pragmatics. Indeed, new ways of analysing speech acts have been proposed. Verschueren has suggested that we treat speech acts as 'reasonably accurate approximations of the prototypical instances of verbal behaviour describable by means of the English verbs used as labels' (Verschueren 1999: 132). This has proved particularly popular within sociopragmatics and, more recently, historical sociopragmatics (see Unit A11). Another criticism that has since been addressed is the focus on single sentences without considering context. Researchers now acknowledge the need to analyse speech acts in a discourse perspective so that we will recognize when they have consequences for the continuation of the discourse, for example (see Unit A6). We would typically expect an apology to be followed by some sort of acknowledgement (i.e. *It's ok. Don't worry about it.*). The function of a speech act can also be dependent on the global context (e.g. whether it occurs in the opening or closing of the conversation. *Thank you* can be used at the end of a discussion and debate to dismiss the speaker (*Thank you Prime Minister*) or as a transition to a new speaker in the debate. In addition, we need to consider combinations of speech acts and their function, such as the combination of thanks and a compliment in the following (adapted from the London-Lund Corpus):

A: and you must have a key of the house and you must look at your map and you
   must know about the telephone and things
B: oh thank you very much that's very nice of you m thank you very much indeed

The function of speech acts is also dependent on the type of activity. *Thank you* can
serve as a signal that the answerer wants to take his leave when it is used at the end
of a telephone conversation, for example:

A: thanks very much
B: thank you look forward to seeing you
A: all right bye bye

Thanking is also an important part of other speech acts. Both acceptance and rejection of offers can be accompanied by thanking and a compliment. The compliment
has a mitigating and/or polite function after a rejection of the offer (*No thanks – it
looks very appetizing*) and also when accepting an offer (*Thank you they look very
nice*, to accept an offer; cf. Golato 2005). These examples of thanking show that
some speech acts are regulated by both social and discourse conventions (see Units
A6 and A8).

Searle has also been criticized because speech acts are only analysed from the
speaker's point of view. For empirical studies we need to take into account the interactional aspect of language and the hearer's role in the communication. For
example, a request is followed by an acceptance or declination of the request. Such
actions are difficult to define in speech act terms but are described in interactional
terms as responses. Less attention has been paid to how an utterance is related to
the preceding and following utterance within speech act theory. For this reason, the
notion of speech act is often replaced by discourse act or communicative act. The
description of a discourse act is based on where it occurs in the interaction and
focuses on what is to be achieved by the act (e.g. to make the recipient accept an
argument). Discourse analysts have focused, in particular, on whether the acts are
initiatory or responsive. The description of speech acts has also played a role in the
development of politeness theory (see Unit A8.2; see also Unit A11). A speech act
can, for instance, be face-threatening or challenging if it imposes on the hearer's
needs for freedom. Speech acts are also used in the organization of conversation as
well as in speech events which have a clear goal, such as classroom discourse (see
Unit A6) and courtroom discourse (see Unit A12).

A4.4 DIRECT AND INDIRECT SPEECH ACTS

A different approach to distinguishing between types of speech acts is to consider
whether they are direct or indirect. Indirectness captures the fact that we do not
always say literally what we mean. However, hearers normally have no difficulty in
interpreting what is said on the basis of inference. When there is a conventional
relationship between sentence type and speech act (illocutionary force) we have a

direct speech act. An example is the relation between an interrogative and a question (*Can you help me?*) or between the imperative and a command (or request). In the next section we will discuss some uses of indirect speech acts.

Sentence type	Speech act
Imperative	Command
Interrogative	Question
Declarative	Statement

Indirect speech acts are cases in which one illocutionary act is performed indirectly by way of performing another (Searle 1975). For example, hearing *Can you pass the salt?* the speaker knows that the utterance should be taken as a request although the form is that of a question.

If the sentence is interpreted indirectly as a request rather than literally as a question we can posit a number of inferential steps explaining the path from a question to a request. Searle (ibid.) has exemplified how inferencing provides the bridge between direct and indirect speech acts. Thus the hearer can infer the intended meaning of *Can you pass the salt?* because it is systematically related to a felicity condition of the request referring to the hearer's ability to carry out the action. Searle spells out in detail the inferential steps the hearer has to go through in order to interpret the question as a request. However, in the psycholinguistic literature the plausibility of the Searlean hypothesis that inferencing is the only route has been questioned. It has been claimed that the indirect requests can be understood without computing their meanings by inference from a literal meaning (Bach and Harnish 1979). The indirect forms have been conventionalized and can be regarded as conversational routines (see below).

Variation in requesting behaviour has also been shown to be affected by social features involving the activity, social roles of the speakers and interpersonal relations. In addition, the social factors relate to gender, class and age. Blum-Kulka *et al.* (1989c: 4) found for instance that, in Israeli society, requests from children to adults and those addressed to people in power were less direct than those in the opposite direction. The importance of social factors for the interpretation of indirect speech acts has also been confirmed in psycholinguistic experiments. Hoppe-Graff *et al.* (1985) showed in experiments that 'very indirect forms' were more likely to be used in standard, routine situations where the risk of misunderstanding was slight while less indirect forms were used in non-standard situations where speakers had to evaluate social factors (such as request goal, power, etc.) against the background of the contextual information (cf. Blum-Kulka *et al.* 1989c: 4).

A4.4.1 Asking someone to do something

We can distinguish a number of conventionalized (or partly conventionalized) markers for asking someone to do something. They can be interpreted without activating the literal meaning of the marker. An indication that they have been conventionalized as requests is the fact that they can occur together with *please* (*Could you please*). *Please* creates problems if the structure is interpreted as a question (**Is it raining please?*).

A large number of requestive markers (the conventionalized form of the request) can be used. The following list illustrates some uses (occurring five times or more in the LLC).

Assertion-based
You can
I would be grateful if you could
I wonder if you could
You had better
You must

Question-based
Could you (please)
Can you
Would you
Will you

Based on permission question
Let me
May I (just)
Can I
Could I

The frequency of indirect speech acts in language raises the question of why speakers are indirect. It has generally been assumed in the speech act literature that indirect speech acts (e.g. indirect requests) are more polite than the corresponding direct form (see also Unit A8). For example, Leech (1983: 108) suggests that the request forms (direct or indirect) can be placed on a scale with regard to (in)directness and politeness:

A.   Answer the phone
B.   I want you to answer the phone
C.   Will you answer the phone?
D.   Can you answer the phone?

> E.   Would you mind answering the phone?
>
> F.   Could you possibly answer the phone?

Notice that the scale suggests that it is more polite to make a request by means of *Could you possibly answer the phone?* than, for example, *I want you to answer the phone.* Alternative A gives the hearer little choice not to comply and is the most direct form. In C–F the modal auxiliary introduces tentativeness and is thus deemed to be more polite. But this condition is not necessarily true of all languages and cultures or, indeed, of all times in history (see Units A10 and A11).

Even in the case of modern data (involving native speakers only), this correlation between indirectness, politeness and apparent choice (on the part of the target) may not hold. For example, a boss might say to his new secretary *Would you like to type these letters?* but the power relationship between the two would suggest that the secretary does not have the right to refuse. In other words, this utterance still functions as an order (albeit an indirect one; ibid.: 127). That is, the let-out is bogus.

Another issue to consider is that utterances are typically multifunctional and, as such, it can be difficult to assign illocutionary force to an isolated utterance. If the utterance is embedded in the discourse this helps us to know what discourse function the utterance has by looking at the hearer's response. However, some speech acts remain fuzzy, i.e. they continue to be characterized by a multiplicity of discourse functions. For example, *If I were you, I'd leave town straight away* can be interpreted according to the context as a piece of advice, a warning or a threat (ibid.: 24).

A linguistic analysis of indirect speech acts as routines or formulae is possible if a speech act recurs in this form and has a (relatively) fixed form and function. According to Manes and Wolfson (1981), to be further discussed in Section B, compliments frequently occur in a (partly) fixed form. Other examples of a close relationship between form and function are apologies and thanking, to be discussed in the next section. They have a fixed form but, unlike requests, are usually expressed directly.

A4.5 SPEECH ACTS AS ROUTINES

There is a long tradition in linguistics that language use is characterized by collocational patterns with variations, multi-word units and idioms (cf. Sinclair 1991). Moreover the routinization of certain polite speech acts is almost taken for granted (cf. Goffman 1971). *How do you do?*, *How are you?*, *I am sorry*, *Thank you* are fixed phrases which we use for ritualized or ceremonious functions such as greeting or apologizing. If a phrase is fixed you cannot change its form and it comes with a ready-made prosodic contour. It is for instance not possible to make any changes in the greeting phrase *How do you do?* However, speech acts can be more or less fixed. Compare the unacceptable *How do you do today?* with *How are you today?* which is acceptable even though something has been added to the phrase.

Speech acts which can be expressed as routines – and hence are conventionally linked to form – include thanking, apologizing, offering, greeting, requesting and complimenting to give a few examples. Routinized speech acts are learnt and used as chunks and do not have to be created anew every time we want to use them. Routine phrases such as *Thank you* or *Sorry* are often used for phatic functions, i.e. to establish solidarity and intimacy with a conversational partner rather than express gratitude or to apologize. It follows that if a gratitude or apology phrase is not forthcoming this may have a disruptive effect on the social relations between the speakers. Both *Thank you* and *Sorry* can be intensified if the speaker wants to express more involvement. *Thank you very much indeed I'm so grateful* would be used in a situation where the recipient wants to express more gratitude and wants to maintain or strengthen an intimate and friendly relationship with the interlocutor. Similarly if an offence is serious the speaker has to choose a phrase such as *I'm terribly sorry* rather than a simple *Sorry.*

The emphasis in philosophical speech act theory was on their universal features. The situation is now changing and there is more interest in studying how speech acts vary synchronically or diachronically depending on the society and culture in which they are embedded. We are now also beginning to find a great deal of research exploring speech acts in regional varieties of English or cross-culturally within the new discipline of variational pragmatics (Schneider and Barron 2008). Variation in the realization of speech acts has often been studied on the basis of politeness (as suggested above). However, although the distinction between the direct form *Answer the phone* and the corresponding *Could you answer the phone?* can be explained in terms of politeness, comparable data from other languages suggest that other factors are needed to explain different ways of asking someone to do something. A potential universal such as 'the want of every "competent adult member" that his actions be unimpeded by others' (Brown and Levinson 1987: 67) explaining the choice of the indirect form *Could you answer the phone?* is consistent with typically Anglo-Saxon values and not with norms in other cultural settings (but see Unit B11.3). The cross-cultural study of speech acts is also of interest for language teaching and second language acquisition and will be discussed in Unit A10.

> **Summary and looking ahead**

The analysis of language in terms of speech acts has also been used in studies of aphasic patients (Wilcox and Davis 2005) and in studies by clinical linguists (Cummings 2005). Speech act theory has for instance been incorporated into pragmatic assessment tools. It has also been used in language teaching, for example, in communicative approaches to second language teaching (Trosborg 1995). In computational linguistics different models for speech act interpretation have been proposed to derive, for example, indirect speech acts by means of the inferential chains.

In Unit B4.2, we include an excerpt from Manes and Wolfson's (1981) pioneering article (which shows how compliments often come in a fixed form, i.e. as a formula). More recent work has demonstrated that many other speech acts (e.g. requests) can occur in a more or less fixed form (cf. *Could you . . .*). Because they are realized in a recognizable way, we can search for them in corpora – something we pick up on in Unit C2.3. A number of different methodologies have been used to study speech acts. It is therefore important to be aware of the advantages and disadvantages of different methods – something we address in Unit B4.3 and again in Unit B4.4, where we discuss how the so-called discourse completion test can be used to study thanking. One reason why the discourse completion test has been so popular is that it makes it possible to make systematic comparisons of speech acts across languages. However, we can also use corpora for comparisons of speech acts such as requests, as you will see in Section C. In Section C we also discuss thanking and the situations where it is used.

Unit A5
Implicature

In previous units, we've touched on the work of philosophers who looked for a theory of meaning based on truth conditions. In this unit, we discuss (in some depth) the work of the philospher H. Paul Grice (1975). As we learned in Unit A3.5, Grice's response to twentieth-century philosophical debates (about the meaning-lessness of some propositions) was to point out that, although much of what we say does not make sense 'literally', it does convey meaning. The utterance, *I sleep all the time Doctor*, will most probably be interpreted by the hearer (H) as an admission/concern on the part of the speaker (S) that she is sleeping more than she seems to think is good for her, for example. Grice's theory, then, is an attempt to explain how H gets from what is said literally to what is meant, that is, from the level of *expressed* meaning to the level of *implied* meaning.

Grice's work has been so influential within pragmatics that it's led to different Neo-Gricean and Post-Gricean approaches to implicature (see Unit A5.1 for a definition). As such, this unit will also introduce you to the Neo-Gricean approaches of Leech, Horn and Levinson, and to the Post-Gricean theory put forward by Sperber and Wilson. Before learning about these various approaches to implicature, however, let's first re-familiarize ourselves with some of Grice's terminology and, in particular, his *conventional/conversational* distinction.

A5.1 MEANING MORE THAN 'WHAT IS SAID'

Although the verb *implicate* is similar in meaning to the verb *imply* – in that both denote the action of suggesting information as opposed to stating information explicitly – implicate is the preferred way of defining this process within pragmatics. This is because Grice's (1969) initial definition sought to capture the central role played by S in conveying to H (or to the audience) information she does not actually state. For example, it's obvious that, when S informs her doctor she is sleeping *all the time*, her words aren't literally true; if they were, she would have to be communicating in her sleep! Rather, the doctor is being invited to look for – or, to use the preferred pragmatic term, *infer* – a meaning beyond the stated words: this could be that the patient is concerned that her excessive sleeping/tiredness is indicative of a health problem and wants the doctor's medical opinion. This generated implicature doesn't come from (the meaning of) the words themselves, however. It comes from:

(1) the patient's *use* of *I sleep all the time Doctor*, in the context of a doctor's surgery, to a person who is responsible for her medical wellbeing, and

(2) that person's ability to infer their patient's implicit message.

To summarize, when discussing implicature and inferencing, we are focusing on S's generation of some meaning beyond the semantic meaning of the word or words (by hinting or suggesting rather than stating explicitly), and on H's understanding of these hints/suggestions.

Because implicature and inference are not a feature of the words themselves, but of interlocutors' intents and interpretations, a hearer's inference may not necessarily be the same as the speaker's intended implicature. The movie, *The 51st State*, provides us with a fictional example of this. A character called Felix De Sousa had told his gangster colleague, Frederick, to 'take care of Laurence, the chemist'. But when De Sousa opened the trunk of his car, he found the chemist's body in there! Confused, De Sousa asked Frederick 'What happened?':

Frederick: You told me to take care of him.
DeSousa: Oh, Shit! I meant to take care of him, not fucking take care of him!

This example is amusing because the pattern, *I meant X not Y*, usually signals a difference between X and Y. However, in this instance, they are filled by the same proposition: *take care of him*. The listener therefore has to infer that there are two possible meanings to *take care of him* and that the addressee has chosen the wrong one (i.e. *kill him*). Our schema for 'gangsters' further adds to the humour at this point for we could argue that Frederick chose the most likely meaning, given their lifestyle; after all, gangsters are not usually known for *caring for* people!

A5.1.1 *Conventional* and *conversational* implicatures

What is implicated is always distinct from what is said, according to Grice, such that even factually incorrect statements can generate implicatures which succeed in context. Grice (ibid.: 142) provides the example, *Jones's butler mixed up the hats and coats* when, in fact, it was the gardener who did so. If said to us when leaving a party, however, we're very likely to ignore the factual mistake – for face reasons (see Units A5.2.1 and A8) – and instead prioritize S's implicit meaning: namely, that he doesn't know whose hat/coat belongs to whom, and needs us to clarify which hat/coat is ours.

The important thing about implicatures is that they do not contribute to the truth-conditional content of a proposition. However, they are not all of the same type.

Grice distinguished between conventional (i.e. non-conversational) implicatures and conversational implicatures, for example.

Conventional implicatures are derived directly from (because of being encoded in) the meaning of the words in use. By way of illustration, *but* conveys an idea of contrast such that, when we hear utterances akin to *She's a professor but she's OK really*, we're likely to infer that professors aren't, normally, okay people (whatever that means)! Similarly, *furthermore* (like *moreover*) conveys the idea of *p* being in addition to *q*, such that, when we read *Laptops are getting cheaper all the time; furthermore, their quality is improving*, we're likely to infer that (S believes) laptops have become relatively inexpensive whilst maintaining a very good quality standard. Conventional implicatures can also conventionally implicate explanation (see, e.g., *therefore, so*) and surprise/contrary expectation (see, e.g., *even*).

Compare the above with conversational implicatures, which must be derived from contextual clues and – according to Grice – can be one of two types: generalized and particularized. The utterance, *I sleep all the time Doctor*, is an example of a generalized conversational implicature (GCI), as the implicature of sleeping too much/most of the time holds across a variety of contexts (medical or otherwise). In fact, *I sleep all the time . . .*, uses adynation: deliberate exaggeration which refers to an impossibility (cf. hyperbole, which involves exaggerating a truth). The adynation relies on the quantifier *all* triggering the related scalar implicature <all, most, many, some>, such that we understand S to mean she sleeps *most* (or too much) of the time (we explore scalar implicatures in some detail in Unit C3.2). The following question-and-answer sequence, in contrast, contains a particularized conversational implicature (PCI) (example from Levinson 1983: 126):

A: What on earth has happened to the roast beef?
B: The dog is looking very happy

The difference between this and our GCI, *I sleep all the time . . .*, is that there is no tangible (extra-contextual) association between *roast beef* and a *dog*, as there is between the idea of someone sleeping too much and the complaint, *I sleep all the time*. Indeed, in this case, it's the juxtaposition of the utterances which leads us to infer that the dog in question is responsible for the disappearance of the roast beef and, further, is *looking very happy*, because he's eaten it! A PCI, then, requires our first understanding the immediate context of occurrence if we are to arrive at the correct inference (i.e. the dog has eaten the roast beef). A GCI, in contrast, arises irrespective of the immediate context-of-use (such that *some* will always implicate <not many/all>).

A5.1.2 Meaning$_N$ and meaning$_{NN}$

Another interesting definition provided by Grice (1957: 213–14), which is also important to his theory of communication and implicature, is that between natural meaning (or meaning$_N$) and non-natural meaning (or meaning$_{NN}$). Marmaridou (2000: 227) provides a lovely non-verbal example to explain the difference between them:

> Suppose that two interlocutors are engaged in a conversation about an absent friend. During the conversation, the addressee happens to cough. At that moment the speaker looks up and by doing so notices the 'absent' friend approaching, whereupon she changes the topic of conversation. Since the addressee's cough was not intended as a sign for the speaker to drop the subject, this instance constitutes an example of natural meaning. Now, if the addressee sees the 'absent' friend approaching and coughs in order to attract the speaker's attention and signal to her that she should change the topic and if the speaker becomes aware of this intention, then it can be said that the addressee by his cough has meant-nn that the speaker should change the topic.

Simply put, meaning$_N$ relates to the meaning that a particular sign has in virtue of its causal relations to other events. Hence, a cough can lead to a change of topic (meaning$_N$) as we saw above. However, a cough will only constitute meaning$_{NN}$ when someone has used this particular sign to mean something and (importantly) their intent to communicate this particular something has been recognized as such by their interlocutor. Meaning$_{NN}$, then, equates to (the successful transmission of) speaker intention.

Grice's interest was in explaining how it is that interlocutors work out meaning$_{NN}$ when this meaning is not part of what is explicitly said/entailed/conventionally implicated (see Figure A5.1 below).

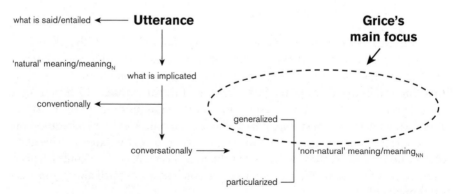

Figure A5.1 Grice's focus on conversational implicatures (adapted from Grundy 2008: 107)

A5.1.3 Grice's Cooperative Principle and the conversational maxims

Grice's understanding of the inferencing process is built on the assumption that:

> Our talk exchanges do not normally consist of a succession of disconnected remarks, and would not be rational if they did. They are characteristically, to some degree at least, cooperative efforts; and each participant recognizes in them, to some extent, a common purpose or set of purposes, or at least a mutually accepted direction . . . We might then formulate a rough general principle which participants will be expected (*ceteris paribus*) to observe, *viz*: 'Make your contribution such as is required, at the stage at which it occurs, by the accepted purpose or direction of the talk exchange in which you are engaged. One might label this the Cooperative Principle.'
>
> (Grice 1975: 47)

Grice famously went on to underpin his Cooperative Principle (CP) with four maxims: Quantity; Quality; Relation; and Manner. He described these maxims as follows:

Quantity	Be informative. (1) Make your contribution as informative as required (for the current purposes of the exchange). (2) Do not make your contribution more informative than is required.
Quality	Be truthful. Try to make your contribution one that is true. (1) Do not say what you believe to be false. (2) Do not say that for which you lack evidence.
Relation	Be relevant.
Manner	Be perspicuous. (1) Avoid obscurity of expression. (2) Avoid ambiguity. (3) Be brief (avoid unnecessary prolixity). (4) Be orderly.

Grice wasn't trying to tell us how to behave as interlocutors. He was suggesting that:

(1) conversation is governed by certain conventions;
(2) hearers tend to assume speakers are conforming with these conventions; and
(3) if speakers are not conforming, they have good reason(s) not to.

A5.1.4 Ways of breaking the maxims

If Grice didn't believe that we satisfy all the demands of the CP all of the time, why did he outline the maxims so specifically? A simplistic answer is that it provided him with the means of explaining how conversational implicatures come to be generated (cf. Unit A5.1.1): hence, Grice's identification of *flouting*, in particular, whereby S deliberately fails to observe a maxim (or maxims) as a means of prompting others to look for a meaning which is different from, or in addition to, the expressed meaning. Consider the following PCI:

Peter: Do you want some coffee?
Mary: Coffee would keep me awake.

Notice that Mary opts to respond with information about what coffee does to her metabolism when a simple *yes* or *no* would have been more useful for Peter; in doing so, she flouts the Relation maxim, 'Be relevant' (but see Unit A5.3). Notice that we need more contextual information if we are to work out what Mary actually meant by her response. Did she mean *no* (because she will be going to bed soon, for example)? Or did she mean *yes* (because Mary has some work to finish, and needs to remain alert)? If this were a real conversation, Peter would have the context-of-utterance to help him to decipher Mary's meaning and/or be able to ask for clarification (if he needed to).

There are ways of breaking the maxims in addition to flouting, of course. For example, a *violation* constitutes a deliberate attempt by S to 'mislead' her interlocutor(s). We might note, here, that we can all-too-easily associate the intention to deceive with a malicious or selfish motive on S's part. But this needn't be the case, as the following example from Cutting (2002: 40) demonstrates: 'Mummy's gone on a little holiday because she needs a rest.' This violation of the second part of the Quality maxim, 'Do not say what you believe to be false', was motivated by a desire to safeguard H's sense of well-being, according to Cutting, for mummy had actually gone away to decide whether she should divorce her husband.

An *opt-out* involves S explicitly indicating his or her unwillingness to cooperate in the way the maxims require. We've taken the following example from a BBC (online) story relating to the cancellation of a 2011 Valentine's Day event at the Cheltenham Racecourse (in Gloucestershire, UK). As you'll see if you access the link below, a racecourse spokesman gives some brief details about a problem concerning the third-party organizers, before stating: 'We are passing the matter to our solicitors and can make no further comment at this time' (13 February 2011: http://www.bbc.co.uk/news/uk-england-gloucestershire-12442689).

An *infringement* constitutes a non-observance on S's part which is not intentional but, rather, stems from imperfect linguistic performance. S may have an imperfect command of the language because of being an L2 speaker, for example, or because of being very young. Alternatively, his linguistic performance may be permanently impaired due to brain damage/a degenerative disease/a pre-existing condition such as autism, etc., or be temporarily impaired because of drink or drugs. Mark Haddon's (2003) *The curious incident of the dog in the night-time* provides some useful examples of infringments by the character, Christopher, who suffers from autism. Christopher has found a dead dog, but his way of communicating to the police is so different to the norm that the police initially suspect him of killing the dog. Christopher has problems with the maxim of Quantity, in particular, such that his answers to the policeman's questions are sometimes uninformative ('The dog is dead', when the dog – who's obviously dead – is in full view) and sometimes over-informative ('I am fifteen years and 3 months and 2 days'). Christopher also struggles with the Relation maxim, such that he doesn't always comprehend the communicative leaps made by his interlocutors. In one instance, for example, a woman at a subway station offers Christopher her help (p. 226):

> And I was sitting on the ground and the woman knelt down on one knee and she said, 'Is there anything I can do to help you?'

> . . . [B]ut she was a stranger, so I said, 'Stand further away' because I didn't like her being so close. And I said, 'I've got a Swiss Army Knife and it has a saw blade and it could cut someone's fingers off.'

> And she said, 'OK buddy. I'm going to take that as a no,' and she stood up and walked away.

Although Christopher's response could be easily heard as a threat by the woman; that was not his intention. He merely wanted her to stand less close to him.

A second means of non-observance – that of *suspension* – was not originally identified by Grice. A suspension is said to come into play when the speech event/ activity type is such that the maxims are not in operation. Consequently, there is no expectation that they will be fulfilled (see, e.g., Thomas 1995). Imagine, if you will, an interrogation. It's very unlikely that an interrogator will start from the assumption that the interrogatee will tell them the truth from the outset. Hence, we can take it that the Quality maxim is probably suspended in such circumstances.

A5.2 RETHINKING GRICE: NEO-GRICEAN PRAGMATICS

We include an extact from Grice's (1975) explanation of the CP and its maxims in Unit B5.2. As you read that extract, you will become aware that Grice believed the first component of the Quality maxim, 'Try to make your contribution one that is true' to be the most important – to the extent that 'other maxims come into operation only on the assumption that this maxim of Quality is satisfied'. Grice also admits to finding his Relation maxim problematic, not least because:

> . . . its formulation conceals a number of problems . . . about what different kinds and focuses of relevance there may be, how these shift in the course of a talk exchange, how to allow for the fact that subjects of conversation are legitimately changed, and so on.
>
> (Ibid.: 46)

In addition, he suggests that, potentially, 'there are . . . all sorts of other maxims . . . such as "Be polite"'. Researchers have since proposed a number of changes to Grice's theory, which address the above, albeit in differing ways. In the following sub-sections, we outline the ideas of three well-known Neo-Griceans – Leech (1983), Horn (1984) and Levinson (1995, 2000) – before moving on to discuss the Post-Gricean approach of Sperber and Wilson (1995) in Unit A5.3.

A5.2.1 Leech's (1983) expansionist approach

Leech (1983) recognized that the pressure to be polite can be very powerful, to the extent that the Gricean maxims are affected. For example, we might find it rude if, in answer to our greeting, *How are you?*, our interlocutor merely replied *Fine* and walked away without returning the greeting. Yet, this 'answer' adheres to the Manner maxim. Leech also suggested that some flouts of the Gricean maxims are undertaken because of politeness reasons (see Unit B5.3). His argument? Indirectness allows us to convey messages which, because they are ambivalent (i.e. have more than one potential pragmatic force), are arguably less face-threatening than they might have been. We might opt to say to the host, *It's hot in here*, or even *Do you think it's hot in here?*, when at a party, rather than request/command our host to open a window, for example. We do so, according to Leech, because such indirect utterances give our targets more freedom (i.e. optionality) in deciding how to respond (see Unit A8).

Leech proposed that we therefore complement Grice's CP with a Politeness Principle (PP) and six interpersonal politeness maxims (tact, generosity, approbation, modesty, agreement, sympathy). Our second reading, in Unit B5.3, outlines Leech's argument for a PP and also how it is that utterances such as *Will/Can you open the window?* function as polite requests. We also discuss Leech's PP (and maxims) in some detail in Unit A8. Hence, we will not outline his approach in any more detail here. Suffice it to say, Leech's consideration of linguistic politeness from the view of speech act types, and his decision to connect politeness to a violation of the CP via indirectness, have been criticized by some (see, e.g., Fraser 1990; Watts 2003).

A5.2.2 Horn's (1984) reductionist approach

Horn (1984) represents our second Neo-Gricean approach. Like Grice, he ascribes a privileged status to the Quality maxim, such that it becomes a kind of felicity condition for all implicatures – on the assumption that it is hard to see how any of the other maxims can be satisfied without it being observed (ibid.: 12). But he reduces the other Gricean maxims to 'two antithetical principles of pragmatic inference', the Q Principle and the R Principle:

Q Principle

'Make your contribution sufficient; say as much as you can' (with R in mind: Horn 1984: 13)

= Gricean maxim of Quantity$_1$ ('Make your contribution as informative as is required') + Manner$_{1+2}$ ('Avoid obscurity of expression. Avoid ambiguity')

R Principle

'Make your contribution necessary; say no more than [you] must' (with Q in mind: Horn 1984: 13)

= Gricean maxim of Quantity$_2$ ('Do not make your contribution more informative than is required') + maxim of Manner$_{3+4}$ ('Be brief. Be orderly') + maxim of Relation ('Be relevant')

The Q Principle is deliberately hearer-based: it centres on the assumption that S will provide sufficient information for H (in a way that eases H's processing effort: see, e.g., Martinet 1962). Hence, if *some* is as much as S can say, H should take it that S implies *not all* (unless he is given evidence to the contrary). Similarly, *may* should be taken to mean 'permitted but not obligated' to (cf. *must*). You'll notice that we've drawn our examples from the scalar implicature relating to quantifiers <all, most, many, some> and the scalar implicature relating to modals <must, should, may>. This is deliberate, as Horn's Q Principle provides us with an excellent means of explaining the phenomenon of scalar implicature. Indeed, we use the term 'Horn scale', within the field of pragmatics, to explain a number of alternative sets (including numbers, colours, etc.).

In contrast to the Q Principle, Horn's R Principle is oriented to reducing the speaker's effort, and centres on the assumption that S should say no more than is necessary to achieve her goals, because her minimal forms will invite pragmatic strengthening (i.e. inferences; cf. Zipf 1949). As we discovered in Unit A3.5, for example, people will often assume 'drink' means *alcoholic drink* in a (Western) party context. Similarly, *if* will be taken to mean 'if and only if' and *can*, 'can and will' (cf. *Can you pass the salt?*).

A5.2.3 Levinson's (1995, 2000) revisionist approach

Levinson has argued for a revision – as well as a reduction – of the Gricean maxims. His first step involved refining Grice's distinction between 'what is said' and what is conveyed. He did so by distinguishing three levels of meaning:

■ Entailment, that is, meaning which is derived from/involves truth relations;
■ utterance-type meaning, that is, default interpretations which are inferable without having to draw on contextual cues (cf. Grice's GCIs); and
■ utterance-token meaning, that is, context-sensitive interpretations (cf. Grice's PCIs).

Levinson has since suggested that utterance-type meaning (i.e. Grice's GCIs) can be accounted for via three *heuristics* related to Grice's Quantity and Manner maxims (see Unit A5.1.3), namely:

H1 (cf. Quantity$_1$): *What isn't said, isn't.*
H2 (cf. Quantity$_2$): *What is simply described is stereotypically exemplified.*
H3 (cf. Manner): *What's said in an abnormal way, isn't normal.*

These heuristics, in turn, have formed the basis for three Neo-Gricean principles; the Q-Principle (Quantity), the I-Principle (Informativeness) and the M-Principle (Manner). As the descriptions below reveal, the Q- and I-Principles broadly correspond to Horn's Q and R Principles (see above) as well as various aspects of Grice's Quantity and Manner maxims. The M-Principle has been included by Levinson as a means of dealing with marked inference, and thus also overlaps with Grice's Manner maxim:

Levinson's Q-Principle

Cf. Quantity$_1$: 'Make your contribution as informative as required'; see also Horn's Q Principle

S: Do not say less than is required (i.e. provide a statement that is informationally weaker than one's knowledge of the world allows, bearing in mind the I-Principle)

H: What is not said is not the case (i.e. assume S has made the strongest statement consistent with what she knows)

Levinson's I-Principle

Cf. Quantity$_2$: 'Do not make your contribution more informative than is required'; see also Horn's R Principle

S: Do not say more than is required (bearing in mind the Q-Principle)

H: What is expressed simply is stereotypically exemplified (i.e. read as much into an utterance as is consistent with what you know about the world)

> *Levinson's M-Principle*
>
> | | |
> |---|---|
> | Cf. Grice's (1975) Manner$_{1+4}$: 'Avoid obscurity of expression . . . avoid prolixity' | S: Do not use a marked expression without reason. |
> | | H: What's said in an abnormal way isn't normal (i.e. assume that if what is said is communicated in a marked way, it is designed to convey a marked message) |

One thing to notice, here, is that Levinson's Q-, I- and M-Principles contain both a speaker and hearer component (like Horn's). The hearer components of the Q- and I-Principles have proven to be particularly useful, as they can explain why stereotypical (or taken-for-granted) aspects of meanings can be left implicit. *I cut a finger*, for example, will be taken to mean the speaker has cut his/her own finger (unless interlocutors are given evidence which contradicts this assumption).

Interestingly, Levinson has suggested that the Q-, I- and M-Principles give rise to Q-, I- and M-implicatures respectively, but that Q- and M-implicatures will have priority over any I-implicatures. Q-implicatures are triggered by a Horn scale or (by choosing an expression from) a contrastive set. For example, if S says 'The flag is white', then H is entitled to assume it isn't white and some other colour(s) from the colour-set; say, red and blue. I-implicatures stand in contrast to Q-implicatures in that they implicate a more expanded interpretation, based on our knowledge of the world. Hence, *Anne's ringing the bells tonight* (without the place explicitly specified) will I-implicate that Anne is ringing the bells at the usual place: a church in Lancaster (in Lancashire, UK). Similarly, *The baby cried. The mommy picked it up* (Sacks 1972) I-implicates that *baby* and *mommy* are related. The M-implicature tends to be used when a correspondingly unmarked expression would not successfully signal the intended message. Compare *Mary caused the car to stop*, which generates the M-implicature that Mary (probably) stopped the car by means other than applying the breaks (i.e. the usual way!): she might have allowed the car to bump into the garage door, for example (cf. *Mary stopped the car*).

Levinson's ideas are prompted by a desire to extend Grice's notion of 'what is said' so that we can allow for much more of a pragmatic contribution than Grice had proposed. But he stopped short of suggesting that there is a level which is intermediate between what is said and what is implicated. As we found in Unit A3.5, the language philosopher Kent Bach has suggested such a level (see, e.g., the discussion of *impliciture*). Moreover, this 'what is implicit in what is said' level is motivated by the belief that there should be no pragmatic intrusion into what is said (cf. Levinson). Relevance Theorists have offered a similar concept to Bach's *impliciture* (see, e.g., the discussion of *explicature*), but for different motivations to Bach: they reject the what is said/what is implicated – and hence semantics-pragmatics – view of Grice and the Neo-Griceans, in favour of explicatures and implicatures; where explicatures constitute a development of a logical form encoded by U (via pragmatic enrichment) and implicatures capture the wider (non explicit) pragmatic meaning. We learn about this cognitive-based approach in some detail in Unit A5.3.

A5.3 SPERBER AND WILSON'S POST-GRICEAN PRAGMATICS

Sperber and Wilson go much further than the Neo-Griceans have done in revising Grice's ideas. They propose that all of the Gricean maxims be reduced to one, that of Relation, on the assumption that relevance is a natural feature of all successful communication. Indeed, they argue that:

> Communicators do not 'follow' the principle of relevance; and they could not violate it even if they wanted to. The principle of relevance applies without exceptions
>
> (Sperber and Wilson 1995: 162; cf. Grice's Relation maxim)

This proposal is more innovative than it might first appear, as relevance theoretic pragmatics assumes a very different view of what pragmatics is and what it entails than Grice and the Neo-Griceans. For example, whereas the latter account for the derivation of implicatures using an inductive, rationalistic perspective (and hence focus on what interlocutors *most probably* mean in context), relevance theorists seek to explain what actually goes on *in* hearers' minds, using deductive means. They argue, for example, that as relevance is a given, interlocutors will treat the context as the variable (ibid.: 142). Moreover, in processing the relevance of an utterance, in context X, they will identify (what they take to be) S's communicative intention by constructing (what they hope will be) an accurate representation of it in their minds. A consistent inability to construct such mental representations, moreover, may be taken to constitute some kind of pathological condition; this helps to explain why many relevance theorists are interested in experimental tests and studies of communication pathologies (as we'll learn in Unit C5).

Relevance Theory is based on a broad understanding of relevance and two Principles of Relevance. Relevance is said to encompass 'all external stimuli or internal mental representations capable of providing an input to cognitive processes', including 'sights, smells, utterances, thoughts, memories or conclusions of inferences' (Wilson 2010: 394). The first of the two principles – the Cognitive Principle – refers to cognition on a general level: 'Human cognition tends to be geared to the maximisation of relevance' (Sperber and Wilson 1995: 260). The second principle – the Communicative Principle – comes about because of the first, and is specific to communication (as its name implies). It captures the notion that interlocutors, by communicating something, are implicitly asserting they have something pertinent to communicate: 'Every act of ostensive communication communicates a presumption of its own optimal relevance' (ibid.). The ostensiveness of the act is important: as we discussed in Unit A5.1.2, a cough can be used by S to communicate intentionally as well as being simply a symptom of ill health. The two Relevance Theory Principles are explained in some detail in our third and final reading in Unit B5 (B5.4).

The presumption of 'optimal relevance' does not mean that every utterance has the same degree of relevance for an addressee. Rather, it means that addressees will use the minimum necessary effort to obtain the most relevant interpretation, implicature or 'contextual effect'. Let's explore this by returning to our Peter/Mary example, where Peter asks Mary if she'd like some coffee, and Mary replies that coffee will keep her awake (which originates from ibid.: 34). Assuming that Mary is trying to be optimally relevant, Peter focuses on finding Mary's most likely meaning (given his question). This is where the context comes into play: if Peter and Mary are shopping for groceries, for example, Peter knows that Mary knows that *want* can be pragmatically enriched to *want to buy*, and *coffee* to *a jar/packet of coffee* (not a drink); as such, Peter can assume that Mary's response means she doesn't want him to buy any coffee (because of the adverse effect it seems to have on her). If Peter and Mary are at home, he would know that Mary knows *coffee* refers to the liquid drink, on this occasion (this assumes that Peter is not writing a shopping list at the time!). At this point, however, he still needs to gauge whether *Mary does not want to stay awake and therefore does not want coffee* or *Mary does want to stay awake and therefore does want coffee*. This is because Mary's response, 'Coffee will keep me awake', constitutes a weak implicature and, as such, generates a number of possible hypotheses. Indeed, much stronger implicatures are *I want to sleep tonight* (which would be heard as a *no*) or *I need to stay awake* (which would be heard as a *yes*). So why does Mary opt for an utterance that doesn't appear to be as optimally relevant as it might have been? Sperber and Wilson claim that the outcome (or cost/benefit) of Peter's extra processing effort will be an extra cognitive effect that would otherwise not have occurred to him: this might be that Peter comes to recognize what Mary plans to do that evening (i.e. sleep or not sleep).

A5.4 THE ROLE OF S AND H IN MEANING MAKING

Sperber and Wilson view communication in terms of *cognitive environment* (i.e. the set of facts that are manifest to an individual) and *mutual manifestness* (i.e. the set of potential assumptions that individuals are capable of perceiving and inferring as a result of an ostensive stimulus). Mutual manifestness, in particular, involves interlocutors' dynamically processing contextual cues 'online' as and when they occur. As the following quotation reveals, however, Sperber and Wilson believe that S has more communicative responsibility than does H:

> It is left to the communicator to make correct assumptions about the codes and contextual information that the audience will have accessible and be

likely to use in the comprehension process. The responsibility for avoiding misunderstandings also lies with the speaker, so that all the hearer has to do is go ahead and use whatever code and contextual information comes most easily to hand.

(Sperber and Wilson 1995: 43)

The responsibility that Sperber and Wilson give to S is understandable, in view of their stance that H always assumes S is trying to be optimally relevant (see above). However, it gives the impression that the roles of S and H are 'fixed' when, in reality, they are transient and continually interchanging – in both everyday conversation and institutional interaction. Moreover, speakers and hearers both play an active part in co-constructing the discourse. That is to say, H evaluates/provides feedback to S which, in turn, may determine S's next move. Some cognitive linguists have thus proposed an alternative cognitive pragmatics approach to RT which acknowledges 'the combined effort of an actor and a partner' who 'consciously and intentionally cooperate to construct together the shared meaning of their inter-action' (Bara 2010: 51). Arundale (2008: 243) goes further still: he proposes that we reject Gricean-influenced approaches altogether (because of their focus on H's *successful recognition of S's intention* and, latterly, on H's *attribution* of intent) and adopt, instead, a model which considers 'utterances in sequence' and focuses, specif-ically, on S and H's ongoing process of 'confirming and modifying' *interconnected interpretings* and their (potential) 'proactive and retroactive effects' (cf. an approach where we focus on one utterance at a time).[1]

Summary and looking ahead

The focus of this unit has been the work of Grice, and subsequent work within pragmatics which has sought to extend, develop or amend his ideas. We continue in this vein in Unit B5; we do so by including excerpts from canonical readings which outline Grice's (1989) motivation for the CP and Leech's (1981) motivation for a PP to complement the CP. We also include an excerpt from Wilson (2010), in which she outlines the two Principles of Relevance (i.e. the Cognitive Principle and the Communicative Principle). In Unit C5, we demonstrate how the relevance theoretic approach, in particular, has recently been drawn upon by experimental pragmaticians as a means of exploring GCIs, scalar implicatures and other pragmatic phenomena.

It should be noted that much of what we have discussed in this unit – and will go on to discuss in Unit B5 – reflects the philosophical/linguistic tradition within pragmatics. As we emphasized in Unit A1.2, however, there is another perspective within pragmatics which is *socio* in orientation. Practioners who adhere to this perspective emphasize not only how we use words to 'do things' (cf. our discussion of speech acts in Unit A4), but also how, as interlocutors, we co-construct our meaning via interactional sequences. We touched on this idea, albeit briefly, in Unit A5.4, when we introduced the work of Arundale. As an adherent of the con-versational analytic approach, Arundale believes that the context needed to interpret what is said is created by the interlocutors themselves in the course of the sequential development of the discourse. As we highlighted in Unit A1.4, some pragmaticians argue that this approach amounts to an investigation of the co-text as opposed to the context as it ignores meaning-shaping factors which are language-external. An approach that considers the meaning-shaping potential of such language-external factors is discourse analysis. We explain these two approaches to interaction – conversation analysis and discouse analysis – in Unit A6.

NOTE

1   Arundale (1999, 2008) is particularly critical of approaches which treat each utterance as though it is independent of other utterances, and that also treat speaker and recipient psychological states (and hence 'meaning') as though they are independent (see also Clark 1996).

Unit A6
Pragmatics and discourse

It is not obvious how the structure of discourse should be analysed and in particular whether it can be described using the same terms that we use for the grammatical analysis of sentences and clauses. We can go back to the early 1950s to find some discussion of this. For example, Zellig Harris, who is well known for his work within structural grammar, proposed that discourse is the next level in a hierarchy where the other levels are morphemes, clauses and sentences. Another 'grammatical' approach is represented by Van Dijk (1972), who claims that we can write a text grammar in the same way as a generative sentence grammar. According to other researchers, the structure of discourse cannot be described by extending the grammatical analysis of sentences and clauses to discourse. However, there is very little consensus on how discourse structure should be described. In Unit A6.1, we focus on two seminal approaches, specifically, Sinclair and Coulthard (1975) and Sacks *et al.* (1974). We then move on to discuss individual aspects of interaction, which are commonly drawn upon in pragmatics such as turn-taking, preference organization, openings and closings (see Units A6.2–6.4).

A6.1 CATEGORIZING DISCOURSE STRUCTURE: TWO SEMINAL APPROACHES

Sinclair and Coulthard's (1975) pioneering research – which is generally associated with the Birmingham School of Discourse Analysis – was based on an attempt to describe the structure of classroom discourse in linguistic terms. But their analytic notions have since been used to describe other 'institutional' discourse types such as the courtroom (see, e.g., Archer 2005).

An important notion in Sinclair and Coulthard's framework is *exchange* – i.e. the conversational unit consisting of an initiation by the teacher followed by a response from the pupil. In a teacher-pupil exchange it is also common for the teacher to express his/her appreciation of the pupil's answer. An example of a three-part structure follows (Sinclair and Coulthard 1975: 51, cited in Thornborrow 2002: 109).

Teacher: What's the name of this cutter? Hands up.
((hand goes up))
Janet

Janet: Hacksaw
Teacher: The hacksaw. And I'll put that other one there.

Sinclair and Coulthard also point out that some kind of feedback is essential for the pupils to understand whether they have answered correctly.

The same questioning format has been described in a conversational–analytical framework (from McHoul 1978, quoted by Thornborrow ibid.):

T: What didju call these
            (1.0) [[indicates on screen]
( ):   @((whispers)) Sand dunes
            (2.9)
B: Sa: :nd dunes @ ( )
T: Sa: : :nd dunes alright any other sensible name for it

The example describes the same kind of pattern consisting of a question, followed by a response from the pupil and the teacher's feedback (see below for a discussion of Conversation Analysis transcription conventions).

The framework suggested by Sinclair and Coulthard is very complex and incorporates a number of hierarchically related units. The following diagram from Stenström (1994: 30) gives some idea of the number of units which are needed to describe spoken discourse on different levels:

Transaction	consists of one or more exchanges dealing with one single topic; one or more transactions make up a conversation
Exchange	is the smallest interactive unit consisting, minimally, of two turns produced by two different speakers
Turn	is everything the current speaker says before the next speaker takes over; it consists of one or more moves
Move	is what the speaker does in a turn in order to start, carry on and finish an exchange, i.e. the way s/he interacts; it consists of one or more acts
Act	signals what the speaker intends, what s/he wants to communicate; it is the smallest interactive unit

The diagram shows how these units can be arranged hierarchically on a rank scale (see Halliday 1961 on the notion of 'rank scale'). For example, a *transaction* (such as a lesson) consists of several *exchanges* which are made up of *turns* (and *moves*). *Act* refers to a discourse or interactional act in Sinclair and Coulthard's model and is not defined in the same way as speech acts. Rather, acts perform functions such as eliciting a response and follow-up.

The analysis by Sinclair and Coulthard has sometimes been thought of as cumbersome because of the large number of (new) categories. In addition, Stubbs (1983: 132) points out several unsolved problems (which are not necessarily unique to this model):

> [T]here are many unsolved problems, such as the following: Is it possible to give formal recognition criteria for exchanges? Are exchanges always well-defined units, with clear-cut openings and closings? Or do they have well-defined openings, but ill-defined ends? As Labov and Fanshel (1977: 62) suggest: 'ending is a more complex act than beginning'. Or are some utterances simply Janus-faced, closing one exchange and opening the next? Is all conversational data analysable into exchanges, or is the concept applicable only to a narrow range of discourse (e.g. teacher-pupil dialogue) whilst other discourse (e.g. casual conversation) drifts along in a less structured way? Can one exchange be embedded within another, giving discontinuous exchanges? And so on. Any work which makes structural claims about the organization of spoken discourse must provide answers to such questions.

The problems pinpointed in the quotation from Stubbs have to do with the deeper-lying fact that conversation is the result of speaker-hearer negotiation (cf. Unit A5.4). The exchange as defined by Sinclair and Coulthard is to some extent open-ended: it is not possible to predict from one speaker's move what the next move will be. This means that in a given context an utterance can be ambiguous between several interpretations and result in different continuations.

A more recent attempt to categorize speech act moves, which draws from Sinclair and Coulthard, is that of Carletta *et al.* (1997). Their coding scheme (of transaction, exchange, move) was proposed for the purpose of analysing the dialogue structure in a map task. Map tasks involve two participants, who have been given slightly different maps. One person has a route marked on the map and has been told to communicate to the other what route to follow. Their moves thus tend to display initiating or responding functions. Typical initiations include the *instruct* move (intended to command the partner to carry out an action), the *align* move (checking the partner's attention) and the *check* move (requesting the partner to confirm information).

A6.2 SACKS, SCHEGLOFF AND JEFFERSON (1974)

A similar interest in the organization of discourse, and its importance as an object of study, was shared by a break-away group of sociologists referring to themselves as 'ethnomethodologists'. The ethnomethodologists were above all interested in describing the methods used by people to account for their own actions and those of others (the so-called 'ethno-methods') (Hutchby and Wooffitt 2008: 27). This approach, as applied to conversational interaction, originates in the lectures given by Harvey Sacks (Sacks 1992) and has since been further developed by Emanuel Schegloff, Gail Jefferson and others.

The approach developed by Sacks, Schegloff, Jefferson and colleagues is generally referred to as Conversation Analysis. The focus of Conversation Analysis researchers is not just institutional exchange systems, but also occurring interactions. Interactions (whether institutional or conversational) are audio- (or video-)recorded and transcribed in order to show where a new speaker enters the conversation, gaps in the conversation, overlap, repetition and repair as well as other performance phenomena. In addition, their analysis is based entirely on what occurs in their datasets (i.e. what is termed participant response). Discourse Analysis (DA), on the other hand, draws from *a priori* theoretical notions (see, e.g., Sinclair and Coulthard's iniation-response-feedback structure). The following is an example of a typical Conversation Analysis transcription (from Wooffitt 2005: 12):

1 E: hh something re:d. ehrm:: i- looks like it might be a
2   porcupine with lots of spines standing hhh standing up
3 S: yeah hh
4 E: and then a frog=a frog's face peering over something
5   (0.8)
6 E: hh a ghost? coming out of door: or a chai:r (0.5) like a mirror. (.)
7   in a funny house,
8 S: yeah=
9 E: =hh shapes (0.3) ahr:: are in this funny house

The transcription shows a lot of detail in comparison with an orthographic rendering. Notice, for example, Speaker S's verbal response (*yeah hh*) in turn 3. Non-lexical words such as *ehrm* (turn 1) and *ahr* (turn 9) have been transcribed. Other features which have been noted are breathiness (*hh*) and laughter (not in the transcription). Notice also that the length of pauses have been marked since this is a fact which may be interactionally important. The use of = in turns 8 and 9 signals 'latching', i.e. the turns are linked without any pause or overlap.

Conversation analysts are concerned with organizational problems in the conversation. Some important principles or techniques in Conversation Analysis designed to deal with conversational problems are also drawn upon quite heavily in pragmatics. These include turn-taking, adjacency (pairs), preference organization and openings and closings, and will be discussed in turn below.

A6.3 SEQUENTIAL ORGANIZATION AND TURN-TAKING

In conversation speakers do not speak at the same time but they take turns as speakers. First one speaker takes the floor and then the next resulting in sequences such as A-B-A-B. There are many questions. How does a new speaker know that 'now it is my turn to speak'? How long can a speaker turn be? How does the current speaker signal that he or she wants to end a turn? Can a pause in the conversation used for planning be misunderstood as a signal to the hearer to take the floor? How do speakers go about suspending, i.e. closing the conversation?

The fact that speakers seem to know when they are allowed to take the conversational turn suggests that there are rules for 'the orderly transition from one speaker to another'. In their pioneering article in the journal *Language* the authors Sacks, Schegloff and Jefferson (1974) suggest a set of rules for turn-taking:

Rule 1 – applies initially at the first TRP [transition relevance place] of any turn

(a) If C [Current speaker] selects N [next speaker] in current turn, then C must stop speaking, and N must speak next, transition occurring at the first TRP after N-selection

(b) If C does not select N, then any (other) party may self-select, first speaker gaining rights to the next turn

(c) If C has not selected N, and no other party self-selects under option (b), then C may (but need not) continue (i.e. claim rights to a further turn-constructional unit)

Rule 2 – applies at all subsequent TRPs

When rule 1(c) has been applied by C, then at the next TRP rules 1(a)–(c) apply, and recursively at the next TRP, until speaker change is affected

(Sacks *et al.* 1974, with some slight changes following Levinson 1983: 298)

The rules suggested account for the fact that only one person speaks at a time although overlapping conversational contributions may occur. Rule 1(a) says for instance that the speaker who occupies the floor can select (or allocate) a new speaker who can take over as a speaker at a 'transition relevance place' (TRP). A TRP occurs at the end of a unit such as a sentence, clause or phrase (a turn constructional unit or TCU) (example from Hutchby and Wooffitt 2008: 50):

1   Rose: Why don't you come and see me some[times
2   Bea: [I would
3   like to

Bea recognizes Rose's utterance as a TCU and what sort of unit it is (an invitation) and responds to it (by accepting the invitation) before Rose has finished talking.

Not surprisingly there are different techniques for explicitly inviting a speaker to take the floor, for example, asking a question or using an address term. If no new speaker is selected the floor is open to the speaker who first takes the turn. If neither rule 1(a) nor 1(b) applies the current speaker may continue as speaker (the speaker 'self-selects'). This cycle may be repeated as soon as there is a TRP, i.e. at the end of a unit projected by the current speaker there is the possibility for a change of speaker.

In authentic conversation we also find overlaps and interruptions in addition to a smooth take-over of the turn. Overlaps often occur at locations where speaker change is possible (that is, at the TRP). However, interruptions can also occur at points in the discourse which are not recognized as TRPs. The turn-taking model described by Sacks *et al.* is not only used to describe casual conversation, but also 'speech-exchange systems' which use different conventions to regulate the exchange of speaker turns (e.g. a classroom, courtroom, etc.). In ordinary conversation the order, size and type of turn can vary. But, in some situations, 'participants are normatively constrained in the types of turn they may take according to their particular institutional roles' (Hutchby and Woofitt 2008: 141). In a classroom lesson, for example, the teacher typically asks the questions and the pupils answer them. Such constraints may be referred to as 'turn type pre-allocation'.

Work within Conversation Analysis has also explored the importance of the speaker gaze (in face-to-face interaction). People may look at each other (or not look at each other) in order to signal their intention to give or keep the turn. Kendon (1967) has for instance shown that at the point in the interaction where the speaker and hearer change roles the speaker ends his/her utterance by looking at the hearer 'with a sustained gaze' and the hearer looks away as he/she is beginning to speak (see Unit A9).

A6.3.1 Adjacency

Conversation analysts use the term adjacency pair to refer to coupled turns where the first part of the pair predicts what will come in the next part. Schegloff and Sacks (1973) characterize an adjacency pair as follows:

Adjacency *pairs* are sequences of two utterances that are:

  (i) adjacent
 (ii) produced by different speakers
(iii) ordered as a first part and a second part
(iv) typed, so that a particular first part requires a particular second part
      (or range of second parts) – e.g. offers require acceptances or rejections, greetings require greetings, and so on
                                        (Quoted from Levinson 1983: 303)

Some typical adjacency pairs are: greeting-greeting, offers/invitation-acceptance/ rejection and question-answer.

The close association between different parts in the adjacency pair is a result of the turn-taking system. Speakers have expectations about what will occur in the next turn (one turn projects the next turn) and that this will be relevant to what is uttered in the first turn. Although the term 'adjacent' is used, it is not always the case that the second part of the pair is produced in the next turn. A question-answer pair can for instance be embedded in another question-answer pair. The following example illustrates a so-called 'insertion sequence' (i.e. an embedded Q&A adjacency pair) (Merritt 1976: 333, quoted from Levinson 1983: 304):

A: May I have a bottle of Mich? (Q1)
B: Are you twenty-one? (Q2)
A: No (A2)
B: No (A1)

The answer to the first question is left hanging until a second question has been answered. It is also not uncommon to find a Q&A sequence preceded by a preface. The following example is from a news interview (Wooffitt 2005: 57, example originally from Heritage and Greatbatch 1991: 99):

Interviewer: hhh <u>The</u>(.) price being asked for these
               Letters is (.) three thousand <u>pou</u>::nds.
               Are you going to be able to <u>r</u>aise it,
               (0.5)
Interviewee: At the moment it . . . ((*continues*))

In Unit B6.2 Tsui (1994) explores an adjacency pair which is expanded into a 'triplet'.

A6.3.2 Preference organization

In Conversation Analysis a distinction is made between two types of responses (second part in an adjacency pair) in terms of preference. This reflects the fact that the turns do not have the same status. Preference in this case is not a psychological one but a structural notion involving markedness. In this light an affirmative response to an invitation is for instance preferred and a declination would be a dispreferred (or marked) member of the adjacency pair. Compare also:

	Preferred	*Dispreferred*
Request	Granting	Denying
Invitation/offer	Accepting	Rejecting
Question	Expected answer	Unexpected answer

What makes this distinction interesting is that the dispreferred member of the pair has a number of structural features distinguishing it from a preferred second part. For example, the denial of a request requires more planning effort reflected in delay markers such as pauses, hesitation and the use of pragmatic markers. The following (often quoted example) shows how 'a dispreferred second' has a structure which can be described in terms of delays and various postponement mechanisms (Schegloff 1972: 98, quoted from Tsui 1994: 58):

> A: Uh if you'd care to come round and visit a little while this morning I'll give you a cup of coffee
> B: hehh Well that's awfully sweet of you, I don't think I can make it this morning . . . hh uhm I'm running an ad in the paper and – uh I have to stay near the phone

The denial of the invitation is fairly long and is structurally complex. There are certain generalizations we can make. For example, B's denial is indirect and contains 'postponement devices' such as pauses and hesitation markers (*hehh, hh, uhm, uh*). It is 'flagged' by a preface (*Well that's awfully sweet of you*). Rather than saying 'no' the speaker provides various reasons for the refusal (*I'm running an ad in the paper, I have to stay near the phone*).

A6.3.3 Openings and closings

The sequential organization of discourse is also visible in the structure characterizing the opening and closing of a telephone conversation. Telephone conversations are more structured than face-to-face conversations especially in their openings and closings. It is therefore of interest to look at the recurring patterns. According to Schegloff (1986: 115), the opening phase of the telephone call is structured as a sequence of four exchanges.

> (1) (ring)
>
> (a) A(nswerer): Hello?
>
> (b) C(aller): Hello Ida?
>   A: Yeah.
>
> (c) C: Hi. This is Carla.
>   A: Hi Carla.
>
> (d) C: How are you?
>   A: Okay
>   C: Good.
>   A: How about you?
>   C: Fine. Don wants to know . . .

The first exchange consists of the summons-answer (a). The second (b) is the identification of each participant (and the subsequent recognition of the speaker's identity by the other party), and the third (c) is the mutual exchange of greetings. The fourth exchange consists of a routine enquiry about the other person's health (*How are you?*) and the routinized response to it (d). This sequence is followed by the introduction of the first topic by the caller.

The closing of a telephone call involves patterning, ritual, repetition, etc. According to Schegloff and Sacks (1973), the telephone call comes to a close in a stepwise manner involving negotiation between the caller and the answerer. The first so-called 'pre-closing' stage is initiated by a mutual agreement to close the conversation. The actual pre-closing can be a sequence built up of adjacency pairs. It typically involves a great deal of ritual; it can be interrupted by the introduction of a new topic and be resumed. The pre-closing sequence is followed by the closing proper (the caller and answerer exchange farewell phrases). The following example (from Levinson 1983: 317) displays many features that characterize the closing of a telephone conversation:

> R: Why don't we all have lunch
> C: Okay so that would be in St Jude's would it?
> R: Yes
>   (0.7)
> C: Okay so
> R: One o'clock in the bar
> C: Okay
> R: Okay?
> C: Okay then thanks very much indeed George=
> R: =All right
> C: // See you there
> R: See you there
> C: Okay
> R: Okay //bye
> R: . . . Bye

What we have here is a sequence made up of adjacency pairs (exchanges) with the function of accomplishing an agreement to close the conversation followed by the actual closing. The caller (C) has accepted the invitation to have lunch. The coming to an arrangement signals a point in the conversation where both caller and recipient are willing to close the conversation. Pre-closing is further characterized by the ritual exchange of okays. The caller first produces *Okay* signalling that he/she has nothing more to say. The recipient's *Okay* echoes this (cf. Levinson's 'topic-less passing turns'). Thanking (in the caller's turn) normally refers back to a favour but can also be used as a pre-closing signal. The exchange of (*good*)*byes* signals the end of the conversation.

There are many variations of the prototypical pattern. Although the closing procedure always involves some negotiation between the caller and recipient it can be shortened; there are also differences in the patterning depending on how well the participants know each other and whether the call is private or a business call. In the example below (from Aijmer 1996: 59, after the LLC) the pre-closing section contains both apologizing (*sorry to bother you*) and thanking (*thanks awfully*):

A: all right
we'll do that Judith
C: that'd be very kind
thanks awfully
sorry to bother you
A: no
not a bit
look forward to seeing you again one of these days

The pre-closing starts with coming to an arrangement (*we'll do that Judith*).

Telephone conversations have also been studied by researchers interested in cross-cultural comparison, with some interesting results. For example, American (and British) speakers have been found to say *Hello*, when answering the call, whereas Swedish (Lindström 1994) and Dutch speakers (Houtkoop-Steenstra 1991) identify themselves by name in the first turn.

Answerer: It is [name]
Caller: Hello it is [name]

Sifianou (2002) has studied the extent to which openings in Greek telephone calls can be described by the patterns established by Schegloff. She found that Schegloff's patterns could occur but that there was a variety of different openings. Moreover, the Greeks in her study used a great deal of playfulness and joking in telephone openings emphasizing the interactional rather than transactional aspects.

A6.4 DISCOURSE STRUCTURE IN INSTITUTIONAL SETTINGS

Researchers in CA have also begun to explore how CA methods can be used to characterize the interaction in different types of institutional and workplace activities. Institutional activities can be more or less formal which affects how participants orientate to the institutional context.

Hutchby and Wooffitt (2008) make a distinction between more formal institutional activities such as courtroom proceedings (Atkinson and Drew 1979), news interview discourse (Heritage 1985; Clayman 1992), formal types of classroom discourse (McHoul 1978) and non-formal types where the conversation is more loosely structured. The latter type is for instance illustrated by doctor and patient interviews (Frankel 1984; Heritage and Maynard 2006), talk-radio interaction (Hutchby 1996a) and business meetings (Boden 1994). In more formal contexts such as the broadcast news interview the turn-taking system is for instance characterized by 'pre-allocation', i.e. 'the participants are normatively constrained in the types of turns they may take according to their institutional roles' (Hutchby and Wooffitt 2008: 141). For example, in a courtroom examination the prosecutor normally asks the questions and the witnesses (and, where relevant, the defendant) answer them.

Conversation analytical techniques have also been used to study sociolinguistic variables such as the use of power in institutional settings. Hutchby (1996a) has for instance shown that power is not a pre-established notion but that the power relation is accomplished in the unfolding of talk in talk-radio interaction. The 'play of power' takes place on the conversational floor and can be described as 'going first' or 'going second'. According to Sacks, who first used these expressions, those who go first (use the first turn) are in a weaker position since going second means that you can use the second position to challenge the other speaker. In talk-radio 'going second' represents a powerful position and one that the host and caller fight about. The host can for instance demonstrate power by using a *So?* to respond to the caller's argument. In the example below the caller is complaining about the number of appeals that she is getting. *So?* challenges the validity of the speaker's claim and forces the caller to provide a reason (*Now the point is*).

```
 1  Caller:  I: have got three appeals letters here this
 2           week. (0.4) All a:skin' for donations. (0.2) .hh
 3           Two: from tho:se that I: always contribute to
 4           anywa:y,
 5  Host:    Yes?
 6  Caller:  .hh But I expect to get a lot mo:re.
 7  Host:    So?
 8  Caller:  .h Now the point is there is a lim i⌐t to (  )
 9  Host:                                          ⌊What's that
10           got to do- what's that got to do with telethons
11           though
12  Caller:  hh Because telethons . . . ((Continues))
```

(Ibid.: 489)

A possible advantage of the conversation analytic approach is that it enables a dynamic account of power relations. This is because power is not associated with the speaker or hearer role but is accomplished in the unfolding of talk. We investigate other approaches to power in Unit A12.

Both Discourse Analysis, as exemplified by Sinclair and Coulthard, and Conversation Analysis, as exemplified by Sacks, Schegloff and Jefferson, provide useful approaches to the study of discourse. The outstanding feature of Conversation Analysis is its concern with the methods used by the participants in the conversation to solve problems. However, a lot of empirical work has pointed to the need for a descriptive framework which provides analytical units as a tool to describe conversational regularities. Many pragmatic phenomena such as pragmatic markers can only be described and understood in relation to units of the conversation (see Unit A7).

Recently there has been a coming-together of Conversation Analysis scholars and discourse-functional linguists in the US and interactional linguistics in Europe (see, e.g., Hakulinen and Selting 2005). The aim is to study the interface between linguistics (linguistic and lexico-grammatical elements) and conversation. The scholars working in this field are not only linguists but also sociologists and anthropologists with an interest in the use of language in social interaction. As in Conversation Analysis, the focus in interactional linguistics is on the sequential context. The context includes both what has preceded the discourse and how the participants produce responses and subsequent turns. Much of the research has concerned the role of phonetic and prosodic cues ('interactional prosody'). We will discuss the interactional linguistic approach in more detail in Unit C4. We will also consider to what extent the insights of Conversation Analysis and DA can be combined.

Unit A7
Pragmatic markers

We pepper our conversation with 'smallwords' (or pragmatic markers) such as *well*, *you know*, *I mean*. At first sight they seem to mean very little. However, they play an important role in making our speech coherent and in establishing or maintaining our relations with interlocutors in conversation. Here is an authentic corpus example (from the BNC), the conversation taking place between two students about their common friend Pete:

A: <u>Well</u> he's so bloody clever. You know?
B: Pete?
A: <u>Yeah, no, yeah well you know</u>, really manipulative, <u>you know</u>, he could <u>just</u>
    <pause> get me round his finger <u>I suppose</u>.
    <pause> I don't know why I get too flattered <u>you know</u>.
B: <u>Well</u> what did he say?
A: <u>I mean</u> he didn't say anything in particular, just the fact that, <u>you know</u>, we were
    <u>just like</u> walking along and <u>just</u> chatting away <u>you know</u> and he was being really
    nice and, <u>you know</u>, it was <u>just</u> <pause> fine.

Well both introduces a speaker turn and expresses some hesitation. *You know* establishes a closer association with the conversational partner (whether she actually knows or not). *I mean*, *just* and *you know* are part of the vocabulary establishing solidarity and rapport among members of the peer group.

In the following sections we will attempt to define pragmatic markers and discuss the syntactic, semantic and functional properties characterizing them.

Well, *I mean* and *you know* have pragmatic meaning (e.g. interpersonal or textual meaning) and do not contribute to the content. Although it is difficult to say what they mean, they obviously play an important part in making the conversation coherent. If we 'dismantle' the utterance from any of these extras, the message gives an abrupt or brusque impression. (Compare A's use of pragmatic markers in A's last turn with the alternative 'he didn't say anything in particular just the fact we were walking along and chatting away'.)

A7.1 WHAT ARE PRAGMATIC MARKERS?

According to Biber *et al.* (1999), pragmatic markers are a type of insert, that is, they are 'stand-alone words which are characterized in general by their inability to enter into syntactic relations with other structures' (ibid.: 1082).[1]

Pragmatic markers can also overlap with speech act routines. For example, thanking can be used as a pragmatic marker closing a discussion (cf. Unit A4) and apologizing (*excuse me*) comes close to an attention-getter. In addition, hesitation phenomena, although not words in the language, can function as pragmatic markers (see, e.g., *um, uh*).

The number of elements analysed as pragmatic markers has been growing and now also includes vocatives (attention-getters), adverbs, interjections and swear words (expletives). Norrick (2009: 83), for example, advocates a broad definition of pragmatic marker:

> Pragmatic markers have been a staple of pragmatic research over the years, but this research has often limited itself to a fairly narrow range of markers. The more frequent pragmatic markers, usually from the sub-class of discourse markers, have now been described fairly well for a number of languages, but the less frequent varieties of pragmatic markers have received little systematic attention, and the historical development of pragmatic markers requires much further study. Corpora are now finally large enough to assemble sufficient data on these less frequent pragmatic markers for significant analysis, so that the topic is especially timely and relevant.

It can be argued that we should also include hedges and vagueness markers.

Expressions such as *like, sort of* (*kind of*) have the functions to modify or soften what is said and can be regarded as pragmatic markers. They can also be used as verbal fillers making it possible for the speaker to pause and search for words or repair his or her own speech. There is a close similarity with general extenders such as *and stuff like that* and *or something*. These can have a number of pragmatic functions including politeness and the 'filler' function.

Another important sub-category of pragmatic markers consists of comment clauses. Comment clauses such as *I mean, I think, you know, you see* are usually placed parenthetically rather than in initial position, but they have the same spectrum of functions as other pragmatic markers. They can for instance have a textual or interpersonal function.

A7.2 DELIMITING PRAGMATIC MARKERS

From a neglected existence, pragmatic markers have recently come into the limelight thanks to the interest in spoken language kindled by the availability of spoken corpora. Pragmatic markers have been intensely studied as evidenced by the large number of books and articles which have come out in the last two decades (Schourup 1985; Schiffrin 1987; Brinton 1996; Hansen 1998; Jucker and Ziv 1998; Andersen and Fretheim 2000; Aijmer 2002).

This does not mean that we have a clear idea of how pragmatic markers should be analysed. There is no agreement on what to call them either. For example, some use the term pragmatic markers, as we have done, some, the terms discourse markers, discourse particle, connective, filler, etc. However, following Fraser (1996), we take 'pragmatic marker' to be an umbrella term encompassing a large number of related pragmatic phenomena with an 'insert' function, and 'discourse marker' to be a term which expresses a relation between utterances such as elaboration, contrast or inference. This is not only a question of terminology but the disagreement reflects deeper-lying differences about what constitutes a pragmatic marker. Moreover, they are difficult to delimit from other categories or word classes and they have functions which are best described in pragmatics or in discourse terms. The large number of theoretical frameworks used to describe pragmatic markers suggests that there may not be a single approach to pragmatic markers. Pragmatic markers have, for instance, been discussed in politeness theory as hedges or softeners but they also have important functions organizing the discourse. The approaches can be synchronic or diachronic. Diachronic studies of pragmatic markers describe how they are used in earlier stages of the language and how they have developed into pragmatic markers from a lexical source (see Unit A11).

It follows that it would be impossible to give a comprehensive list of pragmatic markers although we now have good descriptions of the most frequent markers. According to Carter and McCarthy (2006: 208), the most common pragmatic markers in informal conversation are 'single words such as *anyway, cos, fine, good, great, like, now, oh, okay, right, so, well* and phrasal and clausal elements such as *you know, I mean, as I say, for a start, mind you*'.

Quite clearly, there are many different definitions of pragmatic marker and people mean very different things with the terms they use. What we want to do here is to propose a description focusing on the typical formal and functional features of the most frequent or prototypical pragmatic markers.

A7.3 TYPICAL CHARACTERISTICS OF PRAGMATIC MARKERS

Most researchers would agree that pragmatic markers have little propositional meaning, i.e. they do not belong to the content but to 'pragmatics'. They are pragmatic in the sense that they facilitate for the hearer to interpret the utterance, for example, by signalling how the utterance fits into the context. They have both formal and functional features. Pragmatic markers are often short elements which are not integrated syntactically with the rest of the sentence. They are typically initial in the utterance rather than medial. Pragmatic markers are prototypically 'in symbiosis with' informal conversation (Östman 1982); in other words it would be unnatural to have an informal conversation which contains no pragmatic markers and pragmatic markers are associated with features of informal conversation such as the need for planning. However, pragmatic markers are dependent both on speech type (situation) and speaker. Both *in fact* and *actually* are for instance more frequent in demonstrations and lectures than in conversation.

The following list of features (based on Brinton 1996 and Jucker and Ziv 1998) summarizes some features of prototypical pragmatic markers:

- Phonological and lexical features

  - they are short elements which can be phonologically reduced (*cos 'because'*) and prosodically integrated in a larger tone group; but they can also form a separate tone group (distinguished from the rest of the utterance by a short pause)

- Syntactic features

  - they often occur sentence-initially (but are not restricted to this position)
  - they occur outside the syntactic structure or they are only loosely attached to it
  - they are optional, i.e. they can be omitted without any change to the content (the message)

- Semantic features

  - they have little or no propositional meaning

- Functional features

  - they are multifunctional, operating on several linguistic levels simultaneously

- Sociolinguistic and stylistic features

  - they are a feature of oral rather than written discourse and are associated with informality
  - they appear with high frequency
  - they are stylistically stigmatized and are associated with non-fluency
  - they are gender-specific and more typical of women's speech

Many of these points are formulated in terms of 'often' and 'frequently' suggesting that they are potential features only and not the absolute gospel. Some features may even be contentious, such as the claim that they are more frequent in women's speech. In order to analyse the distribution of pragmatic markers in female or male speech we must identify both the forms and their functions.

A7.4 PRAGMATIC MARKERS AND FUNCTION

Pragmatic markers are above all a functional category with functions in different linguistic domains or functional-semantic components. Many linguists (e.g. Brinton 1996) distinguish two macro-functions although they describe them somewhat differently:

A) Textual function

In the textual function pragmatic markers typically indicate a structural boundary in the discourse. They may point backwards or forwards in the discourse and signal the relationship between the utterances they connect. Some typical textual functions are:

- to initiate or close discourse
- to serve as a filler or turn-holding device
- to mark a boundary in the discourse, e.g. to indicate a new topic or topic shift
- to signal transitions between one element in the discourse and another
- to repair one's own discourse

B) Interpersonal function

In the interpersonal function pragmatic markers are associated with epistemic modality and express an emotion, a reaction or attitude to the hearer or to the text. They can also be used to express shared knowledge or solidarity or to hedge what is said in order to express tentativeness or politeness.

Pragmatic markers can have functions in both components. Focusing only on their discourse (textual) functions or only on the interpersonal function (politeness) may result in only a partial analysis of how they are used. *Well* is a good example of a multifunctional pragmatic marker which functions both on the textual and interpersonal level. Carter and McCarthy (2006: 152–3) distinguish the following functions of the pragmatic marker and many more functions could be found.

> One function of *well* in the textual function is to indicate that the speaker is thinking about things:
>
> A: What do you think of the department's plan?
> B: <u>Well</u>, let's see, it's certainly better than the last one, I'll say that.
> A: Why did she say that?
> B: <u>Well</u> I don't know, I mean, maybe she wants to move house.
>
> *Well* can sometimes signal the opening or closing of a topic or speech event:

Well let's get started, shall we?
Well, that's all for now. We'll see you again at the same time next week.

Well normally occurs at the beginning of a turn. But it can occur in the middle of an utterance, or after a break as a 'filler' or turn-holding device if a speaker is revising what is said or is searching for an alternative expression:

I never said I was happy, well, all right then, I might have said I was not.

Well can have the interpersonal function to express a reaction or response to an earlier utterance. *Well* indicates that the speaker is saying something which contrasts with what has just been said or which does not agree with expectations (a dispreferred response):

A: You always go out to your evening class on a Tuesday.
B: Well, tonight I'm too tired and I'm staying in.
A: D'you live in Cambridge?
B: Well, near Cambridge. (Where *Well* is used in the answer if the question seems irrelevant.)

Well can open a new topic (I've got something to tell you):

You know I said I went to Jill's last night, well, you'll never guess who I saw there.

Well commonly clusters with other discourse markers, adverbs and adverbial phrases especially in 'dispreferred' responses:

Well, actually, I don't think she has agreed.
Well, as a matter of fact, I've bought a flat in the village.

Pragmatic markers can have very complex functions in the social interactions. Bolden (2006) has studied the pragmatic markers *oh* and *so* in social interactions between familiars. Bolden used conversation analytical methodology to show how *so* and *oh* preface utterances that launch a new conversational issue. However they represent different 'discursive practices'. *So* was for instance used with what Bolden described as 'other-attentiveness' (a discursive practice oriented to the interlocutor) while *oh* was used to signal something just remembered (a speaker-oriented discursive practice). The example below (slightly simplified from the original example) illustrates how *so* is used:

(The example is from a telephone conversation. Briar has just finished talking on the other line and returns to Maya)

1 BRI: N-n-no . She's jus-(0.2) she was just calling
2   cause I called her earlier

3	BRI:	.hhh because I: -haven't called her twice.=but-(.) >She
4		was never<involved in the whole free call thing.
5	MAY:	*O. . . .H* ((*breathy*))
6	BRI:	So-congratulations Maya.
7	MAY:	#U-O: # :h tha::nks.

(Adapted from ibid.: 669)

So does not only mark a new topic or return to a topic. *So* has the function both to underscore that the issue is on the speaker's agenda to discuss and that it is concerned with the affairs of the interlocutor. *Oh* on the other hand would have signalled that the speaker had just remembered something.

Pragmatic markers also have clinical applications. The role of pragmatic markers as a compensatory strategy to promote conversation in aphasic patients has for instance been discussed by Simmons-Mackie and Damico (1996).

A7.5 PRAGMATIC MARKERS AND TEXT-TYPE

Pragmatic markers are frequent in narratives. In the following example (taken from an interview) they make the interviewee's description more vivid and dramatic. Notice the frequent use of pragmatic markers after a reporting verb (*one of them'd say well you know; and I'd say well*):

A: And I know a lot of things too with the girls who came to us, we tried to erm give them er a sense of their worth as a women and not to constantly be oppressed and to accept erm what their boyfriends did or said, and so on. <u>You know, like</u> erm maybe one of them'd say, <u>Well you know</u>, <u>I'd say</u>, <u>well</u> why don't you leave her with erm your boyfriend for the day, and you have a day off and have a break? <u>Oh well</u> it's my place to look after <u>you know</u>, the child. And I'd say <u>well</u> if there are two parents there whether it's whether they're married or whether they're not, the parents are there together, it was shared equally. (BNC)

The above text type is informal and the markers have an attitudinal function. For example, *you know* is used to establish and maintain a friendly relationship with the hearer and *like* signals that what follows is only an approximation. In more formal types of speech interaction we would find different markers. The markers in the following examples focus more on structure than on the speaker's attitudes. The situation is a Pensioners' and Trades Union Association meeting. *Now* is typical of formal discourse as an opening signal. *Right* and *okay* would occur in both informal and formal discourse (as responses to thanks):

A: Thank you very much, thank you Chris. <clapping>.
   I'm sure the, I'm sure they'll all go away very <unclear> when you, before you came.
B: <unclear>.

A: Thanks a lot.
B: <u>Well now</u>, now you know that when I disappear with a placard sign, I don't just disappear with a placard, we are doing things behind the scenes.
A: That's right, thanks a lot Chris.
   <u>Okay</u> <unclear>.
C: That's great, thanks very much.
B: <u>Right</u>, were now on other reports. (BNC)

Pragmatic markers are most frequent in informal conversation but they can also be used with 'new' functions in other text types. For instance, *well* is used in commentaries on snooker games to remark on a 'surprisingly successful shot' (Greasley 1994). In the following example from Greasley (simplified) the commentary prefaced by *Well* exhibits an enthusiastic response from the commentator:

Commentator: Well this is absolutely superb and er Terry Griffiths' supporters could even be excused for thinking don't use it all up now save some for the World Championships next month.

Well expresses the commentator's affective reaction (mixed with surprise) to the shot.

Pragmatic markers are also used in new settings such as instant messaging (Fox Tree 2010), in particular with experienced users of the new medium who treat the medium more like conversation and use pragmatic markers to make adjustments.

A7.6 PRAGMATIC MARKERS AND SOCIOLINGUISTIC VARIATION

The relatively new discipline, variational pragmatics, highlights the study of pragmatic variation due to sociolinguistic and regional factors. Existing research has mostly dealt with speech acts across languages and across cultures. Biber *et al.* (1999), for example, have shown that there are differences in frequencies between pragmatic markers in British and American English, such that *well* and *you know* are more frequent in American than in British English.

Pragmatic markers only get their full meaning in a social and cultural context. They must be described with regard to sociolinguistic features such as the social situation, speaker identity and power relations. Moreover they are language-specific and therefore interesting to compare across languages.

Pragmatic markers occur with different functions depending on features of the sociolinguistic situation, for example, the speaker's professional role or identity. For example, *well* is associated with authority and power if used by the cross-examiner in the courtroom, while it expresses a defensive attitude if used by the person cross-examined. The cross-examiner uses *well* together with a 'demanding' tag question:

(Context: the hotel pool has broken and a guest at the hotel has been injured. The hotel owner is being questioned.)

Cross-examining lawyer: Well now things in a hotel may break from time to time
                               may they not (ICE-GB)

Well is used by witness in the following example:

Cross-examining lawyer: How long had you been there before the day of her
                               accident?
Witness: uhm just the night before well I uh got there the early

Of particular relevance in explaining the use of pragmatic markers are the age, gender and social class of the speakers. It has been claimed that women and men use pragmatic markers differently, for example. Holmes (1986) has shown that New Zealand women use *you know* more than New Zealand men for emphasis and to express confidence in the proposition expressed. Pragmatic markers are also said to be used differently by young and old speakers. Young people use a lot of pragmatic markers, especially those expressing vagueness (*like, sort of*) or which could be used for emphasis (*you know*):

> Because, <u>you know</u>, I'd never been skiing before, so I went out all togged up, with <u>like</u>, my tights <u>sort of</u>, <u>like</u>, <u>you know</u>, thermal tights and <u>you know</u>, pair of track suits, <u>sort of</u> bottoms, plus plastic overtop and then I had <u>like</u>, <u>sort of</u> thermal top on, plus the that's a <u>sort of like</u>-shirt, plus the polo-neck plus a jumper, plus a <u>sort of like erm</u>, <u>a sort of</u> sheepskin waistcoat and, and jacket and then this plastic thing over the top.

Pragmatic markers are not useless 'extras' in the utterance but they have important functions to show that the speaker is friendly and cooperative (or to take up a more challenging stance associated with power). They are also important signals directed to the hearer clarifying the speaker's intentions. If they are omitted the speaker may sound abrupt, brusque, unfriendly or negative.

Summary and looking ahead

Pragmatic markers continue to be of interest to researchers with different theoretical leanings and research on pragmatic markers 'grows daily' (Blakemore 2002:11). However, in spite of a large number of publications in this area there is little consensus about issues such as terminology, definition, delimitation of the field and the multifunctionality of the markers. On the other hand, many more lexical items are now being studied as (potential) pragmatic markers and the field has been broadened to include sociolinguistic and regional variation. Exciting cross-linguistic work comparing pragmatic markers across languages and cultures is also being undertaken. Other new areas include the study of pragmatic markers in learner language and in English as a lingua franca.

In Unit B7 we will discuss a few selected pragmatic markers which are less proto-typical. The first reading deals with a marker (*I don't know*) which is a clause rather than a single word. It is shown that as a marker it is not used literally but with a face-mitigating effect. The pragmatic markers in the second reading represent 'hesitation phenomena'. It is shown that they are used for different functions by learners and by native speakers. The third reading illustrates the multifunctionality of the pragmatic marker *like* which is now frequently used by adolescents.

NOTE

1   Notice that inserts can also consist of phrases (rather than single words) such as *I think, I mean, thank you.*

Unit A8
Pragmatics, facework and im/politeness

In this unit, you will learn about Leech's argument that a Politeness Principle should complement Grice's (1975) concept of conversational implicature (Unit A5.1.1; see also Unit B5.3) and become familiar with the work of Brown and Levinson (1978/1987), which draws on the ideas of speech act theorists (Unit A4). We begin, though, with Goffman – a sociologist whose ideas have helped to directly and indirectly shape much of the linguistic facework and im/politeness research; including that of Brown and Levinson.

A8.1 GOFFMAN'S INFLUENCE

Goffman's (1967: 5) definition of face as 'the positive social value a person effectively claims for him' or herself is well known, as is his claim that:

> Face is an image of self delineated in terms of approved social attributes
> . . . as when a person makes a good showing for his [or her] profession or
> religion by making a good showing for him [or her]self.

A less discussed characteristic of Goffman's concept of face is its dynamism: Goffman believed face to be: (i) on loan from society; (ii) liable to be withdrawn if an individual conducts him/herself in a way that is unworthy of it; and, hence, (iii) realized solely in social interaction (ibid.: 10). Fraser (1990: 22; emphasis added) has interpreted this to mean that:

> . . . each society has a particular set of social norms consisting of more or
> less explicit rules that prescribe a certain behaviour, a state of affairs, or a
> way of thinking in context. *A positive evaluation (politeness) arises when an*
> *action is in congruence with the norm, a negative evaluation (impoliteness =*
> *rudeness) when an action is to the contrary.*

For Fraser, then, conversation relies upon our being polite – or operating within the terms of a 'conversational contract' (CC), albeit a CC which can always be renegotiated during actual interaction. Hence, politeness is viewed as an *unmarked norm*, and as the means of ensuring 'socially acceptable' behaviour. Brown and Levinson (1978/1987) and Leech (1983) also associate politeness with normal cooperative behaviour, and they've produced models by which we might categorize such linguistic politeness. Let's explore each in turn, beginning with Brown and Levinson.

A8.2 BROWN AND LEVINSON'S LINGUISTIC POLITENESS MODEL

Brown and Levinson's (1978/1987) study of politeness documents the practices of Tamil speakers (from southern India), Tzeltal speakers (from Mexico) and English speakers (from America and Britain). Even so, the linguistic politeness model they propose is more rationalistic than it is empirical. This is because of their 'playful' adoption of 'Model Persons' (MPs) who recognize that:

> . . . since people can be expected to defend their face if threatened, and in defending their own to threaten others' faces, it is in general in every participant's best interest to maintain each others' face.
>
> (Ibid.: 61)

The challenge MPs face is that they cannot completely eradicate face-threatening acts (FTAs) from their utterances. What MPs do, instead, is choose between a number of politeness superstrategies (see Figure A8.1), which Brown and Levinson situate on a cline of lesser-greater risk. The choice of the strategy is determined, then, by the MPs' assessment of: (i) the social distance between S (MP) and H; (ii) their relative power; and (iii) the size of the imposition in the cultural context.[1]

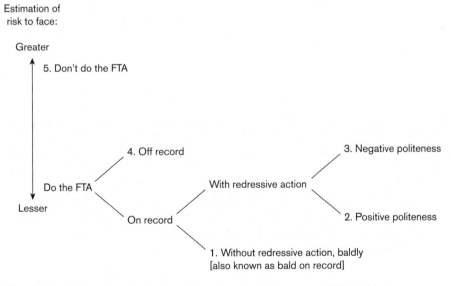

Figure A8.1 FTA strategies (adapted from Brown and Levinson 1987: 60)

Let's consider each superstrategy in turn. The 'without redressive action, baldly' (or bald-on-record) superstrategy is used in contexts where maximally efficient utterances are acceptable because the risk to face (self and other) is considered to be minimal. We're most likely to hear bald-on-record utterances in emergency situations (cf. shouting *Fire!* as a means of getting others to quickly vacate a burning building) and in situations where the status/power differential between interlocutors is obvious (cf. *Get this to accounting asap*, said by a high-ranking boss to his subordinate).

If the risk to face is not considered to be minimal, MPs can use redressive language to help mitigate any face-threatening potential. The two on-record superstrategies used for this purpose – 'positive politeness' and 'negative politeness' – draw explicitly from two 'wants' which Brown and Levinson believe to be universal (but see A8.3): the want to be approved of (also known as positive face) and the want to be unimpeded in one's actions(also known as negative face).

MPs make use of positive politeness when they explicitly want to signal that they are attending to their addressees' positive face. They might treat H 'as a member of an in-group' or 'friend', for example, and/or as someone 'whose wants and personality traits are known and liked'. Additional positive politeness strategies include: noticing H; exaggerating approval of/interest in H; seeking agreement; avoiding disagreement; presupposing/asserting common ground; joking, etc. Similarly, MPs make use of negative politeness when they explicitly signal their addressees' 'want' to be free to act without imposition in some way. If MPs need to make a request, for example, they are likely to redress the potential face threat 'with apologies for interfering or transgressing, with linguistic and non-linguistic deference, with hedges on the illocutionary force of the act' and/or 'other softening mechanisms that give' H 'a face-saving line of escape' and/or the sense that his/her 'response is not coerced' (ibid.: 70). Of course, how much of this mitigation MPs engage in will depend upon the social, familial and/or power relationship between them and their interlocutors as well as the size of the 'imposition'. Hence MPs will likely engage in less negative politeness work when asking a close friend to borrow a pen than they would if they asked the same friend to lend them their car for the afternoon!

The 'off-record' superstrategy comes into play when MPs deem an FTA to be such that an on-record superstrategy is inappropriate (because of being too face-threatening). This superstrategy is particularly useful when MPs want their utterances to have 'more than one . . . attributable intention' according to Brown and Levinson. Consider their example, 'Damn, I'm out of cash, I forgot to go to the bank today', which can be interpreted as a statement of fact or as an indirect request for a (small) cash loan. Yet, the indirectness of the request is such that an MP can deny they ever intended to make a request.

To summarize, the above superstrategies equate to an 'estimation of face risk' scale with the on-record superstrategies being used in situations deemed to be of middle risk (in the case of positive politeness and negative politeness) and minimal/non-existent risk (in the case of bald-on-record). The off-record superstrategy, in contrast, is used when the risk to face is deemed to be quite high. The final superstrategy highlighted in Figure A8.1 – 5. Don't do the FTA – comes into play when MPs judge the threat to face to be too great and thus inadvisable in situations where face maintenance (self and other) is a priority.

A8.3 CRITICISMS OF THE MODEL

Brown and Levinson have been accused of giving undue prominence to FTAs – to the extent that their whole understanding of politeness seems to centre on how to deal with them. They have also been accused of having a Western 'individualist' bias which is at odds with collectivist communities' orientation to the group (see, e.g., the Japanese), and thus for oversimplifying important differences when claiming that all interlocutors share the same 'wants', regardless of their cultural heritage. Matsumoto (1988), for example, has argued that what the model wants to classify under negative politeness actually constitutes a social register in Japanese.

We need to be careful that we don't fall into the trap of thinking that a culture is either 'collectivist' or 'individualist', however, not least because Pizziconi (2003) and Fukada and Asato (2004) have shown that Japanese structures (honorifics, in particular) are subject to individual volition and also the dynamics of particular interactions in some contexts, and thus are more pragmatically determined than Matsumoto and others have previously claimed. One way forward, posited by Grundy (2008: 207), is 'to distinguish situations where deference is given unexceptionally as an automatic acknowledgement of relative social status from situations where it's given exceptionally in a particular situation as a redressive strategy'. We continue our discussion of how the Brown and Levinson model 'can – and can't – help us to understand interaction across cultures' in Unit B8.2.

A different criticism levelled at the Brown and Levinson model relates to their adoption of an MP who uses rational, goal-oriented means to calculate the politeness strategies required in a given interaction. Kopytko (1995: 487), for example, argues that it equates to a 'decontextualized pragmatics' in the sense that it doesn't fully allow for the dynamics of interaction in real time, where interlocutors must respond to turns and not merely plan their own (see, e.g., Unit A5.4). This is particularly problematic for Kopytko (1995: 488), as he believes that 'it is the hearer who assigns politeness to any utterance within the situation in which it was heard'. Watts (2003) and other postmodern researchers share Kopytko's concern that the Brown and Levinson model does not adequately account for H. Indeed, for them, how participants in social interaction perceive politeness – what they call politeness$_1$ or first order politeness – is much more important than any theoretical account of what might constitute politeness – what they call politeness$_2$ or second order politeness. We discuss the issue of whether politeness is most fruitfully analysed not as a normative system of prescripts which are predictive (i.e. politeness$_2$) but rather as a dynamic/interactive social practice (i.e. politeness$_1$) in Unit A8.9. Before doing so, however, we'll outline some of the other well-known goal-oriented politeness and impoliteness models. We begin with Leech's politeness model.

A8.4 LEECH'S POLITENESS MODEL

Leech (1983) advocates a conversational-maxim view to politeness, whereby a Politeness Principle (PP) complements Grice's (1975) Cooperative Principle (CP). The PP is based on the premise that interlocutors seek *to minimize the expression of impolite beliefs* and *maximize the expression of polite beliefs.* Interlocutors draw on a number of politeness maxims to do so: these maxims are relabelled 'constraints' in Leech's 2007 work. The maxims (or constraints) seek to avoid discord first (see A) and seek concord second (see B) (see Figure A8.2).

As the repetition of 'expression of beliefs which imply. . .' in Figure A8.2 suggests, Leech's focus is how interlocutors avoid discord and foster concord *only in so far as these are evident in communication.* For Leech, then, politeness is an aspect of goal-oriented behaviour which is essentially pragmatic. Indeed, the basic question, for Leech, is *What did S mean [to convey] by saying X?* (see Leech 2007 for a more detailed discussion).

Interlocutors choose the most appropriate politeness strategy using three (inter-related) pragmatic scales, according to Leech: (1) the cost-benefit scale; (2) the optionality scale; and (3) the indirectness scale. Let's consider an utterance which involves the generosity maxim: *Have a chocolate!* with, first, the cost-benefit scale in mind. Although imperative in form, it is likely to be heard as benefitting H (unless he/she's on a diet or is lactose intolerant). *Could I have one of your chocolates?*, in contrast, would likely be heard as being 'costly' to H, because he/she would have to supply the chocolate in this case. This is when the optionality scale and indirectness scale become operationalized, according to Leech; for *Could I have one of your chocolates?* constitutes an indirect strategy, and its purpose is to give the addressee a choice as to whether to comply. Compare the imperative, *Give me one of your chocolates!*, which doesn't allow H a choice. Leech suggests that (the scales of) indirectness and optionality often work together in this way when it comes to politeness:

> [i]ndirect illocutions tend to be more polite [. . .] because they increase the degree of optionality, and [. . .] because the more indirect an illocution is, the more diminished and tentative its force tends to be.
>
> (Leech 1983: 108)

Whilst there might be an argument for linking indirectness with politeness in present-day English, we need to shy away from a one-to-one mapping (see, e.g., Unit B11.2). For a direct utterance can be the appropriate form – given the right context. Conversely, indirectness can be used for impolite or face-damaging purposes. Leech (ibid.: 171) provides the example of 'Haven't you something to declare?' spoken by an official at a border checkpoint, which could be argued to be 'progressively more impolite [and] more threatening than the ordinary *yes-no* question', because it seems to presuppose an affirmative response (as opposed to seeking one).

A   Avoid discord by, for example, minimizing (expression of beliefs which imply) . . .

	. . . cost to other	. . . benefit to self	. . . dispraise of other	. . . praise of self	. . . disagreement between self and other	. . . antipathy between self and other
That is	TACT	GENEROSITY	APPROBATION	MODESTY	AGREEMENT	SYMPATHY

B   Seek concord by, for example, maximizing (expression of beliefs which imply) . . .

	. . . benefit to other	. . . cost to self	. . . praise of other	. . . dispraise of self	. . . agreement between self and other	. . . sympathy between self and other
That is	TACT	GENEROSITY	APPROBATION	MODESTY	AGREEMENT	SYMPATHY

Figure A8.2 Maxims subsumed by Leech's Politeness Principle

Leech's interest in impoliteness has grown in his later work (e.g. Leech 2007). Indeed, he suggests that his politeness maxims/constraints might be used to gauge instances when interlocutors appear to transgress the PP for some strategic gain. Bousfield (2008: 51) explains how this might work via an analogy to Grice's CP:

> [. . .] we may be able to say that Leech's PP maxims, or constraints, can be violated (covertly broken), flouted (overtly broken), infringed, suspended, or opted out of . . . intentional linguistic impoliteness [would] occur at the level where one (or more) of Leech's PP maxims is flouted . . . [in order] to generate an impolite implicature. Accidental offences . . . would . . . occur at the 'infringement' level. Emergency or other urgent situations would entail the suspension of the PP (cf. *bald-on-record* . . .), and opting out of the PP would encompass those situations where people choose to *stay silent* when politeness might otherwise have been expected . . . or where . . . stated politeness may be considered to be offensive to the recipient (cf. *don't do the FTA* . . .).

We'll return to the possibility of using Leech's PP in this way in Unit C6. In Unit A8.5 we explore an impoliteness model which has been directly influenced by Brown and Levinson.

A8.5 CULPEPER'S (1996) 'ANATOMY OF IMPOLITENESS'

The politeness models we've explored thus far have tended to concentrate on how we employ communicative strategies to maintain or promote social harmony. This is because of a belief that the norm in social interaction is that of politeness, and hence that 'conflictive illocutions' are 'rather marginal to human linguistic behaviour in normal circumstances' (Leech 1983: 205). Indeed, even Leech's suggestion that his PP could be used to explain impoliteness is based on the premise of politeness as a communicative norm (see, e.g., his description of impoliteness as the 'non observance or violation of the constraints of politeness' in Leech 2007: 18). Yet, it remains the case that interlocutors can – and do – use language strategically to create/cause disharmony, and sometimes systematically so. Consider (American) army training, for example, where sergeants will use 'impoliteness in a systematic way' as a means of reshaping their recruits into the model soldier (Culpeper 1996: 359). For example, one of the recruits in Culpeper's study is told that she is 'a disgrace to the uniform' who doesn't 'even deserve to live in the United States': Alves (the recruit in question) is of Mexican origin. Alves is also advised not to 'have any children . . . because unfortunately there is such a thing as hereditary genes' and it would be unfair for 'anybody' to 'come out like' her (ibid.). This and similar data prompted Culpeper to develop an 'anatomy of impoliteness' model containing five possible strategies. The first three of these strategies – *bald on record impoliteness*, *positive impoliteness* and *negative impoliteness* – 'flip' similarly named Brown and Levinson superstrategies. Hence, the purpose of the *bald on record impoliteness* strategy is to explicitly create the maximum possible face damage (cf. Brown and

Levinson's bald-on-record politeness, where face threat is believed to be minimized or non-existent). Such FTAs are performed in as direct, clear, unambiguous and concise a way as possible (see, e.g., *You fucking shit*).

The *positive impoliteness* strategy captures behaviour which is designed to explicitly damage the addressee's positive face-wants. It subsumes behaviour such as: ignoring the other; being disinterested, unconcerned, unsympathetic; not using identity markers (e.g. address forms) where they are expected (or using inappropriate identity markers for the context); using obscure or secretive language; seeking disagreement; using taboo words; and calling the other names.

The *negative impoliteness* strategy captures behaviour which is designed to explicitly damage the addressee's negative face-wants, for example frightening, condescending, scorning or ridiculing, being contemptuous, not treating the other seriously, belittling the other, invading the other's space (literally or metaphorically), explicitly associating the other with a negative aspect and putting the other's indebtedness on-record.

Culpeper's fourth and fifth strategies demonstrate the influence of Leech (1983). The fourth strategy – *sarcasm or mock politeness* – explicitly draws on Leech's 'irony' concept, which outlines the use of superficial politeness for impoliteness purposes. Consider *You're so kind*, said by someone expecting a door to be held open shortly after it closed on them. The fifth strategy focuses on *withholding politeness* where it would be expected. Culpeper provides the example of failing to thank somebody for a present.

A8.6 CRITICISMS OF – AND REVISIONS TO – CULPEPER'S APPROACH

Mills (2003: 128) is concerned by the 'decontextualised' approach that (she believes) the 'anatomy of impoliteness' promotes, because an 'important aspect of the evaluation of utterances as polite or impolite', in her view, 'is the degree to which institutions have routinised the use of certain types of language' (ibid.: 125). She argues, for example, that the (American) army's 'ritualised and institutionalised codes of linguistic behaviour' are such that 'excessive impoliteness on the part of trainers' is 'the norm' (ibid.: 126) and that the recruits are unlikely, therefore, to classify the sergeants' behaviour as impolite. Notice that Mills seems to be assuming that truly 'impolite' behaviour must therefore be 'above [i.e. beyond] the norm' in some way: as we'll discover in Unit A8.9, this view is typical of the postmodern perspective. Suffice it to say, Culpeper and colleagues have defended the model from some of the criticisms, whilst also remedying some of the model's weaknesses. For example, Culpeper (2005) has countered that because sanctioned impoliteness is used systematically, it does not necessarily follow that the targets of the impoliteness will regard it to have been 'neutralized'. His argument is based on an investigation of the UK version of the *Weakest Link*, a TV show known for the sharp-witted comments of the host, Anne Robinson. Culpeper does acknowledge the importance of considering context when applying the notions of im/politeness, however. In fact, a more detailed consideration of context is first evident in his 2003 paper, which Culpeper co-authored with Bousfield and Wichmann: they show how impoliteness is constructed or countered over stretches of dialogue as opposed to one utterance or a particular adjacency pair. Our third reading, Unit B8.4, is devoted to Culpeper *et al.*'s (2003) discussion of some of these strategies.

A8.7 A RETURN TO GOFFMAN

The later work of Culpeper and colleagues also draws more explicitly on Goffman (1967). Culpeper *et al.* (2003) show how impoliteness can be captured by Goffman's *intentional* level of face threat, for example. The *intentional* level captures acts that have been undertaken 'maliciously and spitefully', with the aim of causing face damage (ibid.: 14). It is therefore distinct from Goffman's *accidental* face threat, which equates to face damage that S is responsible for, but which he/she did not intend at all and would have attempted to avoid had he/she foreseen its offensive consequences.[2] Goffman's *accidental* level of face threat has been used more recently by Culpeper (2005), to explain 'accidental impoliteness'. This is necessary, in his view, to account for instances 'when H perceives and/or constructs behaviour (or communicative acts) as intentionally face-attacking' (ibid.: 38). Culpeper, then, offers a dual perspective in regard to impoliteness – such that impoliteness can come about 'when S communicates an intention to damage face' or 'when H perceives and/or constructs' some behaviour as face-damaging, even though S may not have intended for their actions to be interpreted in this way (ibid.).

Although Culpeper is at pains to point out that prototypical impoliteness will be a combination of both intent on the part of S and recognition of that intent on the part of H, Culpeper's definition is problematic for Bousfield (2008), as he believes that impoliteness must be intentional on S's part and must be perceived by H to be intentional on S's part. This is because Bousfield believes that, to be 'successful', impoliteness must be obvious to both parties and, moreover, that what Culpeper calls 'accidental impoliteness' is actually 'accidental face damage' (because it lacks intent on S's part, and hence cannot be 'impoliteness' in Bousfield's mind). Bousfield (ibid.: 72) therefore offers his own definition of impoliteness which emphasizes that FTAs, which are 'gratuitous', tend to be 'unmitigated in contexts where mitigation . . . is required' and/or are purposefully performed 'with deliberate aggression, that is, with the face threat exacerbated, "boosted", or maximised in some way to heighten the face damage inflicted'.

Bousfield (2008) also reduces Culpeper's (1996, 2005) impoliteness strategies to only two; 'on-record impoliteness' and 'off-record impoliteness'. On-record impoliteness occurs when S explicitly and unambiguously attacks the face of another, in a Goffman (1967) sense, and subsumes Culpeper's (1996) bald-on-record, positive and negative impoliteness strategies. Off-record impoliteness is very similar to the off-record strategy which Culpeper added to his anatomy of impoliteness in 2005 (except for also subsuming Culpeper's sarcasm strategy): indirect utterance(s) which, although they seek to cause damage to H's face, can be readily cancelled (by being denied, for example). As we've discussed earlier, indirectness does not mean something will automatically be more polite. Indeed, after citing Leech's (1983) example of 'Haven't you something to declare?', discussed in Unit A8.4 above, Culpeper (2011: 184) provides his own example of an indirect utterance which he argues is likely to be interpreted as being more impolite than their direct equivalent: cf. *Do you have sawdust for brains?* and *You fool*; see also *Are you stupid?* and *You're stupid.*

A8.8 EXTENDING IMPOLITENESS MODELS TO CAPTURE VERBAL AGGRESSION

Bousfield's (2008) definition of impoliteness as S-intended and H-perceived allows him to side-step an accusation that has been levelled at the other Culpeper-inspired models by postmodern researchers; that the impoliteness strategies they outline are, in fact, strategies for the *aggravation* of or *non-attendance* to face, which can but may not necessarily lead to 'impoliteness' in the lay sense of the term (Locher and Watts 2005). This is important, as there has been a concern over labelling within im/politeness research for some time. Indeed, it is problems relating to terminology which initially prompted Watts (2003) to propose his politeness₁ and politeness₂ distinction. Yet, for Archer (2008), the answer is not to abandon the Culpeper-inspired models completely – as postmodern researchers tend to advocate – but, rather, to *extend* their applicability so that they explicitly capture verbal aggression at a broader level. Put simply, Archer (2008) is proposing that we make use of Culpeper-inspired strategies to investigate *all* of Goffman's (1967) distinctions – *intentional*, *accidental* and *incidental* – rather than focus on *intentional* face damage, that is, 'prototypical impoliteness'. In case you are not familiar with Goffman's (ibid.: 14) *incidental* level of face threat, it captures face damage which, although unplanned on S's part, is undertaken in the knowledge that it might have (potentially) offensive consequences. This is different from accidental face threat, where the utterer would have avoided the face threat, had they known that it may have 'offensive consequences'. It's also unlike intentional face damage, for there is no sense of the action being 'spitefully undertaken'. This acting *in spite of the offensive consequences* as opposed to acting *out of spite* offers an important means of distinguishing impoliteness from verbal aggression, according to Archer (2008). Lawyers have the right (because of their role in the courtroom) to ask witnesses face-threatening and in some instances face-damaging questions during cross-examination. However, they do so in order to develop a crime narrative, primarily, and not to offend the witness (even though they will be aware of the possibility of the witness taking offence; see also Archer 2011c).

Archer's (2008) approach is similar to that of Pearson *et al.* (2001): both are attempting to capture the point at which behaviour transgresses the norms of acceptability or appropriacy (as dictated by the activity type) to become *marked* by 'impoliteness' or 'incivility'. That said, there are some serious terminological differences here too. The most obvious between Archer (ibid.) and Pearson *et al.* (ibid.) concerns their differing understanding of 'aggression': for Pearson *et al.*, 'aggression' cannot be part of a workplace *norm*. Instead, it must be viewed as a type of antisocial behaviour that violates workplace norms *intentionally*. Pearson *et al.* therefore prefer the term 'incivility', which, for them, indicates an ambiguity as to intent. However, as Archer (2008, 2011c) demonstrates with reference to the courtroom, verbal aggression is not necessarily *deviant* in some professional settings and, in fact, only becomes so when the overriding goal is to cause intentional or deliberate face threat, in the Goffman (1967) sense.

A8.9 FACEWORK AND IM/POLITENESS: THE POSTMODERN PERSPECTIVE

Archer's (2008, 2011c) approach can be seen as a second order (i.e. theoretical) approach to facework and im/politeness which is sympathetic to a first order approach. First order (or im/politeness$_1$) approaches, you will remember, argue that impoliteness can only be understood from the perspectives of the participants themselves. As such, her approach is likely to remain problematic for postmodern researchers like Watts – in spite of her return to Goffman[3] – such is their dislike of second order approaches, no matter how participant-sensitive they might try to be (see, e.g., Watts 2003: 25; but see also Unit B8.1). In addition, Archer is still largely focusing on (the prediction of) intentionality – and postmodern researchers tend to emphasize the importance of 'the uptake of a message' by H and others (Locher and Watts 2008). This said, important points of agreement between Archer and postmodern researchers relate to:

1   their both understanding facework or *relational work* as a 'continuum from polite and appropriate to impolite and inappropriate behaviour' (Locher 2004: 51; Archer 2011b, 2011c); and
2   their argument that supportive and aggressive facework can be *politic* (i.e. be considered by participants to be appropriate to the ongoing social interaction).

Indeed, what makes any verbal or non-verbal behaviour *im/polite*, in their respective views, is the extent to which behaviour exceeds participants' expectations of what is politic within a given situation and/or for a given community of practice/activity type (i.e. is *salient* in some way and hence *marked*).

Locher and Watts (2008) demonstrate the power of expectation frames with reference to a political interview dating from 1984. The interview involved two participants, UK presenter Fred Emery and the then-president of the National Union of Mineworkers, Arthur Scargill. British political programmes like *Panorama* tend to exhibit an 'increased level of aggressiveness and a supposed concomitant loss of "respect" on the part of the interviewer towards political interviewees' (ibid.: 85). What is at issue, according to Locher and Watts, is whether Emery was outside the 'frame of normality' for interviewing in seeking to restrict Scargill's action environment by asking him questions and not allowing him the *interactional space* to answer those questions. Are interruptions – especially ones you 'apologize' for ('Sorry if I interrupt you . . .') – acceptable practices for an interviewer or not? Locher and Watts further problematize the issue for us by providing evidence to suggest that Scargill opted to *frame* Emery as someone who was being overtly rude and aggressive, that is, he was acting in a way that was beyond the 'sanctioned' aggression which typifies 'this public form of social practice' in Britain.

By now you will know that politeness and impoliteness are evaluative judgements, which are shaped (in part) by the context-of-utterance and/or the roles of/relationship between the participants. For example, swearing in front of one's grandmother or elderly relatives is likely to be inappropriate in any context, even though swearing in front of one's close friends might be completely acceptable in familiar contexts. Of course, swearing will constitute impoliteness for some, regardless of the roles of the participants and/or the context. What should we glean from this? That our understanding of what is 'politic' in facework terms (i.e. appropriate to the participants, given the activity/context, and their roles/relationship(s)) and what is 'salient' (i.e. is beyond the kinds of behaviour the participants would expect from a particular interlocutor in environment X) is subject to interpersonal differences as well as to socio-cultural and activity-specific expectations. As the Locher and Watts study reveals, what is politic (i.e. appropriate and hence acceptable) and what is salient (i.e. inappropriate and hence unacceptable) is also prone to manipulation. We return to these issues in Unit A12, as part of our discussion of 'Pragmatics and Power' (see also the readings in Unit B8, where we discuss the notions of politic versus salient behaviour in some depth).

> Summary and looking ahead

NOTES

1   Brown and Levinson demonstrate (i)–(iii) via the mathematical sum $W_x = D(S,H) + P(H,S) + R_x$

2   Goffman (1967: 14) also distinguishes an *incidental* level of face threat, which captures face damage which is unplanned, on S's part. This said, S would have known that face damage might be an 'anticipated by-product' of the action they have undertaken. The difference between incidental and accidental face threat, then, is that the utterer opts to perform the act knowing that it may have 'offensive consequences'. The difference between incidental and intentional face threat, in turn, is that the former is not 'spiteful' like the latter (i.e. there is no *intent to harm*).

3   Postmodern researchers tend to draw extensively from Goffman's ideas in regard to facework – or relational work, as they prefer to call it (see, e.g., Locher and Watts 2008).

Unit A9
Pragmatics, prosody and gesture

We all know that it is possible to say the same words in many different ways, and that our tone of voice can have as much effect on the listener as the words we choose. This is evident from our own experience and also through the medium of fiction, where writers often describe their characters' voices in a way that allows us to 'hear' something of their state of mind or attitude. We might find, for example, something like: *Yes, he said firmly*, or *No, she murmured sympathetically*, or *Go away, he snapped abruptly.* Each adverb, and sometimes the verb itself, suggests a way of speaking that conveys how the speaker feels, either about the addressee or about the message itself (Brown 1977). This expression of emotional and attitudinal meaning has been claimed as the primary function of tone of voice, or 'prosody', but it also conveys other less elusive kinds of meaning, including focus of information, utterance type (question, statement), topic structure and the organization of turns in conversation. However, prosody does not have any propositional meaning, and this is the main reason why prosody is considered to belong primarily to the domain of pragmatics rather than semantics. This is not to say that it does not have a clear 'grammatical' structure, just as speech acts have grammatical structure, and much research has been carried out into the underlying phonological system (Ladd 1996). But we are concerned here not so much with the system but with what it means. In order to convey meaning with prosody we exploit a limited number of vocal resources – pitch (intonation), loudness, voice quality and timing (including pauses). Each of these components, that together constitute 'prosody', can be measured separately, and different components have different functions, but they often operate together for certain effects.

In addition to what is conveyed by our tone of voice, an important part of speaker meaning is conveyed by bodily movements. These can include the direction of our gaze, the expression on our faces, the gestures we make with our hands and the spatial orientation of our bodies in relation to others. It is becoming increasingly clear that in order to fully understand the context of an utterance we need to see that context as multimodal, in other words, as deriving from the organized inter-action between what is said, the way it is spoken and visible body movements.

A9.1 PROSODY AND PAUSES

In a written English text, spaces help the reader to see where words begin and end, and punctuation and capital letters signal the boundaries between sentences, clauses and sometimes phrases. In spoken language, these cues are absent and listeners rely on the way in which the speech is phrased to help them break it down into manageable 'chunks'.[1] Many assume that these phrases are marked by pauses, but this is not often the case.

Speakers have, of course, no choice but to breathe occasionally, but very few pauses are solely physiologically determined – most are used strategically in a systematic way. If a written text is read aloud, particularly by a highly proficient reader, pauses are generally found where we might expect them, namely at strong constituent breaks in syntactic structure, especially between sentences and between paragraphs. In spontaneous speech, some pauses also occur at syntactic junctures, but many more do not. Pauses are often linked with the notion of fluency and hesitation, together with filled pauses (*um*, *uh*) false starts and repetitions. Here is an example (silent pauses are transcribed <,>, or <,,>, depending on their perceived length):

> Uh<,> I'm not saying that this is <,> a a a case which uh could be processed
> to trial with the same <,> rapidity as a straightforward <,> uh alleged libel
> in a <,,> newspaper where everything arose in and around London.
> (ICE-GB s2a-063 #004 [from an unscripted legal presentation])

Here we see the co-occurrence of silent pauses, filled pauses and repetition, most of which are not at constituent breaks. However, these features are not to be dismissed as evidence of 'poor speaking'. The fact that several 'hesitations' occur just before noun phrases (*a case, rapidity, alleged libel, newspaper*) is typical evidence for a cognitive explanation for pauses: speakers pause at moments of statistical uncertainty, i.e. before words or phrases that are less predictable. Pauses occur less often before grammatical words than lexical words, which suggests that they are used to signal mental planning. In fact, it is thought that hesitations are an integral part of spontaneous speech, and if speakers are 'punished' for pausing they simply increase the amount of repetition they use (Beattie and Bradbury 1979, cited in Beattie 1983). Some pauses are used to direct the listener to something interesting that they should attend to. For example, when dictating an address or telephone number, a speaker might say . . . *and the telephone number is [pause] 12345*. . . where the pause enables the listener to focus on the important information – in this case, the number. In the classroom, teachers often use an unfinished sentence and a pause to elicit a response from a pupil, as in (holding up a picture) *And this is a [pause].* . . . The teacher hopes that someone will finish the sentence. Culpeper (2005) describes the use of a 'dramatic pause' in a well-known British game show, the *Weakest Link*. When someone leaves the show, their prize is announced with *And you leave with [pause]* . . ., where, according to Culpeper, the pause adds to the 'air of deflation' when the prize turns out to be *nothing*.

Pauses also play a role in turn-taking (see Unit A6). Many occur after the first word in a turn, allowing the speaker to first gain the floor and then plan the rest of the utterance. In English, silences between turns are avoided, and a speaker who paused before taking a turn would probably lose the chance to speak. However, it is important to note that the degree to which pauses between turns are tolerated is culturally dependent; analysis of British and American English suggests that turns either 'latch' or overlap slightly. Aboriginal culture, on the other hand, tolerates long periods of silence as part of conversation (Mushin and Gardner 2009). Such cultural differences can give rise to misunderstandings, as we will see in this chapter.

In some contexts, a pause can actually constitute a turn in its own right and, depending on the context, will generate a range of possible inferences. In the following exchange, B says nothing, but A's response suggests that the silence was meaningful and interpreted as a turn. This would be especially clear if the silence was accompanied by a broad smile or a rueful grimace.

A: What did you think of the performance?
B: [silence]
A: I see

It is clear, then, that pauses, including silent pauses and filled pauses have a strategic function, and are not simply a sign of difficulty. As Clark and Fox Tree (2002: 104) point out: 'Um and uh are signals not symptoms.'

A9.2 PROSODY AND INFORMATION STRUCTURE

When we convey information in a sentence, there are often some parts that we wish to highlight more than others. Sometimes this is simply to underline the meaning of a word such as 'huge' – by emphasizing the word we are making a big gesture with our voices in the same way that we might make a big gesture with our hands, to show just how 'huge' the object is. Whatever the reason, what we are doing is fundamentally iconic – we make the prominence of the word match the 'informativeness' that we ascribe to it, or match the attention we want our hearer to pay to it.[2] Prominence is perceived salience: just as a word can be made prominent in a text, so a syllable can be made prominent in speech. The means of doing this vary – in printed texts we can use *italics*, CAPITALS, underlining, colour, font, or anything else that makes the word stand out from its background. In speech we use prosodic resources, especially pitch, to make a syllable stand out against the rest.

As we pointed out above, speech is naturally divided into phrases, or 'tone groups', and the default position for prominence is on the last lexical word in a group (or more accurately, on the stressed syllable of that word). This default position for prominence placement is shown in the examples below. Note that the last lexical word is not necessarily the last word – a group can end in one or more grammatical words (examples 3, 4, 5 and 7) – and that the last lexical word might actually be a compound (example 6). In example 8, the prominence is, unusually, on a pronoun because it is part of the lexical verb 'to look up', i.e. to consult a dictionary to find the meaning of a word. In example 7, on the other hand, the verb is 'to look'.

1 I think I'll go HOME
2 Can you give me some MOney
3 Don't LOOK at it
4 Can we HELP him
5 It's not a good time to SEE him about it
6 I've cut out an interesting NEWSpaper article
7 There's nothing to LOOK at
8 Pass the DICtionary | there's something I want to look UP

BOX A9.1 PROSODIC PROMINENCE IN ENGLISH

In the example below, the most prominent syllable is *are*, and the prominence can be seen in the fundamental frequency (F0) contour, heard as pitch. It rises to a peak and then falls sharply. The word is also longer than it would be if unstressed – compare its length with the unstressed *the* which follows. The short gap in the F0 contour just before the peak shows that the speaker created additional emphasis by giving *are* a glottal onset. Other interruptions in the contour are caused by non-sonorant consonants (weaKeST linK, GooDBye). Only one gap indicates a pause (between *link* and *goodbye*).

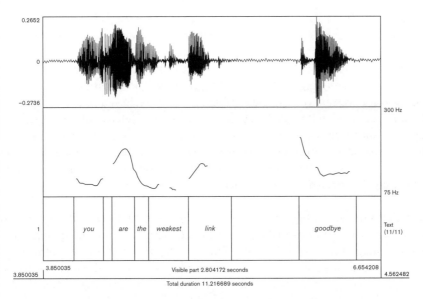

Figure A9.1 Praat picture showing the wave-form and F0 contour of a male speaker saying 'You are the weakest link goodbye'

How is this pattern of accentuation used to convey pragmatic meaning? The default accent placement is the background against which prominence can be used strategically to indicate a different focus, for example in order to set up a contrast. For example, the answer to (2) above might be *Well, I can LEND you some money*. First of all, by being de-accented, the word *money* is being treated as shared or given information. Not all languages, or even all varieties of English, do this, but it is normal for standard British English. Second, by placing prominence on *lend*, a contrast is being set up with *give*, implying, but not saying, that the speaker is not prepared to give. The placement of prominence in an utterance is thus a rich source of pragmatic inference. In the game show the *Weakest Link*, known for the impolite manner of the host, the person with the most mistakes has to leave the programme – they are the 'weakest link'. They are dismissed with *You are the weakest link*. The default place of prominence would be 'link', but since the notion of the 'weakest link' underlies the whole programme and is therefore 'given', we would expect the prominence to shift to 'you', thus contrasting the contestant with the others. In fact, as Culpeper (2005) points out, the host says *You ARE the weakest link* which suggests that it was suspected all along that that person would lose (see Box A9.1 on p. 99).

In speech, to make a syllable prominent, speakers do different things in different languages. It is a common mistake to think that a prominent syllable is simply louder than the others. In English, prominent syllables are generally longer and louder, but most importantly they are typically marked by a jump (up or down) in pitch.

A9.3 PROSODY, SPEECH ACTS AND IMPLICATURE

Another pragmatic role of prosody is to signal speech acts, and it does this partly through the choice of final melody or 'nuclear tone' which is associated with the nuclear syllable – normally the last prominent syllable in the tone group. The exact number of contours available in English is controversial, but most agree that there are at least three: a rising contour; a falling contour; and a contour that falls and then rises (if necessary on a single syllable). These are referred to as *falls*, *rises* and *fall-rises*, illustrated in Box A9.2 on p. 102. The power of pitch contours to generate pragmatic meaning relies, as with prominence placement, on a default pattern typically associated with certain speech acts. Much work has therefore been carried out to establish what these 'default' contours are, from which speakers can then strategically deviate, which they frequently do.

Tonal contours with a high endpoint (rises, fall-rises) are generally assumed to indicate openness or non-finality, and generally occur at a non-final point in an utterance suggesting 'more to come'. Thus, if they occur at a final point in the utterance, it is unsurprising that they are typically associated with questions, so that the suggestion of 'more to come' refers to the answer that is being elicited. Falling contours, on the other hand, are associated with closedness or finality, and are therefore typical of statements. Wh-questions are an exception, since the default tone is a fall. In this respect they sound more like statements, and could perhaps be understood to have the underlying declarative meaning of *I want to know . . .*. When a rising tone is used with a wh-question, as in *What's your name?*, it could be in order to check the name against a list. The rise here usually begins in mid-range. If the rise is extended, beginning lower in the speaker's voice but ending high, it tends to be with children and can sound slightly patronizing if addressed to an adult.

If there is a discrepancy between the form of the utterance and the contour, it is generally the contour that determines how we interpret the force of the utterance. For example, if an utterance with declarative form (e.g. *you are hungry*) normally typical of a statement, is spoken with a rising tone, it is understood as a question and not as a statement of fact (i.e. you are hungry?).

A nuclear tone that lends itself particularly well to conveying some implied meanings is the fall-rise. As we said above, this contour typically indicates non-finality, meaning that more is coming, and therefore frequently occurs on sentence elements that are part of a larger structure. As in:

I went to \/town | and then . . .
\/Sometimes | we like to . . .

However, the fall-rise can also occur on utterances that are pragmatically complete, such as statements. This creates a mismatch between the finality of the syntax and the non-finality of the intonation. According to Wells (2006: 27): '[b]y making a statement with the fall-rise, the speaker typically states one thing but implies something further. Something is left unsaid – perhaps some kind of reservation or implication.' Wells gives a number of examples, including the following (ibid.: 28):

A: What do you think of Hubert?
B: He's very me\/ticulous
A: /But?
B: Utterly boring

As Wells explains, the implicational fall-rise can be used simply to imply that the speaker has reservations. *Is she coming? I \/think so.* The fall-rise here underlies the uncertainty or tentativeness of the reply, but the reason for the uncertainty is not specified. This lack of specificity is sometimes exploited strategically: it enables us 'to imply things without actually saying them . . . to be tactful and politely indirect . . . (or) hypocritical and devious' (ibid.). In the following example (from ibid.):

What's she like as a colleague? Well she \/works very hard. (Or: She works very \/hard)

'. . . the unspoken implication might be *but she has no imagination* or *but she's not a good teacher* or *but she doesn't get on with her colleagues* or something else uncomplimentary' (ibid.: 29; emphasis in original). By using the fall-rise it is possible to say something complimentary but imply (but not say) something critical.

BOX A9.2 NUCLEAR TONES: INTONATION CONTOURS AND THEIR TRANSCRIPTION

In the British tradition, the last accented syllable in a tone group is known as the 'nucleus'. This is the most important accent in the group and is usually the most perceptually salient syllable, although this is less obvious when it occurs at a point in an utterance where the speaker's voice is quite low. The pitch contour that begins on this syllable is known as the 'nuclear tone' or 'nuclear contour'. It can signal whether, for example, the speaker is asking a question or making a statement. It also has the power to generate implicatures (cf. Unit A5).

The most common tunes or pitch contours associated with accented syllables in English are falling (i.e. starting high and ending low), rising and falling-rising (both ending high). It is possible, for example, to say the word *no* with all three tunes (Figure A9.2). The same contours can spread over several syllables.

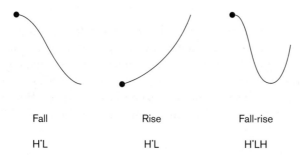

Fall	Rise	Fall-rise
H˙L	H˙L	H˙LH

Figure A9.2 Stylized representations of falling, rising and falling-rising pitch contours (adapted from Wichmann 2000: 11)

The simplest way to present pitch movement in a transcription is to use the forward slash and back slash characters, e.g. \NO (fall), /NO (rise), \/ NO (fall-rise). In polysyllabic words, the character should be inserted immediately before the accented syllable e.g. \elephant, pho\tography, photo\graphic, com\plain. This use of iconic symbols is common in the British approach to intonation (Cruttenden 1997; Wells 2006).

More recently the American Autosegmental system has become widely used (Pierrehumbert 1980; Ladd 1996). This system indicates pitch targets (H high or L low) and describes the contours as interpolations between the pitch targets. The target that is associated with the accented syllable is additionally marked with an asterisk (H* or L*). This means that a falling contour is H*L and a rising contour is L*H, while a fall-rise is H*LH.

Let us return to the example in Unit A9.2 – *A: Can you give me some MOney* – *B: I can LEND you some money*. It is highly likely that this reply would have a fall-rise contour, with the falling part starting on the word *lend* and the rising part on *money* (*I can \/lend you some money*). The prominence alone sets up a contrast with the word *give* in the question, while the fall-rise tone carries an implied *but* . . ., which in this case could be 'but I'm not prepared to give you anything', or even 'but you don't have the right to ask me to give it to you'.

A9.4 INTONATION AND SOCIAL RITUALS

Social rituals, such as thanking and apologizing do not have fixed intonation contours: these depend on the context in which they occur.[3] As we saw in Unit A4, in the case of *thank you* a falling tone conveys genuine gratitude, while a fall-rise or a rise is closer to an acknowledgment of receipt rather than an expression of gratitude. We can imagine then that if someone receives a gift and says /*thank you*, i.e. with a rising tone, effectively just acknowledging receipt, the giver may well be offended.

In the case of apologies, the intonation patterns depend very much on the serious-ness of the offence for which the speaker is apologizing. A detailed study of apologies has been made by Aijmer (1996) including a description of the intonation contours typically occurring with *sorry* and other expressions of apology (*I apologize*, *pardon* and *excuse me*). The use of *sorry* was by far the most common, constituting over 80 per cent (ibid.: 86) of the occurrences in the corpus data. Knowles (1986: 194) suggests that a serious apology normally has a final falling contour, as in *I'm (very)* *sorry*, while if it is more casual, then a fall-rise is more usual (\/*sorry*). Aijmer's study finds that there are many more rising or falling-rising contours on 'sorry' than falling, which suggests that the majority of these apologies are in fact fairly routine, and that there are many fewer expressions of deep regret.

In other expressions with *sorry*, the expression is expanded to include reference to the offence as in *I'm \sorry I'm /late*, or *\Sorry about /that* or to include a vocative as in *\Sorry /Neil*. If the apology is intensified, the prosodic prominence is often transferred to the intensifier: *I'm \so /sorry* or *I'm \so \/sorry* or *I \am sorry*.

At the least apologetic end of the scale, there is evidence that *sorry* in some contexts is routinized to such an extent that it has become a pragmatic marker. This occurs when there is a disturbance in the flow of conversation, for example if the speaker makes a slip of the tongue e.g. *It'll be Tues . . . sorry Wednesday*, or wishes something to be repeated:

A: Pete's arrived
B: /Sorry
A: I said Pete's arrived

Aijmer refers to these as 'talk offences' which require an apology. It is likely, however, that they are no longer perceived as true apologies. Such tokens of *sorry* are spoken quickly, sometimes so quickly that all that remains is something like [soi] or even [so]. This loss of phonetic material is typical of the process of grammaticalization (see Hopper and Traugott 2003), a process of semantic change whereby lexical items lose their propositional meaning over time and take on grammatical, discoursal or pragmatic meaning. You will find more about the use of intonation in speech acts, in this case making a request with *please,* in the reading in Unit B9.1.

A9.5 INTONATION AND DISCOURSE MARKERS

As we saw with *sorry,* there are words and expressions in English which are multi-functional; in some contexts they carry propositional meaning but in others the word has been reduced through frequent use to the status of discourse marker, and carries interpersonal rather than propositional meaning. A particularly interesting case is that of the word *now,* which in initial position can be either a time adverbial (*Now we are going home*) or indicate a shift in the discourse (*Now, what I need to explain is this . . .*). The time adverbial in this position is normally accented, but the discourse marker can be either unstressed or accented. An unstressed initial *now* is fairly clearly a discourse marker, but how do we distinguish between the two meanings when it is accented? The accented time adverbial usually has a high level contour and is part of a larger tone group, but accented discourse markers in initial position usually have a falling contour, and can be followed by a pause. In other words, they consitute their own intonation phrase or tone group. What may be ambiguous on the page is therefore no longer ambiguous when it is spoken.

Extreme contrasting patterns for discourse markers – either completely unstressed, or prominent and carrying a nuclear tone – are analogous to those found on other grammatical words such as conjunctions. Halliday and Hasan (1976) point out that although 'cohesive elements' are normally non-prominent, 'if the cohesive element itself is brought into focus of attention, this is marked in the usual way by tonic[4] prominence' (ibid.: 271). A prominent *and* followed by a pause is a way of emphasizing the conjunction, ensuring that listeners focus on its additive function. Similarly, the initial discourse marker *well* can be very short and unstresssed, but it can also be made prominent with a nuclear tone (fall, rise and fall-rise are all possible) and followed by a pause:

A: Tell us about your experiences
B: \Well [pause] it all began when I . . .

Such an emphatic *Well* suggests that a fairly long turn is to come and the listener should be prepared not to take a turn for a while.

A9.6 INTONATION AND CONVERSATION MANAGEMENT

It has been observed that in the course of an utterance, pitch will gradually decline. This is in part physiologically determined: it requires energy to maintain high pitch, and as the breath is used up, there is less energy available so it is easier to lower pitch than to raise it. The downward trend, or 'declination', is similar to 'going flat' while singing – it does not affect the choice of contours or accent placement.[5] Since it is impossible for a speaker to drift downwards indefinitely, there are points at which the declination is 'reset', and the speaker has to invest new energy to raise the pitch again. However, while this phenomenon has a physiological basis, as with pauses, speakers exploit the impression of a new start strategically to indicate something new in the discourse – e.g. a new idea, a new topic or a new paragraph in a written text read aloud. Prosody is also used to manage topic shift in the course of casual conversation, as we will see below.

The study of conversation fits into the broad view of language as a social phenomenon, and turn-taking is a crucial part of the process of social interaction using language. The role of sound patterns, and also gaze, in achieving turn-taking has been studied for some time, originally relying entirely on auditory impressions but more recently complementing this with acoustic analysis. Of particular interest is the way in which interlocutors are able to anticipate turn ends so that they can take a turn with no intervening pause and with minimal overlap. Participants clearly make use of a range of resources, including their knowledge of syntax and thus what could constitute a complete utterance. This cue functions together with pragmatic and phonetic knowledge so that the imminent end of a turn is judged holistically. Pragmatic completion is observed when the action underlying the turn has been completed, while phonetic signals are a slowing down and lowering of pitch. No single factor is involved, and it is possible for one parameter to override another; for example, a syntactically complete unit can be realized with the intonation of incompleteness, in English usually a rising or falling-rising contour, and thus signal 'more to come' (see Unit A9.3 above). Some studies have also shown that a particular voice quality known as 'creaky voice' can be a cue to the end of a turn.

Of course, turn-taking is not always smooth, and interruptions are common, both collaborative and competitive (cf. Unit A6). We recognize the difference by the prosody of the overlap, as has been shown by Kurtiç *et al.* (2010): the competitive overlap is characterized by a pitch that is higher than the normal reset height for that speaker. This continues until the battle for the floor is decided, with either the incoming speaker gaining the floor or the current speaker retaining it. Speakers are particularly vulnerable to losing the floor when they wish to switch to a new topic but not cede the floor. The relevant signals are contradictory. The upcoming end of a topic is signalled by a narrowed pitch range, but this is also a cue to the end of a turn. Unless the speaker has previously created the right to a lengthy turn (e.g. in answer to *Tell us all about your experiences* as in Unit A9.5 above, in which case a narrative sequence is less likely to be interrupted, speakers are torn between wanting to signal the end of a topic and not wanting to signal the end of the turn. In order to achieve this, as they are coming to the end of one topic they lower their pitch but instead of slowing down they speed up, and accelerate into the high pitch reset for the next topic, thus preventing the interlocutor from taking a turn. This strategy is called 'rush through' (Local and Walker 2004). (Cf. also Schegloff 1979, 1996; Couper-Kuhlen and Ford 2004: 9.)

The importance of prosodic turn-taking signals was highlighted in a study of dyadic (i.e. two participant) conversations between hearing people and people with hearing impairments (Wright 1999). These conversations were marked by many more interruptions than expected. Analysis showed that where there was a potential syntactic completion but the prosody indicated non-finality, the hearing-impaired participants responded to the syntactic cues and, unsurprisingly, not to the prosodic cues. Thus, they thought the turn was complete even when the speaker was signalling prosodically that there was more to come, and the result was an interruption. The hearing participants also interrupted frequently. This was shown to be because the hearing-impaired speakers controlled their pitch less, so that it tended to fall gradually and sometimes inadvertently suggested that they had finished when they actually wanted to continue.

A similar case of conflicting turn-taking signals was described by Beattie *et al.* (1982) concerning a former British Prime Minister, Margaret Thatcher, who had voice training in order to sound more authoritative (for a proposed explanation of this phenomenon see Unit B9.3). This meant encouraging her to lower her voice, but it had the unfortunate side effect of making her sound as if she had finished speaking even when she hadn't, with the result that she was frequently interrupted.

A9.7 BODY LANGUAGE: GESTURE, GAZE AND PROXIMITY

The interplay of prosody and non-verbal communication, including gesture, posture, gaze and facial expression, is clearly important for communication but the relative signalling power of the various components is not yet known. We know, for example, from observing smooth turn-taking in telephone conversations that eye contact is not a necessary cue, and speakers nearly always accompany their speech with gestures, whether or not the interlocutor can see them. However, such features can also play an important signalling role in face-to-face communication.

The function of gaze is both to gather information and to convey it. It is possible to glean affective information from the facial expression of the other person, such as surprise, interest, agreement (Argyle 1988: 109). It also plays an important part in the management of conversational interaction. Broadly speaking, if a speaker looks at his or her interlocutor it can be a signal for the other speaker to take the floor. Thus we find that sometimes a speaker looks at the interlocutor in order to elicit back-channel during a turn (e.g. vocalization, head nod or interested facial expression), and gaze often occurs at grammatical junctures. Glances may also be used to add emphasis to particular words and phrases. A recent study by Allwood (2008) using multimodal corpora shows that during a period of word searching the speaker's gaze is turned away from the interlocutor, and that this serves to help the speaker keep the floor. However, if the speaker searching for a word wants to elicit help he turns his gaze *towards* the interlocutor. If there was no glance towards the hearer, no help was offered. This reflects Beattie's (1983) finding that people look less during hesitant phases of speech, and at the beginning of utterances where the most planning is assumed to be required. At the end of utterances, however, there is a tendency to glance at the other participant. In other words, gaze can act as a turn-taking cue, especially between strangers when there is generally a lower level of eye contact.

The gestures that speakers use are wide-ranging in their nature. Some are unconscious movements that accompany speech, others are more iconic, such as using the fingers to indicate quotation marks in the air (". . .") or holding the thumb and little finger to the ear to signal a telephone. Some are more conventionalized gestures such as the thumbs-up sign to indicate 'positive' or 'good' or 'success'. Other gestures are intended to offend. These vary considerably across cultures and are thus the source of potential misunderstanding. We have, in effect, a continuum of gestures from those that are most idiosyncratic, through those that are conventionalized, to those that are coded, in other words where the shape of the gesture no longer relates to meaning in a non-arbitrary way. At the most conventionalized or coded end of this continuum are sign languages. These hand and body movements are in fact no longer 'gestures' at all, but part of a language.

The question as to what speech-accompanying gestures 'mean' is difficult to answer, just as it is difficult to say what intonation contours 'mean'. It depends to some extent whether they are used deliberately as part of the message or entirely subconsciously as an accompaniment to the message. The gestures made by speakers on the telephone can have little communicative value for the hearers, but in face-to-face interaction it is possible to convey meaning by means of gestures. Within Relevance Theory (see Unit A5.3) both prosody and gestures are taken to have 'procedural meaning': this means that they do not carry any propositional meaning themselves but act as a guide to the interlocutor as to how to interpret an utterance (Wharton 2009). Wharton maintains that gestures and facial expressions (such as a smile) can be unintentional, and simply a sign, for example, that the speaker is happy, but they can also be strategically (i.e. intentionally) employed as a communicative signal, for example to 'show' that the speaker is, or wishes to be seen as, happy (see Unit A5.1.2).

As well as through gaze and gesture, we also convey meaning by the orientation of our bodies, such as how closely we stand to our interlocutors, or the way in which we mirror the stance of the other participant(s). We will see in Unit B10 that the preferred proximity to interlocutors is culturally determined and can be the source of discomfort in cross-cultural interaction. One person's preferred proximity to another speaker may be perceived by them to be too close and thus an intrusion into their personal space. It may, on the other hand, be perceived as too distant, and we may infer that our interlocutor does not really want to continue the conversation or is simply being unfriendly.

The importance of gesture, posture, gaze and facial expression for communication has implications for how we collect data. As we saw in Unit A2, it is already possible to record and annotate speech using special speech annotation software; it is now clear that visual information must also be stored and annotated if we are to fully understand how meaning is made in interaction.

A9.8 TEACHING THE PRAGMATICS OF PROSODY

There are many books, old and new, on the 'art of speaking', which emphasize its importance in a wide range of activities, including public speaking, acting, teaching, preaching, newsreading, story reading and business presentations. It is also of great interest to those developing computer systems and devices that understand human speech and generate a human-sounding voice. On the other hand, in one extremely important area – language teaching – prosody has long been neglected. Pronunciation training has traditionally focused on vowels and consonants, and native speakers are able to recognize pronunciation errors and make allowance for them. Prosody, however, is different. As we said at the beginning of this unit, prosody frequently expresses attitudinal or emotional meaning, which is why it belongs to the domain of pragmatics rather than semantics. Non-native errors are therefore often interpreted by native speakers not as errors but as indicating some unintended meaning. Learners should therefore be aware that, as Wells (2006: 2) puts it, '(s)peakers of English assume that –when it comes to intonation – you mean what you say. This may not be the same as what you think you are saying.' If our prosody, as indeed our gestures, can make us seem abrupt or sympathetic, helpful or offhand, matter-of-fact or interested, then it is important that this is what we really mean, and not something entirely different

Summary and looking ahead

In this unit we have introduced aspects of pragmatic meaning that often seem particularly elusive: prosody, and body language such as gesture, posture and gaze. We explained how prosody is normally used in English, especially pauses, accent placement and pitch contours. We then showed how it can be exploited to generate pragmatic meaning, for example to imply something without saying it. Prosody and gesture have an important part to play in face-to-face interaction and we gave examples of how they are used in conversation management.

The study of non-verbal communication has not typically been part of foreign language teaching, and our first reading in Unit B9 argues the case for its inclusion. You will also read about how choice of pitch contour changes the nature of requests in English, in a study that made use of a spoken corpus. Finally, we present a reading that attempts to explain some of the apparently universal paralinguistic effects of the pitch of the voice. In Unit C7 you will have the opportunity to research for yourself some aspects of prosody and gesture.

NOTES

1 There are many terms in the literature to refer to the 'chunks' or phrases of speech, including: *tone groups, tone units, intonation phrases* and *intonation domains*. These phrases are often around 6–10 syllables long, but there is considerable variation, depending, for example, on how formal the speech is, or how fast it is.

2 An important function of prosodic prominence in English is to indicate the information structure of an utterance by identifying the focus, that is, 'the information in the sentence that is assumed by the speaker not to be shared by him and the hearer' (Jackendoff 1972: 16).

3 And also on the form of the expression used, for example, whether a speaker says a simple *Sorry* or the more elaborate *I am really so sorry*.

4 Their term 'tonic' is equivalent to 'nucleus' as used in this book.

5 The speaker's lowest pitch remains the same while the upper line goes down, so that the pitch 'envelope' narrows. This means that a prominent syllable towards the end of an utterance is in real terms usually lower than at the beginning, but perceived as equally prominent.

Unit A10
Cross-cultural pragmatics

When research in pragmatics focuses on one language such as English, it is tempting to think that one is dealing with universals. However, any idea that Grice's maxims apply everywhere in the same way is undermined by everyday experiences of people around the world. As Wierzbicka puts it, this:

> popular assumption . . . flies in the face of reality as experienced by millions of ordinary people – refugees, immigrants, the children of immigrants, caught between their parents and the society at large, cross-cultural families and their children, and also by monolingual 'stay-at-homes' who suddenly find themselves living in societies which are ethnically, culturally and linguistically diverse.
>
> (Wierzbicka 2003: ix)

In order to learn more about why some of these experiences are negative, confusing and disorientating, researchers have taken two approaches. The first approach is to study pragmatic phenomena in different cultures in order to be able to set up comparisons and thus to predict possible misunderstandings. The second approach is to study representatives of different groups in the process of interacting with each other (see Scollon and Scollon 2001: 539) to see how differences are negotiated. The term cross-cultural communication tends to be reserved for the first approach and intercultural communication for the second.

A10.1 SPEECH ACTS AND INDIRECTNESS

A problem that arises frequently in interaction between people of different cultures is that one participant or group is perceived by the other to be impolite. This can of course be unrelated to language, such as whether or not to take off your shoes on entering a private house: in some cultures it is rude to leave them on, and in others it is rude, or at least odd, to take them off. But we are concerned here with issues of language. Politeness and impoliteness in relation to language is sometimes explained in terms of differing degrees of directness – the English way of uttering indirect requests (*Could you possibly . . ., Would you mind . . .*, etc.) is not necessarily reflected in other languages. For example, a child rejecting an offer (e.g. *Would you like some more juice?*) would be expected to say in English *No thank you*, while in Spain in the same situation a simple *No* is appropriate.

An attempt to compare cross-cultural variation in the realization of speech acts is the so-called CCSARP project (Cross-Cultural Speech Act Realization Project), (Blum-Kulka *et al.* 1989c, see Unit A3). This project focused on the two speech acts – requests and apologies, both of which are considered to be face-threatening acts. The project was designed to study how these speech acts are realized in different communities.[1] To do this, incomplete dialogues were constructed that involved situations requiring a request or an apology. The respondent filled in the missing utterance. Here is an example (from ibid.: 14):

(a) *At the university*

Ann missed a lecture yesterday and would like to borrow Judith's notes.

Ann: ....
Judith: Sure, but let me have them back before the lecture next week.

(b) *At the college teacher's office*

A student has borrowed a book from her teacher, which she promised to return today. When meeting her teacher, however, she realises she forgot to bring it along.

Teacher: Miriam. I hope you brought the book I lent you.
Miriam: ....
Teacher: OK, but please remember it next week.

However, the scope of cross-cultural pragmatics goes beyond speech acts and their realization. In detailed studies, such as a study of *please* in English and its German equivalent, *bitte*, House (1989, 1996) enumerates a number of differences between German and English speakers when they are 'being polite' in their own language and shows that a single parameter is not sufficient to describe the difference. She suggests that the reasons why English speakers sometimes perceive German speakers as impolite (may include) not only greater directness but also greater degrees of explicitness. A request to move further inside a bus (*Can you move up a bit/Können Sie bitte weiter nach vorn rücken*) is similar in English and German. However, on a particular occasion in German, the added explanation (*Andere Leute wollen auch noch einsteigen/Other people want to get on too*) was perceived as impolite by an English participant, not because of the request itself but because of the explicit justification of the request.

A10.2 PRAGMALINGUISTIC OR SOCIOPRAGMATIC FAILURE: WHAT IS GOING WRONG?

Some misunderstandings are the result of inappropriate use of apparently synonymous structures. Thomas (1983: 101) gives the example of the Russian equivalent of 'of course', which is 'used instead of *da* (yes) to convey an enthusiastic affirmative (cf. *yes, indeed, yes, certainly*, in English)'. However, in English, *of course* implies that the speaker has asked something that is self-evident and this, in certain contexts, can be construed as insulting. Thomas gives the following examples of exchanges (in English) between a Russian speaker B and an English speaker A:

> A: *Is it a good restaurant?*
> B: *Of course* [Gloss (for Russian S): Yes, (indeed) it is. (For English H): What a stupid question!]

> A: *Is it open on Sundays?*
> B: *Of course* [Gloss (for Russian S): Yes, (indeed) it is. (For English H): Only an idiot foreigner would ask!]
>
> (Ibid.: 102; emphasis in original)

Problems arising in this way are categorized by Thomas as 'pragmalinguistic failure', while a further category – 'sociopragmatic failure' is intended to capture misunderstandings that arise as a result of culturally different perceptions of, for example, what constitutes an imposition and the evaluation of power relationships in a given context. This distinction is not always easy to make, as we will see in the use of address forms.

A10.3 FORMS OF ADDRESS

An interesting linguistic phenomenon that has pragmatic consequences is the address form. This can include the use of first name or last name with a title (John/ Susan or Mr/Mrs/Ms/Dr/Professor Smith). It can also be coded in the pronoun system. Some languages, such as English, have only one pronominal address form – *you*. Other languages have what is called a T/V (tu/vous) distinction. The T-form is broadly used to address friends and family, while the V-form is used for strangers and as a mark of respect. An early study of the T/V distinction (Brown and Gilman 1960) suggested that the choice of pronoun was determined by two parameters: relative power and degree of solidarity. It can be non-reciprocal, as in the asymmetrical relationship between teacher and pupil, or, in medieval times, between the nobility and common people; it can also be reciprocal as between members of a family. A more recent study (Clyne 2009) suggests that there are many more principles involved in the sometimes difficult decision of which form to use. These principles include the questions: Do I know this person? Is this person much older or younger than me? Does this person belong to the same group as me? Is this person like me?/Should I do what they do? The decision, based on the answers to these questions, depends on the language concerned, personal or group preferences and the context.

Speakers who are accustomed to having the T/V distinction in their own language can feel uncomfortable using only one form, especially if they feel that the single form, such as 'you' in English, sounds too much like the familiar form in their own language (e.g. *tu* in French, *du* in German). For speakers of T/V languages these forms are an important grammatical way of expressing degrees of intimacy, and, deprived of the distinction, they feel either forced to address all and sundry in what seems to them an inappropriately familiar way, or they feel deprived of the means of expressing intimacy when they would like to. Even a linguist like Wierzbicka, with long experience of living in an English-speaking culture, feels this lack of distinction as a loss:

> In my view, a culture where one basic term of address, 'you' is used indis-
> criminately to everyone, cannot be regarded as one which attaches a great
> importance to the value of intimacy. If anything, it is extremely difficult to
> be intimate in English, because of this universal 'you', that is, because of the
> absence of any 'intimate' forms of address.
>
> (Wierzbicka 2003: 106)

However, it seems unlikely that native English speakers actually feel they cannot express intimacy, even though they do not have the grammatical means to do so. There are many other ways of expressing closeness or distance, including tone of voice, modality, use of diminutives and choice of first name, surname, nickname, etc. (cf. Siewierska 2004: 214–15). We must also remember that many languages make other pronominal distinctions, such as according to rank, or according to gender. Wierzbicka's comments highlight the difficulty of using a language with different pronominal distinctions from one's own, and also the temptation to ascribe to a culture what is actually simply one's own perception when operating in that language as a non-native speaker.

Some difficulties, however, are not the result of a different set of address forms, but of the different cultural conventions determining their use. Sometimes the choice is easy but as Clyne points out there is a 'big grey area' where several forms are possible. Judging how to address a new acquaintance is a fine balancing act and the source of considerable anxiety to learners, since an inappropriate choice can severely disrupt relationships or at least be a source of unwanted amusement. Many academics have become accustomed to using first names with other academics at conferences held in English, to whom they would in their own language use the V-form and a title with last name. In Germany, for example, the use of first name is associated with the T-form, so when two Germans meet again after an English-speaking conference they are faced with a dilemma – revert to title and last name, or use the T-form and first name. This is so uncomfortable for some that they prefer to continue to speak English together.

Knowing how to address others is, therefore, a potential source of considerable difficulty in cross-cultural encounters. The main problem is that if there is any violation of a norm in form of address, whether in the choice of V or T, in the use of family or given names, or in any other form (Madam, Sir, mate, my dear) 'the meaning of the act will be sought in the attitude or emotion of the speaker' (Brown and Gilman 1960: 273). In other words, such a violation will not necessarily be perceived as a mistake, but as the expression of an attitude, possibly negative, towards the hearer. This pragmatic interpretation underlies many misunderstandings and even negative national stereotypes, as we will see below.

A10.4 CULTURAL SCRIPTS

Although Thomas' categories of 'sociopragmatic' and 'pragmalinguistic' failure are extremely useful for broadly categorizing mistakes that lead to misunderstandings in cross-cultural communication, Zamborlin (2007) notes that in many cases they are hard to distinguish. While some errors are clearly linguistic failures, others are less easily determined – is an informal term of address being used by mistake or has S misjudged the social distance between S and H? Sometimes what appears to be a linguistic breakdown is in fact due to a lack of cultural knowledge.

While studies such as the comparison of speech acts across cultures have given us excellent insight into some sources of cross-/intercultural misunderstanding, the reasons clearly go deeper than whether we are more or less direct, or whether we use 'supportive moves' preceding a request, or make explicit the reason for the request. It has become clear that our linguistic behaviour is motivated and shaped by cultural beliefs. These beliefs relate to the values of a culture and the values of certain behaviours in that culture, and their study, it is suggested (Wierzbicka 2003), is essential if we are to avoid ethnocentric approaches to, say, notions of politeness. Such cultural beliefs may involve, for example, a view that it is better to tell an untruth than a truth that could be hurtful, or alternatively, that it is better to be spontaneous and say what you really think (ibid.: xii). According to Goddard, who has developed Wierzbicka's ideas, 'people in different cultures speak differently because they think differently, feel differently, and relate differently to other people' (2006: 14). But when we try to describe the cultural values that underlie linguistic behaviour, it is difficult to do so in terms that are not themselves culturally biased. Wierzbicka and Goddard attempt to do this in neutral, universally understood terms by describing certain kinds of interaction in terms of expressions that have a shared meaning across all languages. They call these shared meanings 'semantic primes', and in English these expressions include *good, bad, say, think, want, people, if, because.*

Examples from Goddard's list of semantic primes (ibid.: 4) are given below:

Substantives	I, you, someone/person, something/thing, people, body
Relational substantives	Kind, part
Determiners	This, the same, other/else
Quantifiers	One, two, much/many, some, all
Evaluators	Good, bad

With the help of these simple words it is thought to be possible to express some of the underlying assumptions in each culture that determine linguistic behaviour. Goddard gives the example of what is said in American culture to be a tendency to express positive attitudes, the American Smile Code (Klos Sokol 1997: 117, cited in ibid.: 7). A formulation of such an attitude, using semantic primes, is called a 'cultural script', and it is intended to express the cultural norms against which we should interpret linguistic behaviour.

> *An Anglo-American cultural script for 'cheerfulness' in verbal interaction*
> People think like this
> When I say something to other people
>> It is good if these people think that I feel something good
>> It is not good if these people think that I feel something bad.

(Ibid.: 8)

A10.5 DISCOURSE

A10.5.1 Backchannels

An important feature of turn-taking is the minimal response or backchannel (see Unit A6), which has many functions, from signalling attentiveness to showing agreement or disagreement. These differences are coded in the rhythmic placement of the utterances and also in their prosodic realization, but the cues are clearly not universal. Ishida (2006: 1972) found that 'Japanese back-channel cues, intended to simply signal listening or understanding, are often misinterpreted by speakers as an agreement.'

Hearers are also sensitive to the current speaker's cues as to where a backchannel response is appropriate, and these cues are also not universal. Wichmann and Caspers (2001) suggest that a high level final contour is much more likely to elicit a backchannel response in Dutch than in English. This has important implications for the study of cooperation in interaction between languages: an inappropriately placed backchannel response, or the absence of one where it was expected, can have a dissonant effect, even if unintended.

A10.5.2 Silence

It was already noted (in Unit A9) that silence in conversation has rich signalling power, and cultural norms operate here too. Eades (2003) describes the different values placed on silence in conversation in Australian Aboriginal culture and Australian English culture. She writes:

> silence is an important and positively valued part of many Aboriginal conversations. It is not uncommon for people to sit in silence for lengthy

periods of time while thinking about a serious topic of conversation . . .
Furthermore, in formal or semi-formal contexts, such as meetings or interviews, Aboriginal people like to use silence as they think through topics of
discussion . . . Thus in many Aboriginal contexts, silence signals that the
conversation is working well and that the rights and needs of individuals
to think in silence are being respected . . . On the other hand, in western
societies silence is often negatively valued in conversation . . . silence in
conversation or interviews is frequently an indication of some kind of
communication breakdown.

(Ibid.: 202–3)

As a result of these differences, Eades shows that in the courtroom, for example,
where the powerful participants are almost exclusively Australian English, 'Aboriginal
silence . . . can easily be interpreted as evasion, ignorance, confusion, insolence, or
even guilt' (ibid.: 203).

Australian Aborigines are not the only example of national stereotyping deriving
from discourse behaviour. The 'silent Finn' is a long-standing stereotype in Europe,
based on the fact that Finnish speakers use silence more frequently than speakers
in Anglo-American culture. According to Sajavaara and Lehtonen (1997), this
taciturnity is ascribed by some to a difficulty in communicating. Such negative
stereotyping is the result of interpreting discourse conventions from the perspective
of those, like many British and American speakers, who feel that silence is awkward
and to be avoided. The Finns, on the other hand, value silence. For them, being a
quiet listener is a way of showing respect to the other speaker: 'Finnish politeness
is passive: it is considerate to let other people be in peace' (ibid.: 274). Thus the
pauses between turns that make Anglo-American speakers feel uncomfortable are
quite normal and acceptable behaviour for the Finns.

Different norms for pausing have the potential to cause considerable disruption in
conversation. Speakers who are used to very short pauses may continue to hold the
floor thinking that their interlocutor does not to want to take a turn, while the other
person may feel that they 'can't get a word in edgeways'. Such differences occur,
according to Tannen (1986: 30), not only between speakers from different countries
but also within a single country such as the US. The most serious problem, however,
is not that conversation does not run smoothly. The problem is that people draw
conclusions related not to turn-taking norms but to personality. Those preferring
longer pauses than the perceiver's norm may seem to be slow and dull, or shy and
awkward, while those who have shorter pauses may seem pushy and aggressive or
outgoing and confident. These personality judgements can have serious consequences both in the development of friendships and in institutional settings. Job
interviews, for example, will not go well for someone who comes across as slow and
dull. And, as we saw earlier in relation to Aboriginal Australians, such impressions
can have disastrous consequences in a court of law.

A10.5.3 Interruptions

Closely related to pausing strategies in speech is the phenomenon of simultaneous talk or 'interruptions'. In the fast speech of the New York Jewish speakers, Tannen (1981, 1999) observes a tendency to overlapping speech. This, she says, is 'used cooperatively by New Yorkers, as a way of showing enthusiasm and interest, but it is interpreted by non-New Yorkers as just the opposite: evidence of lack of attention' (Tannen 1999: 463). Many studies have investigated whether patterns of overlap and interruption were related to gender, but with varied and conflicting results (James and Clarke 1993). The assumption behind some of these studies was that interruption was related to dominance, and that men were likely to dominate women in conversation. The fact that there is no clear evidence of this may be due in part to the oversimplified notion of 'interruption'. Edelsky (1981) showed that not all overlapping speech was disruptive, but could be supportive or 'collaborative'. The inferences we draw from overlapping speech should therefore depend not only on an awareness of cultural differences in conversational style, but also on an understanding that an 'interruption' is not necessarily a manifestation of dominance.

A10.6 PROSODY

A10.6.1 Pitch height and range

An important aspect of the voice, and one that can contribute to pragmatic effect, is the pitch range exploited by individual speakers. We know that women tend to have higher voices than men for physiological reasons, but there are also cultural constraints on whether speakers use the higher or lower parts of their range. A study by Van Bezooijen (1995) suggests that the use of pitch height among women may be differently constructed across cultures. She found that the average pitch of adult female speakers varied according to country – higher for Japanese than for Dutch female speakers. Japanese listeners also perceived high pitch in women to be more attractive while Dutch listeners preferred a lower pitch. Van Bezooijen concludes that while 'low pitch in women is part of the Dutch culture, high pitch is part of the Japanese culture' (ibid.: 264).

There are also known cultural differences in how much of their natural pitch range speakers use, i.e. how much their pitch fluctuates while they speak. Finns are thought to use a narrow range, and Chen *et al.* (2004) suggest that Dutch speakers also use a narrower part of their range than English speakers. This can have an effect on perception of attitude: a wider than normal pitch range is often a signal of increased emotional involvement, so an English speaker may sound more emotionally involved to a Dutch or Finnish listener than to a native English listener. Similarly, the narrow range of a Dutch or Finnish speaker may be perceived by an English listener as uninvolved or uninterested.

A10.6.2 Non-verbal communication

We saw in Unit A9 that non-verbal signals – gestures, gaze and body movements – play an important role in communication. However, as with our prosody, we are seldom aware of how we communicate non-verbally, or that such signals vary across cultures and can be misunderstood. A Polish professor newly appointed to a British university complained that too many people smiled at her. This she perceived as over-familiarity from people she did not know. After a number of years, the same professor said how friendly people were in England. We see, then, that it is not only language that can be misunderstood across cultures, but many kinds of non-verbal communication, including smiles. Directness of gaze and body position vary across cultures: for example, Black Americans are claimed to 'look less than whites' (Argyle 1988: 58). It seems that among Black Americans it is felt to be disrespectful to look at someone in authority. This causes difficulties for white teachers who feel it is rude if students do not look at them when they are addressed ('Look at me when I'm talking to you!'). A Black student on the other hand feels it would be disrespectful to look at the teacher. There are also different cultural expectations as to how close one should stand to one's conversation partner. Watson (1970, cited in Argyle 1988) found for example that Southern Europeans tend to stand closer than Northern Europeans, and Arabs closer than Asians.

Summary and looking ahead

There are very many ways in which we can unwittingly cause offence in other cultures. This unit has attempted to describe some aspects of communication that may not be as universal as is sometimes assumed. For example, the notion that indirectness is particularly polite (see Unit A8) does not necessarily apply to all cultures or languages. Building on Unit A9, we have also shown some of the ways in which prosodic behaviour has the potential to create misunderstandings. In Unit B10 you will read more about 'cultural scripts', which are an attempt to identify the cultural beliefs that underlie language behaviour, and you will also read an account of a particular cross-cultural encounter that had unfortunate consequences. Finally, you can read more about research in non-verbal communication and how it varies across cultures.

NOTE

1   Languages studied were Australian, American and British English, Canadian French, Danish, German and Hebrew.

Unit A11
Historical pragmatics

Studying the spoken language of the past may seem impossible if we only have written texts at our disposal. It isn't, however, for the writing of the past (like writing and speech today) was made up of a wide range of communicative practices – from what might be termed the language of distance to the language of immediacy (see, e.g., Koch and Oesterreicher 1985). We see this in computer-mediated communication today: emails, texts and online chat is often very close to speech in its use of emoticons, exclamation marks, abbreviations (e.g. *lol*) and its speech-like use of greetings, exclamatory utterances and other expressions of attitude and stance, not to mention incomplete sentences. A similar hybrid pattern of communicative immediacy and communicative distance is evident in historical text-types such as court records, witness depositions and records of town meetings (cf. Unit A2.2.3). Trial records attempt to record the spoken interaction which occurred during the trial phase, for example, and while we are unable to know how accurate these are, they contain many indications of how participants may have spoken. There are a number of additional text-types, fictional and non-fictional, that also attempt to represent or mimic speech; they include play scripts, conversation in novels and personal letters, and these too provide useful insights into the speech of the past. We highlight studies in this unit which have drawn from these historical text-types to study pragmatic phenomena such as speech acts and address formulae; at specific times in the past and also across different time periods. We also discuss grammaticalization; the process by which content words (such as nouns and verbs) transform through sound change and language migration to become function words, with little or no lexical meaning.

A11.1 THE NEED TO KNOW ONE'S DATA – AND ALSO 'KNOW' WHAT WE DO NOT KNOW

Some of the methods we employ in modern pragmatics are simply not available for historical study. For example, it is no longer possible to elicit information from speakers of the time using questionnaires and discourse completion tasks (DCTs) (see Unit A2). Nor do we have access to 'native speaker' intuitions, which makes it difficult to judge the nuances of one expression compared with another. This is the problem we face when we compare different languages today, of course, so that we sometimes struggle to determine what is considered 'polite', for example (see Unit

A10). Another potential problem we face, when working with historical data, is that it is not easy to find out how contemporary audiences understood and interpreted certain forms or usages unless their response is recorded explicitly in (or can be gleaned indirectly from) the data. Hence, we need to be careful not to impose the way in which we categorize certain forms today on to our historical data. Similarly, we cannot assume that the forms we use today would have been used in the past, or, indeed, would have achieved the same function (Taavitsainen and Jucker 2010). This necessitates that researchers become as aware of the social/cultural/political practices of the historical period/activity-type they are studying as is possible (cf. Unit A12).

A11.2 EXPLORING 'PRAGMATIC NOISE' IN TIMES PAST

We know from modern-day transcription practices that many features of speech – disfluencies such as repetition and hesitations, backchannel responses, etc. – are unconsciously edited out (see Unit A2.4). Nonetheless, there are many remaining features worthy of study that are captured in historical documents. These include 'pragmatic noise' (*oh*, *ah*, *ay*, *ha*, *ho*, *fie*, etc.) and pragmatic markers (*well*, *of course*, etc.). Such items occur in authentic data (trial texts and witness depositions, for example) and also in play texts (constructed data which is designed to be spoken); their presence in scripts (historical and modern) has to do with the 'illusion of spokenness' (they are one of the means by which authors ensure the language they use sounds authentic to the audience, Culpeper and Kytö 2010: 222). Culpeper and Kytö have drawn on the *Corpus of English Dialogues* (CED) (1560–1760) – a corpus containing both authentic and constructed data – to study 'pragmatic noise' items in Early Modern English. They have found that, while many instances of pragmatic noise have since become obsolete (*alas*, *fie*), others are still common today. A good example is the use of *O* or *Oh*. We cannot be certain whether the different spellings indicated different pronunciations. However, the punctuation does give us some idea of the prosody, and from that the different functions. *O* is frequently grouped together with a name or title, and appears to be used as a vocative – *O Sir*, *O Master* – or as an exclamation – *O miserable wretch*; these constitute rhetorical devices which are now obsolete. *Oh* sometimes occurs with a vocative in the CED, but it is more often followed by a comma. This suggests that it was in a separate tone group and hence closer to its use today as an interjection, response or discourse marker (ibid.: 276). There are many subtle ways of saying *Oh* today (as John Local's 1996 study reveals). This phonetic detail is lost to us in historical data, of course. As such, we cannot reconstruct all of the meanings which speakers and hearers will have ascribed to *Oh*.

Other historical texts that provide examples of the language of 'communicative immediacy' include diaries and personal letters, prose fiction containing reported dialogue, and also some books designed for language teaching purposes. Such teaching primers often contained sample dialogues showing the different ways of asking a customer what he/she wants:

What lacke ye?
What doe ye buy?
What will you have?
What will you buy?
What please you to buy? Etc

(From James Bellot, *Familiar dialogues*, 1586,
cited in Culpeper and Kytö 2010)

In the case of written records of actual speech, as in trial proceedings, the best
records are thought to be those which were penned at the time of or shortly after
the event. In the case of fictional texts the best versions are those published first,
because they maintain contemporary punctuation practices. Punctuation, as we will
see, is sometimes important in indicating subtle differences in meaning when we
no longer have access to the way something was articulated.

A11.3 HISTORICAL PRAGMATICS: APPROACHES AND PRINCIPLES

There are two main approaches to historical pragmatics:

1   The study of the pragmatics of a specific time in the past, for example, how
    witnesses were questioned in court between 1640 and 1760 (Archer 2005).
2   The tracing of certain forms or functions diachronically across time, for
    example, how the historical expression *God be with you* became the modern
    Goodbye (Arnovick 2000).

Taking a particular word (form) and tracing the changes in meaning and function
over time is known as a form-to-function approach. A function-to-form approach,
in contrast, takes a particular speech act (function) – such as thanking or complimenting – and examines how this is achieved at different times in history.

A principle that underlies historical research in this area – the Uniformitarian
Principle – assumes that our ancestors' speech is likely to share commonalities with
our own. However, the extent to which pragmatic meaning actually works uniformly
over different periods and societies is dependent, in practice, on the type of linguistic
feature under investigation. Take speech acts, for example: a basic pattern of ritual
insulting can be traced from the Old English (OE) period to the present: that is,
from the flyting of *Beowulf*, to the sounding of today's teenagers in London and
New York. But there are also discernable differences: flyting was meant to be taken
seriously, and thus could lead to actual violence, whereas sounding is more akin
to Leech's (1983: 142–4) definition for banter: something that, being obviously
untrue and obviously impolite, can be used for purposes of solidarity or social
bonding (see Unit A6). Compliments, thanking and other 'inherently polite speech
acts', in contrast, appear to be 'more sensitive to changes of fashion and cultural
variation' (Taavitsainen and Jucker 2008a: 4); which suggests that we – the human

race – have engaged in facework for some considerable time, but may have done so in different ways in the past, at least when it came to thanking and complimenting. We will pick up on our ancestors' use of facework in A11.5, during our discussion of address terms. Before doing so, however, we'll explore Jucker and Taavitsainen's (2000) model for capturing the potential 'fuzziness' of speech acts (past and present).

A11.4 FUZZINESS APPROACH TO SPEECH ACT RESEARCH: *INSULTING* AS A CASE STUDY

In Unit A4, you were introduced to Speech Act Theory, which, by articulating the conditions underlying speech acts, seeks to explain how we do things with words. For example, *I insult you!* does not work as an insult in English. Instead, the focus is very much on S being able to successfully communicate to H their illocutionary intent. Put simply, H has to believe that S made a predication – an example might be *You're a pig!* – with the intention of demeaning him or her in some way. Of course, there are contexts in which people can liken others to a pig without being intentionally insulting and/or being perceived as such. So any rules relating to speech acts cannot be applied without first considering the context of utterance (Searle 1969). If we believed our predication, *You're a pig!*, to constitute banter in context, for example, we would have to generate different preparatory conditions and perlocutionary effects for the utterance: namely, a speaker intent focused around camaraderie and a perlocutionary effect which recognized this intent.

Jucker and Taavitsainen (2000) offer an alternative to the Searlean rule-based approach (see Figure A11.1). At its core is the notion of speech acts as prototypes linked by a shared multidimensional 'pragmatic space'. Specifically, speech acts are said to have fuzzy boundaries that overlap with neighbouring speech acts in a way that allows for variation across time and space. An insult, under this framework, is

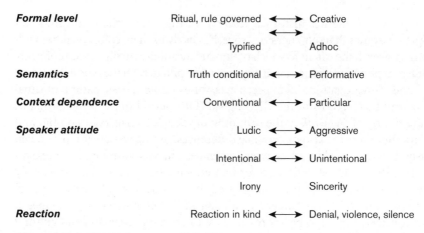

Figure A11.1 Pragmatic space of insults

said to share the same pragmatic space as other evaluative speech acts. Indeed, insults represent the negative end of the pragmatic space relating to S's evaluation of the addressee, and compliments, the positive end. The speech acts to be found at the negative end of this evaluative/pragmatic space can be distinguished using the above clines.

The following extract from *Henry IV, Part I* provides us with a nice example of Jucker and Taavitsainen's *speaker attitude* cline. The ludic (playful) end of the cline would be banter and sounding, according to Jucker and Taavitsainen. That is to say, it captures activities that have more to do with verbal prowess than they do actual enmity. But this dialogue of Hal (imitating his father) seems to be a mix of banter, which is obviously untrue, and comments that are true and also potentially offensive.

Context: The King's son, Prince Hal, and Hal's drinking companion, Falstaff, are acting out a scene-within-a-scene, such that Falstaff becomes Hal and Hal becomes his father, the king.

Prince Hal-as-King:	The complaints I hear of thee are grievous.
Falstaff-as-Prince Hal:	Sblood, my lord, they are false [. . .]
Prince Hal-as-King:	Swearest thou, ungracious boy? Henceforth ne'er look on me. Thou art violently carried away from grace, there is a devil haunts thee in the likeness of an old fat man, a tun of man is thy companion. Why dost thou converse with that trunk of humours, that bolting-hutch of beastliness, that swollen parcel of dropsies, that huge bombard of sack, that stuffed cloakbag of guts, that roasted Manningtree ox with the pudding in his belly, that reverend vice, that grey iniquity, that father ruffian, that vanity in years? [. . .]
Falstaff-as-Prince Hal:	[. . .] whom means your Grace?
Hal-as-King:	That villainous abominable misleader of youth, Falstaff, that old white-bearded Satan.

Although some of the language in the above extract (e.g. *whence, thee, Sblood, swearest thou, dost*) is now old fashioned and/or archaic, it's still relatively easy for twenty-first-century readers to recognize that Hal-as-King is not flattering Falstaff. But how far is it playful and how far aggressive? Here we need to bring into play the irony/sincerity and the intentional/unintentional components of the *speaker attitude* cline. Even so, assigning intentionality is somewhat problematic – to the extent that we are faced with an interesting conundrum: when Hal-as-King asks Falstaff-as-Hal 'why dost thou converse with that trunk of humours . . . that father ruffian' is this banter on Hal's part? Falstaff certainly seems unsure; to the point that he complains he still has 'much to say in the behalf of that Falstaff', when told 'the sheriff . . . is at the door' (i.e. he's in danger). As Falstaff-as Hal, he is also careful to humorously re-frame Falstaff (i.e. himself) as 'sweet', 'kind' and 'true':

Falstaff-as-Prince Hal: My Lord, the man [Falstaff] I know.

Hal-as-King: I know, thou dost.

Falstaff-as-Prince Hal: But to say, I know more harm in him than in myself, were to say more than I know. That he is old, (the more the pity), his white hairs do witness it: but that he is (saving your reverence), a whoremaster, that I utterly deny. If sack and sugar be a fault, God help the wicked! If to be old and merry be a sin, then many an old host that I know, is damned: if to be fat be to be hated, then Pharaoh's lean kine are to be loved. No, my good lord; banish Peto, banish Bardolph, banish Poins: but for sweet Jack Falstaff, kind Jack Falstaff, true Jack Falstaff, valiant Jack Falstaff, and therefore more valiant, being as he is, old Jack Falstaff, banish not him thy Harry's company, banish not him thy Harry's company; banish plump Jack, and banish all the world.

Hal-as-King: I do, I will   [A knocking heard
[Exeunt Hostess, Francis and Bardolph
Re-enter Bardolph running]

Bardolph: O, my lord, my lord; the sheriff, with a most monstrous watch, is at the door.

Falstaff-as-Prince Hal: Out, you rogue! Play out the play: I have much to say in the behalf of that Falstaff.

A very different tone, with no element of playfulness or banter, is found in the following, taken from the Trial of Lady Alice Lisle (1685). The Judge, here, is trying to intimidate Dunne into 'telling the truth' (Jucker and Taavitsainen 2000: 88). As with the Hal/Falstaff examples, name-calling is used. But the Judge does not stop at this; he also accuses Dunne of lying. These accumulated insults lie clearly at the intentionally aggressive end of the *speaker attitude* scale.

LCJ: Why, thou vile Wretch didst not thou tell me just now that thou pluck'd up the Latch? Dost thou take the God of Heaven not to be a God of Truth, and that he is not a Witness of all thou say'st? Dost thou think because thou prevaricatest with the Court here, thou can'st do so with God above, who knows thy Thoughts, and it is infinite Mercy, that for those Falshoods of thine, he does not immediately strike thee into Hell? Jesus God! There is no sort of Conversation nor human Society to be kept with such People as these are, who have no other Religion but only Pretence, and no way to uphold themselves but by countenancing Lying and Villany: Did not you tell me that you opened the Latch your self, and that you saw no body else but a Girl? How durst you offer to tell such horrid Lyes in the presence of God and of a Court of Justice? Answer me one Question more: Did he pull down the Hay or you?

Dunne: I did not pull down any Hay at all.

Unlike Falstaff, Dunne does not attempt to counter the insults, and we have no direct evidence that he feels insulted. However, the context is one in which Dunne is powerless, and it is unlikely that a response would help his cause. It seems, then, that we cannot always point to a perlocutionary effect when it comes to insulting, as the Searlean approach would require.

Taavitsainen and Jucker (2008a) believe that the framework they initially drafted for insults can also be applied to other speech acts/speech act categories. However, they suggest that depending on the speech act (or speech act category) being investigated, some of the components of their multidimensional framework will be foregrounded and others backgrounded. In Unit B11.4, you will learn about their work in regard to compliments: a speech act for which the irony/sincerity component (the third aspect of *speaker attitude*) is especially important.

A11.5 EXPLORING FACEWORK: 'YOU'/'THOU' AND OTHER ADDRESS FORMULAE

Address terms, like speech acts, impact upon facework. Not surprisingly, many studies which investigate address terms – including those focusing on the *you/thou* distinction – also discuss issues of im/politeness. Let's begin, then, with a discussion of the *you/thou* distinction.

A11.5.1 'You'/'thou'

Historically, English had a similar T/V distinction to modern French. The singular forms *thou* and *you* originated from singular (*thou*) and plural form (*ye*), which in turn derived from Old English *ðū* and *ge*. In the thirteenth century, *ye* was extended to singular contexts, when it became a deference marker indicating respect and politeness. During the sixteenth century *ye* was then replaced by *you*, and used among the higher orders of society, with reciprocal *thou* being used among the lower ranks. In addition, *thou* was also used between women friends and by wives to their husbands. As the following example (from Nevala 2003: 147) reveals, the intention in such cases was to signal intimacy/affection:

> *Mine own sweet Thomken*, I have no longer ago than the last night written such a large volume in praise of *thy* kindness to me . . . [THYNNE, 1604, 32: CEEC; emphasis in original]

When higher ranking speakers used *thou* to address lower ranks, they expected the latter to reciprocate with *you*. This asymmetry of use enabled *thou* to be used as a means of signalling disrespect in some contexts (i.e. when directed to someone who wasn't a social inferior). As the following example, taken from the treason trial of Lady Alice Lisle (1685), reveals, the deference marker *you* could also be used ironically when used interchangeably with *thou* so that the effect, in context, was one of contempt (Jucker 2000a: 95). Here the judge switched between *you* and *thou* when questioning Dunne:

LCJ: Why, thou said'st he brought the Light, and gave thy Horse Hay; but I see thou art set upon nothing but Prevarication: Sirrah, tell me plainly, did you see no body else?

This particular extract also provides an example of *sirrah*. Related to the vocative(s) *sir/sire*, *sirrah* quickly developed a condescending or contemptuous meaning when addressed to a social inferior. It would therefore be heard as an insult in this context.

Any investigation we undertake as researchers should seek to (in)validate such *a priori* notions as the above, of course, not least because extant evidence suggests that *thou* and *you* were used in quite specific ways, both by different sectors of Early Modern English society and also within certain text-types. An interesting case is that of the Quakers, who believed in equality of all and therefore used *thou* to everyone. However, its association with disrespect meant that when Quakers like William Edmonson used *thou* to address non-Quakers, their intention could be misconstrued as insulting:

> *When I thee'd and thou'd them* [soldiers] *in our discussion they were very angry and one of them swore, if I thou'd him again, he would cleave my head.*
> (Quoted after Finkenstaedt 1963: 177, in Jucker 2000a: 92;
> emphasis in original)

We have already seen above how the Judge's use of *thou* and *you* in a 1685 treason trial constituted a means of signalling his contempt for the witness, Dunne. Similar evidence of pronoun switching is to be found in witness depositions of the period. For example, Hope (1994) provides an example from the Durham Depositions, involving Bullman's wife and Styllynge. Both insult the other using *thou*, before Styllynge again resorts to *you*:

Bullman's wife [to Styllynge]: Noughtie pak
Styllynge [to Bullman's wife]: What nowtynes know *you* by me? I am neyther goossteler nor steg [gander] steiler, I would *you* knew ytt
Bullman's wife [to Styllynge]: What, noughty hoore, caull thou me goose steiler?
Styllynge [to Bullman's wife]: Nay, mayry, I know *thee* for no such, but I thank you for your good reporte, whills you and I talk further
(Case 139: Deposition of 'Agnes Wheitley [. . .] of Segefield, aged 33'.
Surtees Society 1845: 104; emphasis in original)

Styllynge's *you* does not indicate irony (as it did for Jucker and Taavitsainen in the case of the Judge/Dunne example). Rather, it allows Styllynge to demonstrate 'restraint' and thereby imply 'a superiority in keeping with the formal tone', according to Hope (ibid.: 145).

Drama texts of the period share some of the above similarities, in that the choice of *you* and *thou* can point to the affective attitude of the speaker and the social status of the characters. However, the choice of *you* and *thou* can also be due to rhyme/

metre decisions on the author's part. This raises an interesting issue in regard to historical data: the extent to which a modern reader can truly differentiate actual im/politeness from other motivations (linguistic and socio-cultural). Watts (2003: 62) believes that the answer lies in making use of historical data that contains enough meta-comment for a modern reader to be able to deduce conclusions about the understanding of im/politeness at a certain point in time. A different approach is to (re-)develop data-driven facework models which encompass im/politeness activities so that they become as historically and activity-type sensitive as our current understanding will allow. Researchers interested in address formulae have developed one such model.

A11.5.2 Address formulae

Address formulae have been studied quite extensively in a number of text-types, including written correspondence. Nevala (2004), for example, has studied the openings and closings of letters in the *Corpus of Early English Correspondence* (CEEC). She situates these on a politeness continuum (see Figure A11.2), based on a proposal by Nevalainen and Raumolin-Brunberg (1995), which makes use of Brown and Levinson's (1978/1987) concepts of positive politeness and negative politeness. Specifically, honorifics have been found to display the most negative politeness, and terms of endearment and nicknames the most positive politeness, with occupational titles and kinship terms in the middle of the continuum.

Address formulae include examples at the negative end of the politeness continuum – *Honoured Father, Right worshipful Sir, Good Madam* – as well as the positive end – *Mine own sweet Thomken, my dearest John, right wellbeloved son* (Nevala 2002: 154). Closing formulae demonstrate a similar pattern: *your loving daughter* (positive) to *your most obedient son* (negative). This said, Nevala (ibid.) has observed a general trend from negative to positive politeness across the period.

Nevala (2004: 2138) has also observed some interesting variation within a single family. For example, she has found that writers used strategies denoting 'extreme negative politeness, regardless of the distance' between them when directly addressing Sir Nicholas Bacon, Lord Keeper for Elizabeth I. This reflects Sir Nicholas' superior social status, as well as his role as head of the prestigous seventeenth-century Bacon family in what was a highly stratified society. However, nuclear family members would occasionally use both kinship term and title to address Sir Nicholas. When addressing Sir Nicholas' eldest son, Nathaniel Bacon, in contrast, family members would mostly use positive politeness strategies (first name, last name, kinship or a combination of the three). Family servants opted for negative politeness, however, (*Right Worshipful, Your Worship* or *Your Honour*); with (more) distant writers alternating between neutral and negatively polite formula (*Cousin Bacon, Sir, Right Worshipful*). The possibility of letters being read by others might explain some of these choices, as letters were often written with bystanders and over-readers in mind.

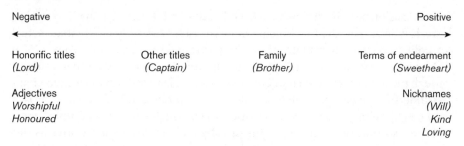

Negative | | | Positive

| Honorific titles | Other titles | Family | Terms of endearment |
| *(Lord)* | *(Captain)* | *(Brother)* | *(Sweetheart)* |

Adjectives			Nicknames
Worshipful			*(Will)*
Honoured			*Kind*
			Loving

Figure A11.2 The politeness continuum (adapted from Raumolin-Brunberg 1996: 171)

A11.6 GRAMMATICALIZATION: 'GOODBYE' AND '(GOD) BLESS YOU'

As intimated above, a particular interest of diachronic investigations is the way in which certain words or expressions change both their form and their meaning over the centuries. Changes in form often involve (phonological and lexical) shortening. The closing 'goodbye' is derived from 'God be with you', for example. Indeed, originally, 'God be with you' had the illocutionary force of both a blessing and a courteous closing. In the late sixteenth century, the phrase then underwent contraction until it gradually came to be treated as one word. At the same time, the closing function of 'God be with you' was becoming dominant such that by the end of the seventeenth/beginning of the eighteenth centuries it had become conventionalized, and the blessing function had fallen out of use. This kind of loss of meaning is referred to as semantic 'bleaching' (Hopper and Traugott 2003).

Another interesting example is that of *marry,* which operated as an oath or an ejaculatory invocation (to the Virgin Mary) in the fourteenth century, but then came to function as an interjection as opposed to a religious invocation. Fischer (1998) suggests that these tendencies (developing into a pragmatically weaker interjection/ losing any religious association) may also account for (the historical development of) other religious oaths. This seems to be true of *bless you* – to some extent. Like *goodbye, bless you* is now part of a fixed adjacency pair in English. Hence, the former constitutes a greeting-greeting, and the latter, the second pair part of a sneeze move. *Bless you,* like *goodbye,* is thus best described as an expression of politeness (or a facework move):

> Responding to a sneeze, the speaker uses the formula to acknowledge the sneezer, to offer comfort and to excuse a disruption of the social interaction. In this way, the formulaic expression encodes linguistic politeness, while the conversational routine advances discourse through its non-salient automaticity.
>
> (Claridge and Arnovick 2010: 176)

Even today, however, the religious function of *bless you* is still relevant for some users. These differing functions can each be linked to the historical development of *bless you*. Like *marry*, its earliest primary use was as a blessing. It then developed a quasi-religious function – that of a wish – in the Middle Ages (i.e. it became an expression of a mental state favourable to H). The sneezing context is merely a progression of the latter, i.e. an implied wish for good health. Hence:

> The diachronic change observed in the sneeze blessing may be understood as a redistribution of pragmatic function, the net result of which represents a pragmatic strengthening. Saying *bless you*, the present-day speaker no longer participates in a religious ritual [generally speaking], but instead engages in a conversational routine that furthers discourse and reinforces sociocultural cohesion through a demonstration of politeness. Finally, the local illocutionary performance of blessing gives way diachronically to a convention, the larger purpose of which is conversational.
>
> (Ibid.: 178)

The English *of course* offers us a more recent example of change in progress. Now generally classed as an adverb, *of course* originates in a structure containing the French/Middle English word *cours* ('the path taken by', Lewis 2003). The expression later came to mean 'predictable' or 'expected' and as late as the eighteenth century could be used as an adjective, as in *these are words of course* 'these are predictable words' (cf. the fixed expression *a matter of course*). *Of course* was also used as an adverb, e.g., *Elizabeth . . . succeeded her of course* meaning 'Elizabeth succeeded her as a matter of course/naturally'. Wichmann *et al.* (2010) have recently found that a new usage is developing – one which has lost most of the meaning of 'naturally' or 'predictably', and now means 'as you (or we) know'. This sometimes occurs when speakers are trying to involve their audience, as when a lecturer says to his students *'And Othello of course calls on Desdemona's father doesn't he'* (ICE-GB S1A-020; emphasis in original). Another example is of a football commentator telling the listeners something they probably know already; *'Rangers of course have been struggling in the First Division'* (ICE-GB S2A-003; emphasis in original). We find, then, that while *of course* is still used today as a sentence adverbial meaning 'predictably', it can be used as a pragmatic marker, in some contexts, and serves to reinforce solidarity.

By now it should be obvious that historical pragmatics is an important approach to language change. Historical linguists aim to find out the path taken by various changes in the language, and it seems that some of these changes are best explained pragmatically. In Unit B11, you will learn more about Historical Pragmatics, generally, and also learn about studies which draw on corpus linguistic techniques to study historical data from a pragmatic perspective.

Summary and looking ahead

Unit A12
Pragmatics and power

Given that language 'is among the social practices through which people enact relations of domination and subordination' (Cameron 2001: 161), it should come as no surprise to find that power generally – and how power is enacted in language, in particular – have been investigated regularly now for nearly half a century. Many of the later studies have drawn upon approaches that we tend to associate with Critical Discourse Analysis (CDA). As A12.2 reveals, these *critical* approaches share an important ideological aim: to show the connections between language, power and ideology and the *hidden effects* they have on people (Fairclough 1989: 2). For example, Teun van Dijk (1992b: 88) has demonstrated how 'political, media, academic, corporate and other elites play an important role in the reproduction of racism' and often in very subtle ways: he points in particular to press reports which engage in *negative other* presentation when discussing the 'exploitation' of the welfare system by 'ethnic minorities'. We'll explore the framing of news stories in more detail in Unit C12.

This unit also examines how people use language to do things in situations where power relationships are asymmetrical – but from a pragmatic perspective. The CDA specialist, Ruth Wodak, is explicit about the debt that CDA owes to pragmatics. Indeed, she goes as far as to assert that an in-depth CDA 'which de-constructs the inferred and indirect linguistic devices as well as explicit prejudiced utterances' would not be possible if it were not for pragmatic theory (Wodak 2007: 204). This said, pragmatic theory constitutes but one of several theories from which a CDA specialist might draw. Wodak's Discourse-Historical Approach, for example, draws on the disciplinary insights of history, socio-psychology, socio-cognition and political science in addition to linguistics. We should also note that another CDA specialist, Norman Fairclough, has criticized a tendency within pragmatics to 'overstate the extent to which people manipulate language for strategic purposes' (1989: 9), even though power is intrinsically bound to a wider set of ideologies, beliefs, opinions and value systems. Indeed, such is the influence of the latter, according to Fairclough, that individuals can either come to accept (unquestioningly) the identity which has been constructed for them by an institutional discourse or find themselves without the appropriate resources to project their own values and beliefs.

Our primary goal in this unit is different from the average CDA study. We focus on specific activity types – courtroom, police interviews, political interviews, doctor-patient discussion – and demonstrate how pragmatic tools (to use Wodak's 2007 term) have been used to account for *powerful/powerless* uses of language therein. Hence, we are as interested in participants' actual behaviour within the different institutional contexts, including any resistance to/negotiation of power on their part, as we are in the activity types themselves – especially when that behaviour seems strategic on their part (cf. Fairclough 1989).

A12.1 WHAT IS POWER?

Power is often seen as a necessary means by which society safeguards its moral and political character; hence, the presence of judicial, penal and legislative institutions. CDA researchers would argue that hegemony is at work here too. Hegemony is the term used to describe the mechanisms through which dominant groups in society succeed in persuading subordinate groups to accept the *naturalness* of their moral, political and cultural values (Gramsci 1971). Hegemonic power, then, is based on consent: it is achieved in large part by institutional discourses which simultaneously inculcate and confirm the ruling group's practices (Louw 2005: 98), whilst also constructing particular subject positions for all groups, dominant and subordinate, to occupy (Althusser 1971).

At this point, it would be easy to conclude that institutional power is a fixed phenomenon, and that access to it is limited (Bourdieu 1992). However, as Foucault (1977, 1980) makes clear, institutional power can be negotiated and contested – especially in interaction. Consequently, even though the strongest form of power may well be the ability to define social reality, that is, to freely impose one's vision of the world on to others (cf. Gal 1992: 160), we need to allow for the fact that some types of power can be emancipatory and/or lead to mutually beneficial outcomes. By way of illustration, French and Raven (1959) identify:

  (i) 'reward power', which involves A controlling (B's) positive outcomes by providing things that B desires and/or removing or decreasing things that B dislikes,
 (ii) 'referent power', where B identifies with and desires to become more like A,
(iii) 'expert power', which involves A having specialist knowledge or expertise that B wants or needs (see also Bourdieu's 1992 *symbolic capital*), and
 (iv) 'legitimate power', which involves A having the legitimate right to prescribe or request certain things of B.

All four of these (power) scenarios could happen in an institutional context and, whilst it's easy to imagine that some of these might lead to an abuse of power in such settings, we should at least allow for the possibility that participants might also use the power they possess in an appropriate (i.e. a legitimate and not merely *legitimized*) way, given their role (cf. Gramsci 1971).

A12.2 CDA INVESTIGATIONS: WHAT MAKES THEM *CRITICAL*?

As Simpson and Mayr (2010: 51) highlight, CDA encompasses a large and loosely grouped body of work which focuses on 'the interconnectedness of discourse, power, ideology and social structure'. The intentions of a CDA researcher, moreover, are overtly interventionist: the *critical* aspect of their work equates to a desire to unravel or denaturalize the ideologies within institutional discourses such that people become aware of the connections between language, power and ideology that are usually hidden from them (Fairclough 1989: 5).

Where does pragmatics come in? The connections to which Fairclough refers are *hidden*, very often, in the pragmalinguistic elements we've explored in this textbook, that is, within presuppositions, implicatures and other linguistic strategies requiring some form of pragmatic enrichment (see especially Units A3 and A5). CDA researchers argue that these devices are used because speakers and writers do not want to be called to account for making explicit statements that would reveal prejudices or stereotypical views. Wodak (2007: 205) provides the example of Dr Jörg Haider, who employed 'latently anti-Semitic utterances' to describe his main political opponent, Dr Ariel Muzicant, in a Vienna 2001 election campaign, but in such a way that he could deny having done so. In one quote attributed to him, for example, Haider stated 'what I don't understand is how someone called Ariel can have so much dirty linen . . .',[1] where Ariel is a play on words: it refers simultaneously to Muzicant and to a washing detergent. The notion of detergent links via semantic association to *dirty linen*, of course. However, as Wodak highlights, *dirty linen* also works as an indirect intertextual allusion to embarrassing personal facts/morally dubious practices, generally, and to *dirty Jew*, specifically, in the Austrian context; hence, it is part of a larger mode of expressing – in a coded way – anti-Semitic prejudices and stereotypes.

As Wodak suggests, such coded anti-Semitic messages will not be deciphered by all. Indeed, they require quite specific socio-cultural, political and historical awareness on the part of the audience – and also the researcher, if such texts are analysed. Without that knowledge, researchers will likely surmise some things – from the language used – but also miss important allusions. For example, they're likely to pick up on Haider's use of *positive self* and *negative other* presentation when he distinguishes himself from Greenberg:

> My friends, you have a choice: you can vote for Spin Doctor Greenberg from the East Coast, or for the Heart of Vienna.
>
> (Haider, 28 February 2001, from ibid.)

This is because *choice/or* set up an obvious US/THEM opposition, with *Heart of Vienna* signalling, in turn, that Haider is prototypically Austrian (in his mind at least) such that *Greenberg/the East Coast* come to represent THEM. What researchers are unlikely to glean – without having Wodak's socio-cultural/political/historical knowledge – are Haider's implicit reference to Greenberg's Jewishness (inferrable from *East Coast*) and his insinuation that Jews are not 'real' Austrians (inferrable from *Heart*; see ibid. for more details).

The need to know the socio-cultural/political/historical context of one's data is Wodak's (ibid.) main motivation for combining a pragmatic approach with CDA, history, socio-psychology, socio-cognition and political science. However, this unit will demonstrate that a pragmatic approach which is sensitive to context in all its guises (i.e. cognitive, social, cultural, historical and/or political) can nevertheless produce extremely insightful findings. We pick up on the issue of context in our Unit B12.2 reading, taken from Van Dijk (2006). In the section that follows, we assess whether pragmatic investigations which focus on power constitute a *critical* pragmatics (cf. Mey 1979, 1985, 2001).

A12.3 DO PRAGMATIC INVESTIGATIONS OF 'POWER' CONSTITUTE A 'CRITICAL PRAGMATICS'?

Mey (1979) first discussed the possibility of a *critical pragmatics* approach in his (German) article, 'Toward a critical theory of language', and went on to explore the ways in which employers and workers 'worded their world' differently in his 1985 monograph, *Whose language?* This period also witnessed the birth of CDA, of course. This helps to explain why Mey (2001) directly links his critical pragmatic approach to CDA researchers such as Teun van Dijk and Norman Fairclough in his textbook, *Pragmatics: an introduction.*

Fairclough, in particular, does not accept that his CDA approach equates to a sub-discipline of pragmatics, as Mey suggests. One possible reason is that Mey's approach prioritizes textual analysis as opposed to the ideological processes which shape institutional texts (see Fairclough 1992). A related reason is Fairclough's (2001: 7–8) concerns in respect to the 'weaknesses' of pragmatics, especially when it comes to accounting for power. This said, CDA has itself been criticized for de-prioritizing textual analysis – and hence linguistic insights – in recent years. The shift away from textual analysis and towards 'how texts fit into the socio-political landscape in which they are produced' (Jeffries 2010: 10) is no more evident than in Fairclough's (2001: 229) claim that 'social issues and problems . . . not . . . texts and interactions' are the starting point for CDA studies. Yet, Fairclough (1989: 26) has previously stressed the importance – within CDA investigations – of the *description* stage (i.e. analysing the formal properties of text) and the *interpretation* stage (i.e. analysing the relationship between text and interaction). 'Texts and interactions' are of primary importance within pragmatics, of course. But this raises an important issue, in our view: does a focus on texts and interactions mean critical pragmaticians must reign in any perceived need to intervene on the side of the powerless – until they've established that the powerless are actually lacking a voice and/or being unfairly disadvantaged in some way, via their close textual analysis? Your answer to this question might shape your answer to the next question we'd like to pose: whether this approach is too *non*-interventionist to be regarded as *critical* (at least in the CDA sense)? We invite you to consider your response(s) to these questions as you read about the power strategies used by participants in the courtroom (Unit A12.4), police interviews (Unit A12.5), (televised) political interviews (Unit A12.6) and medical consultations (Unit A12.7).

A12.4 PRAGMATIC INVESTIGATIONS OF 'POWER IN TALK': THE COURTROOM

We can locate power and its negotiation in a courtroom context by exploring the differing goals of the respective participants, the interactional inferences made by them and any restrictions on the kinds of contributions that they can make (Drew and Heritage 1992: 22; Simpson and Mayr 2010: 10). This is because the question-answer format (within the Anglo-American adversarial tradition) places severe constraints on how an interaction between a lawyer and defendant/witness – or a magistrate and defendant/witness – can proceed. Lawyers, in particular, want to elicit information that is strategically valuable, and so frame their questions in a way that might influence the response. Witnesses and defendants are meant to provide those responses and only those responses: to the extent that they cannot usually pose their own questions – unless they are unsure of a question put to them, in which case they can seek clarification of *that* question (Tiersma 2000: 168). What witnesses and defendants are not meant to do is behave in such a way as to bring into question the 'reasonableness' and 'justness' of the legal system, and thereby undermine the ideological beliefs that underpin that system. This explains the magistrate's attempt to restrict Mr H's contributions to the specific task at hand – paying his fine – in the following extract (taken from Harris 1994: 166–7):

Magistrate: um – well it's up to you Mr H – uh – uh – I'm putting it to you again – are you um – are you going to make an offer – uh – uh to discharge this debt
Defendant: would you in my position?
Magistrate: I – I'm not here to answer questions – you answer my question
Defendant: one rule for one – and one for another I presume [3]
Magistrate: can I have an answer to my question – please [6] the question is – are you prepared to make an offer to the court to discharge – this debt [2]
Defendant: what sort of minimal offer would [be required
Magistrate: [it's not a bargaining situation it's a *straight* question [2] Mr H – can I have the answer
Defendant: well I'll just pay the court a pound annually
Magistrate: that's not acceptable to us
Defendant: what would be acceptable to the court
Magistrate: [. . .] uh we want a sensible offer Mr H

As the above highlights, magistrates (and lawyers) not only have the advantage of being able to set the topic; they can pursue their goal by using follow-up questions. Thanks to their inferential frames, some of their questions also tend to be multifunctional, i.e. serve, simultaneously as requests for information/clarification/confirmation and as the means of making an accusation/controlling the interaction. Their questions can also carry a degree of speaker judgement – especially when they contain presuppositions and/or are preceded by 'facts' that are assumed to be true. Lowndes (2002: 157–8) provides the following example:

Barrister: . . . did you put in that conversation or did you suggest that that conversation happened because you wanted to get across to the judge that this person was agreeing he had knocked you down . . . Is that why you made it up?

Notice that *Is that why you made it up?* is cleverly designed so that, irrespective of how the defendant responds, she appears to be buying into the presupposition contained in the utterance that preceded it (that she *put in* a *conversation*). In this instance, the defendant failed to deny the presupposition. In our Unit B12.3 reading, taken from Harris (1995), the defendant does deny one of the magistrate's presuppositions – that he has money on him – but he does not invalidate the magistrate's implicit accusation that he 'has money which he is wilfully using for purposes other than to pay his fines'.

Witnesses (like defendants) are in a subordinate position in the courtroom. But, as they have less to lose than defendants, it is easier to find evidence of witnesses resisting the strategies of their questioners.[2] Lowndes (2002: 158; emphasis in original) provides an example of such resistance:

Barrister: but I think *you recognise that it sometimes might happen* that you started the bouldering activity and the children don't like it and you've got to come off the river isn't that right
Witness: Yes uhuh occasionally not often
Barrister: Yes but that is always a possibility isn't that right
Witness: Yes it always is a possibility
Barrister: Yes so therefore you may end up in fact being more out of the river than on the river isn't that right
Witness: Yes that's a chance

The witness, here, qualifies his initial agreement to the lawyer's framing utterance, *you recognise that it sometimes might happen . . .*, by rearticulating (and hence reshaping) the lawyer's own epistemic modality ('always a possibility', 'may end up'). The resulting vagueness is particularly interesting, as we tend to think of reformulations as a way of disambiguating meaning/enforcing explicitness. For example, *So you're saying that . . .* can be used to seek confirmation and, more importantly, to reshape an earlier utterance so that it is given a different meaning.

A12.5 PRAGMATIC INVESTIGATIONS OF 'POWER IN TALK': POLICE INTERACTION

Thornborrow's (2002: 41) investigation of a 1980 televised interview – between two UK police officers and a woman making a complaint of rape – also shows resistance on the part of the subordinate participant. The resistance is fuelled by conflicting assumptions between A (as complainant) and the two police interviewers, B and C. Police interviewer C, in particular, seems unconvinced by A's complaint that she has been raped by three men. Indeed, he constructs an alternative account of what happened to A which implies she'd willingly had sex with the men she is now accusing. How C does this is extremely interesting: first, he gets A to confirm that she had been arrested a 'coupla times . . . under the mental health act', and, in doing so, insinuates that she is unstable and, in all likelihood, dishonest too; C then explicitly states that A was 'not frightened at all' when with her alleged attackers, before insinuating that A herself is frightening. For example, C tells A he 'wouldn't take [her] on'. This prompts A to ask:

A: why would I frighten [you [xxx]] only a little (wife)
B: [you you (jus-)]   it doesn't matter (.) you're
   female and you've probably got a hell of a temper (.) if you were to go=
A: =I haven't
   got a temper [(xxx) a hell of a temper
C: [(oh I dunno)
B: I think if things if if things were up against a a wall (.) I think you'd fight and
   you'd fight very hard

Notice that Police Interviewer B steps in at the point at which A challenges his colleague; and demonstrates that, like C, he does not believe A's account. Notice, also, how *and* in *you're female and you've probably got a hell of a temper* triggers the implicature that females tend to be bad tempered (see Unit A5). A continues to resist B and C's (ideological) assumptions, nevertheless, and this prompts B to suggest that, given her (mental) history, A would have fought 'very hard' had she really been in danger. The implication? What happened was not rape: it was consensual.

Conflicting assumptions are much more common in interviewer/suspect interactions, as our Unit B12.4 reading (taken from Haworth 2006) will make clear: the extract relates to the questioning of Dr Harold Shipman in regard to the suspicious death of his patient, Mrs Grundy. The conflicting assumptions signal, in turn, that police interviewers tend to assume guilt when interacting with suspects, prompting some researchers to suggest that Grice's Quality maxim is suspended in such activity types (see, e.g., Thomas 1995). Evidence that the Quality maxim has been suspended is also apparent in the interviewer(s)/complainant data above; indeed, Police Interviewer C directly informs A, *you don't fool us*, immediately after signalling that he found A frightening (thereby implicating his belief that A was trying to deceive the two officers). What is less clear is why the officers chose not to believe A (who, after all, was not a suspect).

Limberg (2008) has also investigated televised police-related data – this time drawn from a German documentary series broadcast in 2005. Limberg focused primarily on the threats made by both police and citizens at points when the police were dealing with 'minor offences perpetrated by citizens in several German cities' (ibid.: 160). As we might expect, police officers have a right to threaten or counter-threaten, when the need arises, but 'offenders' do not. Hence, when a tenant who told a police officer, 'Are you from Stendal – well then have fun',[3] he was immediately reprimanded for 'threatening' him and by so doing 'going to the end of the line' (i.e. too far, see ibid.: 175–6). Police officers, in contrast, can legitimately make use of 'manipulation' tactics. Limberg (ibid.: 172) provides the example of a conditional threat; 'YOU PUT THAT HERE ON ITS STAND NOW, OR I'LL GET REALLY UNPLEASANT'. The threat was made to a motorcyclist, who attempted to escape from a routine traffic control because he did not want to accompany the police officers to the station. His reluctance was partly due to not wanting to leave his motorcycle in a hedge in the German countryside and partly due to being over the drink-driving limit. Limberg suggests that, although slightly menacing, the threat was nevertheless 'in accordance with the professional rights of police officers, and only implemented after other, less threatening strategies failed' (ibid.). Its purpose, moreover, was to dissuade the offender 'from behaving in an unacceptable manner' (ibid.: 177) rather than to threaten him personally (cf. Units A8 and A11). This said, Limberg is very aware that some offenders 'may not realise that threats are regarded as an accepted practice in police encounters' of this kind, and hence have a very different view of their appropriacy (ibid.: 166).

A12.6 PRAGMATIC INVESTIGATIONS OF 'POWER IN TALK': POLITICAL INTERVIEWS

The media interview constitutes another activity type in which question-and-answer sequences predominate (cf. A12.4). Generally speaking, interviewers want their interviewees to answer their questions at length. However, in political interviews, we can encounter conflicting agendas such that the interviewer begins to restrict the interviewee – by asking them questions but not allowing them the interactional space to answer those questions, for example. Locher and Watts (2008: 88–9) provide the example of Fred Emery's 1984 *Panaroma* interview with the then-president of the National Union of Mineworkers, Arthur Scargill. Emery asked Scargill a question but almost immediately interrupted him so that Scargill struggled to give his answer:

E: peter taylor reporting \ well with me in the studio watching the film \ is mr arthur scargill \ president of the national union of mineworkers \ mr scargill \ (..) the issue causing (..) the breakdown (.) was all last week / the issue (..) at the front of the news \ and in everybody' minds \ was the union's refusal to accept the closure of uneconomic pits \ are you now willing to discuss uneconomic pits\
S: (..)
  we're not prepared to go along to the national coal board \ and start—

E: you're not \ sorry if I interrupt you (.) there \ y/I-I/let me just
S: [er::] [er::] are
E: remind you that—
S: you – are you going to let me answer the question \ you put a question \ for god's
  sake let me answer \
E: you-you said you're not \ let's - let's have the (.) question again \ and see
  of we (..) get it right clear \ are you now willing to discuss uneconomic pits \
S: (..)
  can I answer \
E: go ahead \

British political programmes like *Panaroma* are known to exhibit 'an increased level
of aggressiveness and a supposed concomitant loss of "respect" on the part of the
interviewer towards political interviewees' (ibid.: 85). However, there is still a 'frame
of normality' for interviewing which is not meant to be breached. Hence, Scargill's
complaint and counter-framing move:

> Scargill represents Emery as having acted rudely and aggressively . . . His
> reassertion of the right to answer the question is accompanied by the
> emotional utterance 'For God's sake let me answer!' indicating a negative
> evaluation of Emery's behaviour as violating the norms of appropriateness,
> as he frames them.
>
> (Ibid.: 90)

Framing, then, does not only relate to how participants draw from expectation
frames as a means of gauging in/appropriacy (see, e.g., Tannen 1993: 14–15), but
can also relate to the way(s) in which interlocutors opt to 'represent the character
traits, ideas', opinions and statements 'of others' (Locher and Watts 2008: 99, n9).

As our second *Panorama* extract – from the 2007 programme, *Scientology and Me*
– reveals, power is not fixed, even in an institutional context (Locher 2004: 39).
Hence, it can be taken from (or surrendered by) the interviewer. In this particular
case, the reporter, John Sweeney, is arguing with a spokesman for the scientology
movement, Tommy Davis. Sweeney's first utterance (below) is not part of his conversation with Davis but, rather, is directed to the TV audience. It therefore acts as
a framing device for the quarrel. Sweeney explains: I find Scientology's hijacking of
the holocaust sickening. After 90 minutes, I feel as though they're taking control of
my mind and I can't bear another second of it. Then Tommy Davis launches into
me yet again for the uncritical way he believes I interviewed Shaun Lonsdale back
in Clearwater and I lose it big time.

Davis: You should have said to him: 'What evidence, Shaun Lonsdale, do you
          have that people have been tortured.' You didn't do that.
Sweeney: Well no, hold on a second Tommy . . .
Davis: . . . the point I'm getting to . . .
Sweeney: No, no, no, stop there Tommy. No, no . . .

Davis: (shouting aggressively) No, I'm not stopping here! You listen to me for a second. You're accusing members of my religion of engaging in brainwashing . . .
Sweeney: (shouts louder) No, Tommy, you stop now . . .
Davis: (still shouting) Brainwashing is a crime.
Sweeney: (out-shouts) No, listen to me . . . you were not there at the beginning of the interview! You were not there . . .
Davis: (subdued but persistent) brainwashing is a crime . . .
Sweeney: (battles on, superior in volume . . .) You did not hear or record all the interview . . . do you understand?
Davis: Brainwashing is a crime against humanity . . .
Sweeney: Do you understand? Do you understand . . . (continues shouting)

Davis' criticism of Sweeney's interviewing style ('You should have said . . .') immediately follows Sweeney's framing utterance. This is followed by a challenge ('hold on a second', 'stop there Tommy') and counter challenge ('I'm not stopping here! You listen to me . . .'). When coupled with the repetition ('no'/'brainwashing is a crime'/'do you understand'), and the increasing volume of both parties, the implication is a loss of control. Sweeney confirms this, on his part, when he offers his second *framing* overview following his last utterance above:

> I apologise there and I apologise now. It was wrong and I'd let my team down. I lost my voice but not my mind.

Sweeney's final clause, 'but not my mind', provides some justification for acting as he did; self preservation. Having the last say also enabled Sweeney to regain some of the discursive power that had been lost: discursive power, in this context, refers both to the structural level (i.e the turns/space that speakers are given or claim for themselves) and also the interactional level (i.e. what speakers accomplish in that space; see, e.g., Thornborrow 2002: 8).

A12.7 PRAGMATIC INVESTIGATIONS OF 'POWER IN TALK': DOCTOR-PATIENT INTERACTIONS

The activity types explored thus far have been conflictive, in the main. In this section we discuss an activity type which is not usually conflictive: doctor-patient interactions. We do so so that we might gauge whether a different type of power is likely to be in evidence. Questions we might consider include:

- Are the linguistic means used above to (try to) dominate conversation being used by doctors and patients, here, to establish rapport (Tannen 1994: 23–4)?
- Is 'expert power' in evidence (French and Raven 1959)?
- Is there evidence of hegemonic practices (Gramsci 1971)?

The following extract is taken from a doctor-patient interaction which has been discussed at length by Mishler (1984), Fairclough (1992) and Thornborrow (2002).

The extract captures a conversation between D (a doctor, who is male) and P (a patient, who is female). P has complained of stomach pain, and is being examined by D:

P: [...] there's a pain right here [...
D: [Hm hm
P: and and then it goes from here on this side to this side.
D: Hm hm Does it [go into the back?
P: [It's a:ll up here. No. It's all right [up here in front
D: [Yeah   And when do
    you get that?
P: Wel:l when I eat something wrong.
D: How- How soon after you eat it?
P: ... Wel:l ...
    probably an hour ... maybe [less
D: [about an hour?
P: Maybe less ... I've cheated and I've been drinking which I shouldn't have done.
D: [Does drinking make it worse?
P: [(...)   Ho ho uh ooh Yes ... especially the carbonation
    and the alcohol.
D: Hm hm ... How much do you drink?
P: I don't know ... enough to make me go to sleep at night ... and that's quite a bit.
D: One or two drinks a day?
P: O:h no no no humph it's (more like) ten [... at night.
                At night.
D: [How many
    drinks- a night. ... Whaddya ta- what type of drinks? ... I[(...) -
P: [Oh vodka ... yeah
    vodka and ginger ale.
D: How long have you been drinking that heavily?
P: Since I've been married.
D: How long is that?
P: (giggle ...) Four years. (giggle)

(Ibid.: 16–17)

According to Fairclough (1989: 12), institutional talk is not simply 'an accomplishment of the social actors who produce it'. Rather, it is subject to the social and institutional constraints of the context in which it is produced. As such, institutional talk (doctor-patient interaction included) will always reproduce existing relations of power and status, according to Fairclough (1992). What we have, here, is a hegemonic reading, of course (Gramsci 1971). Indeed, Fairclough points to D's use of an activity-specific three-part structure (question/response/assessment) as a means of controlling P's turns. D's aim? To glean relevant medical information from P. Fairclough also draws on Mishler's (1984) 'voice of the lifeworld' and 'voice of the medical world' which, for both researchers, are said to be in conflict in this interaction: in fact, both have argued that the 'voice of the lifeworld' will always be subordinate to the 'voice of the medical world' in medical contexts.

Thornborrow offers a different perspective: she believes D and P construct their discourse collaboratively. To validate her argument, Thornborrow points to the instances when: P and D take the roles of both initiator and responder; P self-selects as continuing speaker; P introduces new information, which has not been directly requested, etc. In this way, P is able to make the most of D's expert power (French and Raven 1959). Moreover, although the overarching aim is the transmission of information/the solving of problems (i.e. *report talk*), D's frequent use of feedback signals could be seen as an attempt, on his part, to connect with P (cf. Tannen 1994). Thornborrow goes on to conclude that, although it is obvious that this extract (and longer versions of the same) constitute a particular form of institutional discursive practice, there is asymmetry between P and D, and that D has an obvious agenda (i.e. diagnosis and treatment):

> . . . when we begin to look at the detail of the talk, it becomes less clear that we can describe the operation of power in discourse in terms of one participant 'controlling' the turn-taking organisation.
>
> (Thornborrow 2002: 21)

The suggestion that discourse is co-constructed, even in medical interaction, will most likely remind you of Arundale's (2008) remarks in regard to *interconnected interpretings*, that is, the notion that utterances are continually confirmed and modified by speakers and hearers (see, e.g., Unit A5.4). The co-construction of meaning does not prevent interlocutors using language 'for strategic purposes', however (cf. Fairclough 1989: 9). Indeed, our examples of the different institutional activity types demonstrate that people will regularly manipulate language when it serves their purposes, regardless of whether they are deemed to be 'powerful' or 'powerless'. But is such manipulation characteristic of these specific activity types only? Let's find out.

Task A12.7

➤ Have you ever consciously used language strategically (i.e. to achieve a specific goal) with:

- ■ A family member?
- ■ A friend?
- ■ Your partner?
- ■ A work colleague?

➤ What was your goal (or goals)? What strategy (or strategies) did you employ? How successful were you?

A12.8 POWER, TALK AND THE WORKPLACE: A SNAPSHOT

There is plentiful evidence to suggest that language can be used as strategically in, for example, staff meetings and face-to-face workplace interaction as it can be in the courtroom, in police interaction, in political interviews and in medical inter-action (i.e. the activity types discussed above). Somewhat predictably, directives, turn-taking patterns and other *task-oriented* aspects of workplace discourse con-stituted the focus of much of the early linguistic research in this area (see, e.g., Francis 1986; Willing 1992; Boden 1994; Bargiela-Chiappini and Harris 1996). But the focus seems to have switched, more recently, to work colleagues' conscious use of small talk and humour – as a means of building, for example, solidarity and collegiality (see, e.g., Holmes 2000; Holmes and Stubbe 2003; Holmes and Marra 2006; Mullany 2006; Vine *et al.* 2009). Of course, the early research by Laver (1975), Boden (1994) and Tannen (1994) allowed for such relational language strategies to be used in the workplace, but at the beginning of workplace interactions as a means of enabling the 'real work' to commence on a positive note. Work coming out of the Wellington Language in the Workplace Project (http://www.victoria.ac.nz/lals/lwp/), in contrast, appears to suggest that task-oriented and relational language usage is interlinked in workplace settings:

> In research on workplace directives, for instance, the [overriding] focus is on the way people use language to get things done, and [yet] issues of power and politeness together with their implications for solidarity building and relationships, are [also] always relevant.
>
> (Vine 2010: 330)

Holmes and Stubbe (2003) have found, further, that small talk and/or humour can be used as a way of creating a more informal atmosphere and/or as a means of relieving tension during more task-focused activities. Humour might be used as a means of softening directives or criticism, for example. Hence, a colleague might opt to include the modification devices *well*, *perhaps* and *just* within a directive such as 'Tell them where it is.' They may even modify the directive further via the use of a conditional structure, 'Well perhaps if we just tell them exactly where it is' (dSAI-04, cited in Vine 2004: 93; see also Mullany 2004).

Power remains a factor within such (modified) usage, of course. Indeed, small talk and humour are proving to be extremely useful devices for 'doing power' in the workplace, albeit in a less direct/more covert way. For example, Vine *et al.* (2009) have found that some work colleagues will use humour as a distancing device when they want to emphasize how an 'out-group' member (working in another depart-ment) is different to them (we pick up on the notion of *othering* in Unit C9.1). Humour – and small talk – can also provide subordinates with a means of resisting power and/or challenging power structures. Taylor and Bain (2003) found, for example, that humour was used within one call centre as a means of undermining management authority.

Holmes and Stubbe (2003: 117) also document this 'darker side' of humour in the workplace – 'to mask risky negative messages' – in their New Zealand datasets. 'The advantage' of using such a strategy, as Vine (2010: 337) highlights, is that 'it gives the speaker the option of saying they were "just joking"' (cf. Unit A5). It remains a 'risky' strategy nevertheless – which may help to explain why many researchers (see, e.g., Holmes and Marra 2002; Schnurr 2010) maintain that contestive uses of humour are likely to be much less frequent in the workplace than supportive uses of humour. The following example of 'subversive humour' in a work-based context – an email sent by 'Richard' to staff members in his department – is taken from Schnurr and Rowe (2008: 116–17):

Dear all

Please note that there will be no air conditioning in offices this Friday (public holiday) and the summer regime will come into force next week, which means that air conditioning will only be available for restricted hours (I think it is going off at 7pm). Last summer after heroic resistance led by Henry 'rage against the machine' Morris we were able to get exemptions up to 9.00pm. If you wish to make a case, I will forward your request to the air conditioning czar: please give the dates you will be in HK and a reason, i.e. you are working on a research project.

Thanks

Rich

As Schnurr (2010: 315) highlights, 'Richard's humour clearly has a critical edge to it as it evokes connotations of the misuse of power, arbitrary decision making, and non-democratic gaining and exercising of power.' Many of the strategies Richard uses as part of his 'subversive humour' are those we've discussed above or in other parts of this textbook. For example, he uses names to frame individuals in particular ways – some of which are intended to be flattering (*Henry 'rage against the machine' Morris*), some of which are intended to be unflattering (*air conditioning czar*) and some which are intended to signal congeniality (*Rich*: cf. Unit A8; see also the framing project we outline in Unit C9.3). By so doing, he is able to distance himself from management and side with his 'team'.

Drawing from a range of (mainly institutional) activity types, Unit A12 has demonstrated that language is not powerful or powerless per se. Rather, speakers have access to discursive resources which help them to use language powerfully (Wodak 2007) or, alternatively, find that their access to such discursive resources can be limited or even non-existent in some instances (Thornborrow 2002). The institutional context is largely responsible for assigning these 'powerful' and 'powerless' roles to interlocutors, of course. And these constraints, in turn, can point to obscured societal ideologies: it is here that we can see hegemony at work, for a given society's ideologies or worldview are often the 'naturalized' beliefs of the dominant (Gramsci

> **Summary and looking ahead**

1971). As we have seen, however, participants can nevertheless resist the strategies of others – even when their discursive practices are severely curtailed. This brings into play Foucault's (1977, 1980) view of power, that is, the idea that power is not a 'given', or something which is merely maintained through the ideological operations of society; it is something which can be negotiated and contested in interaction. We share this view – hence our belief that *it's important to determine how power is being used within a particular activity*, and our argument that we can do this by engaging in the type of detailed linguistic analysis that a pragmatics approach affords.

The three readings in Unit B12 have been chosen because they explore language in institutional contexts – i.e. a political speech (given in the UK House of Commons), an interaction between magistrate and defendant (in a UK Magistrates Court) and an interaction between police officer and suspect (in a UK police station). All touch on the concept of power. The third reading also discusses, in some detail, how discursive power is negotiated by a suspect in a context that grants him no institutional power. At the end of Unit B12, we provide you with some further reading regarding these particular institutional contexts and also the workplace more broadly. In Unit C9, you will be encouraged to undertake newspaper-related investigations using an existing corpus of newspaper front pages, LexisNexis and/or other sources. Specifically, you will have an opportunity to use a combination of pragmatics and corpus linguistic techniques to tease out (any) underlying ideological messages.

NOTES

1   This and other translations relating to Haider have been translated by Wodak (2007).
2   As defendants are not always questioned, there also tends to be less lawyer/defendant data available overall than there is lawyer/witness data.
3   This and other translations have been translated from German by Limberg (2008).

SECTION B
Extension

Unit B1
The origins of pragmatics

B1.1 INTRODUCTION

Pragmatics is a fairly recent discipline tracing its roots to Morris' tripartite division of semiotics into syntax, semantics and pragmatics. Pragmatics has had what Mey (2001) describes as a 'spectacular development'. However, pragmatics as a linguistic discipline 'didn't happen of itself' but is founded in traditions and approaches in different disciplines. In order to understand how it has developed so quickly and in many different forms it is necessary to take a look at its history. Our first extract from Nerlich discusses the foundations of pragmatics in pragmatics and rhetoric and draws attention to certain keywords shared by pragmaticians of different schools. Our second extract from Leech describes the development of pragmatics from a different starting point: pragmatics is seen as a reaction against Chomskyan generative grammar. It thus complements the picture of the rise of pragmatics in Britain from philosophical foundations. Leech also draws attention to 'independent thinkers' in the British tradition such as R.J. Firth whose 'contextual theory of meaning' has had an influence on functional theories of language such as Halliday's systemic functional linguistics.

B1.2 NERLICH (2010)

We are used to associating pragmatics with its British roots in (and hence its development of ideas which came from) ordinary language philosophy. As Nerlich points out, however, we can also discuss 'a French school of pragmatics', a 'German school of pragmatics' and 'an American school of pragmatics'. The work of the French linguist, Benveniste, was influenced by the British philosophers and had as its main thesis *Nihil est in lingua quod not prius fuerit in oratione* ('there is nothing in language that was not first in language use'). Jürgen Habermas is a German sociologist in the tradition of critical theory. His interest in the links between language and society is comparable to (but not the same as) the critical linguistic approach we discuss in Unit A12.

Text B1.2.1
B. Nerlich

B. Nerlich (2010) 'History of pragmatics'. In L. Cummings (ed.) *The pragmatics encyclopedia*. London and New York: Routledge, pp. 192–3.

Pragmatics, the study of language use in social situations, is a fairly recent addition to the language sciences. The term 'pragmatics' is generally said to date back to the 1930s work of the semiotician and behaviourist Charles Morris and his distinction between the three parts of semiotics: syntactics, semantics and pragmatics. The foundations for pragmatics as a linguistic discipline are rooted in the work of ordinary language philosophers and speech act theorists, such as Ludwig Wittgenstein, John L. Austin, John Searle and Herbert P. Grice. From the 1970s onwards pragmatics split into a more formal (Huang 2007) and more functional enterprise (Mey 2001). This discussion focuses on the history of pragmatics (from the Greek *prāgma* = act) as a study of linguistic action and interaction in society (Nerlich and Clarke 1996) and in particular on its origin in five approaches which one can distinguish in Europe and America: (1) the British approach which emerged from ordinary language philosophy with Wittgenstein, Austin and Searle, and which has dominated the field until the present; (2) the school of British contextualism and functionalism; (3) the French approach which is based on the theory of enunciation elaborated by Emile Benveniste; (4) the German approach, which is associated with the critical theory movement around Jürgen Habermas and Karl Otto Apel, and saw pragmatics as part of a general theory of (communicative) action. The Austinian conception of pragmatics was successfully amalgamated with those developed in France and in Germany. These traditions were affiliated in various ways with (5) the development of American pragmatism as a new philosophy which emerged in the United States in the latter part of the nineteenth century, and which made the three-way split between syntactics, semantics and pragmatics popular in linguistics, philosophy and semiotics.

A pragmatic perspective on language has its deeper roots in antiquity, that is in rhetoric, as one of the three 'liberal arts' or the 'trivium' (rhetoric, grammar, logic).

. . .

The various strands of thought which built on these older foundations clustered around certain pragmatic keywords which are still central to pragmatic thinking today:

British (1) speech act, meaning, use, intention
British (2) context, situation, function
German agenthood of (transcendental) subject, dialogue, pronouns, speech act
French subjectivity, markers of subjectivity, indexicals, enunciation
American meaning as action, the triadic sign relation.

 Task B1.2.1

➤ A pragmatic perspective on language implies that language is used to influence others and to make them act in certain ways. There is therefore a link between rhetoric and pragmatics. How would you characterize this relationship? Should rhetoric be subsumed under pragmatics (or the other way round)?

B1.3 LEECH (1983)

The emergence of pragmatics as a linguistic discipline happened very quickly. In this extract Leech discusses how and why this shift from formal grammar to pragmatic issues took place. In particular Leech argues in favour of a unified pragmatics where grammar and pragmatics are distinct but interacting domains of linguistics.

G. Leech (1983) *Principles of pragmatics*. London: Longman, pp. 1–5.

Text B1.3.1
G. Leech

The subject of 'pragmatics' is very familiar in linguistics today. Fifteen years ago it was mentioned by linguists rarely, if at all. In those far-off-seeming days, pragmatics tended to be treated as a rag-bag into which recalcitrant data could be conveniently stuffed, and where it could be equally conveniently forgotten. Now, many would argue, as I do, that we cannot really understand the nature of language itself unless we understand pragmatics: how language is used in communication.

How has this change come about? In part, the whole of the recent history of linguistics can be described in terms of successive discoveries that what has gone headlong into the rag-bag can be taken out again and sewed and patched into a more or less presentable suit of clothes. To the generation which followed Bloomfield, linguistics meant phonetics, phonemics, and if one was daring – morphophonemics; but syntax was considered so abstract as to be virtually beyond the horizon of discovery. All this changed after Chomsky, in the later 1950s, discovered the centrality of syntax; but like the structuralists, he still regarded meaning as altogether too messy for serious contemplation. In the earlier 1960s (for by this time the pace of linguistic advance had quickened) Katz and his collaborators (Katz and Fodor 1963; Katz and Postal 1964; Katz 1964) began to find out how to incorporate meaning into a formal linguistic theory, and it was not long before the 'California or bust' spirit led to a colonization of pragmatics. Lakoff, with others, was soon arguing (1971) that syntax could not be legitimately separated from the study of language use. So pragmatics was henceforth on the linguistic map. Its colonization was only the last stage of a wave-by-wave expansion of linguistics from a narrow discipline dealing with the physical data of speech, to a broad discipline taking in form, meaning, and context.

But this is only part of the story. First, all the names mentioned in the preceding paragraph are American, for it describes the progress of mainstream American linguistics. It is probably more true of linguistics than of other subjects that its dominating influences have been American; but we should not forget that many influential scholars, both in the USA and elsewhere, have continued to work outside the 'American mainstream'. We should not overlook independent thinkers such as Firth, with his early emphasis on the situational study of meaning, and Halliday, with his comprehensive social theory of language. And equally important, we should not overlook the influences of philosophy. When linguistic pioneers such as Ross and Lakoff staked a claim in pragmatics in the late 1960s, they encountered there an indigenous breed of philosophers of language who had been quietly cultivating the territory for some time. In fact, the more lasting influences on modern pragmatics have been those of philosophers; notably, in recent years, Austin (1962), Searle (1969), and Grice (1975).

The widening scope of linguistics involved a change in the view of what language is, and how linguistics should define its subject. The American structuralists were happiest with the idea that linguistics was a physical science, and therefore did their best to rid the subject of appeals to meaning. But by accepting ambiguity and synonymy as among the basic data of linguistics, Chomsky opened a door for semantics. Subsequently, Chomsky's disaffected pupils in the generative semantics school went a stage further in taking semantics to be a base for their linguistic theories. But once meaning has been admitted to a central place in language, it is notoriously difficult to exclude the way meaning varies from context to context, and so semantics spills over into pragmatics. In no time the generative semanticists found they had bitten off more than they could chew. There is a justifiable tendency in scientific thought to assume that an existing theory or paradigm works until it is shown to fail. On this basis, the generative semanticists tried to apply the paradigm of generative grammar to problems – such as the treatment of presuppositions and of illocutionary force – which most people would now regard as involving pragmatics. The attempt failed: not in the spectacular way in which theories are supposed to fail on account of a crucial falsifying observation, but in the way in which things tend to happen in linguistics, through a slowly accumulating weight of adverse arguments.

[. . .]

While the generative semanticists were exploring the outer limits of this paradigm in semantics and pragmatics, Chomsky himself, with others of similar views, was interested in a narrower definition of the scope of this paradigm, that of the so-called Extended Standard Theory, which then evolved into a narrower Revised Extended Standard Theory. These versions of generative grammar have maintained the centrality of syntax; semantics has been relegated to a peripheral position in the model, and has to some extent been abandoned altogether. Pragmatics does not enter into the model at all, and indeed Chomsky has strongly maintained the independence of a grammar, as a theory of a 'mental organ' or 'mental faculty', from consideration of the use and functions of language.

This more limited definition of the scope of linguistic theory is, in Chomsky's own terminology, a 'competence' theory rather than a 'performance' theory. It has the advantage of maintaining the integrity of linguistics, as within a walled city, away from contaminating influences of use and context. But many have grave doubts about the narrowness of this paradigm's definition of language, and about the high degree of abstraction and idealization of data which it requires.

One result of this limitation of generative grammar to a strict formalism is that, since about 1970, it has been progressively losing its position as the dominant paradigm of linguistics. More and more linguists have found their imagination and intellect engaged by approaches more wide-ranging than those allowed for in generative grammar. These approaches do not yet add up to an integrated paradigm for research, but they have had the effect collectively of undermining the paradigm of Chomsky. Socio-linguistics has entailed a rejection of Chomsky's abstraction of the 'ideal native speaker/hearer'. Psycholinguistics and artificial intelligence place emphasis on a 'process' model of human language abilities, at the expense of Chomsky's disassociation of linguistic theory from psychological process. Text linguistics and discourse analysis have refused to accept the limitation of linguistics to sentence grammar. Conversational analysis has stressed the primacy of the social dimension of language study. To these developments may be added the attention that pragmatics – the main subject of this book – has given to meaning in use, rather than meaning in the abstract.

At this point, I shall merely state the major postulates of this 'formal–functional' paradigm.

[. . .]

The postulates are:

Text B1.3.1
G. Leech

P1: The semantic representation (or logical form) of a sentence is distinct from its pragmatic interpretation.

P2: Semantics is rule-governed (= grammatical); general pragmatics is principle-controlled (= rhetorical).

P3: The rules of grammar are fundamentally conventional; the principles of general pragmatics are fundamentally non-conventional, *i.e.* motivated in terms of conversational goals.

P4: General pragmatics relates the sense (or grammatical meaning) of an utterance to its pragmatic (or illocutionary) force. This relationship may be relatively direct or indirect.

P5: Grammatical correspondences are defined by mappings; pragmatic correspondences are defined by problems and their solutions.

P6: Grammatical explanations are primarily formal; pragmatic explanations are primarily functional.

P7: Grammar is ideational; pragmatics is interpersonal and textual.

P8: In general, grammar is describable in terms of discrete and determinate categories; pragmatics is describable in terms of continuous and indeterminate values.

The effect of these postulates is to define two separate domains, and two separate paradigms of research, making up a single 'complex' paradigm for linguistics. Arguments in favour of this paradigm are based on the simplicity and naturalness of the explanations it offers. There is no clear way of testing the validity of scientific paradigms: they exist on a more abstract plane than the scientific method which Popper described as 'the method of bold conjectures and ingenious and severe attempts to refute them'. Nevertheless, by exploring, formulating, and refining paradigms of research, we are determining the background assumptions on which the search for truth about language will proceed with increased understanding.

Task B1.3.1

➤ According to Leech, there is no reason to talk about rules outside grammar. In pragmatics we refer instead to the principles which people follow when they communicate. These principles can explain why we can mean more than we actually say, for instance. A number of different pragmatic principles have been discussed above. In Unit A5 we deal with the cooperative principle proposed by the philosopher Grice and also Sperber and Wilson's relevance principle, which is based on a broad understanding of relevance. Another principle advocated by Leech is the politeness principle (see Unit A8). Leech's view of pragmatics raises certain problems about what we mean by pragmatics and its delimitation from semantics:

◾ Leech proposes what Mey (2001) refers to as 'a "pragmatic" definition of pragmatics'. He argues in favour of distinguishing between grammar and pragmatics (the complementary view). An alternative view of pragmatics is to regard pragmatics as a particular perspective on language. In such a view pragmatics permeates all components of linguistics including grammar, semantics and lexis. What difference does the perspective view make to how we do pragmatics? What are the problems of delimiting semantics from pragmatics?

▓ According to Leech, 'more and more linguists have found their imagination and intellect engaged by approaches more wide-ranging than those allowed for in generative grammar. These approaches do not yet add up to an integrated paradigm for research, but they have had the effect collectively of undermining the paradigm of Chomsky'. Is this equally true today (Leech's book *Principles of pragmatics* came out in 1983)? Has pragmatics become an integrated paradigm for research?

FURTHER READING

There are a number of introductions to pragmatics:

Leech, Geoffrey N. (1983) *Principles of pragmatics.* London and New York: Longman. The author argues that semantics and pragmatics are distinct but complementary. Pragmatics is studied by means of principles such as the cooperative principles and politeness principles.

Levinson, Stephen N. (1983) *Pragmatics.* Cambridge: Cambridge University Press. Provides a ground-breaking overview of pragmatic issues. It includes a chapter on discourse analysis and conversation analysis.

Thomas, Jenny (1995) *Meaning in interaction. An introduction to pragmatics.* London and New York: Longman. The book does not presuppose any previous knowledge of pragmatics. The theoretical points are illustrated with copious examples from fiction, newspapers and authentic interactions.

Verschueren, Jef (1999) *Understanding pragmatics.* London: Edward Arnold. Looks at pragmatics in a broad sense including social, cultural and cognitive aspects. The focus is on pragmatics as a special perspective on language.

Mey, Jacob L. (2001) *Pragmatics. An introduction.* Oxford: Wiley-Blackwell. Represents a broad view of pragmatics. It includes a discussion of the critical orientation of pragmatics and chapters on literary pragmatics and cross-cultural chapters.

Cummings, Louise (2005) *Pragmatics. A multidisciplinary perspective.* Edinburgh: Edinburgh University Press. It is argued that pragmatics cannot ignore neighbouring fields such as philosophy, psychology, artificial intelligence and language pathology and vice versa.

Yule, George (2006) *Pragmatics.* Oxford: Oxford University Press. A brief introduction to pragmatics for beginning students which describes and explains a number of basic pragmatic notions such as deixis, speech act, implicature, etc.

Huang, Yan (2007) *Pragmatics.* New York: Oxford University Press. An introduction to central topics in pragmatics. Explores the interface between pragmatics and cognition (including relevance theory), pragmatics and syntax and pragmatics and semantics. The examples are drawn from a range of different languages.

Grundy, Peter (2008) *Doing pragmatics*. London: Hodder Education. Combines pragmatic theory and practice. It is intended for both beginning and advanced students. Includes chapters on language evolution and intercultural pragmatics.

Cummings, Louise (ed.) (2010) *The pragmatics encyclopedia*. London and New York: Routledge. Covers traditional and more recent theoretical and empirical concerns and establishes interdisciplinary links with other areas of research.

O'Keeffe, Anne, Svenja Adolphs and Brian Clancy (2011) *Introducing pragmatics in use*. London: Routledge. An introductory textbook in pragmatics which draws on language corpora to illustrate pragmatic phenomena.

Archer, Dawn and Peter Grundy (eds) (2011) *The pragmatics reader*. London and New York: Routledge. Contains both key classic texts and extracts illustrating developments in contemporary pragmatics.

Unit B2
Research methods in pragmatics

B2.1 INTRODUCTION

We have seen that there are many different ways of assembling empirical evidence for pragmatic meaning, and that the choice depends very much on the focus of the research. In Unit A2.2 we described the various ways to collect examples of actual language usage, mostly in the form of recordings. In Unit A2.5 we showed how the development of large electronic corpora of spoken and written language has contributed to the availability of data for pragmatics research. Corpora allow us to see what people actually say, and provide information on the social context in which it is said – the participants, their relative power relations and the activity itself. Before automatically searchable corpora became widely available, researchers often found it more efficient to use a Discourse Completion Task to find out what people might have said in a given situation as in the CCSARP project (see Unit A10.1). While this provides evidence of what people think they *would* say rather than what they actually *did* say, it is a very useful source of data. The first reading (Kasper 2000) describes this method in detail and discusses its value for research.

An important approach to pragmatics is Relevance Theory (see also Unit A5), which assumes that speakers take account of their hearers in their choice of language. While sociopragmatics studies how people take account of social context in their formulation of a message, Relevance Theory suggests that we adjust our utterances to the needs of our hearers. The second reading describes an experiment designed to test whether this is so. Experimental pragmatics, which this reading exemplifies, adopts methods similar to those in psychology and cognitive science, and aims to develop theory-driven predictions which can be tested in a controlled way.

None of the methods described in the first two readings is helpful in the study of the language of the past. We cannot record people in action, we cannot ask them what they would say in a certain situation and we cannot ask them about their intuitions. The only source of insight into historical speech is what has been preserved in writing. This means that historical research into pragmatics has to address special problems. The final reading shows how we can use historical corpus data in a systematic way to study how specific speech acts were realized in the past.

B2.2 KASPER (2000)

If we are interested in what people say in different contexts, the best way is to record them doing it. However, as we have seen, what they say and do might be affected by the presence of the observer, the 'observer's paradox', so that we are not sure how they might have responded when not being observed. In addition, it is difficult to collect a large enough number of cases to be able to make generalizations. In order to have more quantifiable data, one approach is the use of questionnaires in which people are asked what they might say in a certain hypothetical situation. These questionnaires vary in format: in each case a situation is described to which the user may respond, but the response can be written or spoken, and can be more or less constrained. One important question raised by Kasper is whether these different formats are likely to elicit comparable results. For example, is a written reponse likely to be very different from an oral response? And how might such responses compare to naturally occurring data?

These questions are discussed in the following extract.

G. Kasper (2000) 'Data collection in pragmatics research'. In H. Spencer-Oatey (ed.) *Culturally speaking – managing rapport through talk across cultures.* **London: Continuum, pp. 316–41.**

Text B2.2.1
G Kasper

An obvious question to worry about is whether and how the written mode as opposed to spoken production may result in different responses. Rintell and Mitchell (1989) addressed this question by comparing spoken and written requests and apologies from native and non-native speakers of English, elicited by oral (open role-play) and written (open response format) versions of the same production questionnaire. They found that non-native speakers' oral responses were significantly longer than their written responses; however, this was not true for the native speakers, suggesting that language proficiency rather than research procedure was a crucial factor. Moreover, in some situations both groups were more direct in the written than in the spoken mode, suggesting that respondents were more influenced by face and politeness issues in procedures involving face-to-face interaction. However, these differences were out-weighed by the similarities of the written and oral responses, suggesting that strategy choice and wording of single-turn responses to production tasks may be fairly stable across modalities.

A serious concern is how production questionnaires compare to authentic data. Beebe and Cummings (1996, originally presented 1985) compared refusals elicited through a single-item questionnaire with refusals performed in telephone conversations in response to the same request. Interlocutors in these interchanges were native speakers of American English. The questionnaire responses did *not* represent natural speech with respect to the actual wording, range of refusal strategies, and response length, but they modelled the 'canonical shape' of refusals, shed light on the social and psychological factors that are likely to affect speech act performance, and helped establish an initial classification of refusal strategies.

Hartford and Bardovi-Harlig (1992) examined the rejections by native and non-native graduate students of their academic advisers' suggestions for the students'

Text B2.2.1
G. Kasper

course schedules. The production questionnaire elicited a narrower range of semantic formulae and fewer status-preserving strategies than the authentic data, yet it proved an adequate instrument to test hypotheses derived from the authentic interactions. The questionnaire data confirmed Hartford and Bardovi-Harlig's (1992) hypothesis that the non-native speakers were more likely to use unacceptable content to reject advice than the native speakers.

Task B2.2.1

➤ How reliable are such questionnaires? Why do the authors think they are useful, even if in a real situation we do not actually say what we think we would say?

➤ What is the value, according to the authors, of using such questionnaires in the context of language teaching? Is it important to find out what learners *know* as well as what they *do*?

➤ What would you say to someone who had lent you their pen but you had lost it? Would it matter who it was? Would the kind of pen make a difference? What else might determine what you said?

B2.3 VAN DER HENST AND SPERBER (2004)

This reading is an example of research undertaken in the framework of Relevance Theory (Sperber and Wilson). Relevance Theory assumes that all contributions are intended to be maximally relevant to the conversation, and that speakers design their contribution for the benefit of the hearer. This extract is from Section 5: 'Testing the principle of relevance with a speech production task'. In it, the researchers ask participants the same question (What's the time?) but accompanied by different information about why the questioner needs to know. This means that if the hypothesis is correct, the answer to the question will take into account what is relevant for the hearer.

Text B2.3.1
J.-B. van der
Henst and
D. Sperber

J.-B. van der Henst and D. Sperber (2004) 'Testing the cognitive and communicative principles of relevance'. In I.A. Noveck and D. Sperber (eds) _Experimental pragmatics_. Basingstoke: Palgrave Macmillan, pp. 141–71.

Testing the Communicative Principle of Relevance with a speech production task

According to the Communicative Principle of Relevance, utterances convey a presumption of their own optimal relevance, and do so whether or not they actually are optimally relevant [. . .] In the study that we report in this section, we investigate the degree to which speakers actually aim at being relevant, even when talking to perfect strangers from whom they have little to expect in return.

Imagine the following exchange between two strangers in the street:

Text B2.3.1
J.-B. van der
Henst and
D. Sperber

(15) Mr X: Hello, do you have the time, please?
      Mrs Y: Oh yes, it is 4:30

In fact, Mrs Y's watch does not indicate 4:30 but 4:28. She has chosen to round her answer even though she could have been more accurate [. . .] What explains this behaviour? We recently proposed that rounding is in part explained by considerations of relevance (Van der Henst, Carles and Sperber, 2002). A rounded answer is generally more relevant than an accurate one, and speakers round in order to be relevant to their hearer.

      [. . .]

In order to find out whether a tendency to optimize relevance was a factor in rounding the time, we approached people on the campus of the University of Paris VII and just asked them: 'Hello, do you have the time please?' (Van der Henst, Carles and Sperber, 2002). We took note of their response and of the type of watch they were wearing: analogue or digital, and distinguished two groups, the 'analogue' and the 'digital' group. For people with a digital watch, it requires less effort to just read aloud the exact time indicated by their watch than to round it to the closest multiple of five. If people asked for the time were just trying to minimize their own effort, then they should always round when their watch is analogue, and never do so when it is digital. On the other hand, if people are also motivated by the goal of reducing their audience's effort, then, not only people with analogue watches, but also a significant percentage of people with digital watches should round.

What we found is that people rounded in both conditions. The percentage of rounders is calculated on the basis of the percentages of responses which indicate the time in a multiple of five minutes. If people never rounded there should be 20 per cent of such responses (this is the theoretical distribution of numbers which are multiples of 5). However, the percentages we observed in the two conditions were much higher: [. . .] 97 per cent of people rounded in the analogue condition and 57 per cent in the digital one [. . .] Hence, even though participants of the digital group rounded less than participants of the analogue group, a majority of them did, remarkably, make an extra effort in order to diminish the effort of their audience.

Some people with analogue watches may round just in order to save their own effort, but the case of people with digital watches shows that a majority of people are disposed to round, even when this means making an extra effort. We attributed this disposition to a more general disposition, that of trying to produce optimally relevant utterances. Still, an alternative explanation could be that people round in order to minimize their commitment: they may not be sure that their watch is precise to the minute, and be more confident that it is accurate within a five-minute interval. Indeed, this desire to minimize commitment may account for some of the rounding we observed, but could it be enough to make the relevance-based explanation super-fluous? To investigate this possibility, we created a situation where accuracy manifestly contributed to relevance.

Although rounded answers are easier to process than non-rounded ones, there are some situations [. . .] where optimal relevance depends upon cognitive effects that are carried only by a more accurate answer. Speakers guided by the goal of producing an optimally relevant answer should, in this condition, provide, if they can, a more precise answer than in the ordinary kind of situation in which our first experiment took place.

We tested this prediction in Experiment 2 with two groups of people. In the control group, participants were approached in the same way as in the previous experiment

Text B2.3.1
J.-B. van der
Henst and
D. Sperber

and were just asked for the time. In the experimental group, the request for the time was framed in a context in which an accurate answer was obviously more relevant. The experimenter approached the participant with a watch held in his hand and said: 'Hello! My watch isn't working properly. Do you have the time please?' In this context, it was clear that the experimenter was asking for the time in order to set his own watch and that, for this purpose, an answer precise to the minute would be more relevant. Only the answers of participants with an analogue watch were recorded. Participants had therefore to make an extra effort in order to provide an accurate answer. We found that participants were much more accurate in the experimental than in the control condition: there were 94 per cent of rounders in the control condition and only 49 per cent in the experimental one [. . .] This means that 51 per cent of participants of the experimental group gave the requester a time accurate to the minute. Note that rounded answers may nevertheless have been in conformity with the presumption of optimal relevance: even if approximate, they were relevant enough to be worth the hearer's attention, as required by the first clause of the presumption, and, as required by the second clause, they may have been the most relevant ones compatible with the speakers' abilities (if they had doubts about the accuracy of their watch), or preferences (if they were reluctant to work out a more precise answer). Our results show anyhow that a majority of the people not only understood that accuracy was more relevant in this condition, but also were able and willing to make the effort of giving an accurate answer.

That accuracy to the minute is relevant to someone setting his watch is easy enough to understand. It need not involve the kind of refined concern for relevance that Relevance Theory presupposes. In a third experiment, we manipulated the relationship between relevance and accuracy in a much subtler way.

Suppose you want to know how much time you have left before an appointment at 4:00pm. The closer you get to the time of the appointment the more accuracy is likely to be relevant. At 3:32, being told that it is 3:30 is likely to have practically the same effect as being told, more accurately, that it is 3:32. On the other hand, being told at 3:58 that it is 4:00 is likely to be misleading. Two minutes may, for instance, be the time you need to reach the place of your appointment. In other words, the closer you are to the time of the appointment, the more accuracy becomes relevant.

In the third experiment, all participants were approached in the same way and told 'Hello, do you have the time please? I have an appointment at T'. We then divided participants into two groups: the 'earlier' group who gave a time between 30 to 16 minutes before the time of the appointment and a 'later' group who answered with a time between 14 minutes before the time of the appointment and the time of the appointment itself. As we had predicted, the results show that participants rounded less in the 'later' group (75 per cent of participants) than in the 'earlier' group (97 per cent): 22 per cent difference may not seem so impressive until you realize that those people in the later group who did give an accurate answer not only were willing to make the effort of reading their analogue watch more carefully and had enough confidence in its accuracy, but also made the extra effort of taking the perspective of the stranger who was addressing them and of inferring that accuracy, at this point in time, would contribute to the relevance of their utterance.

The experiments described in this section show how subtle aspects of people's spontaneous speech behaviour can be predicted on the basis of the Communicative Principle of Relevance: speakers tend to produce utterances that justify the presumption of optimal relevance these utterances automatically convey.

Task B2.3.1

➤ What was the reason for comparing responses from people with analogue and digital watches?

➤ What could be the advantage of giving a rounded answer to the question 'What's the time?' (i.e. 4.30 when it was in fact 4.28) (a) for the hearer (b) for the speaker?

➤ What do the authors infer from the fact that there was less rounding up of the time in the answer when the questioners said they had an appointment within the next quarter of an hour?

B2.4 KOHNEN (2009)

Our final reading shows the problems of pragmatics research in relation to historical speech. In the absence of sound recordings we rely entirely on what is written. As we suggested in Unit A2.5, electronic corpora are now frequently used for the study of historical pragmatics. Kohnen reminds us that the relationship between form and function in speech acts is not fixed. We can search a corpus for the forms we know, but have to accept that there may be others which remain hidden. This means also that we cannot be sure of the frequency distributions of the forms we know about. In addition, unless we take note of the different genres and registers in which we find occurrences of a particular speech act, we cannot know to what extent certain forms are typical of certain contexts. In this extract, Kohnen considers how researchers can and do deal with these problems.

T. Kohnen (2009) 'Historical corpus pragmatics'. In A.H. Jucker, D. Schreier and M. Hunit (eds) *Corpora: pragmatics and discourse.* **Amsterdam: Rodopi, pp. 21–3.**

Text B2.4.1
T. Kohnen

Speech-act verbs and the ways they give access to speech acts in corpora

One way researchers deal with these problems relies on speech-act verbs and the ways they give access to speech acts in corpus data. [For example] . . . Taavitsainen and Jucker (2007) use speech-act verbs of verbal aggression in order to access insults in a large corpus. The set of speech-act verbs of verbal aggression can be determined for the major periods in the history of English and can thus be systematically retrieved in a historical corpus. This approach can cover all the items in a historical corpus where speech-act verbs of a certain kind are mentioned and can thus [. . .] provide a highly instructive ethnographic picture of the respective speech acts. It can also serve to access explicit performative manifestations of speech acts (see Kohnen 2000a, 2000b). But it cannot cover all the manifestations of a specific speech act in a historical corpus.

Fixed, recurring manifestations of speech acts

Another approach relies on the fact that many speech acts are realised by more or less fixed, recurring patterns. A corpus-based analysis can start with such common patterns of linguistic expressions, convert them to more abstract search strings approximating them and then test their precision and recall in large corpora, that is, test whether they achieve correct identification and comprehensive coverage of the speech act under investigation.

For example, Jucker, Schneider, Taavitsainen and Breustedt (2008), while "fishing for compliments", look at linguistic patterns which are typically used as compliments and work out approximations to the number of compliments in the *British National Corpus*. Valkonen (2008) investigates explicit performatives containing speech-act verbs of promising. One of his interesting results is that 97 percent of all instances in his large corpus are based on the verbs *promise*, *swear* and *vow*.

These and similar studies certainly yield instructive results, but their reliability is based on the extent to which a speech act is realised by fixed and routinised expressions. Since they always begin with a formal specification of the speech act under investigation, they risk missing the more creative, indirect or simply uncommon manifestations and thus cannot solve the problem of the "hidden manifestations".

A genre-based empirical bottom-up methodology

In a more or less complementary approach to the studies mentioned [. . .] I suggested a genre-based bottom-up methodology (for a more detailed account of this methodology, see Kohnen 2008). This methodology starts with relatively small diachronic pilot corpora of selected genres (for example, sermons, letters, prayers etc.) and analyses all the manifestations of a particular speech act (for example, directives) in these pilot corpora. This analysis necessarily proceeds 'by hand', that is, all the text excerpts have to be read, considering carefully which sections of text might serve the function of the relevant speech act. This microanalysis will produce a preliminary inventory of the manifestations of the speech act under investigation. With more genres, the list of different realisations will probably grow. However, it seems reasonable to assume that the more genres included, the less 'new' manifestations will be found. In a final step, selected manifestations and their distribution can be tested in larger multi-genre corpora in order to assess the frequency and distribution of the various manifestations in a more comprehensive setting of language use.

Given an appropriate number of genres and pilot corpora, such a methodology should produce a fairly detailed inventory of the different manifestations of a speech act across time, approaching a reasonable level of completeness and representativeness. This, it is hoped, should significantly increase the retrievability of speech acts in diachronic corpus-based studies, thus reducing the impact of the problem of unpredictable and hidden manifestations. With regard to the third problem mentioned above (mixing genres and registers), this method will also enhance our knowledge about the distribution of speech acts and their different manifestations across genres.

Task B2.4.1

➤ Speech act verbs such as 'promise' (as in 'I promise to . . .') are a useful starting point but inevitably miss many cases. How else would you look for promises in a corpus?

➤ Corpus-based studies of speech acts tend to be restricted to those using 'routinized' expressions. What is the disadvantage of this approach?

➤ What is the advantage of the 'bottom-up' approach described here?

➤ What is the importance of genre differences?

FURTHER READING

For an overview of methods used in historical pragmatics, you can read Fitzmaurice and Taavitsainen (2007). Rose and Kasper (2001) provide insights into the study of pragmatics in relation to language teaching. For methods used in Experimental Pragmatics, see the book of the same name, edited by Noveck and Sperber (2004). Cameron (2001) provides detailed discussion of the process of collecting and transcribing spoken language.

LOOKING AHEAD

In Unit C1, you will be given the opportunity to develop and analyse your own data, not only for your own research but to give you a critical insight into the research methods of others.

Unit B3
The semantic-pragmatic interface

B3.1 INTRODUCTION

The readings in this section each deal with the semantics-pragmatics boundary dispute. The first excerpt, by Kasia M. Jaszczolt (2010), is taken from his encyclopedic entry, 'Semantics-pragmatics interface', in the Routledge *Pragmatics encyclopedia*. The excerpt (as it is reproduced here) will help you to situate the boundary dispute in its historical context. You'll learn more about the debate between the ideal and ordinary language philosophers as well as the proposal which ultimately allowed each group to co-exist with the other: that we see semantics as a theory of linguistic meaning and pragmatics as the study of language use (cf. Grice 1989). You'll also learn more about the notion of semantic underdetermination. As previously discussed (see Unit A3.5), semantic underdetermination was one of the first ideas put forward to account for lingusitic features which – like reference, deixis and presuppositons – transcend the semantics-pragmatics interface. Our second excerpt, from Robert Stalnaker's (1974) article on 'Pragmatic presuppositions', takes one of these phenomena – presupposition – and argues that they should be seen as being pragmatically derived only: not least because 'presuppositions are related to the particuar contexts or situations in which statements are made, and reflect, not properties of language, but the common background beliefs and assumptions of speakers and addressees' (Archer and Grundy 2011: 17). Our third excerpt, by Nick Enfield (2003), picks out similar themes to Stalnaker when exploring deixis, namely, that their meaning comes from S and H's understanding of S's use of 'pointing devices' in a given context. But he suggests that such phenomena have both pragmatic and semantic properties.

B3.2 JASZCZOLT (2010)

We focus below on the first section of Jaszczolt's article (pp. 428–9). This means we capture Jaszczolt's discussion in regard to semantic and pragmatic researchers studying the same thing – 'meaning' – (albeit from different perspectives) as well as Grice's enduring influence in regard to the semantics-pragmatics boundary debate. The reading also points to the various ways in which researchers have since developed Grice's ideas in regard to what is said explicitly and what is derived implicitly via the context-of-use (see Unit A3.5 and also Unit A5).

Text B3.2.1
K. M Jaszczolt

K.M. Jaszczolt (2010) 'Semantics-pragmatics interface'. In L. Cummings (ed.) *The pragmatics encyclopedia*. **London and New York: Routledge, pp. 428–32.**

Semantics and pragmatics have both developed sophisticated methods of analysis of meaning. The question to address is whether their objects of study can be teased apart or whether each sub-discipline accounts for different contributions (in the sense of qualitatively different outputs or different types of processes) that produce one unique object called 'meaning'. Traditionally, semantics was responsible for compositionally construed sentence meaning, in which the meanings of lexical items and the structure in which they occur were combined. The best developed approach to sentence meaning is undoubtedly truth-conditional semantics. Its formal methods permit the translation of vague and ambiguous sentences of natural language into a precise metalanguage of predicate logic and provide a model-theoretic interpretation to so construed logical forms. Pragmatics was regarded as a study of utterance meaning, and hence meaning in context, and was therefore an enterprise with a different object of study. However, the boundary between them began to be blurred, giving rise to the so-called semantic underdetermination view. Semantic underdetermination was a revolutionary idea for the theory of linguistic meaning. It was a reaction to generative semantics of the 1960s and 1970s which attempted to give syntactic explanations to inherently pragmatic phenomena. We have to note the importance of the Oxford ordinary language philosophers (John L. Austin, H. Paul Grice, Peter F. Strawson) and Ludwig Wittgenstein in Cambridge in the late phase of his work, and subsequently the work of Gerald Gazdar, Bruce Fraser, Jerry Morgan, Jay Atlas, Ruth Kempson, Deirdre Wilson, Stephen Levinson, Larry Horn, and many others, in opening up the way for the study of pragmatic inference and its contribution to truth-conditional representation, now understood as Gricean, intended meaning with intuitive truth-conditions. I list below some important landmarks.

Grice (1978) remarked that pragmatic processes of disambiguation and reference assignment to indexical expressions sometimes have to be taken into consideration before the sentence's truth conditions can be assessed. At the same time, Kempson (1975, 1979, 1986) and Atlas (1977, 1979, 1989) suggested that negation in English should not be regarded as ambiguous between narrow-scope and wide-scope as Bertrand Russell had proposed, but was instead semantically underdetermined. In other words, the celebrated example (1) is not semantically ambiguous between (1') and (1") but instead the scope of negation is pragmatically determined in each particular utterance on the basis of the recovery of the speaker's intentions.

(1)   The king of France is not bald.
(1') $\exists x \, (KoF(x) \land \forall y \, (KoF(y) \rightarrow y = x) \land \neg Bald \, (x))$
(1") $\neg \exists x \, (KoF(x) \land \forall y \, (KoF(y) \rightarrow y = x) \land Bald \, (x))$

(1') is a presupposing reading: there is a person who fulfils the property of being the king of France, there is only one such person, and whoever fulfils this property is not bald. The reading in (1") is non-presupposing: the king of France is *not* bald because there is no such person. Since (1') entails (1"), the semantic underdetermination (sense-generality) view has both formal and cognitive support: the logical forms in (1') and (1") are not disjoint and (1') and (1") do not correspond to separate, independent thoughts. A battery of tests was proposed in order to tell ambiguity and underdetermination apart (Zwicky and Sadock 1975; *see also* Jaszczolt 1999). The boundary became

Text B3.2.1
K.M. Jaszczolt

more and more blurred. Linguists began to adopt the underdetermination stance to an increasing set of expression types and we can talk about the beginning of an orientation called radical pragmatics (Cole 1981), sense-generality (Atlas 1989), or contextualism (Recanati 2004, 2005). According to this view, semantic analysis takes us only part of the way towards the recovery of utterance meaning and pragmatic enrichment completes this process. In other words, the logical form becomes enriched (or, to use a more general term, modulated; *see* Recanati 2004, 2005) as a result of pragmatic inference and the entire semantic-pragmatic product becomes subjected to the truth-conditional analysis (*see*, for example, Carston 1988, 1998, 2002; Atlas 1989, 2005; Wilson 1975; Recanati 1989, 2004, 2005; Sperber and Wilson 1995). For example, sentence (2) is normally enriched with the consequence sense of *and* before being subjected to the truth-conditional analysis as in (2').

(2) Tom dropped the vase and it broke.
(2') Tom dropped the vase *and as a result* it broke.

This widening of the content of semantic representation resulted in the reallocation of some of the meanings which Grice classified as implicit to the truth-conditional content of the utterance. One of the main research questions now became to delimit the scope of such an enriched, truth-conditional representation, called what is said (Recanati 1989) or explicature (Carston 1988; Sperber and Wilson 1995) vis-à-vis implicatures. Carston (1988) argued that enrichment stops as soon as optimal relevance (in the sense of relevance theory of Sperber and Wilson) is reached. She proposed that a criterion for classification is provided by the functional independence principle, according to which implicatures have their own, independent logical forms and they function as separate premises in reasoning. Identifying some problems with the formal definition of functional independence, Recanati (1989) offered the availability principle. According to this principle, an aspect of meaning is part of what is said when it conforms to our pre-theoretic intuitions (but *see* Carston's 1998 response).

B3.2.1 Task

> Jaszczolt suggests that, for some researchers, 'semantic analysis takes us only part of the way towards the recovery of utterance meaning and pragmatic enrichment completes this process'. How does 'pragmatic enrichment' help us to understand the following example utterances (taken from Meibauer and Steinbach 2011: 5–6)?

> - The omelette left without paying.
> - Anne married and got pregnant vs. Anne got pregnant and married.
> - I didn't have breakfast.

> *And* is said to have a 'consequence sense' in 'Tom dropped the vase and it broke' such that it can be enriched to 'Tom dropped the vase *and as a result* it broke.'

>> - How is this 'consequence sense' of *and* derived in your view? Is it implicit in what is said – because this is what *and* can mean (i.e. it represents one

of the [conventionalized] senses of *and*) – or is it implied – because it has to be triggered by the context-of-utterance?

■ What other senses does *and* have and how do these different senses come to be triggered? Rather than adopting an armchair approach (i.e. constructing made-up examples or drawing examples from memory) to answer this particular question, use a dictionary such as the *Oxford English Dictionary Online* to derive a list of the possible uses of *and* and then compare these possible uses with the actual occurrences of *and* in the *British National Corpus* (BNC) or the *Corpus of Contemporary American English* (COCA). These corpora are available from Mark Davies' website – http://corpus. byu.edu/ – and are free to use.

B3.3 STALNAKER (1974)

Our second and third readings explore phenomena which are often described as straddling the semantics-pragmatics interface – presuppositions and deixis. Here, we focus on Stalnaker's argument that, as presuppositions constitute 'constraints on the contexts in which statements can be made', they are determined not by truth/falsity values (cf. the truth-conditional semanticists' approach) but, rather, by the common background beliefs and assumptions of interlocutors. This makes presuppositions 'pragmatic' in Stalnaker's view.

R. Stalnaker (1974) 'Pragmatic presuppositions'. In M.K. Munitz and P.K. Unger (eds) *Semantics and philosophy*. New York: New York University Press, pp. 197–214.

Text B3.3.1
R. Stalnaker

[A semantic] . . . account draws the distinction between presupposition and assertion in terms of the content or truth-conditions of the sentence uttered or the proposition expressed. Here is an example of such a definition: a proposition that P presupposes that Q if and only if Q must be true in order that P have a truth-value at all. The presuppositions of a proposition, according to this definition, are necessitated by the truth, and by the falsity, of the proposition. When any presupposition is false, the assertion lacks a truth-value.

[Within a pragmatic account] . . . [t]he distinction between presupposition and assertion should be drawn, not in terms of the content of the propositions expressed, but in terms of the situations in which the statement is made—the attitudes and intentions of the speaker and his audience. Presuppositions, on this account, are something like the background beliefs of the speaker—propositions whose truth he takes for granted, or seems to take for granted, in making his statement.

The pragmatic account is closer to the ordinary notion of presupposition, but it has frequently been assumed that the semantic account is the one that is relevant to giving a rigorous theoretical explanation of the linguistic phenomena. I want to argue that this assumption is wrong. I will suggest that it is important for correctly understanding the phenomena identified by linguists to give the second kind of analysis rather than the first. In terms of the pragmatic account, one can give intuitively natural explanations of some facts that seem puzzling when presupposition is viewed as a semantic

Text B3.3.1
R. Stalnaker

relation. The pragmatic account makes it possible to explain some particular facts about presuppositions in terms of general maxims of rational communication rather than in terms of complicated and ad hoc hypotheses about the semantics of particular words and particular kinds of constructions [. . .]

Let me begin by rehearsing some truisms about communication. Communication, whether linguistic or not, normally takes place against a background of beliefs or assumptions which are shared by the speaker and his audience, and which are recognized by them to be so shared [. . .] The more common ground we can take for granted, the more efficient our communication will be. And unless we could reasonably treat *some* facts in this way, we probably could not communicate at all.

Which facts or opinions we can reasonably take for granted in this way, as much as what further information either of us wants to convey, will guide the direction of our conversation—will determine what is said. I will not say things that are already taken for granted, since that would be redundant. Nor will I assert things incompatible with the common background, since that would be self-defeating. My aim in making assertions is to distinguish among the possible situations which are compatible with all the beliefs or assumptions that I assume that we share. Or it could be put the other way around: the common background is defined by the possible situations which I intend to distinguish among with my assertions, and other speech acts. Propositions true in all of them are propositions whose truth is taken for granted.

Although it is normally inappropriate because unnecessary for me to assert something that each of us assumes the other already believes, my assertions will of course always have consequences which are part of the common background. For example, in a context where we both know that my neighbor is an adult male, I say "My neighbor is a bachelor," which, let us suppose, entails that he is adult and male. I might just as well have said "My neighbor is unmarried." The same information would have been conveyed (although the nuances might not have been exactly the same). That is, the *increment of information*, or of content, conveyed by the first statement is the same as that conveyed by the second. If the asserted proposition were accepted, and added to the common background, the resulting situation would be the same as if the second assertion were accepted and added to the background.

[. . .]

[To summarize] . . . it is persons rather than sentences, propositions or speech acts that have or make presuppositions [. . .] It is true that the linguistic facts to be explained by a theory of presupposition are for the most part relations between linguistic items, or between a linguistic expression and a proposition. They are, as I interpret them, facts about the constraints, of one kind or another, imposed by what is said on what is appropriately presupposed by the speaker, according to various different standards of appropriateness. But I think all the facts can be stated and explained directly in terms of the underlying notion of speaker presupposition, and without introducing an intermediate notion of presupposition as a relation holding between sentences (or statements) and propositions.

Task B3.3.1

> Stalnaker's argument that presuppositions are pragmatic in nature is based on his belief that 'it is persons rather than sentences, propositions or speech acts that have or make presuppositions'. Do we lose anything by making presuppositions a pragmatic phenomenon only? (cf. Units A3.4–A3.4.1).

➤ 'My neighbor is a bachelor' and 'My neighbor is unmarried' presuppose the same thing, according to Stalnaker: that S's neighbour is an adult male. As Baker (2006: 106–8) has shown, however, (the 'unmarried' sense of) *bachelor* can also trigger other connotations: for example, a *happy* and *agreeable* life or, conversely, a *solitary* and *lonely* life. It can even trigger a 'playboy' or 'homosexual' connotation. Baker's study makes use of the BNC. Undertake your own study of [some of!] the 424 'hits' for *bachelor* in the BNC (and/or the 3,579 'hits' for *bachelor* in COCA):

▪ How many of these usages denote the neutral information 'adult unmarried male'?

▪ How many allude to something in addition to this? What meaning(s) do they suggest?

▪ Are these additional meanings presuppositional in respect to *bachelor* in the same way that *old*, *unmarried* and *male* are said to be? (Recall Stalnaker's notion of 'common ground' above; if the nuances are part of the 'beliefs or assumptions which are shared by the speaker and his audience, and which are recognized by them to be so shared' to the extent that they constitute an uncontroversial background assumption, then they are presuppositional.)

B3.4 ENFIELD (2003)

Our final reading in this section explores a specific phrase: *what-d'you-call-it*. This non-specific expression is often used when an interlocutor cannot bring to mind the name for something (even though they are thinking of something very specific at the time). In a section of his paper not included here, Enfield discusses how important shared background knowledge is when such phrases are used deictically by interlocutors. His main argument, however, is that such phrases are conventionalized to some degree; such that they display semantic as well as pragmatic properties. Simply put, when we hear *what-d'you-call-it*, we assume S means to signal '*something*' and that it is a *something* which – if we use our shared background knowledge – we will be able to readily identify (in spite of S not producing '*the word for this thing* right then').

N.J. Enfield (2003) 'The definition of what-d'you-call-it: semantics and pragmatics of recognitional deixis', *Journal of Pragmatics* 35: 101–17.

Text B3.4.1
N. J. Enfield

Suppose Mary is power-drilling and John is nearby. She mislays the chuck key while changing drill-bits, and the following exchange ensues:

(1) Mary: *John, where's the* WHAT-*d'you-call-it?*
     John: *I put it back in the toolbox.*

[. . .]

Text B3.4.1
N.J. Enfield

Mary chose the word WHAT-*d'you-call-it* in the context of (1) [. . .] [because t]he term is to some degree *conventionalised* [. . .] and as such has a relatively stable meaning and [hence] can be relied upon in just such contexts to lead the hearer to the right interpretation.

[. . .]

[A] definition (in the form of a paraphrase of the speaker's message; Goddard, 1998: 18) for WHAT-*d'you-call-it* [is]:

> (2)   WHAT-*d'you-call-it*:
> - Something
> - I can't say the word for this thing now
> - By saying WHAT-*d'you-call-it* I think you'll know what I'm thinking of.

The details of this definition account for restrictions on the usage of the expression. First, Mary had to be talking about *something*, which best refers to objects [. . .] [(be they count nounts or mass nouns)] [. . .] That WHAT-*d'you-call-it* should refer to 'something' accounts for its relative oddity (but not necessarily infelicity) in place of adjectives, and especially in place of inflected verbs and determiners:

> (3)[1]   ?Mary said she would WHAT-*d'you-call-it* the council on John's behalf.

[. . .]

Second, [. . .] Mary's use of the word WHAT-*d'you-call-it* conveys that she *cannot think of the word* for the thing she wants to refer to [. . .] This accounts for the following contrast:

> (4)   Where's the WHAT-*d'you-call-it*?. . . you know, the chuck key?

> (5)   *Where's the chuck key?. . . you know, the WHAT-*d'you-call-it*?

In (4), the speaker at first cannot think of the word, and then is able to be more specific a moment later when the word comes to mind. This represents a natural and common flow of events. Example (5) presents the opposite sequence, which does not make sense, as predicted by (2). The speaker who utters WHAT-*d'you-call-it* in (5) obviously *can* think of the word for the thing she is thinking of, since she has just uttered it.

Third, [. . .] in saying WHAT-*d'you-call-it* the speaker conveys that she assumes the addressee knows (or *can* know) what she is thinking of once she has said the word. Given the context of her utterance in (1), Mary can quite well make this assumption of John. However, if John were somewhere on the other side of town, with no idea of what Mary was doing, and she called him on the telephone and uttered the string in (1) with no contextual set-up [. . .] communication would fail.

Task B3.4.1

> ➤   Enfield claims that WHAT-*d'you-call-it* refers to 'something' the label for which S 'can't recall' at the time of utterance, and that by saying WHAT-*d'you-call-it* S thinks H will know what she's thinking of. Enfield maintains that this also applies 'mutatis mutandis, to WHAT's-her-name and WHAT's-his-name'. Do you

think this is true? For example, when you use these non-specific phrases, do you always assume that your interlocutor will know who you are thinking of? If not, does this undermine Enfield's argument that such phrases are semantic (because of having conventionalized meanings)?

NOTE

1 From this point onwards, the numbering of the examples differs from the original paper.

FURTHER READING

We recommend that you read Jaszczolt's (2010) overview of the semantics-pragmatics interface in its entirety, and also read Huang's (2007) valuable and quite detailed discussion of the same (see especially chapter 7). For a specific (albeit short) discussion of 'pragmatic enrichment' – a phenomenon discussed by Jaszczolt (2010) in some detail – see Meibauer and Steinbach (2011: 5 and 6). Seuren's (1995) classic work, *Western linguistics: an historical introduction*, contains a chapter on presupposition (see chapter 6). Like Stalnaker, Seuren concludes that presupposition is a pragmatic phenomenon. For a critique of the position taken by Stalnaker, we would recommend Atlas' (2004) chapter on 'Presuppositions' in *The handbook of pragmatics*. Levinson's (2004) discussion of 'Deixis' – also in *The handbook of pragmatics* – provides an extremely insightful overview of this particular linguistic phenomenon, as does Marmaridou (2000), in her monograph, *Pragmatic meaning and cognition* (see chapter 4). In addition, chapter 3 of this work covers presupposition. You might find it useful to begin with Marmaridou's (2010) overview of 'Presupposition' in Cummings' (2010) *Pragmatics encyclopedia* prior to reading any of the more detailed accounts highlighted here, however, as the arguments they contain tend to be quite complex.

LOOKING AHEAD

We return to the notion of a semantics-pragmatics interface in Unit C3: specifically, we discuss some studies which have been undertaken by experimental pragmaticians. If you are not very familiar with this particular approach, we would recommend that you familiarize yourself with the chapters in Noveck and Sperber's (2004) edited collection, *Experimental pragmatics*. Given that the studies we discuss in Unit C3 also touch directly upon the notion of implicature, we further recommend that you reread Units A5 and B5 before attempting these tasks.

Unit B4
Speech acts: doing things with words

B4.1 INTRODUCTION

When we talk we do something with language. However speech acts can be of different kinds. They can be creative, i.e. created ad hoc in the communication situation or they can be routinized, i.e. they come in a more or less fixed form. Thus for example speech acts such as greetings, thanks, apologies have a fixed form and are processed as units rather than word for word. We can recognize a routinized speech act such as thanking from the fact that it contains *thank* or *thanks*. It might come as a surprise that also compliments are usually routinized and not created spontaneously. The article by Manes and Wolfson (1981) is interesting because it shows empirically that American speakers prefer to express compliments in a routinized form. Manes and Wolfson's article has been followed by a number of studies on compliments using different methodologies and studying compliments both synchronically and diachronically.

In the second extract, Jucker (2009) draws attention to the diversity of methods which have been used to study speech acts. These include, for example, the ethnographic methods used by Manes and Wolfson and techniques involving informants such as discourse completion tasks and role-plays. The different methods are discussed from the point of view of their strengths and weaknesses.

The last extract in this unit (Eisenstein and Bodman 1993) illustrates the use of the discourse completion task to collect examples of thanking. This test enables researchers to have control of the data and has therefore been the predominant methodology in cross-linguistic studies and in studies comparing native and non-native speakers' production and understanding of speech acts such as requests and apologies.

B4.2 MANES AND WOLFSON (1981)

Manes and Wolfson analysed compliments collected by the authors or by students in 1977–8 through observation of a variety of speech situations. Their analysis showed that syntactically, semantically and functionally compliments in American English are formulaic (routinized). They have a fixed syntactic form and they are appropriate in particular social situations.

J. Manes and N. Wolfson (1981) 'The compliment formula'. In F. Coulmas (ed.) *Conversational routine. Explorations in standardized communication situations and prepatterned speech.* **The Hague: Mouton de Gruyter, pp. 115–32.**

Text B4.2.1
J. Manes and
N. Wolfson

The semantic formula

It is obvious that since compliments are expressions of positive evaluation, every compliment must include at least one term which carried positive semantic load. What is interesting is that, despite the almost unlimited number of terms which may be chosen, the overwhelming majority of compliments contain one of a highly restricted, set of adjectives and verbs.

The range of adjectives which can be used in compliments is enormous. In our data alone we find no fewer than seventy-two different adjectives. Some are topic specific (*delicious, curly*) while others are extremely general (*nice, beautiful, fantastic*); some are quite strong in their expression of positive evaluation (*fantastic, gorgeous, stupendous*) while others carry a much weaker semantic load (*nice, good*). Out of this wide variety of terms, however, only a very few occur with any degree of regularity. Not surprisingly, *nice* and *good*, with their weak semantic load, are by far the most common. Of the six hundred and eighty-six compliments in our data there are five hundred and forty-six in which the positive semantic load is carried by an adjective. Of these, one hundred and twenty-five, or 22.9 per cent, make use of *nice* and another one hundred and seven, or 19.6 per cent, use *good* [. . .]

[T]hree other adjectives, *beautiful, pretty* and *great*, appear in more than 5 per cent of adjectival compliments. *Pretty* and *beautiful* occur in 9.7 per cent and 9.2 per cent of such compliments respectively, while *great* occurs in 6.2 per cent.

    (7)   That's such a pretty sweater.
    (8)   You did a beautiful job of explaining that.
    (9)   That book you lent me was great. It was great. What an ending!

Thus two thirds of all adjectival compliments make use of only five adjectives. In the other one third (one hundred and fifty-six compliments) we find a total of sixty-seven different adjectives, most occurring only once or twice.

The fact that we find only seventy-two different positive adjectives in our corpus does not, by any means, imply that these are the only adjectives which occur in compliments. Indeed, we are certain that further research would uncover a much greater variety of adjectives than that so far collected. What the figures presented here suggest is that, although the possible choice of complimentary adjectives is very great, speakers prefer to use one of a very restricted set of semantically vague adjectives. The compliments thus created are, to all intents and purposes, semantic formulas.

    [. . .]

In contrast to the wide range of semantically positive adjectives found, only a very few semantically positive verbs appear in compliments. The only such verbs which occur in our corpus are *like, love, admire, enjoy* and *be impressed by*. This limited set of verbs, moreover, forms a pattern of usage similar to but even more striking than that of adjectives: just two verbs, *like* and *love*, occur in 86 per cent of all compliments which contain a semantically positive verb. As with adjectives, most other positive verbs occur only once or twice in our data. Here again we find speakers making use of what amounts to a semantic formula: I *like/love* NP.

Text B4.2.1
J. Manes and
N. Wolfson

Although 96 per cent of the data consist of compliments using semantically positive adjectives and verbs, other forms which are clearly intended and interpreted as compliments do occur [. . .] Another semantic pattern which deserves notice is the use of intensifiers. As can be seen from the example so far cited, *really* and other intensifiers are quite common in compliments, occurring in over one third of our data. We have noted above that verbs which are not verbs of liking normally occur with intensifiers (see examples 13 and 14). Furthermore, *quite a* and *some* appear in compliments in what would normally be the adjective position:

(19) That's quite a record collection you've got.
(20) That's some birthday cake.

This suggests that intensifiers, perhaps because of their frequent association with clearly complimentary terms, can themselves function as semantically positive items. Although they are by no means a necessary part of the compliment formula, intensifiers occur frequently enough to be considered a typical feature of compliments.

Another typical feature of compliments is the use of certain deictic elements, specifically second person pronouns and demonstratives:

(21) That's a sharp suit and tie you're wearing.
(22) I love your skirt and your blouse.
(23) That's a nice piece of work.
(24) Wow, you've got a great apartment.
(25) This is pretty.

The use of these elements is related to the fact, discussed below, that compliments are typically independent of the utterances which precede them. If a compliment appears as an aside in the middle of a conversation or, as is frequently the case, begins the conversation, the listener may well be confused as to the intended object of the compliment. The purpose of deixis in compliments, then, is to identify clearly the person or object to be complimented. The reason deictic elements are not invariably part of compliments is that identification may be accomplished through other means. We have many examples in our data in which the object of the compliment is identified by the verbal or nonverbal context. However, second person pronouns and demonstratives occur in 75 per cent of all compliments in our data. Furthermore, in 40 per cent of the cases in which there is no deixis, the compliment is preceded by another compliment which does include such an element, or the object of the compliment is actually named:

(26) Mary, I like that coat on you. It looks just super.
(27) I love your skirt, Betty. It's very attractive.
(28) Mmm. The chocolate sauce is good.

Thus deixis in compliments, in the form of second person pronouns and demonstratives, may be seen to serve an extremely important discourse function.

Task B4.2.1

➤ Reread the Manes and Wolfson excerpt, focusing in particular on the way(s) in which Manes and Wolfson use the notion semantic formula. What are the most frequent adjectives used in the formula? What are the most frequent verbs? What other features are typical of the formula?

➤ Manes and Wolfson define compliments as 'expressions of positive evaluation'. To what extent does their definition make it difficult to distinguish compliments from flattery, praise, appreciation? Discuss how these speech acts may be distinguished from each other (you might find it helpful to draw from the A and B sections relating to Unit 8 as well as Unit A4).

➤ Manes and Wolfson based their study of compliments on field notes (participant observation) and statistics. What are the limitations of the approach suggested by Manes and Wolfson? What other possible approaches are there to studying compliments?

B4.3 JUCKER (2009)

Many types of data have been used to study the realization of speech acts such as questionnaires, role-plays, ethnographic data and corpora. The different methodologies are discussed at length in Unit A2. Manes and Wolfson (Text B4.2.1 above) used an ethnographic method based on observation of everyday interaction. In the extract below, Jucker discusses the limitations and problems of the ethnographic method, when studying compliments.

A. Jucker (2009) 'Speech act research between armchair, field and laboratory. The case of compliments'. *Journal of Pragmatics* 41: 1621–5.

Text B4.3.1
A. Jucker

[. . .]

How are compliments realized? Are there typical syntactic patterns? Are there typical adjectives? Are there other features that typically occur in compliments?

Manes and Wolfson (1981: 115) open their seminal paper on compliments with the observation that "one of the most striking facts of compliments in American English is their almost total lack of originality". By this they refer both to the syntactic patterns and to the range of adjectives that are being used in compliments. They base their claim on data collected by the notebook method. They collected 686 compliment sequences in a large range of speech situations in which they participated or which they observed, and they made sure that the complimenters and the recipients of the compliments were both men and women and represented different educational and social backgrounds.

According to their data the positive evaluation of the compliments is regularly carried by an adjective with a positive semantic load, but only a few different adjectives

173

are used for this purpose. The two most frequent ones are *nice* and *good*. In addition to these only three more appear regularly: *beautiful*, *pretty* and *great*. They also present a range of syntactic patterns that occur regularly in their data.

[. . .]

These results have been replicated by Holmes (1988: 453, 1995: 128), who finds that the same syntactic patterns dominate her notebook data of New Zealand compliments.

There are, however, several problems connected with this method. First, the method depends on researchers or research assistants who spot a compliment when they see one. This may seem to be a trivial point, but in real conversations, the researcher's attention may momentarily be absorbed by other things and a compliment may easily pass unnoticed. There is no possibility to go back and listen to the conversation again. It seems likely that researchers are more alert to stereotypical compliments, and, therefore, compliments that fit their preconceived ideas of what a compliment should look like are more likely to be included in the collection. This makes it less likely that unusual patterns are attested in the data.

And second, the method depends on the researcher's memory because he or she often notes down the compliment a considerable time after the event. It is plausible to assume that they may reliably remember the general content of the compliment but not the actual wording. Thus they may reproduce the compliment in a more stereotypical manner than it was originally uttered.

Yuan (2001: 287–288) provides empirical evidence for this. On one occasion of her research, she interviewed two elderly ladies and tape-recorded the interaction. She also took field notes and wrote down the compliments in the typical fashion of the notebook method. After transcribing the tape-recorded interaction, she could analyse the differences between the field notes and the transcription, and – as her examples show – they were quite considerable. Extracts (28) and (29) give only the translation of the interaction but not the Chinese original.

(28) [Field note data, Respondent 82-F-O-H]
Researcher: In fact, you don't look old at all. (You) don't have any wrinkles on your face.
Respondent: Yeah. I just turned 49 this year. (Yuan, 2001: 288)

(29) [The actual exchange in the transcription]
Researcher: You also look very young (Particle)
Respondent: But I've only retired for a little over a year. I'm 49.
Researcher: Gosh, you look very young. (You) don't have any wrinkles. (Yuan, 2001: 288)

The field notes failed to record one significant turn, and they failed to record the respondent's information about having retired. The compliment, which in the transcription is spread out over two turns, is merged into one in the field notes. Yuan concludes on this basis:

It seems, then, that what can be recorded accurately in field notes are the topics of compliments and information about interlocutors. Some supportive moves such as elaboration and explanations may fail to be recorded in field notes through the loss of turns. In addition, the actual wording may not be totally reliable.

(Yuan, 2001: 288)

[. . .]

A corpus search for speech acts depends on the availability of typical conventionalized patterns for a particular speech act. Deutschmann (2003), for instance, found that apologies regularly include expressions such as *sorry, pardon, excuse*, which allow the identification of many, perhaps even most, apologies in a large computerized corpus, such as the BNC. For compliments this is more difficult since compliments are less conventionalized than apologies. They do not display standard illocutionary indicating devices.

Text B4.3.1
A. Jucker

Task B4.3.1

➤ The different research methods which can be used to discuss speech acts are subsumed in the article under the headings 'armchair', 'field' and 'laboratory'. The corpus method fits under the heading 'field' and involves looking for conventionalized patterns which are defined by the analyst from the outset. What are the advantages of using corpora to analyse speech acts rather than experimental methods? It is possible that different speech acts require different methods. Thanking and apologizing, for example, lend themselves to corpus investigations. What about speech acts such as complaining or invitations?

➤ Assuming that there is not an ideal method to study speech acts discuss how we could combine different methods (armchair, field/corpus and laboratory) to analyse speech act routines (e.g. requests and apologies).

B4.4 EISENSTEIN AND BODMAN (1993)

The following excerpt describes the use of gratitude by native speakers of American English. Gratitude phrases are used in a large number of situations to foster interpersonal relationships such as intimacy and rapport or because they are expected or appropriate in a certain situation. The excerpt is based on a questionnaire (discourse completion test) describing a number of situations designed to elicit the expression of gratitude.

M. Eisenstein and J. Bodman (1993) 'Expressing gratitude in American English'. In G. Kasper and S. Blum-Kulka (eds) *Interlanguage pragmatics*. Oxford: Oxford University Press, pp. 64–81.

Text B4.4.1
M. Eisenstein
and J. Bodman

We began investigating how gratitude is expressed by observing its use in natural contexts by native speakers of American English. Data were either audiotaped and transcribed at a later time or written down as field notes. We focused on only those utterances whose illocutionary force was that of gratitude in response to receiving a gift, favor, reward or service. Fifty situations were identified in which expressions of gratitude occurred. These ranged from short, formulaic expressions that appeared to be highly ritualized to intricate and lengthy interchanges conveying deeply felt emotions. As a result of a series of pilot studies, we constructed a questionnaire containing

Text B4.4.1
M. Eisenstein
and J. Bodman

fourteen of these situations designed to elicit expressions of gratitude. The pilot studies revealed the importance of describing the roles and relationships of the interlocutors in the questionnaire in detail as well as carefully describing specific contexts for the situations; we found that small changes in these variables significantly affected the nature of the responses. Fifty-six native speakers of American English, representing both males and females, a range of ages, diverse social backgrounds, and natives of a variety of regions within the United States, were asked to write responses to each of the fourteen situations.

[. . .]

Some of these items produced phatic, ritualized responses, such as brief comments to a bus driver (Item 2), a cashier (Item 5), a garage attendant (Item 13), and a friend handing over a newspaper (Item 12).

[. . .]

Some other items on the questionnaire produced relatively short, but more creative responses than those described above. Swift thanking followed by a single brief comment was typical for Item 6 (a friend bringing attention to a bit of food on a diner's face) and Item 8 (thanking a spouse for spontaneously helping around the house). Typically, our respondents felt (although a great more could have been said) that comments like:

Thanks. You're a sweetheart.

(coded as Thanking + Expressing Affection) and

Thanks. That was really nice of you.

(coded as Thanking + Complimenting the Giver) were sufficient in recognizing a spouse's thoughtfulness.

The remaining items elicited and seemed to require much more complex and lengthy expressions of gratitude. These were most successfully analyzed as speech act sets (Cohen & Olshtain, 1981), groups of semantic formulae that together achieve the appropriate language for a particular situation. In appreciation for a generously offered $500 loan, a characteristic response was:

You're a lifesaver. Thanks. I'll never forget it. You really can't imagine what this means to me.

(coded as Complimenting the Person/ Action + Thanking + Expressing Indebtedness + Expressing an Inability to Articulate Deep Feelings). Our respondents, when interviewed later, indicated that in these situations gratitude was much more challenging to express. It was not uncommon for the respondents to state with humility that their linguistic skills were inadequate for the task. American native speakers, rating the appropriateness of the utterances, found humbling admissions such as this not only expressed the depth of the feelings in a satisfactory manner, but also adequately expressed gratitude.

It is useful to consider two characteristics that Goffman (1967) describes that are operant in social interactions—"demeanor" and "deference"—in order to understand the complex linguistic task speakers face. "Demeanor" refers to the social desirability of an individual reflected through his or her appearance and behavior. "Deference" is the appreciation an individual exhibits to another through his or her

Text B4.4.1
M. Eisenstein
and J. Bodman

words and actions. Expressing gratitude requires that the recipient of a gift, favor, or service exhibit both proper demeanor and proper deference in situations in which he or she is feeling especially vulnerable. The recipient must show humility and gratitude without losing dignity and control. The giver must remain sensitive to the needs of the receiver and also behave with adequate deference and demeanor. The struggle to find the words and exhibit acceptable demeanor and deference that are mutually satisfactory is highly challenging. In addition, the difficulty of the task is further compounded by the fact that both demeanor and deference in expressing gratitude are culturally bound and, hence, difficult to translate from one sociolinguistic context to another.

The lengthiest speech act sets were produced by situations that caused the recipient to feel unusually grateful or indebted to the giver. None of the individual semantic formulas constituting a set could be identified as more salient or of a higher order than the others. Instead, the members of each set interacted synergistically to express gratitude appropriately. Furthermore, the functions within the speech act set did not appear in a fixed order. The direct expression of thanking, for example, could be stated at the beginning, the middle, or the end of the set.

While greater emotion sometimes provoked longer speech act sets, this did not occur when there was considerable social distance between interlocutors. Item 4 (a vice president of personnel offers a relatively new employee a raise) elicited surprisingly brief expressions of gratitude. This confirms one aspect of Wolfson's Bulge Theory (1989), identifying brevity in communications between socially distant interlocutors. However, we did not find in all cases the terseness that Wolfson (1989) identified in communications among intimates. While the situation in which a spouse is helpful around the house did produce a brief response, the situations involving gift giving and loaning a large amount of money evinced quite lengthy responses despite the intimacy of the interlocutor relationship.

Our data revealed that, although speakers are free to say anything they wish in expressing gratitude (and there were occasional examples of highly creative speech act sets), most speakers seemed to draw from a finite pool of conventionalized expressions and ideas. Within the speech act set of expressing gratitude for a gift, many native respondents referred to the lack of necessity for such generosity by using expressions such as "Oh, you shouldn't have" and "You didn't have to." In accepting the loan, native speakers stated their inability to express their appreciation sufficiently:

God, I don't know how to thank you.
I can't tell you how much I appreciate this.
I can't thank you enough.
I can't tell you what this means to me.

Task B4.4.1

> Notice that thanking can be expressed in many different ways. There are 'terse' expressions as well as intensified gratitude expressions of thanking. In addition, there are semantic sets or sequences where not all components need to express thanking. Give some examples of such sets and situations in which they are appropriate.

➤ Why can the situation of thanking be described as vulnerable? How is this description related to Goffman's analysis of the social situation in terms of 'demeanor' and 'deference'?

➤ Wolfson's 'Bulge Theory' suggests that speech acts such as thanking occur more frequently between friends than between acquaintances. How do Eisenstein and Bodman's results either confirm or disconfirm the Bulge Theory?

FURTHER READING

A number of speech act accounts will reward further investigation. For example, Aijmer (1996), Deutschmann (2003) and Adolphs (2008) all adopt a corpus-based approach: Aijmer investigates thanking, apologizing and requesting as routines in the London-Lund Corpus; Adolphs explores the realizations of the speech act of suggesting in a number of spoken corpora (including CANCODE); Deutschmann explores apologies using the BNC. Blum-Kulka *et al.* (1989a) also study apologies and requests. In their well-known Cross-Cultural Speech Act Realization Project (CCSARP), however, the approach adopted is one of discourse completion tasks (see Unit A2.2.4.1). Trosborg (1995) also adopts an intercultural perspective: she investigates the communicative acts of complaining and apologizing among learners and native speakers (as well as discussing the teaching of communicative functions to foreign learners). Additional non-English studies include Golato (2005). Golato's interest is German compliments, and the approach adopted is conversation analysis. Speech acts in the history of English are studied in an edited volume by Jucker and Taavitsainen (2008). Some of these touch on issues of politeness and impoliteness and, in so doing, draw on Jucker and Taavitsainen's (2000) notion of 'pragmatic space' (discussed in Unit A11.4) rather than a strict Searlean-based account (see Unit A4). Eemeren and Grootendorst (1984) are also interested in facework issues. However, they expand (rather than reject) Searle's theory of speech acts by stressing that when speakers perform an illocutionary act they do so in order to get a response. The authors have further developed Searle's notion of perlocutionary acts by introducing a distinction between inherent perlocutionary effects and consecutive perlocutionary consequences. Last but not least, we recommend Labov and Fanshel (1977), who suggest that the crucial speech acts needed to establish coherence in conversation are not requests and assertions, for example, but, rather, challenges and defences.

LOOKING AHEAD

In Unit C2 you have the opportunity to further explore speech act patterns on the basis of corpus data. In Unit B11 you can also acquaint yourself with Taavitsainen and Jucker's (2008b) historical analysis of English compliments. Compliments are closely related to insults which are studied in a historical perspective in Unit A11 (Jucker and Taavitsainen 2000). The relation between speech acts and politeness is further discussed in Unit A8.

Unit B5
Implicature

B5.1 INTRODUCTION

The three readings in this section highlight a progression of ideas in regard to implicature. We begin with an extract from H. Paul Grice's canonical work, 'Logic and conversation', in which Grice (1989) outlines the motivation for his Cooperative Principle (CP). Our second extract in this section is taken from Geoffrey Leech's (1981) *Semantics* monograph. As will become clear, Leech accepts Grice's approach to implicature, by and large. However, he argues for a Politeness Principle (PP) to complement Grice's CP, as a means of giving the latter explanatory power. Simply put, Leech believes his PP can explain why people sometimes opt to implicate their intended message and hence violate the CP (cf. Grice's focus which involves explaining *how* participants violate the CP). Leech's reading as it is reproduced here also intimates his belief that the PP is, in fact, a higher order principle than the CP: this is something Leech makes much more explicit in his 1983 work, when he argues that the aim of the PP is 'to maintain the social equilibrium and the friendly relations which enable us to assume that our interlocutors are being cooperative in the first place' (p. 82). Our final reading in this section is taken from Deirdre Wilson's (2010) encyclopedic entry on 'Relevance Theory' (in the Routledge *Pragmatics encyclopedia*). As we highlighted in Unit A5.3, relevance theorists are not interested in producing 'rational reconstructions of how a speaker's meaning *might be* inferred'. Rather, their aim 'is to produce a psychologically plausible theory of communication' by documenting 'empirical hypotheses about what actually goes on in hearers' minds' (Wilson 2010: 393). An inferencing process guided by the CP and multiple maxims is therefore rejected by them, and replaced by a cognitive approach to implicature whereby H is said to interpret every act of ostensive communication as having at least minimal relevance to him/her such that it is worthy of his/her processing effort. Wilson's reading (as it is reproduced here) explains in some detail the two Principles of Relevance which are said to underpin Relevance Theory: the Cognitive Principle (i.e. cognition on a general level) and the Communicative Principle (i.e. the notion that participants will always try to find meaning).

B5.2 GRICE (1989)

Grice originally delivered the work from which this excerpt is taken, 'Logic and conversation', as part of his 1967 William James Lecture series. We focus specifically on Grice's discussion regarding which of the Maxims was the most important, in his view, and why.

Text B5.2.1
H. P. Grice

H.P. Grice (1989) 'Logic and conversation' [1967]. Reprinted in *Studies in the way of words*. Cambridge, MA and London: Harvard University Press, pp. 22–57.

Our talk exchanges do not normally consist of a succession of disconnected remarks, and would not be rational if they did. They are characteristically [. . .] cooperative efforts; and each participant recognizes in them [. . .] a common purpose or set of purposes, or at least a mutually accepted direction. This purpose or direction may be fixed from the start (e.g., by an initial proposal of a question for discussion), or it may evolve during the exchange; it may be fairly definite, or it may be so indefinite as to leave very considerable latitude to the participants (as in a casual conversation). But at each stage, *some* possible conversational moves would be excluded as conversationally unsuitable. We might then formulate a rough general principle which participants will be expected (ceteris paribus) to observe, namely: Make your conversational contribution such as is required, at the stage at which it occurs, by the accepted purpose or direction of the talk exchange in which you are engaged. One might label this the Cooperative Principle.

On the assumption that some such general principle as this is acceptable, one may perhaps distinguish four categories under one or another of which will fall certain more specific maxims and submaxims [. . .] I call these categories Quantity, Quality, Relation, and Manner.

[. . .]

It is obvious that the observance of some of these maxims is a matter of less urgency than is the observance of others; a man who has expressed himself with undue prolixity would, in general, be open to milder comment than would a man who has said something he believes to be false. Indeed, it might be felt that the importance of at least the first maxim of Quality is such that it should not be included in a scheme of the kind I am constructing; other maxims come into operation only on the assumption that this maxim of Quality is satisfied. While this may be correct, so far as the generation of implicatures is concerned it seems to play a role not totally different from the other maxims, and it will be convenient, for the present at least, to treat it as a member of the list of maxims.

There are, of course, all sorts of other maxims (aesthetic, social, or moral in character), such as "Be polite," that are also normally observed by participants in talk exchanges, and these may also generate nonconventional implicatures [. . .]

Task B5.2.1

➤ Grice's notion of 'cooperative interaction' equates to a willingness, on the part of interlocutors, to participate in a talk exchange, regardless of whether they have or share the same goal(s). Indeed, they could be having an argument, yet still be cooperating in a Gricean sense. Write down instances where you have found yourself to be 'in conflict' with someone, yet have continued to 'cooperate' in the Gricean sense of continuing the talk exchange.

- Identify instances where you've *flouted* the maxims identified by Grice –
  Quantity, Quality, Relation, Manner (see Units A5.1.3–A5.1.4) – for
  example, by exaggerating, using irony or bringing in seemingly irrelevant
  information.
- Identify instances where you've *violated* the maxims, that is, broken the
  maxims covertly such that your interlocutors do not know to look for
  'hidden' meanings (cf. Unit A5.1.4).

B5.3 LEECH (1981)

Leech's work on implicature extends 'Grice's concept of conversational implicature
to include other principles, apart from the CP, and in particular to include a
Politeness Principle'. As we have already outlined Leech's PP in Unit A5.2.1, and
discussed the PP in some depth in Unit A8.4, we focus here on Leech's explanation
of how the PP and CP work together such that we understand *Will/Can you open
the window?* as a polite request. The excerpt (brief though it is) also points to the
influence of Searle (1975: 74), who had earlier argued that politeness was the 'chief
motivation – though not the only motivation – for using . . . indirect forms' of
directives.

**G. Leech (1981) *Semantics: the study of meaning*. Second Edition.
Harmondsworth: Penguin Books, pp. 338–9.**

Text B5.3.1
G. Leech

Both Grice, in his account of conversational implicature, and Searle, in his account of
indirect illocutions, allude to politeness as an important factor omitted from their
analyses [. . .] I propose that the most promising approach to indirect illocutions is to
extend Grice's concept of conversational implicature to include other principles, apart
from the CP, and in particular to include a Politeness Principle. We can then include
in our account of pragmatics not only what means exist in a given language for making
particular illocutionary acts [. . .] but an explanation of why it is that certain semantic
types of structure are appropriately used for particular illocutionary purposes. Thus
the interpretation of a question such as *Will/Can you open the window?* as a polite request
might be roughly spelt out, in terms of Gricean implicature, as follows (cf. Searle
1975):

> S has asked me whether I am willing/able to perform X. This question, interpreted
> most directly as a request for information, is irrelevant to the conversation
> (Maxim of Relation). Therefore there must be some more relevant, less direct
> interpretation of this question. Now, this question is relevant if S wants me to
> do X. It is relevant, because one of the pre-conditions for my doing X is that I
> should be willing/able to do X. Moreover, if S is observing the Politeness Principle
> to the required degree and is assuming that I am also observing the Politeness
> Principle, this is as precise and perspicuous a way as any of getting me to do X
> (Politeness Principle, Maxims of Quantity and Manner). Therefore, the most
> natural assumption is that S has uttered *Will/can you X?* in order to get me to
> do X.

Text B5.3.1
G. Leech

We do not have to suppose that such a laborious piece of reasoning goes on in a hearer's mind whenever an indirect illocution is interpreted. The main point, as Grice affirms, is that the implicature should be 'capable of being worked out' – that it is a rational and interpretable thing to say, given the purposes of the conversation, and the need to observe pragmatic principles such as the CP and the Politeness Principle.

The essence of the Politeness Principle is, in its positive aspect, 'Give credit to the other person', and in its negative aspect, 'Do not cause offence to the other person'. This establishes an asymmetry between speaker and hearer, such that what is polite to the hearer is in some degree impolite to the speaker, and vice versa. A *polite belief* is one that gives credit to the hearer, and an *impolite belief* is one that indicates credit to the speaker or indicates discredit or cost to the hearer. Hence a statement such as *You will open the window* or a command such as *Open the window* express impolite beliefs, and it is advisable for the speaker to adopt some more indirect tactic of getting the message across, if he wants the hearer to perform such an action. In this light, we may think of pragmatics as involving problem-solving strategies both for the speaker and for the hearer. Pragmatics cannot be reduced to rule, but at least through such techniques of analysis as are suggested by Grice's notion of conversational implicature, we can partially explain, in rational terms, aspects of language behaviour which would otherwise seem perplexing and haphazard.

Task B5.3.1

> Do you agree with Leech's statement that *You will open the window* and *Open the window* 'express impolite beliefs', and hence that it's 'advisable for the speaker to adopt some more indirect tactic of getting the message across, if he wants the hearer to perform such an action'? What kind of indirect utterances might S use to achieve his/her aim? Are such utterances more 'polite' than the direct utterances above – or does their level of im/politeness depend on the context of utterance, the roles of the interlocutors, the power a/symmetry between them, their cultural norms, etc.? For example, if a visitor hinted that the window needed to be closed by asking you for a blanket, would you feel that they were being impolite or polite? Can other non-verbal tactics be used to communicate the same message (of wanting the window closed)? For example, what if your guest opted to shiver overtly? Issues relevant to this particular task are covered in Units A8–10, A12 and C6.

B5.4 WILSON (2010)

We have discussed earlier how relevance theorists have replaced Grice's CP and its attendant maxims with two Principles of Relevance (see Unit B5.1 above and also Unit A5.3). Wilson outlines these principles in some detail for you. She also discusses an inferencing heuristic. Based on the Communicative Principle ('every utterance conveys a presumption of its own optimal relevance'), the inference heuristic seeks to show how H will follow 'a path of least effort' and 'stop at the first overall interpretation that satisfies the expectations of relevance that the utterance itself has raised'. H can act in this way, according to Wilson, because S 'is expected (within the limits of his or her abilities and preferences) to have made the utterance as easy as possible for [H] to understand'.

D. Wilson (2010) 'Relevance Theory'. In L. Cummings (ed.) *The pragmatics encyclopedia*. London and New York: Routledge, pp. 393–7.

Text B5.4.1
D. Wilson

A fundamental problem for human cognition is that at any point in our waking lives, a huge variety of potential inputs are competing for our attention [. . .] The central claim of relevance theory is that, as a result of constant selection pressures, the human cognitive system has developed a variety of dedicated (innate or acquired) mental mechanisms or biases which tend to allocate attention to inputs with the greatest expected relevance, and process them in the most relevance-enhancing way. This claim is expressed in the First, or Cognitive, Principle of Relevance (Sperber and Wilson 1995: 260–6):

> *Cognitive Principle of Relevance*
> Human cognition tends to be geared to the maximization of relevance.

It follows from the Cognitive Principle that the human cognitive system is capable (at least to some extent) of monitoring expected cognitive effects and processing effort and allocating resources in such a way that a competing potential input is helped by a comparatively high level of expected effect and hindered by a comparatively high level of expected effort. As a result, the spontaneous working of our perceptual mechanisms tends to pick out the most relevant potential inputs, the spontaneous working of our memory retrieval mechanisms tends to activate the most relevant potential contextual assumptions, and the spontaneous working of our inferential mechanisms tends to yield the most relevant conclusions.

 [. . .]

The Cognitive Principle of Relevance has important consequences for pragmatics. In order to communicate, a speaker needs the addressee's attention. If attention tends automatically to go to what is most relevant at the time, then the success of communication depends on the addressee taking the utterance to be relevant enough to be worthy of his or her attention. Thus, a speaker, by the very act of communicating, indicates that the addressee is intending to see the utterance as relevant enough to be worth processing, and this is what the Communicative Principle of Relevance states (Sperber and Wilson 1995: 266–78):

> *Communicative Principle of Relevance*
> Every utterance conveys a presumption of its own optimal relevance.

The Communicative Principle of Relevance is a law-like generalization about what happens when an utterance is addressed to someone. It is not a rule or maxim that speakers are expected to follow, but which they may occasionally violate (e.g. because of a clash with other maxims, or in order to trigger an implicature, as in Grice's account of figurative utterances). Relevance theorists have consistently argued that the very act of communicating creates precise and predictable expectations of relevance, which are enough on their own to guide the hearer towards the speaker's meaning. In this framework, there is no essential connection between (real or apparent) maxim violation and the derivation of implicatures, and many of Grice's examples must be reanalyzed (on clashes, *see* Sperber and Wilson 1995: 272–6; on blatant maxim violation, *see* Wilson and Sperber 2002; *see also* Sperber and Wilson 1995: 158–63).

The presumption of optimal relevance mentioned in the Communicative Principle has a precise content. The addressee is entitled to presume that the utterance is at least relevant enough to be worth processing. This follows directly from the Cognitive Principle. If attention and processing resources are automatically allocated to inputs with the greatest expected relevance, then the speaker manifestly intends the addressee to presume that the utterance is more relevant than other inputs competing for his or her attention at the time. In many circumstances, the hearer can also presume that the speaker has aimed higher than this. The speaker wants to be understood. An utterance is most likely to be understood when it simplifies the hearer's task by demanding as little effort from him or her as possible, and encourages the hearer to pay it due attention by offering him or her as much effect as possible. It is therefore manifestly in the speaker's interest for the addressee to expect not merely relevance enough, but as much relevance as is compatible with the speaker's abilities and preferences, and this is what the presumption of optimal relevance states (Sperber and Wilson 1995: 266–78):

Presumption of optimal relevance
a. The utterance is at least relevant enough to be worth processing.
b. It is the most relevant one compatible with the speaker's abilities and preferences.

The Communicative Principle and the definition of optimal relevance ground the following practical heuristic for inferring the speaker's meaning (Sperber and Wilson 2002; Wilson and Sperber 2002):

Relevance-guided comprehension heuristic
a. Follow a path of least effort in constructing an interpretation of the utterance (and in particular in resolving ambiguities and referential indeterminacies, adjusting lexical meaning, supplying contextual assumptions, deriving implicatures, etc.).
b. Stop when your expectations of relevance are satisfied.

A hearer using this heuristic should proceed in the following way. The aim is to find an interpretation that satisfies the presumption of optimal relevance. To achieve this, the decoded sentence meaning must be enriched at the explicit level, and complemented at the implicit level by supplying contextual assumptions which will combine with it to yield enough cognitive effects to make the utterance relevant in the expected way. What route should a hearer follow in disambiguating, assigning reference, adjusting lexical meaning, constructing a context, deriving contextual implications, etc.? According to the relevance-guided comprehension heuristic, the hearer should follow a path of least effort, and stop at the first overall interpretation that satisfies the expectations of relevance that the utterance itself has raised.

What makes it reasonable for the hearer to follow a path of least effort is that the speaker is expected (within the limits of his or her abilities and preferences) to have made the utterance as easy as possible for the hearer to understand. Since relevance varies inversely with effort, the very fact that an interpretive hypothesis is easily accessible gives it an initial degree of plausibility (an epistemic advantage specific to communicated information).

What makes it reasonable for the hearer to stop at the first interpretation which satisfies the expectations of relevance raised by the utterance is that a speaker who knowingly produced an utterance with two or more significantly different interpretations, each yielding the expected level of cognitive effect, would put the hearer to the gratuitous extra effort of choosing among them, and the resulting interpretation (if any) would not satisfy clause (b) of the presumption of optimal relevance. Thus, when a hearer following the path of least effort finds an interpretation that is relevant in the expected way, in the absence of contrary evidence, this is the best possible interpretive hypothesis. Since comprehension is a non-demonstrative inference process, this hypothesis may well be false. This can happen when the speaker formulates the utterance in a way that is inconsistent with the expectations raised, so that the normal inferential routines of comprehension fail. Failures in communication are common enough. What is remarkable and calls for explanation is that communication works at all.

Task B5.4.1

> We have discussed the following adjacency pair from both a Gricean perspective (see Unit A5.1.4) and also a relevance-theoretic perspective (see Unit A5.3).

Peter: Do you want some coffee?
Mary: Coffee would keep me awake.

- Which perspective did you find most convincing? Why?
- In our Gricean account of the above (see Unit A5.1.4), we suggested that Mary's response constituted a flout of the Relation maxim. According to relevance theorists, however, relevance cannot be reduced to a maxim which can be broken. Do you agree with Sperber and Wilson (1995: 142) and other relevance theorists that relevance should be seen as a given, and context should be treated as the variable (cf. Unit A5.3)? Why/why not?

> Do you think that S will always construct their utterance in such a way that it is as easy for the hearer to understand as is possible, as Wilson claims here? When might S not do so?

> To what extent is a focus on H or a focus on S problematic in your view? Do you think Arundale (2008: 243) is right to point out that (implicature) theories should not be based on either speaker intent or hearer perception but, rather, should allow for S and H to mutually 'confirm and modify' their jointly constructed interpretings (cf. Unit A5.4)? What evidence can you provide to support such a view?

FURTHER READING

For extremely useful overviews of implicature, see Horn's (2004) chapter in Horn and Ward's *The handbook of pragmatics*, Huang's chapter in his 2007 book on *Pragmatics* and also Huang's (2010) entry, aptly titled 'Implicature', in Cummings' *Pragmatics encyclopedia*. You will glean a sense of Grice's enormous contribution to pragmatics by reading Chapman's (2005) *Paul Grice, philosopher and linguist*. Wharton's (2010) entry 'H.P. Grice' in *The pragmatics encyclopedia* provides a more succinct yet equally useful summation. Wilson and Sperber's (1981) paper is a good starting point, if you want to learn more about Relevance Theory, as is their monograph, *Relevance* (Sperber and Wilson 1995). Carston's (2002) *Thoughts and utterances* will also reward close scrutiny.

LOOKING AHEAD

In Unit C3, you will learn more about the Neo-Gricean/Post-Gricean debate in respect to the best way of explaining implicatures. In Unit C6, we give you an opportunity to test Leech's PP for yourselves. We would recommend that you read the relevant A and B sections on Facework and Im/politeness (Unit A8 and Unit B8) prior to undertaking this particular exercise, however. This will ensure that you are very familiar with Leech's Politeness approach and also other facework and im/politeness approaches.

Unit B6
Pragmatics and the structure of discourse

B6.1 INTRODUCTION

Conversational structure has been studied both in Discourse Analysis and Conversation Analysis. It is also important not only to show how the conversational organization is built up but to motivate the proposal in pragmatic terms. In this spirit we will look at the motivations for proposing a three-part exchange structure (Initiation-Response-Follow-up; adjacency triplet in Conversation Analysis).

B6.2 TSUI (1994)

One of the conversational patterns we have discussed above is the adjacency pair. Some characteristic pairs are for instance question-answer or request-compliance. The notion adjacency pair suggests a two-part structure. Especially in classroom discourse a pair such as question-answer may be followed by an additional part. Thus, according to Sinclair and Coulthard (1975) a typical classroom discourse consists of an initiating move, a responding move and a follow-up. There has been a lot of discussion about this third conversational move, for example whether it is obligatory and what function it has in the exchange, whether it is text-type specific, and whether it is at home in ritual exchanges only. Mishler (1975), for example, argues that a three-part unit is acceptable in classroom discourse and some interview situations but would be unnatural in natural conversation. Tsui on the other hand argues that a third 'follow-up' move is also found in some non-classroom exchanges and should be regarded as an obligatory structural unit which can be omitted under certain conditions, for example if the speakers know each other well. The follow-up move has the general function of acknowledging or evaluating the outcome of the interaction. However, when we move outside classroom discourse the follow-up move can be shown to have a large number of different functions in addition to evaluation.

A. Tsui (1994) *English conversation.* **Oxford: Oxford University Press, pp. 30–5.**

Functions of the follow-up move

[. . .]

From the above debate, it is apparent that the function of the follow-up move is perceived by some as solely evaluative (e.g. Berry 1981; Burton 1981; Coulthard and Brazil 1981). If providing an evaluation of the correctness of information supplied in the response were indeed the *only* function of this third move, then I would agree with Burton's observation that it seldom occurs outside the classroom. I would also agree with Berry (1981, 1987), and Coulthard and Brazil (1981) that the third move is optional in speech events other than quizzes or puzzle-solving sessions. However, Heritage's study of 'oh'-receipt tokens supports the observation that providing an evaluation is not the *only* function of the follow-up move.

This has also been noted by Mehan (1979: 194) who maintains that the third component in a three-part sequence which occurs in classroom discourse is different from that which occurs in everyday conversations. For example:

(12) [Mehan 1979: 194]
 A: What time is it, Denise?
 B: Two thirty.
→ **A:** Very good, Denise.
(13) [ibid.]
 A: What time is it, Denise?
 B: Two thirty.
→ **A:** Thank you, Denise.

He points out that while the third component in (12) evaluates the content of the response, that in (13) seems to be more an acknowledgement of the previous reply than an evaluation of it.

Berry (1987: 47), on examining three-move exchanges in doctor–patient interviews, revises her initial position, and asserts that third moves of these exchanges are usually different in character from those of classroom exchanges: they do not have an evaluative function. For example:

(14) [Coulthard and Ashby 1976: 80]
 Doctor: How long have you had those for?
 Patient: Well I had'm a week last Wednesday.
→ **Doctor:** A week last Wednesday.
(15) [Coulthard and Montgomery 1981: 21]
 Doctor: How long have you had these quick pains on the right side of your head?
 Patient: Well again when this trouble started.
→ **Doctor:** Again for about two years.

Berry (1987: 84) comments, 'And intuitively, one feels that they are not so much commenting on the quality of the patient's reply as acts of noting and/or reinterpreting the reply for the doctor's own benefit.'

Clearly, the follow-up move has functions other than making an evaluation of the response. An investigation, in the following section, into what these functions are will help us decide whether it is an important element in conversational organization.

[. . .]

From the above examples, we can see that the follow-up move is a very important element of an exchange, not only in classroom discourse, but in conversation as well. It is the element on which further interaction is based. We may say that it has a general function of acknowledging the outcome of the interaction that has taken place in the initiating and the responding moves. As Heritage and Atkinson (1984: 10) observe:

> Any third action, therefore, that implements some normal onward development of a sequence confirms the adequacy of the displayed understandings in the sequence so far. By means of this framework, speakers are released from what would otherwise be the endless task of explicitly confirming and reconfirming their understanding of one another's actions.

In other words, a three-part exchange is the basic unit of organization in conversation. The three moves are related to each other in such a way that each move sets up the expectation of the subsequent move. This does not mean, however, that in all conversational exchanges, the three moves *actually* occur, but rather that whatever occurs will be interpreted in the light of this expectation. As Berry (1981: 38) points out:

> a rule such as A *predicts* B is not to be taken as a claim that A always *will* be followed by B; it is a claim that A will always be *expected* to be followed by B and that whatever does follow A will be interpreted in the light of this expectation.

Hence, when the third move does not occur, we may say, following Sacks (1972: 341), that it is absent. However, as Sacks points out, in order to show that the absence of something is not trivial, that its absence is not just one among a host of other things that might equally be said to be absent, we need to show its *relevance of occurrence*:

> Nontrivial talk of an absence requires that some means be available for showing both the relevance of occurrence of the activity that is proposedly absent and the location where it should be looked for to see that it did not occur. (ibid.: 342)

Task B6.2.1

➤ As we can see from this extract the notion adjacency pair is not without problems. It is for instance not clear whether it represents a two-part or a three-part structure. Intuitions about discourse structure are unreliable and corpus data are of little help. For example, in conversational data we find both two-part and three-part structures. There are in fact several possible endings to a small interchange depending on text-type, how well the speakers know each other, the type of feedback, etc.

➤ The strength of Tsui's argumentation is that there is a pragmatic motivation for the third move in some cases.

- Which is the motivation for the third move?
- What is meant by saying that the third move is 'noticeably absent'?
- Some typical follow-up moves are *oh, ah, all right, okay, really*, each with a separate function. What functions do they have and what generalizations can we make about these functions?

B6.3 STUBBS (1983)

Drew and Heritage (1992) make a distinction between informal and more formal discourse such as interviews or discussions. A news interview, for example, consists of questions and answers associated with speaker roles reflecting the fact that turn allocation is more fixed. In more formal discourse, questions may be introduced by a preface focusing on the topic of the speaker contribution. The hearer or the audience recognize what is said as a preface to something else because of its position at the beginning of the utterance or the larger discourse or their knowledge about the activity. For example, in an interview there is an interviewer introducing the topic that the interviewee is supposed to talk about and in a broadcast discussion the participants have expertise relating to a particular topic. In such contexts the preface is part of a little ritual pointing forwards to and focusing on the topic.

Prefaces can be of many different types. Prefaces can be what Stubbs refers to as misplacement markers whereby speakers signal a lack of coherence with the preceding talk. Misplacement marking is associated with taking control in the discourse in order to create coherence. Misplacement markers (originally a term used in Conversation Analysis) are identical with what Sinclair and Coulthard (1975) refer to as 'frames' in their study of classroom discourse. Such items are minimally little words such as *well* or *by the way*. In more structured discourse prefaces can be quite long and have internal structure as shown by Stubbs. The following extract from Stubbs discusses the use of prefaces in committee meetings.

Text B6.3.1
M. Stubbs

M. Stubbs (1983) *Discourse analysis*. Oxford: Blackwell, pp. 184–6.

. . .

In data I have studied from committee meetings, if speakers are going to produce an utterance which is out of place in this sense they typically preface it by an elaborate item such as:

9.18 just one other comment – Mike – er – you asked just now what
9.19 can I – I must just say that – I think that . . .
9.20 John – you know this other information

Such items claim their lack of connectedness to the immediately preceding talk as recognized and therefore accountable.

[. . .]

Text B6.3.1
M. Stubbs

[S]ome speech events are characterized by much overt signalling of discourse organization. S. Harris (1980) argues that overt references to the discourse and to the speech acts performed are common in courts of law. Thus a magistrate might say to a defendant:

9.29   I'm putting it to you again . . .

However, defendants do not preface utterances with forms such as I *want to make it clear*, although in terms of propositional content alone, there is every reason for using such a preface.

A subcategory of such prefaces is interruption prefaces. Interruptions are an important turn-taking mechanism in certain speech situations, but are an almost entirely unstudied aspect of conversation. (However, see Jefferson, 1973, and Lycan, 1977, for some discussion.) Interruptions turn out to be a very complex speech act. They are clearly not defined by the mere overlap of two speakers in time. The interpretation of an utterance as an interruption depends on a complex of facts, including the status of the speakers, and the perceived relevance of the utterance, which relates interruptions to the kind of preface discussed here. Interruptions could be studied from many points of view: their synchronization in time; the points, for example defined syntactically, at which speakers tend to interrupt; whether speakers of higher status interrupt differently from speakers of lower status; and recognizable prefaces (e.g. *could I just come in there?* . . .).

There are various surface markers which typically preface utterances designed to break into the flow of discourse. Examples are:

9.30   can I add to that er . . .
9.31   can I ask organization-wise why . . .
9.32   we've got two people in sales if I can just come in here . . .
9.33   if I could ask a question again . . .
9.34   look – look – let me – let me – make it patently clear . . .

There is probably no way of specifying all the surface forms that an interruption preface will take. On the other hand a large number have a form which makes them a subcategory of the type of preface defined above:

1   term of address
2   can I/could I/I must/let me (i.e. forms of mitigation)
3   self-referential metastatement

In addition the first few syllables are often repeated.

Task B6.3.1

➤   Prefaces can be subclassified as noted by Stubbs above.

▪   What types of prefaces can we distinguish?
▪   To what extent are they text-type specific?
▪   What is their relationship to the status and social role of the users?

> As Stubbs makes clear in regard to the courtroom, a defendant would not be likely to use a preface such as 'I want to make it clear.' How can we explain this in terms of the social event and power?

> Stubbs suggests that interruption prefaces are complex speech acts which are difficult to define. How could a corpus be of help to study interruptions and which surface forms might we start with?

B6.4 McCARTHY (2003)

Speaking turns are both initiating and responding. An important area of spoken discourse analysis therefore concerns the listener's responses. The listener uses 'small' response tokens such as *yes, right, I see,* which are 'squeezed into' the turn-initial slot where he/she attends to the preceding turn and signals an upcoming contribution. McCarthy's notion of 'responsive item' includes elements which occur in the second move (in an adjacency pair) or as the third responsive move (referred to above as the follow-up move). When response items are 'free-standing' they are referred to as backchannels. Response elements do more than simply mark the listener's response. *Yes* or *no* would have functioned as response signals but the speaker prefers expressions characterized by a more active interaction with the interlocutor. However, response can function on different levels in the discourse. Besides the use to establish and maintain social relationships, they also have a discourse-marking function to signal boundaries for example in conversational closings. As you read the article, notice also the broad spectrum of devices which can be used as back-channel responses ranging from lexical items or short clauses to vocalizations and gestures.

The data represent both British and American English. The British data come from the spoken CANCODE Corpus and are compared with data from the North American spoken sample of the Cambridge International Corpus.

Text 6.4.1
M. McCarthy

M. McCarthy (2003) 'Talking back: "small" interactional response tokens in everyday conversation'. *Research on language and social interaction* **36(1): 33–63.**

[. . .]

RESPONSE TOKENS IN THE CORPUS: QUANTITATIVE DATA

Word-frequency lists were generated for both corpora using corpus-analytical software. The 2,000 most frequent words in both the British and American corpora were then scrutinized manually and the most likely items (based on the previous studies reviewed earlier and on observation and intuition) for consideration as response tokens were listed. The initial search through the frequency lists produced the items in Table 1, in descending order of frequency, for the British and American data combined.

Text 6.4.1
M. McCarthy

Table 1 Total frequency of potential response items occurring more than 200 times in the combined corpora (British and American)

Item	Frequency
Really	27,481
Right	27,767
Good	16,442
Quite	6,688
Great	3,729
True	2,984
Sure	2,328
Exactly	2,290
Fine	1,698
Wow	1,440
Absolutely	1,368
Certainly	1,305
Wonderful	1,231
Lovely	1,145
Definitely	1,112
Gosh	934
Cool	766
Excellent	418
Perfect	286

"Perfect" represents a cutoff point. The next word below it, "marvelous," makes the 100+ British list at 104, but fails to make the 100+ American list and is thus out of the running (similarly, "brilliant" makes the British 100+ list but not the American list). All of these items occur in nonminimal responses, but Table 1 shows their total occurrences in all turn positions.

[. . .]

CONTEXTS AND USES

In this section we look at the environments in which samples of these response tokens occur and illustrate broadly the kinds of functions they typically fulfill. Each extract is labeled according to its variety, British (Br.) or American (Am.), and items for comment are in bold.

Nonminimal Responses Without Expanded Content

The first set of examples shows response tokens occupying the whole response move, or only minimally accompanied by "yes/yeah/no/okay/oh," after which the turn reverts to the previous speaker. Extracts 1 and 2 show the typical use of items such as "lovely," "fine," and "right" marking transactional or topical boundaries, where speakers jointly coordinate stages of conversational business such as making arrangements or agreeing on courses of action. However, as asserted several times already, the response tokens are nonessential transactionally and do more than just signal boundaries; they seem to signal affective and social well-being between interlocutors, and both British and American varieties display the same functions. Note how both

Table 2 Occurrences of relevant tokens in nonminimal responses[a]

Item	*As response*
Right	1,150
Wow	1,099
True	880
Exactly	872
Gosh	746
Absolutely	594
Great	493
Definitely	365
Sure	349
Fine	348
Good	313
Cool	229
Really	214
Excellent	200
Lovely	196
Wonderful	195
Certainly	101
Perfect	32

[a] Turn-initial position or post-function word ("yes," "no," etc.).

social arrangements are concluded by "Lovely" in extract 1 and especially how speaker A returns with "Lovely" even after the arrangement has been adequately confirmed with "Yeah" in transactional terms. "Lovely" thus seems to be displaying both a responsive function and (simultaneously in its second occurrence) a discourse-marking one as follows:

Extract 1 (Br.) [Telephone call between friends, arranging a barbecue]

A: I would love it if you could bring a salad.
B: Yeah.
A: It would be very nice.
B: I will do then. I'll do that this afternoon then yeah.
A: Lovely.
B: What time do you want us then?
A: When were you planning?
B: Well you said about fiveish didn't you.
A: Yeah.
B: Yeah.
A: Lovely.

Extract 2 (Am.) [Social chat among friends]

A: Well please promise me that you won't carry any heavy things.
C: No I can't. I can't lift anything.
A: It's not worth it.

Text 6.4.1
M. McCarthy

C: No.

A: There's no reason to.

C: Well anything. Even a heavy pot or a dish.

A: No.

C: You know you don't realize. I said to dad you've got to take the cake out.

A: Right.

C: Cause when you do (1.0) that's the weakness.

A: Right.

Extract 3 illustrates sociable agreement asserted with "right" and reinforced with "definitely":

Extract 3 (Am.) [Social conversation between acquaintances]

A: You know, I, I wouldn't, couldn't tell you if we sentenced someone tomorrow how long he'd actually be in jail.

B: Uh huh.

A: Could you?

B: No. Me either.

A: I couldn't. And I think they kind of depend on that, these criminals.

B: Right, yeah, definitely.

Note here how "Uh huh" seems to be considered an insufficient contribution at this moment of listening-response relevance (Erickson and Shultz, 1982): Speaker A persists with a follow-up tag question and then with an expansion of the main argument; it is only then that B responds with an emphatic confirmation of convergence and agreement.

"Wow" and "gosh" potentially express strong affective responses of surprise, incredulity, delight, shock, horror, and so forth, as part of their lexical meaning (though in particular contexts these could also, of course, be ironic, sardonic, etc.). Here "wow" responds repeatedly to a progressive report of exorbitant charges in an educational setting, an example of the restricted options for the listener to respond with an extended turn, as discussed earlier, but also an example of the importance of responding at transition relevant points, and feeding back to the teller: [. . .]

Task B6.4.1

➤ Backchannel items are typically little items such as *uh* and *huh*, *I see* and *good*.

▪ Why is it problematic to describe backchannel items in terms of their formal qualities?

▪ What other criteria can we use to distinguish a backchannel from a turn or a follow-up move?

FURTHER READING

Sinclair and Coulthard (1975) give a detailed picture of the different categories of their 'rank scale' and its correlations with grammatical units. The model has been used – and further developed – by Stenström (1994) to provide additional categories needed to describe patterns of question-answer. An early, somewhat different, analysis of the structure of discourse is proposed by Labov and Fanshel (1977). Labov and Fanshel study the conversational interaction in a therapy session. They are primarily interested in determining the actions performed by speakers through their utterances. However, the acts which are crucial for the analysis are not requests and assertions but challenges, defences and retreats. Levinson (1983), chapter 6, is an excellent introduction to Conversation Analysis. Wooffitt (2005) explains the concepts used in Conversation Analysis and illustrates conversation analytical methods on empirical material. Hutchby and Wooffitt (2008) give an overview of the methods used in Conversation Analysis with illustrative examples. The edited volume by Drew and Heritage (1992) applies Conversation Analysis to the study of language in a variety of settings, including doctor–patient consultations, legal hearings, news interviews, visits by health visitors, psychiatric interviews and calls to the emergency services. The articles in Antaki (2011) show how Conversation Analysis can be used to identify communicative practices in different work situations.

LOOKING AHEAD

In Unit C4 you will have the chance to further explore prefaces on the basis of your own corpus work. Response items are easy to ignore when one studies discourse although they are important for the flow of the conversation. In one of the tasks you will explore the differences between British English and American English in the use of response elements. The final task deals with the closing of a telephone conversation. This shows a more fixed structure than the closing of face-to-face conversation and both the caller and the receiver have special tasks.

Unit B7
Pragmatic markers

B7.1 INTRODUCTION

In this section we will look at some selected pragmatic markers and their functions. The first extract deals with the discourse functions of *I don't know*. Very little work has been done on this pragmatic marker: this may be because it is not immediately obvious that it is a pragmatic marker at all. Indeed, it is generally taken in its literal sense – 'the speaker does not know' – and is used as a reply to a question. However, *I don't know* can be used when the speaker is able to supply the information. The functions of *I don't know* in this case can be explained with reference to the notion of 'face'. As you learned in Unit A8, 'face' has to do with the 'public self-image speakers want to create for themselves' (a notion derived from Goffman 1967). *I don't know*, for instance, enables the speaker to preserve the other's face by avoiding expressing his or her own opinion.

B7.2 DIANI (2004)

The data in Diani's article are taken from the COBUILD/Birmingham Spoken corpus which consists of about two million words representing everyday casual conversation, meetings and discussions.

G. Diani (2004) 'The discourse functions of *I don't know* in English conversation'. In K. Aijmer and A.-B. Stenström (eds) *Discourse patterns in spoken and written corpora*. Amsterdam: John Benjamins, pp. 157–71.

Text B7.2.1
G. Diani

3. I *don't know*, semantic or pragmatic marker?

Collins COBUILD *English Language Dictionary* (1987: 802) defines the verb *know* as follows:

1   If you know a fact, a piece of information, or an answer, you have it in your mind and are certain that it is correct;
2   . . . you have heard of something;
3   . . . you have information about a subject;
4   . . . you are familiar with a place, a work of art, an idea, someone, etc.;
5   . . . you are aware of something;
6   . . . you have the necessary skills and knowledge to do something.

Text B7.2.1
G. Diani

People say I *know* when they are familiar with a piece of information. When they use I *don't know*, i.e. a declaration of insufficient knowledge, we need to distinguish a number of possible pragmatic functions.

In her research, Tsui (1991) has identified a variety of functions of I *don't know*. Here I limit myself to describing the ones that emerge from the data. She observes that I *don't know* is generally taken to be a reply to an information question when the speaker is unable to supply the requested information:

(5) <F02> Oh that's quite <ZGY>
  <F01> It's great isn't it? Ein Haus. Or is it Eine Haus?
  <F02> **I don't know**.
  <F01> There you go. The extent of my German.
  <F02> You know it always used [. . .]
  (Cobuild: ukspok/04. Text: S000000030)
(6) <M01> [. . .] why is the government going to sell more BT shares? I would have thought.
  <M02> **I don't know**.
  <M01> with all these big profits that's money coming in for us isn't it?
  (Cobuild: ukspok/04. Text: S0000000230)

However, Tsui has noted that I *don't know* is produced even when the speaker is able to supply the information requested in the question, as in (7) and (8) below:

(7) <M07> [. . .] in anything else after twelve years of the sort of rule we haven't isn't it?
  <M01> Well **I don't know** I mean I don't think we can blame the government for all our ills I think it's the way we are.
  (Cobuild: ukspok/04. Text: S0000000142)
(8) <M01> Don't the two things sometimes go hand in hand?
  <M04> Well **I don't know**. Well no I mean if some if one shop's selling something for say a pound and another one's selling [. . .]
  (Cobuild: ukspok/04. Text: S0000000304)

In examples (5)–(7), the production of I *don't know* is a way of avoiding that disagreement is expressed overtly and disclaiming what has been said in the previous turn. Prefacing a disagreement with a declaration of insufficient knowledge reduces the speaker's commitment to the truth of the proposition expressed in the disagreement, hence mitigating its face-threatening effect. In general, disagreement sequences are structured so as to minimize the effects of explicit disagreement (Pomerantz 1984). An illustration is given in (8), where we see the addressee prefacing his disagreement with Well I *don't know*, thus displaying reluctance and discomfort (cf. Tsui 1994).

Throughout the examination of the data, I have noticed that I *don't know* may serve as a 'marker of uncertainty', as Tsui (1991: 619) calls it. This is illustrated in (9) (=2):

(9) [. . .] that can do a really good job like Maggie Thatcher.
  <M01> Now there seems to be I mean **I don't know** this is not scientific at all but a bit of a sexual divide here. It seems the women like [. . .]
  (Cobuild: ukspok/04. Text: S9000000810)

By using *there seems to be* the speaker hedges the opinion that there is *a bit of a*

Text B7.2.1
G. Diani

sexual divide here. I mean I don't know further emphasises the speaker's uncertainty and unwillingness to commit himself. Example (10) is somewhat different:

(10) [. . .] I mean how would we feel if erm **I don't know** Holland owned the Isle of Wight or something like that I mean I suppose we'd feel a [. . .]
(Cobuild: ukspok/04. Text: S000000074)

Here I *don't know* seems to match Brown and Yule's (1983: 109) description of 'fillers', the principal function of which, they say, is 'to fill the silence and maintain the speaker's right to speak, while he organizes what he wants to say' (cf. Stenström 1984: 206).

We can see from the data that I *don't know* is also used for minimizing compliments. Examples (11) and (12) illustrate this:

(11) <M01> Well I'll tell you something shall I Margaret?
 <F01> Yes please.
 <M01> Well speaking as a school governor
 <F01> Well I'm sure you qualify.
 <M01> Ooh **I don't know** I mean er it frightens me the fact that we're supposed to look after all this money and and run school and run it like a business. It worries me immensely you know.
(Cobuild: ukspok/04. Text: S0000000156)
(12) <M01> You were lucky it's worth a lot more than that now.
 <M03> Oh **I don't know** er it's it's not something that I deal with because it was given to me by a friend [. . .]
(Cobuild: ukspok/04. Text: S0000000463)

[. . .]

Following Tsui's analysis, we have seen that I *don't know* does not necessarily occur in response to an information question. It can occur in a number of conversational environments, such as in reply to an assessment or a request, where it functions to:

– avoid explicit disagreement;
– avoid commitment;
– minimize face-threatening acts;
– mark uncertainty.

Task B7.2.1

> Summarize the different pragmatic functions of *I don't know*. To what extent are they dependent on the sequential context (what comes before in the discourse)?

> *I don't know* often co-occurs with other markers. What is the effect of clustering such as you find in examples (7) and (8) (*well I don't know*), (9) (*I mean I don't know*) or (11) and (12) (*Oh I don't know*)?

B7.3 GILQUIN (2008)

In spontaneous speech speakers have to plan what to say 'on the fly'. This is reflected in vocalizations such as *uh* and *mm*, false starts, repetitions, as well as in little words such as *well* or *I mean* which do not contribute anything of importance to the message itself. A popular idea is that elements like *uh* and *um* are hesitation signals or 'fillers' which should be avoided. However, as pointed out by Gilquin, hesitation markers are not meaningless fillers: rather, they are closely associated with speech management and have functions such as searching for words, self-repair and turn-taking.

Hesitation phenomena can look different in native and non-native speaker performance. We are now lucky to have access to spoken learner corpora which makes it possible to make comparisons between non-native speakers (the LINDSEI Spoken Corpus) and native speakers (the LOCNEC Corpus). It is shown in Gilquin's study that some categories of hesitation markers are overused by (French) learners while others are underused. A number of explanations are suggested for this situation.

**Text B7.3.1
G. Gilquin**

G. Gilquin (2008) 'Hesitation markers among EFL learners: pragmatic deficiency or difference?' In J. Romero-Trillo (ed.) ***Pragmatics and corpus linguistics. A mutualistic entente.*** **Berlin: Mouton de Gruyter, pp. 119–43.**

Smallwords

While French-speaking learners tend to overuse silent and filled pauses to express hesitation, they do not exploit the full range of smallwords that may be used to perform this function, as is clear from [Table 4], which give[s] the relative frequency of a number of markers of hesitation regularly discussed in the literature. For some of them the difference in frequency is not statistically significant between the two groups, but in the majority of cases (12 out of 18) there is a significant underuse among the learners. Particularly striking is the underuse of *like*, illustrated by (12) which is extremely common in native speech (527.05 occurrences per 100,000 words) but is hardly ever found in learner speech (6.36 occurrences per 100,000 words).

(12) I don't wanna swim any more people come out with **like** bruises all over their legs where they've hit rocks at the bottom <LOCNEC 025>

A notable exception to learners' tendency to underuse smallwords of hesitation is *well*, which as Table 4 shows, is significantly overused by learners (sentences (13) and (14) are just a couple of illustrations taken from LINDSEI-FR). To paraphrase Hasselgren (1994), one could say that *well* is a "pragmatic teddy bear" for learners, who cling to it because it is familiar, safe and widely usable. This over-reliance on *well* probably explains why learners do not feel the need to use other smallwords of hesitation, which results in an overall overuse of this category of hesitation markers.

(13) but <laughs> er **well** when I've seen the number of my room . **well** I I noticed that it wasn't the case <LINDSEI-FR002>

Pragmatic markers

Table 4 Relative frequency of smallwords of hesitation shared by native speakers and learners (per 100,000 words)[1]

	LOCNEC	LINDSEI-FR
all right	12.78	3.18
all that	3.99	2.12
anyway	45.52	33.90
I mean	352.16	152.53
in a way	15.97	3.18
just	746.65	274.35
kind of	86.24	67.79
like	527.05	6.36
or so	3.19	7.41
or something	43.92	13.77
right	99.02	5.30
something like	27.95	40.25
sort of	456.77	34.96
stuff	67.88	5.30
thing	142.14	49.78
things like	55.90	23.30
well	415.25	1076.20
you know	479.13	190.67
Total	3581.52	1990.34

Text B7.3.1
G. Gilquin

(14) er . with the school .. th first time I was **well** about fifteen or sixteen secondary school .. er . the second time . **well** in fact .. er I've been studying in a: teachers training college before I was here <LINDSEI-FR 048>

6. Assessing learners' use of the hesitation function

[. . .]

One may wonder whether these differences between native speakers' and learners' use of the hesitation function are just that – differences, or whether they should best be viewed as pragmatic deficiencies, which should somehow be remedied. This is the issue that is addressed in this section.

Pragmatic differences have been given considerable attention in the literature on English as a Lingua Franca (ELF), i.e. English as a means of communication between speakers with different mother tongues (see e.g. Seidlhofer 2005). According to the advocates of ELF, only those features which cause misunderstanding should be eradicated. Features which differ from native English but still allow mutual intelligibility, on the other hand, are tolerated (or even promoted). In this context many cross-cultural encounters are claimed to be successful, and according to Aston (1993: 245), "interlanguage pragmatics should operate with a difference hypothesis rather than a deficit hypothesis". Hesitation phenomena such as those investigated here do not normally lead to misunderstanding or communicative breakdown. They are at best "'ripples' on the pragmatic surface" (Seidlhofer 2001: 147). As such, they should not qualify for the label of "deficiencies", but should instead be considered as mere differences, which are "non-fatal" (Jordan and Fuller 1975) to the conversation. In what follows, however, I would like to argue that markers of hesitation may have a role to

201

play in the success (or otherwise) of interactions, and that it is precisely those markers that are overused by learners which may be detrimental to the conversation, whereas the markers they underuse help make the pragmatic "ripples" smoother.

[. . .]

The key issue here seems to be fluency, that is, "the ability to contribute to what a listener, proficient in that language, would normally perceive as coherent speech, which can be understood without undue strain, and is carried out at a comfortable pace, not being disjointed, or disrupted by excessive hesitation" (Hasselgren 2002: 148). Although fluency would not be considered as one of the "core" features of ELF, since it is not crucial to intelligibility (it just helps to be "understood without undue strain"), it is nonetheless an important aspect of oral language, As Lennon (1990: 391–392) explains, "fluency reflects the speaker's ability to focus the listener's attention on his or her message by presenting a finished product rather than inviting the listener to focus on the working of the production mechanisms". In other words, it makes it possible for the listener to concentrate on what should be central to an utterance, namely its content.

Note

1 Thus, for example, while learners used *well* more than a thousand times, the corresponding figure for native speakers is only 415.

 Task B7.3.1

➤ Hesitation markers may be both overused and underused. Which markers are most interesting because of the differences between native speakers and non-native speakers?

➤ The Gilquin excerpt gives rise to many questions, in our view. They include the following:

- How should we look upon the differences between the native speakers' and the non-native speakers' use of hesitation markers?
- Should we tolerate differences which do not lead to conversational break-down or do the differences reflect learner deficiencies which need to be remedied?
- What is the importance of using hesitation markers for fluency and for native-likeness?
- Can pragmatic markers be taught or are they acquired naturally by immersion in another culture?

➤ Jot down your own responses to these questions (you might find it helpful to reread the excerpt a couple of times).

B7.4 RÜHLEMANN (2007)

Like as a discourse marker is a newcomer in British English. Some of its uses (such as *be like* introducing reported speech) are above all typical of American English. *Like* in British English is used especially by young speakers in new uses including the quotative use, although other functions are more common. Christoph Rühlemann found many uses of it in the BNC, as our third excerpt in this unit makes clear.

C. Rühlemann (2007) *Conversation in context. A corpus-driven approach.* London: Continuum, pp. 143–7.

> Text B7.4.1
> C. Rühlemann

Like is one of the most common words in conversation. Indeed Adolphs and Carter (2003: 49) claim that the word *like* 'is over five times more frequent in spoken English than in written English'. The reason for this is that in informal speech *like* acts as a discourse deictic with various sub-functions. In the following two sections I will first test Adolphs and Carter's claim and, then, investigate what the subfunctions of *like* in discourse are.

Like is an extremely versatile word that can take over more functions than most other words. A lemmatized word search for LIKE in the BNC lists six distinct functions. They are labelled PRP (preposition), VERB, CONJ (conjunction), ADJ (adjective), SUBST (noun) and ADV (adverb). The six uses are illustrated below. In the discussion we will see that the ADV category requires the most scrutiny and differentiation.

(6.47) PRP: There's nothing **like** forward planning.
(6.48) VERB: Yeah I used to **like** their pork er dripping.
(6.49) CONJ: [whispering] Just feel **like** I'm not learning anything [. . .].
(6.50) ADJ: in a church you are being . . . to by people who are of **like** mind
(6.51) SUBST: but I suppose the **likes** of me, bit old-fashioned aren't we?
(6.52) ADV: Er you'll you'll make it rough, **like**.

Discourse functions

Browsing occurrences of *like* tagged ADV in C [conversation], the observer is presented with a broad range of different uses of *like*. These are illustrated in (6.53)–(6.59).

It will be observed that the functions *like* carries out in (6.53)–(6.59) are of a different nature from the ones considered in (6.47)–(6.52). While these latter can be described as *grammatical* functions, the functions of *like* in (6.53)–(6.59) are *discourse* functions.

In (6.53), *like* seems to serve to qualify a particular word choice (*reminder*), indicating that the word may not be exact or appropriate and should not be taken literally (Adolphs and Carter 2003; Andersen 2001: 241ff.).

(6.53) PS 007>: Oh yes, I was assuming that ... erm... a I do, I didn't really set it
                out as a formal agenda just as a
       PS002>: Just as a not
       PS007>: a reminder, **like.**

Like may be linked to politeness (cf. Andersen 2001: 229), as in (6.54), where it downtones a directive that might otherwise be taken as face-threatening.

Text B7.4.1
C. Rühlemann

(6.54) PS029>: and it peels like rubber. Peels off like rubber. You can get it off [. . .]
PS02D>: Mm [. . .]. Perhaps it's sort of [. . .] on there yeah.
PS029>: Yeah. You gotta paint it **like**.

In (6.55), *like* serves to focus attention to an upcoming illustration of a preceding statement (Adolphs and Carter 2003; Miller and Weinert 1998; Andersen 2001: 241 ff.).

(6.55) PS01F1>: think it's the way he looks, **like**, if you know what I mean, you **like** [. . .] pull his face and **like**, look over glasses

In a few cases, as in (6.56), *like* may be seen as a pause filler granting the speaker planning time (note the co-occurrence with the hesitation form *er* and the phrasal restart) (cf. Jucker and Smith 1998: 189; Andersen 2002: 256).

(6.56) PS03T>: well you should wipe the outside of the frame didn't you?
PS03S>: er, yes, **like**, you like just flick round it

In (6.57), *like* co-occurs with two vague items (*sort of* and *-ish*) and would thus appear to act itself as a vagueness marker (cf. Adolphs and Carter 2003; Jucker and Smith 1998: 186).

(6.57) PS04U>: . . . And you said cos it'll be so busy could you stop over, you wasn't coming down to me till sort **like** after threeish.

In (6.58), *like* indicates that the numerical information given is approximate rather than precise (cf. Andersen 2001: 233 ff.):

(6.58) I mean I've been in two shops now there's fifty pound difference **like**, you know

Finally, in (6.59), *like* introduces a direct DP [discourse presentation; reported speech] (Cf. Jucker and Smith 1998: 189 ff.; Andersen 2001: 250 ff.; Adolphs and Carter 2003).

(6.59) PS000>: Yeah that's what I, why, that's what I said to Susanna and she was **like** don't be ridiculous

Like as quotative

Frequency

Adolphs and Carter claim with regard to *like* that 'one of its most frequent uses is as a marker of reported speech' (2003: 54). On the face of it, this claim seems open to challenge. It is unclear whether quotative *like* is indeed frequent in contemporary British English. Romaine and Lange (1991: 248f.) observe that '[a]t the moment the use of *like* as a quotative complementizer appears to be confined to American English, though there are perhaps traces of a similar development in British English'. Miller and Weinert (1998: 311) found quotative *like* to be absent from their data of spontaneous conversations altogether. In Andersen's (2001: 266f.) analysis of the functional distribution of discourse marker *like* in COLT, the quotative function was found to account for 7 per cent only. In my data, *like* as a marker of DP does occur but is clearly not one of the most frequent uses of discourse marker *like*.

Task B7.4.1

➤ *Like* also needs to be characterized formally. What observations can you make about *like* and its position in the clause?

FURTHER READING

There is an extensive literature on different aspects of pragmatic markers. Schiffrin's (1987) pioneering work on the functions of the discourse markers *oh, well, now, then, you know, I mean* and the connectives *because, and, but* and *or* has greatly influenced later work. Hansen (1998) is a valuable overview of previous studies and of topics such as spoken and written language, discourse structure and different methodologies to study pragmatic markers. The empirical description deals with French pragmatic markers. Aijmer (2002) is a study of some selected pragmatic markers (*now, oh, ah, just, sort of, and that sort of thing, actually*) on the basis of the London-Lund Corpus. Blakemore (2002) analyses *so, however* and *well* within a relevance-theoretical framework. Fischer (2006) is a collection of articles giving an up-to-date overview of the state of the art in studies of pragmatic markers. The contributors to the volume were asked to give their views on problematic issues such as terminology, definition, the multifunctionality of pragmatic markers and the relation between the description of pragmatic markers and general linguistic issues such as the semantic-pragmatic interface. Not surprisingly there was little agreement on these issues.

Research on pragmatic markers also includes studies of pragmatic markers by non-native speakers (e.g. Müller 2005). Müller studies how well non-native speakers master the use of pragmatic markers such as *well, so, you know* and *like* by making a comparison with native speakers. Aijmer and Simon-Vandenbergen (2006) are concerned with the methods and theories used to study pragmatic markers cross-linguistically. A wide range of language pairs are represented. Aijmer and Simon-Vandenbergen (2011) discuss recent tendencies and future challenges in pragmatic marker studies. The authors point out that pragmatic markers are indexical, and suggest a number of contextual dimensions to which the markers are attached.

The historical study of pragmatic markers is represented by Brinton (1996, 2008) amongst others. The focus here is on the pragmatic developments of selected pragmatic markers or comment clauses in the history of English.

LOOKING AHEAD

In Unit A7 you were presented with some criteria which have been used to define prototypical pragmatic markers. In Unit C5 you will be requested to test how well these criteria work on a sample of expressions which have been considered to be pragmatic markers. In Unit C5 you will also be asked to look in more detail at the quotative *like* which seems to be spreading rapidly to new areas. Finally, we will ask you to consider the functions of pragmatic markers in social terms. What happens for example if they are omitted?

Unit B8
Pragmatics, facework and im/politeness

B8.1 INTRODUCTION

In our summary to Unit A8, we suggested that what is 'politic' in facework terms – that is, is appropriate to the participants, given the activity/context, and their roles/relationship(s) – and what is 'salient' – that is, beyond the kinds of behaviour the participants would expect from a particular interlocutor in environment X and hence open to the interpretation of being overly polite or gratuitously impolite – is prone to interpersonal differences as well as to socio-cultural and activity-specific expectations. In this unit, we include excerpts from articles which will help us to explore, in further detail, when behaviour is politic and when it is salient and, if the latter, when it becomes impolite and how interlocutors might deal with such impoliteness. We begin with O'Driscoll's (2007) article on 'Brown and Levinson's face . . .'. O'Driscoll is particularly interested in the extent to which Brown and Levinson's ideas in regard to (positive and negative) face can 'help us [to] understand interaction across cultures'. This is controversial, to some extent, as plentiful research has suggested that negative face, in particular, is problematic when it comes to collectivist cultures (see Unit A8.3). O'Driscoll's excerpt also indicates a coming together (in part) of a first order and a second order approach (cf. Units A8.8 and A8.9). Specifically, he suggests that the concepts of positive and negative face are best seen as 'second-order ones which . . . do not in themselves describe social values and do not depend for their existence on their salience for interactants'. The implication, then, is that saliency (i.e. politeness or impoliteness) should be considered separately to whether interlocutors are engaging in positive or negative facework. The excerpt from Watts' (2003) monograph on *Politeness* constitutes our second reading in this section. Watts, of course, has made much of the politic/saliency distinction. His particular focus, here, is determining how politic behaviour differs from polite behavior, that is, behaviour which is more attentive to face than we might expect, as interlocutors, in a given situation. The third reading also discusses salient behaviour. In this instance, however, we focus on impolite behaviour. More specifically, the excerpt from Culpeper *et al.* (2003) discusses the strategies which are available to interlocutors when they believe themselves to be faced with impoliteness strategies.

B8.2 O'DRISCOLL (2007)

In Unit A8.3, we discussed some of the criticisms which have been levelled against the Brown and Levinson (1978/1987) approach to politeness. One of these criticisms related to the universality of Brown and Levinson's positive face and negative face. In this excerpt taken from O'Driscoll (2007), we focus on the applicability of positive and negative face(work) in the context of cross-cultural transactional encounters.

In the introduction to his full paper, O'Driscoll eludes to the furore that Brown and Levinson's ideas have propagated. He also highlights an observation that we made in Unit A8 which makes clear his position in this regard – that 'people are not cultural clones' or, put another way, that 'the undoubted existence of culture-specific norms cannot reliably predict how a person will behave on an occasion of IAC [interaction across cultures]', not least because 's/he may have reasons for wanting to diverge from these norms' (ibid.: 465). O'Driscoll's stance helps him to set the scene for his later analysis of a shop assistant's question to a customer, which we include here in full. Not included here, explicitly, is O'Driscoll's argument that Brown and Levinson's notions of negative and positive face 'have wide currency', once we see them as 'two oppos[ing] directions of a single dimension' whereby 'B&L's positive politeness is free-ranging' and, hence, 'related to a much wider range of potentially valued personal attributes' and Brown and Levinson's negative politeness is more 'specific and focused' (ibid.: 473–4). This view is important, however, as it constitutes the crux of his argument in regard to 'the shop question' (and also his argument for considering positive/negative face and saliency separately).

Text B8.2.1
J. O'Driscoll

J. O'Driscoll (2007) 'Brown and Levinson's face – how it can and can't help us to understand interaction across cultures'. *Intercultural Pragmatics* **4(4): 463–92.**

[. . .]
   [T]he problem [with negative face] is its apparent limited cross-cultural applicability. The solution to it is to construe the concepts of the positive and negative faces as firmly second-order ones which therefore do not in themselves describe social values and do not depend for their existence on their salience for interactants. That is to say, the concepts have to be extricated from B&L's construal of face as wants. Negative facework, I propose, is behavior which predicates or implies a person's singularity, but no claim of any value is implied by its identification.
   The problem with positive face is its breadth [. . .] Instead of subdividing 'positive' [face, as some researchers have proposed], I suggest constraining it. This can be done by picking up on the suggestion of polarity in the terminology and regarding positive as exclusively and specifically the opposite of negative [. . .] [Hence,] negative face(work) pertains to separation and individuation, [and] positive face(work) [. . .] to connection and belonging [. . .]
   This stripped-down conceptualization of positive and negative is not tied to other aspects of the B&L model. Positive and negative are not values or desires—they are

just end points on a scale on which some interactive behavior can be mapped (and sometimes values and desires uncovered thereby) [. . .]

An example: The shop question

To demonstrate the potential relevance of the positive-negative spectrum within even the most quotidian sorts of interaction, I consider here a very mundane encounter. I consider this one because it is, in my direct experience, subject to cross-cultural variation. In the following two paragraphs, I outline the bare situational bones by underlining; the other parts offer comment on these.

A customer is buying food items in a shop. It could be a (green) grocers or the delicatessen counter of a supermarket, but in any case the immediate situation is not self-service; [. . .] it is an occasion where [. . .] the customer asks for the items from a shop worker, who then performs the required action (cuts a piece of cheese, fills up a paper bag with a certain amount of a vegetable) and hands the item over. At the precise point in this encounter on which I focus, the customer has already been served two items. There has been nothing in his/her manner to indicate to the shop worker whether s/he now desires a third item. Of course, such clues are often forthcoming. But sometimes they are not, and in these cases the shop worker needs to find out. One possibility is an attentive silence which waits for the customer to make his/her intentions clear. Another is use of body language—raised eyebrows perhaps. No doubt there are cultures and situations where such moves occur. But a very common way for the shop worker to find out is through speech; that is, s/he asks the customer.

Now, because context makes it clear there are only two alternatives (either the customer wants something else or s/he doesn't), the shop worker is very likely to phrase this request for information as a yes/no question; that is, *either* s/he asks if the customer wants something else (e.g. English "Anything else?") *or* s/he asks if the customer has finished (e.g. English "Is that all?").

At first sight, this verbal move in this situation appears very unpromising for a B&L-inspired face analysis. For one thing, as the participants are already in verbal communication and it is a request with transparent relevance to the encounter, it could not constitute an FTA. Second, it cannot be described as a polite act, in either a first-order sense (neither actors nor observers would evaluate it as such) or a second-order sense (no theory so far would accommodate it). On Kasper's politeness continuum (1990: 205), it is very close indeed to the transactional pole. Third, it is not, by the greatest stretch of the imagination, *strategic* with respect to face. It is a norm, a formula. Fourth, the use of a yes/no question as opposed to an either/or one conforms perfectly to Grice's maxim of quantity (which the latter would flout by predicating both alternatives unnecessarily). In view of B&L's starting point, which was to explain cases where Grice's maxims of efficient conversation (Grice 1975) are flouted, this is ironic.

And yet, despite all these apparent contra-indications, face *is* involved here, waiting in the wings. It comes to the fore when the customer receives the form of the yes/no question to which s/he is not routinely accustomed. (Because I do not want language specifics to intrude, I refer henceforth to these two alternatives as MORE? and FINISHED?.) At the very least, s/he will feel momentarily nonplussed and a small hiatus in communication will result. As this is not the question s/he was unconsciously expecting, s/he may deduce it is some other query that s/he has failed to catch and will ask for repetition. But when s/he does comprehend the question, s/he will experience a small loss of composure. S/he will feel "put out." Why?

First, imagine that the customer is accustomed to MORE? (In my experience, this is the case with British and Greek customers.) If s/he gets asked FINISHED? instead, s/he may suspect s/he is being insulted. Is the shop worker implying a wish to be rid of me? How rude! Now imagine the customer is accustomed to FINISHED? (very common in Flanders and, I am told, in Portugal). If s/he gets asked MORE? instead, s/he is likely to feel uneasy at this apparently unwonted salesmanship and consequently imposed upon.

We may ask at this point how a simple—and relevant—yes/no question can have these face consequences. Presumably, it is partly to do with what in conversation analysis is called preference organization (see, e.g., Atkinson & Heritage 1985). That is, many conversational turns appear to be prejudiced in favor of a particular kind of response. B&L themselves argue convincingly (B&L: 38–39) that this is the case partly for reasons of face. In the case of this yes/no question, we might speculate that the preference is for "yes." Leaving aside such speculation, however, what is irrefutable is that in asking the question in this Gricean manner the shop worker unavoidably *predicates* one alternative at the expense of the other. In doing so, s/he *implies* a preference, not for a particular verbal response as such but for what is to happen next in his/her dealings with the customer. S/he implies a preference either for prolonging the encounter (MORE?) or for terminating it (FINISHED?).

By asking MORE? the shop worker makes a 'move toward,' predicating continued contact with the customer and thus paying symbolic attention to positive face. By asking FINISHED? s/he makes a 'move away,' predicating a ceasing of contact and thus paying symbolic attention to negative face. Either alternative can be construed as giving face to the customer. Both attend to the customer's wishes and imply the customer is a valued person. But they do so in diametrically opposed ways, MORE? does it by implying the desire to continue having dealings with him/her; FINISHED? does it by implying that such an important person must be very busy and must not have his/her time wasted any more than is necessary.

All these considerations are normally below the level of participant consciousness [. . .] However, whenever the 'unexpected' alternative is used, the relevance of the positive-negative distinction as formulated here reveals itself. The customer who expected MORE? but gets FINISHED? experiences a threat to positive face; the one who expected FINISHED? but gets MORE? feels a threat to negative face. Thus an FTA emerges. But this FTA is not inherent to the speech act itself; rather it depends on the customer's emotional response.

 Task B8.2.1

> Positive face (the desire to be approved of) and negative face (the desire to be unimpeded) may 'not depend for their existence on their salience for interactants'. However, a positive face move or negative face move can be intended to be (and/or perceived as being) politic or salient, given a certain set of circumstances. This is because what is salient/politic for an individual (or individuals) will depend on the extent to which their interlocutor's behaviour adheres to what they might expect given the activity type, their role(s)/relationship(s) and/or their cultural schema, that is, on whether the behaviour is

'appropriate' or 'inappropriate' for them given their assessment of the context. Working in groups (where possible), come up with scenarios of different encounters (the airport, doctor's surgery, hotel reception, hotel bar) where you might hear *Anything else?* and *Is that all?*

■ Are these questions always politic to the situation, regardless of the encounter?

■ Do either or both of these questions sound salient in a particular encounter you've explored? What socio-cultural factors help to account for this salience?

➤ In the introduction to this extract, we outlined O'Driscoll's claim that Brown and Levinson's notions of negative and positive face 'have wide currency', across many cultures, once we see them as 'two oppos[ing] directions of a single dimension'. Now you've read O'Driscoll's extract, what do you think we gain by seeing positive and negative face in this way? Does it allow for a coming together of first order and second order ideas, for example? (Cf. Unit A8.9.)

B8.3 WATTS (2003)

In this excerpt we focus on Watts' discussion of the characteristics of politic as opposed to polite behavior. This politic/polite distinction was an extremely important one at the time of publication as Watts was using *politic* to explain (what for him constituted) 'appropriate' behaviour, given the activity type or context of utterance. Yet, other researchers had been labelling the same kinds of behaviour using (linguistic) *politeness* terms.

R.J. Watts (2003) *Politeness*. Cambridge: Cambridge University Press, pp. 257–9.

Text B8.3.1
R.J. Watts

[. . .] consider the following example. Imagine that you have booked two tickets to see a play and that they are numbered P51 and P52. Twenty minutes before the play is due to begin you locate row P and move along it to seats 51 and 52 only to find that someone else is already sitting there. What is the appropriate mode of behaviour in this situation? [. . .] [T]he first thing [you might] do is make clear to those sitting in P51 and P52 that you have booked them on that particular evening and that there must be some mistake. If you say any of the following:

(1) a. Excuse me. I think you're sitting in our seats.
     b. Excuse me but those are our seats.
     c. I'm sorry. I think there must be some mistake.
     d. I'm sorry, but are you sure you've got the right seats?

I maintain that you open the verbal interaction within the verbal framework of the politic behaviour that can be expected in this type of situation [. . .]
   [. . .]

On the assumption that an utterance similar to (1a–d) is made, it is unlikely that those sitting in the seats will apologise and simply vacate them. This would be equivalent to admitting that they knew all along that they were sitting in someone else's seats – although of course this does sometimes happen. What is now likely to ensue is a sequence in which the people occupying the seats compare their tickets with yours to try to ascertain where the mistake might lie. For example, you or those sitting in P51 and P52 may have missed a capital R printed in the bottom right-hand corner of the auditorium. Alternatively, your tickets or those of the people already sitting in P51 and P52 may actually be R51 and R52 but with the extra stroke in the capital letter R printed rather unclearly. [Once again, t]his kind of negotiation sequence constitutes politic behaviour. It's what the participants would expect to happen in this situation [. . .]

We can conclude from this discussion that politic behaviour is not equivalent to [socially] polite behaviour, although certain utterances that lie within the scope of politic behaviour may indeed be open to interpretation as polite. [. . .]

[. . .]

[. . .] This is exactly what we want to achieve in a politeness theory that conceptualises politeness as a first-order notion constantly open to discursive dispute.

Task B8.3.1

> Watts' main conclusion here is that 'politic behaviour is not equivalent to polite behaviour, although certain utterances that lie within the scope of politic behaviour may indeed be open to interpretation as polite'.

▪ Make a list of five utterances that, for you, are (i) politic but not polite and (ii) both politic and polite. Do your two lists share anything in common? Are there any commonalities within the lists?

▪ What merits are there in understanding politeness as being 'constantly open to discursive dispute'?

▪ What are the disadvantages of holding such a view (if any)? Think here about how you might 'capture' different *types* of politeness if they are 'constantly open to discursive dispute'.

B8.4 CULPEPER, BOUSFIELD AND WICHMANN (2003)

The final reading in this section is taken from Culpeper *et al.*'s (2003) article, 'Impoliteness revisited: with special reference to dynamic and prosodic aspects'. As the title intimates, this paper considers prosodic aspects in relation to facework and im/politeness – in fact, it was one of the first to do so. However, we do not focus on that particular aspect of the paper here. Rather, we focus on Culpeper *et al.*'s discussion of 'impoliteness and responses to it' (pp. 1562–8, with omissions). In this section of their paper, Culpeper *et al.* allude to the importance of both parties (S and H) when it comes to impoliteness and facework more generally: a focus that had tended to be overlooked by researchers of 'both politeness and impoliteness' up to this point (p. 1562).

J. Culpeper, D. Bousfield and A. Wichmann (2003) 'Impoliteness revisited: with special reference to dynamic and prosodic aspects'. *Journal of Pragmatics* 35: 1545–79.

Text B8.4.1
J. Culpeper,
D. Bousfield
and
A. Wichmann

Theoretically, when a recipient of an utterance perceives a strategic impoliteness act [. . .] they have two choices open to them: they can either *respond* or *not respond* (i.e. stay silent) [. . .] [T]he [latter] option presents particular problems for both the other participants in the original speech event and the researcher, who must depend solely on contextual factors in interpreting the meaning of the silence. Participants who choose to respond to the impoliteness act have a further theoretical set of choices open to them: they can either *accept* the face attack or they can *counter* it. In accepting the face attack, the recipient may, for instance, assume responsibility for the impoliteness act being issued in the first place. Thus, repeated, strong and personalized complaints (i.e. an impoliteness act) might be met with an apology. Note that this option involves increased face damage to the responder [. . .] The alternative option, to counter the face attack, involves a set of strategies which can be considered in terms of whether they are *offensive* or *defensive*. Offensive strategies primarily counter face attack with face attack; [. . .] [d]efensive strategies primarily counter face attack by defending one's own face [. . .] As we will illustrate below, [. . .] these strategic groupings are not mutually exclusive. Offensive strategies have, to some degree, the secondary goal of defending the face of the responder; defensive strategies may have, to some degree, the secondary goal of offending the speaker of the original impoliteness act. As a consequence, the distinction is best conceived of as a scale. The response options we have described are represented in Fig. 1.

   [. . .]
   One specific defence strategy . . . in our data [of traffic warden/parking violator interactions] was 'abrogation': the abrogation of personal responsibility for the action(s) or event that caused the interlocutor to issue a face damaging utterance in the first place. In Labov's (1972b) terms, this is a type of denial. It works by deflecting the FTA. In our data, abrogation involves attempting to switch either social role (from being addressed as private citizen to that of a public servant) or discoursal role (where an interactant emphasises that they are merely acting in a representative role such as a 'mouthpiece'). Abrogation by social role switching is like saying 'I'm not to blame, I'm just following orders!', whilst abrogation by discoursal role switching is like saying 'Don't shoot the messenger!' An example of defensive social role switching by S1 (a

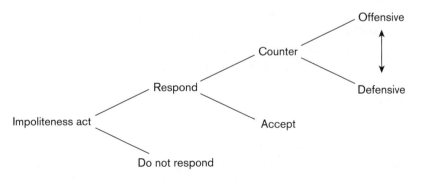

Fig. 1 A summary of response options

Text B8.4.1
J. Culpeper,
D. Bousfield
and
A. Wichmann

clamper) (and of implicit discoursal role switching) can be seen in |14| below. This example also illustrates, on the part of S2 (a car owner), how role triggering or role enforcing can be a more offensive strategy.

[14] S1:   =well you see *I'm just doing a job* but I've come
S2: *don't you think this is a bit stupid=*

S1: along here and   yeah
S2: *yeah   well so was Hitler all I'm asking you as a person don't you think this is a bit stupid*

S1:   well <exhales loudly> yes and no
S2:

The sequential organisation of this example is thus:

> (S2) OFFENSIVE (enforce role switch + implicate impolite belief) *don't you think this is a bit stupid*
> (S1) DEFENSIVE (abrogation) *well you see I'm just doing a job*
> (S2) OFFENSIVE (implicate impolite belief + reiterate enforced role switch) *Yeah well so was Hitler all I'm asking you as a person don't you think this is a bit stupid*
> (S1) DEFENSIVE (compromise) *well <exhales loudly> yes and no*

Note that the identification of the first offensive strategy 'enforce role switch' is only sustainable in the light of his second turn, when he makes the metapragmatic comment *I'm asking you as a person* to clarify his intent. In S1's final utterance, the hedge *well* and the exhalation signal that agreement (the preferred response) is not forthcoming, and the following *yes and no* attempts to negotiate a compromise. The interaction is interrupted at this point.

[. . .] |O|ther specific defensive strategies that occurred in our data |include| *opt|ing| out on-record*. This strategy attempts to 'seal off' the FTA. In the following example, S2 (an adjudicator) refuses the appeal of S1 (a car owner) on the basis that he 'prefers the council's evidence', despite S1's claims that the traffic warden who ticketed him (*this woman* in the extract) has falsified her records:

[15] S1   so you're quite happy that this woman perjured herself in
S2:

S1: writing
S2:   *I'm not saying anything more Mr Langarth and that is the end of the*

S1:   so you are happy   you're happy that she
S2: *proceeding*   *I'm not saying anything*

S1: perjured herself
S2:   I *I'm not making any further commentthank you* .. If you'll be

S1:
S2: kind enough to wait in the foyer

A further type of defensive strategy is *insincere agreement*, which manages the impoliteness act by allowing its speaker to 'let off steam'. A variant of this strategy is to express surface agreement with the face attack. In this example, S1 (a car owner) has stopped his car to heckle S2 (a traffic warden), who has just ticketed him for illegal parking.

Text B8.4.1
J. Culpeper,
D. Bousfield
and
A. Wichmann

[16] S1: One day you're going to get a lot of problems .. and you create the problems
S2:

S1: . we don't create the problems . ban the bloody cars all over London and
S2:

S1: we have no worries
S2:   *yeah*

S1: you give us authority to put them <indistinct > and then you come and give
S2:   *all right all right I agree with you*

S1: us a ticket   bar the cars take the cars off London
S2:   *all right I agree with you sir*   *yeah too*

S1:   do it today not tomorrow
S2: *many c*   *yup too many cars yeah too many cars on the road*

S1: don't give us this bloody headache all the time
S2:   *yeah too many cars .. anyway*

S1:
S2: you gonna shift

Note the lack of synchronisation between S1's accusations and S2's responses, particularly towards the end where the repeated *yeah too many cars* does not seem to address S1's immediately prior discourse. This betrays the fact that S2 is on 'automatic pilot', simply allowing S1 to let off steam. A*nyway*, towards the end of the extract, marks S2's shift back to serious business.

Yet another defensive strategy, though one which has some similarities with the previous strategy, is to ignore the implied face attack. This is particularly clear in cases of sarcasm, where the surface meaning of the utterance is accepted, rather than the implied sarcastic barb. In [one] example [. . .], a van owner, who has just been clamped, says *have a good day*, to which the clamper replies *I will do*. Clearly, the clamper complies only with the surface meaning of the van owner's sarcastic utterance. This defensive counter strategy may also be offensive at the same time, given that it is such a blatant misunderstanding of the van owner's meaning. This is not a rare occurrence: counter strategies which operate both offensively and defensively with respect to face occurred elsewhere in our data [. . .].

[. . .]

We conclude this section with two brief points. First, it should be remembered that in other discourses other impoliteness patterns may emerge, as well as other defensive strategies. Second, one area that we have neglected, but would obviously benefit from research, is how these confrontational encounters are resolved (see Vuchinich, 1990 and Hutchby, 1996b: chapter 6, for some first steps).

Task B8.4.1

➤ Look for two examples of each of Culpeper et al.'s (2003) response options – i.e. *abrogation, opting out on-record, insincere agreement, ignoring/deflection via sarcasm*. You might use examples from your own life, examples from fiction or examples from corpora. Now answer the following:

■ Which was the easiest strategy to find? Is there any reason for this and, if so, what might that be?

■ Are some response options more 'offensive' than others in your view? If so, which – and why?

➤ What is your default style when it comes to responding to face attack? Does your style change at all depending on (the power/status of) your interlocutor? If so, why is this (in your view)?

FURTHER READING

Eelen (2001) and Bargiela-Chiappini (2003) provide extremely useful overviews of the links between face and politeness, and Bousfield (2008) and Culpeper (2011) provide in-depth discussions of impoliteness. More specifically, Fraser (1990) provides a distinction between the 'social-norm' view, the 'conversational-maxim' view, the 'face-saving' view and the 'conversational-contract' view of politeness which you might find useful (not least because we've discussed a number of these approaches in Unit A8). An approach which we haven't discussed is the 'pragmatic scales' approach (see, e.g., Spencer-Oatey 2000, 2002). Spencer-Oatey's approach tends to be popular with intercultural researchers in particular, and might therefore provide you with a useful link to our discussions in Unit A10 and the readings in Unit B10. Collections of papers relating to impoliteness that will reward investigation include Bousfield and Locher (2008) and Bousfield and Culpeper (2008). Bousfield and Locher, in particular, include theoretical papers (which discuss the difficulties of defining impoliteness), and more applied papers (which draw on different datasets in their discussions of facework, im/politeness and their interface with power) and, as such, provide a useful link to our discussions in Units A12 and B12.

LOOKING AHEAD

In Unit C6, you are given the opportunity to undertake some facework and im/politeness studies of your own. We also touch upon facework and im/politeness issues in other chapters of this textbook (see, in particular, Units A12, C6 and C9).

Unit B9
Prosody: intonation

B9.1 INTRODUCTION

We saw in Unit A9 that speech communication involves much more than words alone. Both prosody and gesture play an important role in structuring the talk, enhancing the content of what we say, and expressing interpersonal meanings. We will return to gesture and other body language in Unit B10 and again in Unit C8. In this unit, however, we will focus on prosody, and in particular on one important component: speech melody, or intonation.

One of the important functions of intonation is to convey speaker attitudes and emotions, but how we do this is not so easy to explain. Some features of the voice relate directly to emotional states – we often hear quite clearly how someone is feeling by the sound of their voice. But even here things are not always clear-cut; we may think someone is excited and happy and then realize from their faces that they are actually agitated and anxious; someone may at first seem depressed but is actually just tired or relaxed. Animals, too, can give ambiguous signals: a dog wags its tail when it is pleased, but also when it is on alert for possible danger. Some people analyse emotions by positing different dimensions: positive and negative, high and low arousal (Cowie *et al.* 2000). On this basis, tail-wagging would be a sign of arousal, but whether positive (excited) or negative (anxious) would depend on the situation. It is also important to recognize that some meanings described as 'attitudes' are not necessarily related to emotion. If someone sounds 'condescending' or 'authoritative', or 'firm' this may relate more to how the speaker perceives his/her role in relation to the other person. Unlike emotions, these are pragmatic effects and can only be examined in context.

Most work on intonation over the last few decades has focused on its structure, i.e. intonational phonology. This enables us to see the intonational system, including what units it is composed of and how these units are arranged together, very much like identifying word classes and how they are arranged in phrases and sentences. But a sequence of phonological 'events', can be performed ('realized') in different ways, just as the same musical melody can be played in different keys. The whole sequence might be high or low in the speaker's range, or a prominence on an individual syllable might be large or small. These differences are gradient differences – both localized ones, i.e. associated with a particular point in the utterance, and longer-term ones that affect a whole stretch of speech. These gradient differences are generally thought of as paralinguistic, while the events themselves are linguistic (phonological). Unfortunately, a speaker only has one channel to speak with, and the final melody is a combination of the linguistic and the paralinguistic, which are very difficult to tease apart.

Our first reading (Mennen 2007) considers the importance of intonation for language learners, both in terms of the phonological inventory to be learned and in terms of phonetic implementation. The second reading (Wichmann 2004) looks at how basic choices between intonational categories (falling vs. rising contour) may signal something about the Speaker-Hearer relationship. The third (Gussenhoven 2004) takes an ethological approach and suggests some very fundamental meanings embodied in pitch that are common to signalling across the animal world.

All papers have something to say about intonational meaning that is not specific to English. Perceived attitudes may be pragmatic inferences generated by both linguistic and paralinguistic features of an utterance or sequence of utterances. In the case of linguistic features, the effect has to be seen in the context of the prosodic system of the language concerned. In the case of paralinguistic features, while these too may be in part culturally determined (see Unit A10) there is evidence that this may be more universal in effect. Gussenhoven's paper takes a very wide view, seeing human communcation as closely related to, or derived from, animal behaviour.

B9.2 MENNEN (2007)

Mennen is concerned with the place of intonation in language learning and teaching. She argues that making pronunciation mistakes in a foreign language is not quite so problematic as getting the intonation wrong. Native speakers can usually identify pronunication errors and make allowances for them. However, they tend to be less aware of their own use of intonation and are therefore less able to identify inappropriate use by a learner. Instead they are likely to assume that an 'attitude' is being expressed, but possibly not what the speaker intended.

<table>
<tr><td>Text B9.2.1
I. Mennen</td><td>**I. Mennen (2007) 'Phonological and phonetic influences in non-native intonation'. In J. Trouvain and U. Gut (eds) *Non-native prosody: phonetic description and teaching practice*. The Hague: Mouton de Gruyter, pp. 53–76.**</td></tr>
</table>

There is no doubt as to the importance of intonation in communication. Intonation not only conveys linguistic information, but also plays a key role in regulating discourse and is an important indicator of speaker identity [. . .] The use of an inappropriate intonation pattern may give rise to misunderstandings. Such misunderstanding can be major or minor depending on the context in which the intonation pattern is used. As there is no one to one correspondence between intonation and meaning, an appropriate meaning can often be found that fits with the 'wrong' intonation pattern [. . .] Nevertheless, some patterns will clearly not be acceptable in some varieties, and the cumulative effect of continuously using slightly inappropriate intonation should not be underestimated. Given that we derive much of our impression about a speaker's attitude and disposition towards us from the way they use intonation in speech, listeners may form a negative impression of a speaker based on the constantly occurring inappropriate use of intonation [. . .]

In order to establish intonational differences and similarities across languages which could cause the L1 and L2 intonation systems to influence one another, a generally agreed framework for analysing intonation needs to be used [. . .] A model which has been used successfully to describe a wider range of languages [. . .] is the model of intonational analysis developed by Pierrehumbert (1980) and Pierrehumbert and Beckman (1988) [. . .] The most important principle of Pierrehumbert's model is that it separates the phonological representation from its phonetic implementation, and intonation is viewed as consisting of a phonological and phonetic component [. . .]

The distinction between a phonetic and phonological component in intonation is important as it suggests that languages can differ at both these levels. As a result, L1 and L2 intonation systems may influence one another both at the level of phonological representation as well as at the level of their phonetic implementation. A *phonological* influence would result from intonational differences in the inventory of phonological tunes. A *phonetic* influence would result from a difference in the phonetic realisation of an identical phonological tune (Ladd 1996). An example of *phonological* influence is the use of rises where native speakers would use falls and vice versa [. . .] An example of *phonetic* influence is the finding of a different pitch range [. . .] compared to the monolingual norm [. . .]

Task B9.2.1

> Are you aware of any national stereotypes that might arise from inappropriate prosody, including intonation? (You can read more about this in Unit A10.)

> The model of intonation referred to here (Autosegmental) is illustrated in Unit A9.3, Box A9.2, which shows some of the contours available in English. Using the wrong one would count in Mennen's terms as an error in phonological choice. What does she mean by phonetic implementation?

B9.3 WICHMANN (2004)

Wichmann's paper is concerned with the pragmatic effects of phonological choice. It demonstrates how the intonation of a simple polite request (*can you . . . please*) varies according to the context. The study is based on the ICE-GB, a corpus of British English containing 1 million words in all, of which 600,000 words are orthographically transcribed speech. It is not possible to search automatically for requests in this corpus (see Unit A2.5.1), so the method used was a lexical search on the word *please*. This corpus also has sound recordings, so that the researcher can listen to each example found. Some examples can be analysed instrumentally, using speech analysis software, but this is not always possible with this data, since it was recorded in many natural environments – the kitchen, the office, the classroom, etc., and the recording quality is sometimes poor. All the examples in this study were transcribed auditorily on the basis of repeated listening. In cases such as this, the reader has no choice but to trust the analyst, or go back to the original data. Even experts can disagree, but increasingly the data is made available (often on publishers' websites) in the form of soundfiles, so that readers can listen for themselves. Despite the relative subjectivity of auditory analysis, it would be a mistake to think that instrumental analysis is more objective. The analyst needs to know which parts of the contour are important and which are not, and also how to interpret the effect of the vowels and consonants on the F0 contour. (See Box A9.1, in Unit A9.2.)

This study is concerned particularly with final intonation contours on requests that contain *please*. Rising and falling final contours are thought to be important for distinguishing between sentence types such as statement and question. However, this study found that *please*-requests occurred with both rising and falling contours, and it was therefore important to know whether they mean the same, and if not, when each is used. The most common type of request had the word *please* in utterance-final position, and it was particularly these that were studied closely. Wichmann found that *please*-requests ending in a rising contour occurred in situations where the participants were equal in power and status. Those with a falling contour, on the other hand, occurred in unequal encounters, and were much closer to commands than requests.

Text B9.3.1
A. Wichmann

A. Wichmann (2004) 'The intonation of *please*-requests: a corpus based study'. *Journal of Pragmatics* 36: 1521–49.

5.3. Contextual effects: public vs. private

Typical of a modal interrogative in a private situation is the use of *can*, the word *please* in final position, and ending high; typical of a modal interrogative in a public situation is the use of *could*, the word *please* in final position, and ending low. Mitigated commands occur in private speech but vary in form and realisation; in public speech they are more uniform, usually positive commands, with an initial *please*, and the pitch usually ends low. Typical intonation contours of indirect requests and mitigated commands according to situation are summarised in Fig. 1.

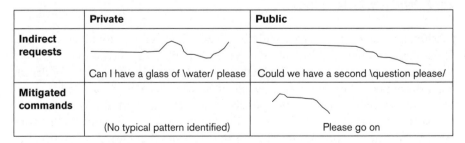

	Private	Public
Indirect requests	Can I have a glass of \water/ please	Could we have a second \question please/
Mitigated commands	(No typical pattern identified)	Please go on

Fig. 1 Summary of the typical forms and contours of indirect requests and mitigated commands in public and private speech. (Real examples from the corpus.)

6. Discussion

Text B9.3.1
A. Wichmann

Requests in 'public' speech, whether using strategies of indirectness or mitigated commands, tend to be spoken with a final falling contour. In this data that means that where social distance is greater, and the power relationship asymmetrical, a request (spoken by the more powerful) is likely to end low, regardless of the type of utterance chosen. In the 'private' texts, where power relations are more symmetrical and the social distance between participants is smaller, we can predict a higher frequency of requests ending high (with a final rise). This is entirely consistent with what is known about the discoursal effects of terminal contours. Falling intonation contributes to what has been described as 'a feeling of closure' (Croft, 1995). A final fall is typical of a 'citation'—a word, phrase, sentence read aloud in isolation: in other words the intonation signals the closure of a complete text. In interactional terms, the sense of closure or finality can signal the end of a turn, and in some contexts it can convey the sense that there is no more to be said on the matter, the matter is closed or non-negotiable. A final rise, on the other hand, signals 'openness' (Cruttenden, 1997) or 'non-finality' (Wichmann, 2000), and when it occurs at a point of syntactic completion it can mean that a response is possible or that there may be more to be said on the matter.

The notions of openness and closure relate to the speech act 'request' as follows: the public requests are mostly the kind where the hearer does not have the right to refuse because of the social roles and power relationships involved. The private requests are the kind where the hearer is unlikely to refuse because the imposition is minimal but has the option to comply or not. Speakers distinguish prosodically between these situations. A falling tone, with its inherently low endpoint, assumes compliance; a rising tone, with its inherently high, or at least non-low, endpoint, does not. This contour suggests that the matter is still 'open', if only notionally, e.g., for negotiation or for non-compliance. Brown *et al.* (1980: 30) observe a similar distinction:

> Low terminals are regularly associated with the end of topics, with the end of a turn when a speaker has no more to say on a topic, and with conducive questions where the speaker has a high expectation of the correctness of the assumption that lies behind his question . . . Not-low terminals are associated with more to come on the same topic, in the same turn, and with nonconducive questions.

Task B9.3.1

➤ The rising contour is said to be 'open' and the falling contour 'closed'. Can you explain why the intonation of these *please*-requests is different in the situations described? What motivates the choice between 'open' and 'closed'?

➤ Do you think the version with the falling contour might sound impolite in certain situations? How would that come about?

➤ Do you know how the differences described in the reading might be expressed prosodically in any other language or another variety of English?

B9.4 GUSSENHOVEN (2004)

In this reading, Gussenhoven discusses why paralinguistic choices such as high or low pitch, either at certain points or over a longer stretch of discourse, might create certain impressions. To do this he examines observations of animal behaviour, particularly how it relates to trying to appear 'big' to a potential aggressor. This is an example of looking at possible universal features of intonation, features that may explain perceived attitudes or 'tone of voice' and even, in a grammaticalized form, explain some apparent universals in intonational phonology.

Text B9.4.1
C. Gussenhoven

C. Gussenhoven (2004) *The phonology of tone and intonation.* **Cambridge: Cambridge University Press, pp. 80–2.**

5.6 The Frequency Code

The Frequency Code was proposed by Ohala (1983) as an explanation of the striking similarity across languages in the use of rising or high question intonation and falling or low statement intonation. Essentially, Ohala extended the explanation for the widespread similarities in patterns of avian and mammalian vocalizations in face-to-face competitive encounters to human speech given by Morton (1977). Vocalizations by dominant or aggressive individuals are low-pitched, while those by subordinate or submissive individuals are high-pitched. Lower pitch suggests the organ producing the vocalization is larger. In fact, the exploitation of this correlation in nature is not confined to meaningful variation by individuals. In many species, it is hard-wired in the sexes through dimorphism, the different biological developments of the male and female members of a species. In the front to back dimension, the male human larynx is almost twice the size of the female larynx, exactly the dimension which affects the fundamental frequency most. It arises at puberty, the age at which boy becomes man, ready to assume the role of defender or aggressor. To underscore the effect, the male larynx is positioned lower in the throat, causing the vocal tract, the tube leading to the lips, to be some 3.5 cm longer than the female vocal tract. The effect is that formant frequencies are lower in men, again suggesting a larger creature. Other aspects of dimorphism in animals and humans point in the same direction: males may have extra feathers to be erected, antlers, thicker manes, or, in the case of humans, peripheral facial hair, all of which serve to make the creature look more imposing. Ohala (1983, 1984, 1996) claims that we associate pitch with this package of evolutionary meanings, for which reason intonation contours have come to have the distributional bias we observe. The Frequency Code, therefore, is a 'size code': just as effort is here seen to lie behind the meanings to be discussed [in a later section], so size is the explanatory concept behind the meanings discussed in this section.

5.6.1 *Affective interpretations of the Frequency Code*

It is tempting to think of the anatomical differences between men and women as just a relic of an earlier evolutionary functionalism, with no relevance for present-day social interaction beyond signalling the sex of the speaker. However, people will project what they perceive as their social role in their voice, and gender roles are no exception. Voice characteristics that are manipulated include type of vocal fold vibration (breathy

Text B9.4.1
C. Gussenhoven

voice, creaky voice), formant frequencies (as a result of vocal-tract manipulations like lip rounding, nasalization, habitual tongue posture, and pharyngeal constriction), but also fundamental frequency (e.g. Laver 1980). For instance, while men will produce lower average formant frequencies than women as a result of their longer vocal tracts, speech communities vary in the social significance they attach to the gender difference, which suggests that one or both sexes might well exaggerate the effect (Henton 1995; Henton 1999). Henton and Bladon (1988) find that creak is a marker of British male speech, and that at least in some varieties it is used to signal masculinity. Similarly, different speech communities may have different average pitch levels, for one or both sexes. Thus, American men speak at a lower pitch than German men (Scherer 1979), Japanese women speak at a higher pitch than American women (Ohara 1992), and Dutch spoken by Belgian women is higher than Dutch spoken by Dutch women (Bezooijen 1993). Biemans (2000: 157), who also gives a survey of the recent literature (2000: 19ff.), found a positive correlation between five artificial registers superimposed on a set of spontaneous male and female utterances and the scores on a 'femininity' scale, and a negative correlation with the scores on a 'masculinity' scale. That is, raising our register will make us sound more feminine and lowering it will make us sound more masculine.

There are several different affective interpretations of the Frequency Code. 'Feminine' vs. 'masculine' values are associated with 'submissiveness' and 'dominance', respectively. Other meanings include (for higher pitch) 'friendliness' and 'politeness'. A closely related one is 'vulnerability' (for higher pitch) versus 'confidence', which may play out as 'protection', or as its counterparts 'aggression' and 'scathing'. They can be grouped as affective interpretations of the Frequency Code, as they signal properties of speaker. Positive scores for high pitch on semantic scales for 'polite', 'non-aggressive', and 'friendly' are a commonplace finding in perception experiments with intonation. Uldall (1964) found that listeners associated high-ending rises with both 'submissiveness' and 'pleasantness'. In a recent experiment, Rietveld, Haan, Heijmans, and Gussenhoven (2002) found that the scores on four scales measuring affective meanings for eight Dutch intonation contours correlated highly with the mean fundamental frequency of the contours. Even stronger correlations were found between these scores and the mean fundamental frequency of the last quarter of the contours, suggesting that contour endings are used more for this purpose than other parts.

Task B9.4.1

➤ In Unit A9.6.1 we referred to a study of a female British politican who was trained to lower her pitch when speaking. Why might this have made her sound 'more authoritative'?

➤ The authors claim that the frequency code can explain a number of perceived attitudes, such as friendly, aggressive, polite, etc. These are similar to the effects suggested in literature by writing 'she said aggressively' or 'he said gently' (see Unit A9.1) Sometimes, however, the same 'tone of voice' can have different effects, depending on the context. For example, a voice that sounds reassuring to one person might sound condescending to another. Can you explain how these apparently contradictory effects might arise?

FURTHER READING

Much work on the interface between prosody and meaning has been carried out in the Conversation Analysis framework, and many useful papers are collected in Couper-Kuhlen and Selting (1996), Couper-Kuhlen and Ford (2004) and Barth-Weingarten *et al.* (2010). A recent article by Gorisch *et al.* (2012), also in the Conversation Analysis tradition, examines how the pitch of 'insertions' (short responses) indicates a positive or negative alignment with the other speaker.

A wider variety of theoretical approaches are represented in Barth-Weingarten *et al.* (2009) and also the Special Issue of the *Journal of Pragmatics*, Volume 38 Issue 10 (2006), which contains a good overview, for example, of the relevance theoretic approach to prosody (Wilson and Wharton 2006). The Special Issue also contains a paper (Peppé *et al.* 2006) taking a developmental perspective, which addresses the pragmatic ability of children with autism. For a book-length account of non-verbal communication and Relevance Theory, read Wharton (2009).

The most extensive overview of research into all aspects of body language is by Argyle (1988). Kendon (2001) is a review article on gesture that considers alternative views of gesture, for example, whether gestures are co-produced with speech or actually aid speech production. A more recent book-length account of gesture is that by Kendon (2004).

LOOKING AHEAD

In Unit C7 we invite you to explore some of the paralinguistic uses of prosody, and make comparisons with other languages or other varieties of English that you are familiar with.

Unit B10
Cross-cultural pragmatics

B10.1 INTRODUCTION

Communication between speakers of different languages is fraught with difficulty, even between speakers who appear to know each other's language well. We find that there are considerable cultural differences operating at all levels of behaviour, verbal and non-verbal, and that these affect our ability to communicate. Such differences also exist closer to home, between speakers of the same language, as Tannen found in her study of New York speakers (see Unit A10.5.3). Misunderstandings arising from cultural differences have been categorized by Thomas (1983) as either pragma-linguistic or sociopragmatic (see Unit A10.2) The first is caused by misusing 'apparently synonymous' expressions (such as 'of course' in English and Russian) but others are more to do with not knowing the cultural norms, such as what counts as an imposition or what the power relations are in a given situation. The consequences of cultural and linguistic misunderstandings are evident in the courtroom, and have implications for the way in which judges and juries understand defendants; where an interpreter is used, the challenge for the interpreter is to understand not only the sense of what a defendant is saying but also the broader cultural and interpersonal meanings being conveyed. Finally, the potential for misunderstandings is a constant threat to international diplomacy.

There are some researchers such as Kecskes (2011) who claim that cross-cultural misunderstanding is less common than we think. Many conversations take place in a language that is not the native language of either or any of the speakers, but they choose English as a lingua franca. Kecskes suggests that in this situation formulaic language is used very little, and speakers rely on 'semantically transparent language' to make sure that others understand them (ibid.: 378). He claims that pragmatic theories tend to idealize human communication and that intercultural communication is more of an emergent achievement, reached by a process of trial and error.

Nonetheless, we believe that the study of cross-cultural pragmatics is important for a number of reasons, both practical and theoretical: the claims to universality of some theoretical models can only be challenged if they are tested against a range of different languages. In practical terms, if we wish to avoid some of the serious consequences of miscommunication, we must consider the implications for language teaching, where focus on words and grammar often crowds out pragmatic and social considerations.

The readings in this section cover a range of different foci in cross-cultural communication, starting with Wierzbicka (2003) who looks at directness and indirectness, features that are commonly closely associated with politeness. The second reading (Thomas 1983) concerns not how to say something but whether or not to say it – it describes a setting in which the local cultural conventions are in direct conflict with those of the speaker, touching on deeply held moral beliefs. Finally, in Argyle (1988) we look at how non-verbal behaviour varies across cultures, and consider the potential for misunderstanding that can arise.

B10.2 WIERZBICKA (2003)

In attempting to describe the communicative norms of other cultures it is very hard not to impose the values and categories from our own culture, and some effort has been made to express these in a very simple terminology (see Unit A10.4). In this reading Wierzbicka explains the need for a very general way of describing the different beliefs that underlie different ways of saying things.

Text B10.2.1
A. Wierzbicka

A. Wierzbicka (2003) *Cross-cultural pragmatics*. Berlin: Mouton de Gruyter, pp. 88–9, 92–3.

12. 'Directness'

The terms 'directness' and 'indirectness' are often used in linguistic descriptions as if they were self-explanatory. In fact, however, they are applied to totally different phenomena, which are shaped by totally different values.

The confusion which surrounds this notion is linked with the widely accepted distinction between so-called 'direct' and 'indirect' speech acts, and, in particular, between imperatives and the so-called whimperatives. Thus, it is widely assumed that if one says to somebody *Close the door!* this is a 'direct' speech act, whereas if one says *Could you close the door?* or *Would you mind closing the door?* this is an 'indirect' speech act. But although these particular examples may seem clear, it is by no means clear how the distinction in question should be applied to other phenomena and to other languages. Thus, in many languages, for example, in Russian, Polish, Thai, or Japanese, the imperative is often combined with various particles, some of them somewhat impatient, others rather friendly, some of them described as 'softening' the directive, others as, on the contrary, making it harsher or more peremptory, and so on. Are such combinations of the imperative with a particle 'direct' or 'indirect' speech acts? There is no general principle which would allow us to answer this question.

I suggest, therefore, that the whole distinction between 'direct' and 'indirect' speech acts should be abandoned – at least until some clear definition of these terms is provided; and also, that the distinction between 'direct' and 'indirect' ways of speaking in general should be abandoned, and that the different phenomena associated with these individually examined. I believe that when this is done, cultural explanations for the cross-linguistic differences associated with these terms can be provided.

[. . .]

Blum-Kulka (1982: 30–31) mentions that it is not common in English to express refusal by saying 'No' as one does in Hebrew, or to say 'No' in response to a request for information (for example in shops, hotels, and restaurants): 'Do you have such and such?' In English, when someone indicates that they want something from us we are free to say 'No', but not to say just 'No'. The label 'directness' is not helpful in describing this aspect of the Anglo-American ethnography of speaking, though one can use here, more illuminatingly, the label 'bluntness'. (It should be noted, however, that 'bluntness', though clearer here than 'directness', is not self-explanatory either, and that for example Geertz (1976: 245) attributes 'bluntness' to Anglo-American culture, contrasting it in this way with Japanese culture.) 'Bluntness' in saying 'No' is viewed positively in Israeli culture but not in Anglo-American culture. These different attitudes to 'bluntness' in saying 'No' can be represented as follows:

Anglo-American culture
I say: No
I don't want you to feel something bad because of this
I will say something more about it because of this
Israeli culture
I say: No
I think I don't have to say anything more about it

In Japanese culture, the norm seems to be to avoid saying 'No' altogether (in particular, to refuse an offer or a request, to express disagreement, and so on). Thus, Nakane (1970: 35) notes: ". . . one would prefer to be silent than utter such words as 'no' or 'I disagree'. The avoidance of such open and bald negative expressions is rooted in the fear that it might disrupt the harmony and order of the group". This norm can be represented as follows:

Japanese culture
I can't say: No
I will say something else because of this

Task B10.2.1

➤ It is claimed that saying 'No' in Japanese culture might disrupt the harmony of the group. Do you think that other cultures value harmony less?

➤ What are the implications of this article for the relationship between indirectness and politeness?

B10.3 THOMAS (1983)

Thomas distinguishes between pragmalinguistic failure, such as might occur in situations described by Wierzbicka above, and sociopragmatic failure, which involves underlying conventions that may be unfamiliar to a participant. The latter can be particularly problematic because the conventions are not transparent. It may, for example, seem hypocritical to a learner of English to be asked how they are (*How are you?*) but find that the speaker is not really interested in their well-being.

However, we accept it in English as a conventional greeting rather than a genuine question. We sometimes apologize out of politeness to someone for bumping into them in the street, even if we think it was their fault. But if this is not the convention in another culture, a learner from that culture might feel angry at being expected to apologize for something when not actually at fault. This kind of cultural convention underlies the problem described by Thomas in this reading.

Text B10.3.1
J. Thomas

J. Thomas (1983) 'Cross-cultural pragmatic failure'. *Applied Linguistics* 4: 91–112.

It is not always easy to distinguish between moral principles and pragmatic principles. What (for me) was a painful illustration of this fact came when I was teaching in Russia. At the end of each semester, the Rector of the University called a meeting of each department to discuss how well the teaching staff had fulfilled its plan. This particular semester—my first—had started six weeks late because the students had been despatched to the state farms to help bring in the potato harvest. Nevertheless, the Rector criticized each teacher individually for having underfulfilled his/her norm and, ludicrous as the situation seemed to me, each teacher solemnly stood up, said that s/he accepted the criticism and would do better next time. I felt particularly aggrieved, since not only had I taught every class I had been scheduled to teach, but a number of others besides. I might, perhaps, have accepted in silence what I saw as totally unfair criticism, but to *say* I accepted it was more than I could bear. The anger I aroused, by saying quite politely that I did not think I was to blame, was quite appalling and the reverberations lasted many months. What offended my Soviet colleagues so deeply was that they felt I was being intolerably sanctimonious in taking seriously something which *everyone* involved knew to be purely a matter of form; behaving like the sort of po-faced prig who spoils a good story by pointing out that it is not strictly true. I, for my part, had felt obliged to sacrifice politeness in the greater cause of (overt) truthfulness!

This type of situation arose frequently, and all the British and Americans I knew in the Soviet Union reacted as I had, bristling with moral indignation. Yet, if it is inconceivable that an entire people is actually less truthful than another, we must look for different pragmatic principles in operation. In my view, every instance of national or ethnic stereotyping should be seen as a reason for calling in the pragmaticist and discourse analyst!

Task B10.3.1

➤ What would you have done in Thomas' situation?

➤ What exactly is a lie in your view? Are there any occasions when you think a lie is acceptable?

B10.4 ARGYLE (1988)

In Unit A9 we described how bodily gestures can play a part in interaction. We showed how gaze can send important signals during turn-taking, for example, to indicate whether the speaker is ready for a contribution from the other participant. Sometimes bodily signals convey attitudinal information – exaggerated staring, or standing 'too close' to someone may be perceived as aggressive. Other non-verbal features may contribute to perceived politeness, such as handshakes, pats on the back, standing straight and smiling. However, these patterns of behaviour are by no means universal, but vary considerably across cultures. The following extract shows the extent to which this variation occurs, and underlines the fact that behaviour must be judged according to cultural norms.

M. Argyle (1988) *Bodily communication*. London: Routledge, pp. 57–60.

Text B10.4.1
M. Argyle

Gaze

The level of gaze varies quite a lot between cultures. Watson (1970) studied 110 male foreign students at the University of Colorado. He used a scoring system and obtained results showing that the Arabs, Latin Americans, and southern Europeans looked more than those from non-contact cultures. The numbers were small, but the differences between contact and non-contact cultural groups were significant. Other studies have confirmed that there are higher levels of gaze for Arabs, South Americans, and Greeks. A pair of Arabs in conversation in the laboratory look at each other more than two Americans or two Englishmen. Gaze and mutual gaze are very important to Arabs, and they find it difficult to talk to someone wearing dark glasses, or when walking side by side. Not facing directly enough is regarded as impolite.

Black Americans look less than whites, both while talking and while listening, and this applies to males and females, children and adults. A meta-analysis of eleven studies found an average effect size of 0.73σ, but it was greater than this, $1-42\sigma$, for people being interviewed (Halberstadt 1985). The low level of gaze by blacks in interviews combined with the use of very slight head-nods while listening can give the impression that they are not attending or do not understand (Erickson 1979).

The meaning of gaze can also be different. Black Americans are reluctant to look at people in authority since it is felt to communicate equality and hence disrespect (Hanna 1984). Students in south India are excited but embarrassed by a direct gaze from a member of the opposite sex; it is seen as bold but rude; there is no tradition of courtship in this region (L'Armand 1984). Since Roman times it has been believed that some people have the 'evil eye'. This is still the case in Naples, where it is ascribed to some priests, and monks, though formerly to old ladies with squints or deep-set eyes. It is believed that those who are looked at by the evil eye are cursed.

Spatial behaviour

E. T. Hall's original observation that Arabs stand closer than Americans (1959) was confirmed by Watson (1970) in his study of foreign students in the USA. Arabs also stand at a more directly facing orientation, and southern Europeans even more so. People from contact cultures stand closer, face more directly, touch and look more, and speak louder.

Text B10.4.1
M. Argyle

Genuine cross-cultural studies are few, but it has been found that Indonesian students use less space than similar Australians (Noesjirwan 1978). Latin Americans on average need less space than North Americans, but there are regional variations: Costa Ricans stand closer than the Columbians or Panamanians (Shuter 1976). Within the USA, hispanics stand closer than anglos. The evidence on black Americans is conflicting: most studies find that they interact at greater distances, though this may vary with the situation (Hayduk 1983). Black children stand closer than whites, but black adolescents and adults stand further away from one another; there is a strong correlation of distance with age for blacks. Blacks also adopt a less direct orientation (from meta analyses by Halberstadt 1985). Blacks move about more when standing talking in a group, and a speaker may move away and turn his back to the group, to add emphasis.

What is the explanation of these differences in spatial behaviour? They may derive from wider aspects of the environment, such as the size of houses and the degree of crowding. Cultures develop more or less explicit rules about proper spatial behaviour. Those who stand or sit too far away are seen as cold, aloof, and withdrawn, while those who come too close are seen as embarrassingly intrusive and over-intimate.

One of the most remarkable sets of cultural rules about spatial behaviour is that governing how close the members of each Indian caste may approach one another. These rules are still kept in rural areas of southern India:

Brahmins	7 ft
Nayars	25 ft
Iravans	32 ft
Cherumans	64 ft
Nayadis	

This works additively, so that a Nayadi must not come closer to a Brahmin than 128 ft.

There are rules governing spatial behaviour for different situations in any culture. In Britain and the USA, for example, Cook (1970) found that two people sitting in a pub prefer to sit side by side, with their backs to the wall. In a restaurant or cafeteria, on the other hand, they sit opposite each other. When they are seated people adopt a considerably greater distance than when standing: 5–8 ft as opposed to 1½–3 ft.

 Task B10.4.1

➤ How do the various behaviours described above relate to the power relation-ships between people? What misunderstandings could arise between different groups of people for example between white teachers and black students?

➤ A number of studies are mentioned here that have investigated gaze and spatial behaviour. What methods do you think were used to establish what people actually do? What methods can one use to establish how various non-verbal behaviours are perceived by others?

➤ Do you remember being taught, e.g. as a child, or as a language learner, any non-verbal signals as being 'polite' or 'impolite' when interacting with other people?

FURTHER READING

Following your reading of Thomas (1983) in Unit B10.3, we suggest you read the important discussion by Coleman and Kay (1982) on what constitutes a prototypical lie. In relation to address forms, Gu (1990) provides an interesting discussion of politeness in modern Chinese, including the use of personal names. His study questions the universal applicability of the models of Brown and Levinson and of Leech. For a recent overview of impoliteness from a cross-cultural perspective read Culpeper *et al.* (2010).

For further discussion of English as a lingua franca and the implications for teaching, see Seidlhofer (2001, 2005). Kaur (2011) presents a study of the sources of misunderstanding in communication using English as a lingua franca. This article, as well as that by Culpeper *et al.* (2010), appeared in the journal *Intercultural Pragmatics*, which publishes a wide range of studies in the field.

Many studies of pragmatic development among learners focus more on the object of acquisition – inferring meaning from indirect speech acts, for example – than the theoretical assumptions about the learning process. Kasper (2009) offers a comprehensive overview of research on L2 pragmatics under a number of theoretical approaches, including cognitive theories, socio-cultural theory and conversation analysis.

LOOKING AHEAD

Units A10 and B10 have introduced a wide range of pragmatic phenomena that can lead to miscommunication between speakers of different languages. In Unit C8 you will have the opportunity to investigate for yourself some of these issues – forms of address, and the relation between indirectness and politeness – using a variety of methods including the analysis of corpus data. You will also be invited to consider what implications cross-cultural miscommunication has for language teaching and to carry out a comparative study of how pragmatic meaning is addressed in textbooks for learners of English.

Unit B11
Historical pragmatics

B11.1 INTRODUCTION

The readings in this section have been chosen because they provide (i) a general overview of historical pragmatics, (ii) an overview of the (prevalent) use of corpora/corpus-based approaches within historical pragmatics and, finally, (iii) a sense of some of the results which can be achieved from applying corpus linguistic techniques to historical data. We begin with Jonathan Culpeper's (2010) entry on 'Historical pragmatics', which is taken from Cummings' *Pragmatics encyclopedia*. We then move on to Thomas Kohnen's (2009) paper on 'Historical corpus pragmatics'. As the title indicates, one purpose of Kohnen's paper is to define the sub-field of historical corpus pragmatics. We do not include that discussion here. Instead, we summarize Kohnen's views in this regard in our introduction to his reading and focus, in our excerpt, on Kohnen's discussion of the diachronic development of English directives, with special reference to politeness and in/directness issues. The final reading in this section, by Irma Taavitsainen and Andreas Jucker (2008b), also explores a speech act which is commonly associated with politeness: the compliment. As we have discussed Jucker and Taavitsainen's (2000) fuzziness approach to speech acts in some detail in Unit A11.4, we focus here on their explication of a data extract taken from the *Dialogue Between Two Young Ladies Lately Married, Concerning Management of Husbands* (1696), which was found by them using the search string: *(more) beautiful.*

B11.2 CULPEPER (2010)

Culpeper's excerpt touches upon some of the issues and topics we have already explored in Unit A11, namely, the validity of using written texts to learn about the speech of the past, the research approaches commonly used to investigate such data and the pragmatic phenomena commonly discussed. Culpeper stresses the role that Elizabeth Traugott has played within the more micro approaches. Representative of the Anglo-American tradition within pragmatics (see Unit A1.1), Traugott is especially well-known for her grammaticalization work (Unit A11.6). Culpeper does not point to a representative researcher for the Continental European approach, but he does highlight how macro studies which explore im/politeness in a historical context have drawn on Goffman, for example (cf. Unit A8). By so doing, Culpeper is able to touch on 'the crucial issue of the applicability or otherwise' of a modern 'theory or concept' when applied to historical data. Towards the end of the excerpt, Culpeper also summarizes some of the methodological difficulties facing historical pragmatics. As such, he provides us with a useful lead in to our later papers in this section, which use corpus linguistic techniques to study pragmatic phenomena.

J. Culpeper (2010) 'Historical pragmatics'. In L. Cummings (ed.) *The pragmatics encyclopedia*. London and New York: Routledge, pp. 188–92.

Text B11.2.1
J. Culpeper

The conceptual and theoretical apparatus of historical pragmatic studies is various, but, broadly speaking, as we move from the more micro to the more macro, we move from the more cognitive and universal to the more social and local. Elizabeth C. Traugott's work has played a significant role in shaping the theoretical input to the more micro approaches. Traugott (1982) hypothesized that meanings of linguistic expressions tend to shift from propositional to interpersonal meanings, with quite often an intermediate stage of textual meaning (these categories of meaning, of course, echo those of Halliday, e.g. Halliday 1978). A good example is Jucker's (1997) discussion of how *well* developed into a pragmatic marker with the potential for expressing interpersonal meanings (compare 'I am never well', an assertion about health or well-being, and 'Well, I never!', an expression of surprise). Such processes of change are sometimes discussed under the label 'grammaticalization', to which Traugott's work has contributed much (*see also* Traugott's later notion of 'subjectification' (Traugott 1989, 1995) and her notion of 'intersubjectification' (Traugott 2003)). Other authors (e.g. Erman and Kotsinas 1993) have preferred to talk of 'pragmaticalization', because items such as pragmatic markers can be seen as lying outside the grammar and not having grammatical functions. This, however, rather depends on what you consider 'the grammar' to be. Traugott and Dasher (2002: 158–59) argue that pragmatic markers belong to the grammar, just as one would consider, for example, sentence adverbials to be part of the grammar. Whatever the label, the processes of change discussed are in fact fairly similar, both involving the increasing importance of meanings considered typically pragmatic. The development of pragmatic meanings in relation to semantic change has been explained in terms of Grice's conversational implicature (particularly as developed in Neo-Gricean pragmatics). Thus, one-off, context-sensitive, particularized implicatures are said to evolve into preferred, contextually-stable generalized implicatures, which may then become part of the semantic meaning of the item (*cf.* Levinson 2000). Of particular note here is Traugott's invited inferencing theory of semantic change, which aims at providing a full, step-by-step account of how pragmatic meanings develop (Traugott 1999; Traugott and Dasher 2002).

More macro historical pragmatic work (leaning towards pragmaphilology) is not in fact generally atheoretical, despite non-pragmatic historical language philology often being so. Theories or at least concepts, often cultural and/or social in orientation and drawn from diverse fields of study, are used to account for how pragmatic meanings are generated and interpreted in particular contexts, and for how those very contexts are to be analyzed and understood. To take just one example, the work of the cognitive-sociologist Erving Goffman is deployed both indirectly via face-oriented politeness theories, and directly in studies such as Bax (2001), which uses Goffman's notion of frame analysis (Goffman 1974). Typically, the theories and concepts used were not devised for historical purposes, which leads to the crucial issue of the applicability or otherwise of a particular theory or concept.

Text B11.2.1
J. Culpeper

In fact, pragmatic theories are not only based on and devised for relatively recent language, but are also largely based on and devised for spoken data. But there are no actual records of spoken data prior to the invention of the tape-recorder.[1] All, however, is not lost. For one thing, as we go further back into the past the gap between the characteristics of writing and of speech narrows [. . .] Further, much can be inferred about spoken interaction from historical speech-related text-types (e.g. trial proceedings, play-texts, didactic works in dialogue form), as well as from more colloquial written genres such as personal letters (*see* Culpeper and Kytö 2000). It is worth noting that how colloquial a particular genre is at a particular point in time is partly culturally determined. Thus, personal letters in East Asia are traditionally considerably more formal than their European counterparts. There is also secondary data available in the form of conversation manuals, prescribing modes of approved conversational behaviour. A more radical approach, and one that is gaining ground, is to recognize that pragmatics need not be constrained by medium (*cf.* Stein 1992). Indeed, more recent research has pointed out the interactional qualities of written language (*cf.* Myers 1999). Jacobs and Jucker (1995: 10) rightly argue that 'written texts can be analyzed as communicative acts in their own right'. Any pragmatic discussion of a linguistic feature in a historical text must, therefore, take on board the fact that a, if not the, key contextual aspect of that feature will be the genre of which it is a part.

Methodologically, historical pragmatics encounters huge challenges (see the discussions in Jacobs and Jucker 1995; Jucker 2000b; Fitzmaurice and Taavitsainen 2007). One particular difficulty attends diachronic pragmatics. If one tracks a particular function and how it changes the forms it employs, one needs to assume that the particular function one is tracking is stable (if the enterprise is to be meaningful). But this assumption cannot be strongly held. For example, if tracking the speech act of apology over time, one may observe different forms being employed. Simultaneously, however, what actually counts as an apology may be changing as well, so that the forms one observes do not have a stable relationship with a function. As Jacobs and Jucker (1995: 19) point out, illocutionary force is not clearly the best *tertium comparationis*. A further methodological problem for historical pragmatics is that many of the methods of synchronic pragmatics (e.g. questionnaires, discourse completion tasks or role-plays) are unavailable because the interactants of that period are dead. Instead, methodological approaches include [. . .] detailed qualitative analyses, often drawing upon social historical research and/or contemporary social commentaries in order to help reconstruct contexts [and approximations of] speaker meaning ([cf.] Stetter 1991: 74, 79, cited in Arnovick 2000: 12) [. . .] [T]he use of corpus-based methods by which researchers reveal and/or track patterns of usage, relationships with the co-text and aspects of context, are [also] becoming increasingly popular (e.g. Jucker and Taavitsainen 2008).

 Task B11.2.1

> Grammaticalization studies like those undertaken by Elizabeth Traugott seek to show how changes in language are not merely the result of language-internal factors but, rather, are triggered by verbal interactions among speakers: simply put, speakers invite their hearers to infer some meaning beyond that which they literally state and, over time, some of these 'one-off, context-sensitive, particularized implicatures' evolve first into GCIs (cf. Unit A5.1.1) before becoming

'part of the semantic meaning of the item'. In Unit A11.6, we introduced you to an adverb – *of course* – which might be undergoing such change. A search of *of course* using the BNC will give you sixty-five hits. Undertake this search for yourself, and (once you're familiar with the examples) answer the following:

- How many of the sixty-five examples have the sense 'as you (or we) know'? Has 'as you (or we) know' proven to be the most frequent sense? If not, what sense is the most common? You might find it useful to have a good dictionary next to you when working out the different senses of *of course*.
- Given the BNC is not up to date (because of being put together in the 1990s), what other sources might you draw from in order to check for this supposed developing sense of *of course*?

NOTE

1   This is not strictly accurate, since sound recording begain with the invention of the phonograph in 1877, and not with the invention of the tape-recorder in the 1950s. However, the tape-recorder made it much easier to study spoken data.

B11.3 KOHNEN (2009)

Many historical pragmatic studies could be said to be corpus-based, if by corpus-based we mean that they glean their data from corpora. *Historical corpus pragmatics* is not merely the use of corpora to study pragmatic phenomena, however: it is an approach which makes systematic use of corpora and the principles of corpus-linguistic analysis. This new partnership between historical pragmatics and corpus linguistics 'has brought to light some [thorny] methodological problems' and also 'triggered innovative solutions to corpus-based methodology', according to Kohnen (2009: 14). Two problems highlighted by Kohnen in his paper which we do not include here are:

- The fuzzy relationship between speech act form and function – we don't insult people in English using the word *insult*, for example (cf. Unit A11.4).
- 'Hidden manifestations' – which can lead to us having a fragmented picture in regard to how a particular speech act (e.g. a directive) has evolved over time.

Recent studies which have sought to capture speech acts over time (see, e.g., the papers in Jucker and Taavitsainen's 2008 edited collection) demonstrate how researchers are beginning to make use of quite sophisticated search strings, or are turning to pragmatic annotation (cf. Units A2.5.1–A2.5.3) as a means of improving our current understanding of speech acts of times past. Our excerpt from Kohnen documents two of his historical corpus pragmatic studies of English directives as well as a study undertaken by Culpeper and Archer (2008). The excerpt begins by describing how directives are linked with indirectness and politeness today.

Text 11.3.1
T. Kohnen

T. Kohnen (2009) 'Historical corpus pragmatics'. In A.H. Jucker, D. Schreier and M. Hundt (eds) *Corpora: pragmatics and discourse*. Amsterdam: Rodopi, pp. 13–36.

[. . .] The following [. . .] manifestations of directives typically imply different assumptions about the relative politeness or directness of the speech act [today], with the explicit performative (1) at the less polite end and the interrogative (4) at the more indirect end of a scale:

(1) I order you to leave.
(2) Go!
(3) I would like you to leave.
(4) Could you please leave?

Was [this] range of manifestations [. . .] already available in earlier periods of the English language [. . .] or did they gradually develop in the course of time? [. . .]
      [. . .]
      Kohnen (2004) deals with [a] prominent direct realisation of directives, the imperative. I looked at imperatives in the religious treatises in the tagged [. . .] version of the *Helsinki Corpus* (PPCME2) and in the *Brown* and LOB corpora [. . .] Whereas the frequency of imperatives between 1200 and 1375 is fairly high (4.5 in 1,000 words), it is only 1.9 in Late Middle English and 0.6 in the LOB corpus and 0.83 in the *Brown Corpus*. [Hence, one direct] manifestation [. . .] seems to decrease in the course of the history of English.
      Kohnen (2002) looked at the development of two typical indirect manifestations of directives in the *Helsinki Corpus*, the speaker-based declaratives expressing speaker volition (I *would like you to leave*) and hearer-based interrogatives questioning the volition/ability of the addressee (*Could you please leave?*). Here the data showed that speaker-based manifestations develop slowly during the sixteenth and the first half of the seventeenth century, whereas hearer-based interrogatives do not really spread until the end of the seventeenth century. In all, the general frequency of both constructions is still rather low at the end of the Early Modern period (1.1 and 0.82 in 10,000 words).
      [. . .] The late advent of indirect directives was supported by a very recent study of conventional indirectness. Culpeper and Archer (2008) looked at the manifestations of requests in their socio-pragmatic corpus of trials and plays dating from 1640 to 1760 [. . .] [T]hey found that requests in their data are quite different from those found to be prevalent in modern [English], with a low proportion of conventional indirectness and a large share of so-called impositives (that is, imperatives, performatives, hedged performatives, obligation- and want-statements) [. . .] [T]he authors argue that lack of indirectness may not necessarily imply lack of politeness, [however,] since the correlation of directness with less politeness may in fact be culture-specific and [moreover] is not borne out by the data.

Task B11.3.1

➤ Kohnen concludes his paper by claiming that these and similar findings should encourage us to question and/or qualify 'the picture of directives becoming less explicit, less direct and less face-threatening' over time.

▨ Why are directives often explained in terms of in/directness and im/politeness today? (You might find it beneficial to go back to some of our discussions in Units A4 and A8).

▨ In a section of his paper not included above, Kohnen suggests that the requirements of politeness could be 'suspended by genre conventions' in times past. Can you think of any modern activities where the requirement to be polite seems to be suspended? Do these activities have any (socio)linguistic features in common? Are the power relationships between the interlocutors aysmmetrical, for example? (Cf. Unit A12.) Is directness a feature of these activities?

▨ When researchers wish to study speech-act types, they often identify forms as a first step. Kohnen, for example, searched for words such as *Go!* and phrases such as *I order you to* *, *I would like you to* *, *Could you please* *? How would you go about finding directives in a corpus? Which would be the easiest to find, in your view, and why?

B11.4 TAAVITSAINEN AND JUCKER (2008b)

You learned about the ethnographic approach to the study of compliments in Unit A4. Taavitsainen and Jucker have used a similar computer-aided approach to study English compliments in a historical context, using literary texts as their data source. Specifically, they searched for the speech-act label *compliment* in conjunction with lexical items likely to indicate positive evaluation. These items included: *beautiful, (really) nice, (really) great, lovely, well done, like/love your, what a, you look/'re looking.* One of their findings was that historical compliments 'are gendered speech acts, connected with positive politeness' (cf. Holmes 1988). Below, we reproduce part of their discussion in respect to *A Dialogue Between Two Young Ladies Lately Married, Concerning Management of Husbands* (1696). As a qualitative analysis, the reading offers a useful contrast to Kohnen's quantitative analysis of directives (see above). For ease of reference, we have reproduced Taavitsainen and Jucker's utterance-by-utterance summary of their main observations in bold.

I. Taavitsainen and A.H. Jucker (2008b) '"Methinks you seem more beautiful than ever". Compliments and gender in the history of English'. In A.H. Jucker and I. Taavitsainen (eds) *Speech acts in the history of English*. Amsterdam and Philadelphia: John Benjamins, pp. 195–228.

Text B11.4.1
I. Taavitsainen
and A.H. Jucker

[. . .] The [following] passage was located by the evaluative adjective (*more*) *beautiful*; the word *compliment* does not occur in this text. The text is a conversation between two newly married ladies from the year 1696 [. . .] The beginning of the dialogue sounds almost like a parody of the modern compliment. [. . .]

Amy. Welcome, my dear *Lucy*! I have long'd to see you.	Greeting, address with endearment Compliment
Lucy. Sweet *Amy*! I have had no less impatience for your dear Company. Lord! how you're alter'd, methinks you seem more beautiful than ever: A very Angel!	Greeting in response, address with endearment, compliment Return of compliment (hyperbolic) Mild swearing. Exclamation of positive evaluation, exaggeration
Am. Fie, *Lucy*, do you begin to abuse me thus already?	Response. Mock disapproval by interpreting the compliment as a mock insult
Luc. No, I vow; you appear such in my eye, really.	Response, assurance of honesty
Am. Perhaps my new Mantua adds to my little Beauty: You like the Fashion then? 'Tis the newest Stuff.	Attribution of the positive evaluation to a piece of garment. Asking for more praise. Bragging.
Luc. As I live, I never saw any thing more pretty; sure 'tis all Spanish Wool.	Compliment, exaggeration. Asking for details.
Am. Yes, yes, the Wool is Spanish, but it was Dyed at *Venice*.	Bragging.
Luc. There is no Silk can wear neater – And what a delicate Colour! – For Heaven's sake, from whence had you this Noble Present?	Compliment continued. Affective language use. Admiration. Request for more information. Rhetorical counter question
Am. From whence, *Lucy*? From whom should a Vertuous Wife receive it but from her Husband?	Topic shift. Compliment/envious statement (?)
Luc. Oh happy you, who have such a Husband! wou'd I had Married a Cobler when I met with my Bargain.	Self-blame, disparaging one's own
Am. How now, Friend! do you repent already?	Response. Surprise, request for more information
Luc. How is it possible I shou'd do otherwise?	Counter-question, topic continued

(Anonymous. A *Dialogue Between Two Young Ladies Lately Married, Concerning Management of Husbands*. London: Printed in the year 1696, pp. 3.1–37.8)

The rest of the dialogue turns out to be highly didactic, giving advice to Lucy, the unhappy newly married lady, on how to improve her situation. The text belongs to the category of didactic handbooks, although it employs mimetic characters. The text is revealing of women's position at the time of writing. The cause of Lucy's unhappiness is revealed little by little. She continues:

> *Luc.* How is it possible I shou'd do otherwise? do you see these Rags, and how I am dizen'd? Thus it goes with my Husband's Wife. Let me dye, if I am not ashamed to appear in Publick, when I perceive how genteel other Women go, whose Husbands are much inferior to mine both for Quality and Estate.

Amy starts to preach in biblical terms, with references to St Peter, for instance, about women's status. The argument goes according to the traditional lines, but between the lines, we can read about the social conditions as well. The identity of a married woman was completely dependent on her husband's status. Women were totally subordinate to men and could not, for example, own property (see Shoemaker 1998):

> *Am.* The true Ornament of Wifes does not consist in Apparel, or Dress, as we are taught by St. *Peter*,. . . we, that are Marry'd, ought to esteem our selves fine enough if we please our Husbands only.

> *Luc.* But, in the mean time, my good Man, tho' he be so very penurious to his Wife, is other ways sufficiently profuse in wasting that fair Estate which I brought him.

Lucy's troubles do not end here, the treatise enumerates all possible vices and hardships to be tolerated. Women were under their husbands' rule, and the offered role is extremely submissive. There was no remedy:

> *Am.* But St. *Paul* Teaches, That Wives ought to be subject to their Husbands with all reverence: And St. *Peter* proposes to our Imitation the Example of *Sarah*, who call'd her Husband Lord. . . .

The advice contained in the dialogue is for the unhappy wife to adopt a strategy of pleasing her husband in all:

> *Am.* My principal Care was to appear to my Husband always in a good humour, that so I might give him no occasion of disquiet; I observ'd his Affections and Inclinations; I observ'd proper times, and methods, by which he was most apt to be appeas'd, or offended; just as those do who reclaim your Elephants, and Lions, and such like Creatures, which are not to be overcome with force.

The beginning of the dialogue serves to create the atmosphere of intimacy between the participants in the communication, and the talk constructs women's friendship as containing support, empathy, trust, and understanding.[1] Compliments play an important role as social "strokes" reaffirming and strengthening friendship. In this context, they are part of what Tannen (1990: 77) calls "rapport talk", where the phatic function overrides the informational. Without the opening scene between Amy and Lucy, the intimate discussion with private confessions would be much less credible.[2] The topics are identical to Present-day compliments to women: looks and garments. To modern ears, the bragging elements in the dialogue are reminiscent of children's talk, but the young ladies [. . .] cannot be very old, as the average age for marriage was very low at the time. [. . .]

Notes

1 These characteristics are considered key components of women's friendship. The most noticeable feature in the talk of women friends is the construction of talk as a joint effort, in which all participants construct a shared text. In this written dialogue of 1696, the interaction achieves almost the same effect (*cf.* Coates 1996: 23, 117).

2 Compliments play a similar role to gossip in creating mutual trust and confirming interpersonal relations (see Coates 1989: 98).

Task B11.4.1

➤ Taavitsainen and Jucker stress how 'compliments play[ed] an important role as social "strokes" reaffirming and strengthening friendship'. They further suggest that the compliments used by Amy and Lucy were 'gendered', because they exhibited 'characteristics' that 'are considered' to be 'key components of women's friendship', namely, 'support, empathy, trust, and understanding'.

▪ Write a list of those words or utterances which, for you, suggest 'support, empathy, trust, and understanding' between Amy and Lucy.
▪ Tannen (1990) contrasts such 'rapport talk', that is, 'strokes' which establish friendships and/or consolidate relationships, with 'report talk', that is, conversations which are purpose driven and/or about imparting information. Is there any evidence of 'report talk' in the conversation between Amy and Lucy (for example, could the advice Amy gives be seen as purpose driven)? Identify any 'report talk' which you believe to be evident.
▪ According to some researchers, males use mostly 'report talk' and women use mostly 'rapport talk'. Is this your experience? Can you think of conversations you have had where you've used (i) 'rapport talk' only, (ii) 'report talk' only, (iii) both 'rapport talk' and 'report talk'? What is it about the conversation and/or situation, if anything, which encourages you to use (i), (ii) or (iii)?

FURTHER READING

A good starting point in regard to historical pragmatics is Jucker's (1995) edited collection of the same name, not least because it's now regarded as an important landmark in the development of this field. More recently, Jucker and Taavitsainen have co-edited a second volume entitled *Historical pragmatics* (2010); like Culpeper's (2010) entry in Cummings' (ed.) *Pragmatics encyclopedia*, the purpose of the volume is to both situate historical pragmatics and also bring readers up-to-date in regard to recent developments. A chapter from that volume, Archer (2010), provides a summary of the evolution of speech acts over time in a way that picks up on the use of im/politeness approaches and also the idea of a shared pragmatic space (see, e.g., Unit A11.5). The Jucker and Taavitsainen edited collection also has chapters on 'Address terms' (Mazzon 2010), 'Politeness' (Nevala 2010) and 'Grammaticalization' (Traugott 2010). Specialist monographs on grammaticalization (which seek to tease out related processes such as 'subjectification', 'intersubjectification' and 'pragmaticalization') include Rossari (2009) and Hansen and Visconti (2009). To learn more about English speech acts in a historical context, see the papers in Jucker and Taavitsainen (2008); for those interested in the use of corpus linguistic techniques in a historical context, we particularly recommend Culpeper and Archer (2008) and Kohnen (2008). Kytö's (2010) chapter on 'data in historical pragmatics' also touches upon the use of corpus linguistic techniques – as well as providing a brief outline of some computational tools which have been specially designed for historical language analysis.

LOOKING AHEAD

As our focus has largely been upon speech acts in this section, we would recommend that you reread both Units A4 (relating to modern speech acts) and A11 (relating to the study of speech acts of times past) so that you gain a better sense of the similarities of approaches but also what is (and is not) possible when it comes to the study of the speech acts of times past (when compared to modern studies). In Unit C2, you are given an opportunity to extend your understanding of the latter, by engaging in speech act studies relating to compliments, thanks and requests.

Unit B12
Analysing power

B12.1 INTRODUCTION

As this textbook has made clear, the notion of context is central to pragmatics. Indeed, it is the means of distinguishing pragmatics from semantics, according to some (see, especially, Units A1, A3 and A5). The first reading in this final unit, taken from Van Dijk (2006), takes up the discussion of context once again, but from a socio-cognitive perspective. The approach that Teun Van Dijk outlines in this paper is labelled 'socio-cognitive' because there is a deliberate linking of the cognitive to the social; more specifically, Van Dijk suggests that participants draw on mental models from their episodic memory and that these models 'function as the interface between situational and societal structures and discourse structures' (ibid.: 163). To illustrate his approach, Van Dijk draws on a political speech made by the then-Prime Minster, Tony Blair, in the UK House of Commons.

Whilst Van Dijk's approach could be seen as an extension of the critical discourse analytic approach (cf. Unit A12.2), Sandra Harris' (1995) approach is more explicitly pragmatic. Drawing from UK Magistrate Court data, Harris focuses in particular on the use of questions as a means of control (cf. Unit A12.4). Her motivation for so doing, however, is not primarily to analyse courtroom interaction, but to assess whether 'universal pragmatics', and in particular 'Habermas' validity claims, can provide a sustainable conceptual framework for understanding the relationship between pragmatics and power' (ibid.: 117). Habermas' (1984) ideas respecting power and, in particular, the differences between 'communicative discourse' and 'strategic discourse' are well known – and are often applied to data by CDA specialists (cf. Unit A1). However, his wider ideas in respect to formal (universal) pragmatics are not usually applied to natural language data (by himself and/or others, regardless of discipline). One explanation for this is Habermas' own view that the formal (universal) pragmatics approach 'seems to be hopelessly removed from actual language use' (ibid.: 328).

Our final reading by Kate Haworth (2006) explores a third conflictive context: that of a police interview (cf. Unit A12.5). Like Van Dijk, Haworth advocates an 'integrated' approach. However, by this, Haworth means a combination of Conversation Analysis, Critical Discourse Analysis (CDA) and Pragmatics. Like Harris, Haworth points out that some institutional roles are more associated with power and control than others. However, she also shows how such power can be contested and resisted by the subordinate participants.

B12.2 VAN DIJK (2006)

In the following excerpt, Van Dijk (2006) explores a political speech, made by the then-UK Prime Minister, Tony Blair, to the House of Commons. As highlighted above, his primary motivation is to explicate his socio-cognitive approach to context. However, we focus, specifically, on Van Dijk's discussion of Blair's understanding of how discourse 'works' in this political context and his manipulation of that knowledge (based on his mental constructs of the parliamentary context).

T. Van Dijk (2006) 'Discourse, context and cognition'. *Discourse Studies* **8(1): 159–77.**

Text B12.2.1
T. Van Dijk

On 18 March 2003, Tony Blair, UK Prime Minister, held a speech in the House of Commons that began as follows (according to [. . .] the official *Hansard* [transcript]):[1]

> At the outset, I say that it is right that the House debate this issue and pass judgment. That is the democracy that is our right, but that others struggle for in vain. Again, I say that I do not disrespect the views in opposition to mine. This is a tough choice indeed, but it is also a stark one: to stand British troops down now and turn back, or to hold firm to the course that we have set. I believe passionately that we must hold firm to that course. The question most often posed is not "Why does it matter?" but "Why does it matter so much?" Here we are, the Government, with their most serious test, their majority at risk, the first Cabinet resignation over an issue of policy, the main parties internally divided, people who agree on everything else?
> ['Hon. Members: the main parties?']
> Ah, yes, of course. The Liberal Democrats – unified, as ever, in opportunism and error.
> [Interruption]

[. . .]
[. . .] Blair's position [. . .] [means that] he is permitted to address the House of Commons, he is allowed to speak first, and hence to order and influence the sequence of the debate, and to use deictic expressions such as 'we' [. . .] referring to the government [. . .]. That Blair knows that he is addressing the MPs as such, and in the House of Commons, also shows in his use of deictic expressions such as 'the House'.
[. . .]
[. . .] [C]ontext as participant construct also controls the more explicitly interactional properties of the debate, as we see in the last lines of this fragment. MPs interrupt [Blair] after his reference to some political parties as the 'main parties', by repeating that phrase as a question – a repetition and question that may 'be heard as' an objection, disagreement or criticism [. . .]. That Blair actually does understand it that way is shown by his lightning-fast reaction, 'Ah yes . . . ', seemingly agreeing and going to correct himself, but then negatively describing the Liberal Democrats, the major party opposed to military action in Iraq [. . .]

Text B12.2.1
T. Van Dijk

[. . .]

[. . .] [I]n a political context the interruption may be heard (interpreted, represented, modeled) as 'doing opposition', and the same is true for Blair's reaction to it, namely as attacking the opposition, and hence as defending both his policies as PM, and as leader of Labour. It is only within the framework of this context-controlled production and understanding that an expression such as 'unified, as ever, in opportunism and error' is heard – as the following protests (not transcribed by *Hansard*) suggest – as an ironical *political* attack against the Liberal Democrats. In sum, Blair not only engages in an interactional side-sequence of responding to an interruption or a disagreement, but given his definition of the current political situation, he is engaging in 'doing politics' by taking advantage of the interruption to attack the opposition. Obviously, a 'pure' or 'autonomous' account of interaction that ignores participants' contexts cannot account for this *political* aspect of this fragment of the parliamentary session.

Task B12.2.1

➤ According to Van Dijk, much of Blair's/the MPs' social and political:

> knowledge is presupposed, and only manifested occasionally and indirectly, and hence must be part of the context as defined by the participants: Blair must know the now relevant things the MPs know, and hence not only must represent his own and their roles, positions, memberships or identities, but also his own knowledge and that of his recipients. Only then is he able to distinguish between the knowledge or beliefs he is (re)stating in his speech, and those that are presupposed and taken for granted.

▪ Undertake your own analysis of the Hansard transcript as a means of identifying any presupposed knowledge (Blair's and the MPs').
▪ Are there features in this transcript that are suggestive of 'power'? If so, what are they? Could you categorize any 'power' manifestation according to *type* (cf. Unit A12)?
▪ Having undertaken your own analysis, in what ways would you say Van Dijk's socio-cognitive approach is similar to CDA (cf. Unit A12.2)? In what ways is it similar to a critical pragmatics perspective (cf. Unit A12.3)? What makes the socio-cognitive approach distinctive?

NOTE

1   The numbering that Van Dijk included in his original paper has been removed.

B12.3 HARRIS (1995)

Harris has explored the linguistic structure of magistrate/defendant interactions previously (see, e.g., Harris 1984). In that work, she has aluded to the magistrate(s)'s specific goal orientation (i.e. eliciting appropriate answers) and their use of inferential frames such that questions become multifunctional (i.e. serve simultaneously as accusations and requests for information). She has identified, in addition, that defendants adopt a respondent role in the main – and tend to be reprimanded for their 'inappropriate' behaviour when they seek to move out of that role (see also Unit A12.4). In this excerpt, Harris extends her discussion regarding the multifunctionality of the magistrates' questions by linking this characteristic to Habermas' 'validity claims' of comprehensibility, truth, truthfulness (i.e. sincerity) and rightness (i.e. appropriacy).[1] Validity claims are especially important when considering Habermas' ideas in regard to strategic discourse and its orientation to success (cf. communicative discourse, which is oriented to reaching an understanding). For strategic discourse shares many of the characteristics we have already noted above in respect to magistrate/defendant interaction: namely, that speakers have differing speaking rights and that the interaction tends to be goal oriented. We focus here on pages 119 and 122–4 of Harris' paper, where she explains how the asymmetrical distribution of speech acts can be such that only the institutional representatives (i.e. those with 'power') can successfully raise/challenge validity claims (as to comprehensibility, truth/fulness and rightness).

S. Harris (1995) 'Pragmatics and power'. *Journal of Pragmatics* 23: 117–35.

Text 12.3.1
S. Harris

By focusing on communication as social action, Habermas foregrounds language not only as the primary means of understanding and consensus, but also as the potential instrument of power and inequality. The data cited here was recorded in the Arrears and Maintenance Court of the Nottinghamshire County Magistrates Courts, the lowest tier of courts in the United Kingdom system. The recordings involved twenty-six cases, with five magistrates. [. . .]

The prototypical pattern of speech acts in court is the question/answer sequence [. . .] [Q]uestions in court appear to be used by institutional representatives (i.e. judges, lawyers, magistrates) as a mode of control, making it difficult for non-institutional participants (i.e. defendants, witnesses) to put forward propositions of their own. A defendant or witness who is limited to the role of respondent may find it difficult to raise or challenge validity claims for the following reasons.

Firstly, questions sit much less easily with Habermas' concept of a 'validity claim' than do assertions, promises or even directives. [. . .] A question can put forward a truth claim, but only inasmuch as it contains a presupposition or a proposition which is embedded in its interrogative structure. The following questions (all magistrate or clerk utterances addressed to a defendant) provide relevant examples:

(a) would you like to explain to the magistrates why *since then you've chosen to ignore the order of the court*, please (presupposition)
(b) who (*someone*) *wrote this letter for you* (presupposition)
(c) *everybody else seems to have done something but you*, don't they *you didn't choose to pay it off then*, did you (proposition + tag)

Although it is possible for a defendant to raise a validity claim with regard to the above presuppositions/propositions, in effect, interactively, it is extremely difficult; and few defendants in the data base challenge the 'truth claim' of presuppositions or propositions which are embedded in conducive syntactic forms.

Secondly, questions in court are often multi-functional. Accusations which a defendant might want to challenge explicitly on the basis of a truth claim are often posed as questions. The following sequence follows an account given by the magistrate addressed to the court, including the defendant, concerning the 'facts' of the latter's case, i.e. that he has two fines on which he still owes the court money.

M: yes – what are you going to do about it
D: well – uh – I would like to ask your worships if it would be all right if I had fourteen days to pay the three pound one – and uh – and still have to pay the fifty pence on the other – your worship
M: why is it you've suddenly become flush with money
D: well as I say – uh – they've put an increase on and uh – but I daren't draw out again until Monday (they = Social Security)
M: how much money have you got on you
D: I haven't got any on me – your worship
M: how'd you get here
D: I uh got a lift – part way here

Though on the surface these questions request information, their underlying function is as accusations – that the defendant has money which he is wilfully using for purposes other than to pay his fines. While the defendant's responses indicate that he recognises the accusation, he does not directly challenge the validity of the presupposition in the magistrate's second question or the implied accusations which underlie the final two questions. [. . .] [I]t is also interesting to note that these questions function as accusations only in relationship to a specific asymmetrical context and in a questioning sequence. It would be quite possible to pose such questions ("How much money have you got on you?", "How'd you get here?") in a different context without any accusatory intent. Questions used as indirect accusations tend to prevent defendant validity claims (denial of truth) which a direct accusation would make possible.

Thirdly, it is illuminating to match Habermas' validity claim based on 'rightness', on normative social rules, with instances of actual discourse. [. . .]

C: In May of this year you were before this court for motoring offences when you were fined a total of – thirty-five pounds and for costs fifteen pounds making a total of – fifty and uh you were ordered to pay within twenty-eight days – you haven't as yet paid anything or been in touch with the court – can you explain why you haven't paid and what your situation is at the present time
D: yes – the reason I haven't paid is – A that I haven't got the fifty pounds and also – secondly – that I feel I was totally unfairly judged to be guilty at the time

Clearly, the validity claim being raised by the defendant in this instance does not relate to the 'truth' of the clerk's previous assertions. Both participants accept the circumstances and the amount of the fine and that the defendant has not as yet paid any money. Propositional truth is not in question. Nor is the 'truthfulness' or sincerity of the clerk being called into question. The validity claim which is raised would intuitively seem to be concerned in some way with 'rightness' but not in the sense of the appropriacy of 'social norms'. The defendant is not challenging the 'right' of the clerk as

Text 12.3.1
S. Harris

representative of the court to impose a fine on him but the 'rightness' of the action itself on other grounds (unfairness).

In other words, he is not calling into question the validity of the clerk's statements on the basis of a normative rightness which depends on legitimately ordered interpersonal relations but on a matter of 'justice'. This would seem an example of a defendant explicitly 'moralising' the world of institutionally ordered relations, attempting to engage in moral argumentation (in Habermas' terms) from a position of inequality in terms of power.

Task B12.3.1

➤ According to Harris, a 'defendant or witness who is limited to the role of respondent may find it difficult to raise or challenge validity claims'. Reread the example above between C and D, where the defendant challenges the 'rightness' of paying the fine because of being 'totally unfairly judged to be guilty'.

■ In Harris' explanation, she states that 'propositional truth is not in question' here. To what 'propositional truth' is she alluding (cf. our discussion of presuppositions and the courtroom in Unit A12.4)?

■ What does the defendant (D) seem to presuppose that the Clerk (C) might not? To what extent might their different stances account for the 'power struggle' between them?

B12.4 HAWORTH (2006)

Notice that Harris is careful to state that defendants and witnesses who find themselves in a respondent role 'may find it difficult to raise or challenge validity claims' as opposed to stating categorically that they will not be able to do so. In this final excerpt, you will be able to explore the notion of resistance in more detail. As previously highlighted, the context is that of a police interview. The data relates to the case of Harold Shipman, a UK doctor who was convicted of murdering fifteen of his patients in 2000 (and is suspected of murdering many more).

K. Haworth (2006) 'The dynamics of power and resistance in police interview discourse'. *Discourse & Society* 17(6): 739–59.

Text B12.4.1
K. Haworth

[. . .] [T]here is an expectation that the police interviewer (P) will control the topical agenda. Yet right at the start we see something different. P goes though the formulaic opening to the police interview, namely the mandatory caution, and then starts to set up his agenda for this interaction. But as soon as P has completed enough of his utterance to make it clear that he is about to introduce a topic, Shipman (S) interrupts:

P: . . . there's one or two points we'd like to pick up [on from]
S: [err] can I clarify something first

Text B12.4.1
K. Haworth

P: yeah

S: I've had the chance to mull over the questioning this morning, (,) and perhaps I've made clear what ha-happened when Mrs (.) Grundy asked me to witness the will. . .

P defers to S and lets him continue, thus abandoning his own topic introduction. S then introduces his own topic instead. Bearing in mind the expected balance of power in favour of P in terms of seeing the topical agenda of the interview, this marks a significant breach of that order right at the start of the interaction.

[. . .]

P now gets to introduce the first main topic, namely Mrs Grundy's medical records. P makes it explicitly clear that he is unilaterally changing the topic:

P: OK (-) I want to go back to the (.) computer (.) medical records. . .

Throughout this sequence S picks up P's topic. However that is not to say that his responses are straightforwardly co-operative. S's first response in this section simply does not answer P's question:

P: . . . the entry for (.) Mrs Grundy's visit on the 9th of June, (.) will you tell me why (.) there's no reference there (.) to you taking any blood from her.
(-)

S: normally (all) the blood results came back two days later.

P: no but (can you tell me) why there's no (.) mention on that date.

S: I cannot give you an explanation

His answer does give the surface appearance of conformity, in that taken on its own it sounds like a legitimate and helpful answer – but not to the question asked. This is therefore a subtle form of subversion rather than a blatant challenge. The *illusion* of compliance is at least worth maintaining.

P recognises this challenge and sanctions S, repeating his question . . . failure to answer for a second time *would* have been a blatant challenge, and sure enough this time S replies. But although P maintains some control here, this demonstrates that his grip on it is by no means firm.

The chosen topic allows S to display his institutional status:

P: . . . it doesn't actually say you'd taken a blood sample from her.

S: errm (-) it's not the custom of most general practitioners to write, (.) "I have taken a a blood sample which would consist of this this and this" most general practitioners just write down what the blood test is that they're doing.

This is another interesting evasive tactic, in that S does not address what he actually did but instead refers to the 'custom' of his peers: he implies he has merely followed standard practice for his profession. He thus uses his professional status as a shield, shifting focus of blame onto the institution to which he belongs, instead of on himself as an individual member. Further, due to the subject matter belonging entirely to S's medical domain, P has no choice but to defer to S's knowledge and professional status at this point, leaving himself in a weak position discursively.

[. . .]

Through the above analysis several factors emerge as being of particular significance in the balance of power and control in this interview. The ascribed discursive roles of the participants are of paramount importance, providing the 'default' positions from which each participant must operate. As we have seen, these are very unequal in the resources they make available to each participant, giving P a considerable advantage in terms of power and control in this interaction. However, although this 'starting position' may be fixed, what each manages to achieve from there is not.

In line with the asymmetrical default position, we have seen that P does have overall control of the interaction, whereas S is generally left in the position of attempting to resist that control, rather than being able to actually seize it for himself. Yet the level of resistance he manages to achieve is quite remarkable given the circumstances. Through his constant attempts to challenge and undermine P's position he significantly reduces the default advantage with which P started out.

In addition, the institutional roles of the participants have been shown to have a strong influence on the interaction. S uses his professional status to bolster his discursively weaker position and place himself on a more equal footing with P. He also constantly undermines P's status, both as investigative officer and as questioner. It is interesting to note that P rarely alludes to his own institutional position – but this is hardly necessary in the context. His stronger discursive role as questioner is itself a manifestation of that status.

Task B12.4.1

➤ How does Shipman go about resisting/contesting the restrictions imposed upon him by his role as responder? Is such resistance unusual or predictable, given the activity type? Is it risky? How successful is Shipman's strategy, in your view?

➤ In her abstract to her full paper, Haworth makes it clear that she is adopting 'an integrated approach, [which] draw[s] on Conversation Analysis, critical discourse analysis (CDA) and pragmatics' (2006: 739). Provide a summary of these approaches in your own words: you might find it useful to look again at Units A1 and A6 as well as Unit A12. If possible, compare your summary with that of a colleague, friend or fellow student and then produce a visual map (together) which shows where the disciplines overlap and where they remain distinct from one another. You might also consider adding Van Dijk's socio-cognitive approach to your visual map of analytical approaches.

NOTE

1   Habermas' validity claims share some similarities with Grice's conversational maxims (see, e.g., Unit A5.1.3).

FURTHER READING

Thornborrow (2002) and Simpson and Mayr (2010) discuss power both in relation to the Conversation Analysis and CDA approaches and also specific institutional contexts. Mey (2001) looks at power from a pragmatic perspective, but his discussion is largely in the abstract. A monograph relating to the courtroom which largely adopts a pragmatics perspective is that of Cotterill (2003). A feature of the courtroom which we have not discussed in this section but which is very relevant within, for example, cross-cultural pragmatics, is the effect of interpreting on the message being conveyed. Issues discussed in some detail by Hale (2004) include whether an interpretation should be verbatim *translation* as opposed to one that signals intention and propositional content. Very useful book-length accounts of the language of the workplace include Holmes and Stubbe (2003) and Vine (2004). Holmes and Stubbe's main focus is how and why people 'do' power and politeness in the workplace. For example, they look at the discourse strategies involved in balancing the demands of meeting workplace objectives/getting things done on time and the need to maintain good collegial workplace relationships. Vine's focus is similar – but there is a more explicit emphasis on three types of 'control acts', i.e., directives, requests and advice, which are used by four women and their colleagues to achieve different purposes. As Holmes and Stubbe and Vine adopt an approach that is largely akin to sociopragmatics (see Unit A1), we'd also recommend that you explore the various readings in Antaki's (2011) edited volume, *Applied conversation analysis: intervention and change in institutional talk.* The volume brings together works devoted to the use of CA, and include some insightful discussions relating to different types of interview context (medical, job-seeker, telephone, etc.). A Conversation Analysis specialist who has explored the enactment of power in radio talk from a Conversation Analysis perspective is Hutchby (see especially 1996b). Baker (2006) and Semino (2008) will also reward the reader: see, especially, Baker's discussions relating to corpus building (chapter 2), collocates (chapter 5) and modality and metaphor (chapter 7), and Semino's discussions of metaphor in politics (chapter 3) and corpora and metaphor (chapter 6). To learn more about Lakoff's more recent work in relation to metaphor and framing (and its political implications) see, e.g., *Don't think of an elephant* (Lakoff 2004) and *Whose freedom?* (Lakoff 2006).

LOOKING AHEAD

In Unit C9, we encourage you to undertake your own 'pragmatics and power' studies. We also touch on power in other units in Section C – in particular, Unit C6 (Facework and im/politeness).

SECTION C
Exploration

Unit C1
Choosing, transcribing and annotating a dataset

As we have seen, there are many different ways of gathering data for pragmatic analysis, depending on the focus of study. Sometimes a method seems straightforward until you do it yourself, and then you realize that it is not. It is therefore useful to practise gathering data for yourself, not only for your own research but also to make you more critically aware of the basis for other researchers' claims.

C1.1 USING INTERNET SOURCES TO CREATE A CORPUS

An important way of finding examples of actual language usage is to search an existing corpus, or to create a corpus of your own. A simple way of starting your own corpus is to search for a word or phrase (known as a 'string' of words) in a search engine such as Google. You will soon find that there are many decisions to be made as you go along. Try, for example, to do a search for *terror*: how many hits does this give you? If you have too many, how might you go about choosing a much smaller corpus set? One possibility is to limit the search in some way, for example by choosing the Google link to 'Pages from the UK', and then perhaps only those hits from the last 24 hours, or the last month. If there are still too many hits, you might consider being more specific. For example you could use certain websites such as 'newsbank' (see Baker 2006: 31–2) or an electronic database such as LexisNexis.

If you are interested in the meaning of discourse markers you could search for a string such as *I was like*.

The size of the corpus you create is not the only issue to consider. You may, for example, want to determine whether all of the hits you have chosen to use are representative of British English, or of other international varieties of English. One way of trying to limit yourself to one variety is to choose newspapers published in a particular country (although this does not necessarily accomplish 100 per cent success). Why might using different varieties of English be a problem, in your view? It may also be important to know something about who has written the text and for whom. The choice of the terms *terrorist* or *freedom fighter* may depend, for example, on the socio-cultural perspective of the user.

C1.2 DESIGNING AND USING A DISCOURSE COMPLETION TASK

1   One of the situations described by Kasper (2000: 327) as a discourse completion task reads as follows:

> (5) It's your birthday, and you're having a few friends over for dinner. A friend brings you a present. You unwrap it and find a blue sweater.
>
> You say:
>
> _____
> _____
> _____

(Eisenstein and Bodman 1993)

Does the above strike you in any way as age and/or class-related? For example, would you talk about 'having a few friends over for dinner' yourself? If not, reword the above example so that it is more relevant for your own situation. Once you are happy with the wording, we'd like you to use it to collect some data. You need to decide how many people you need to ask, who those people are (i.e. are they strangers to you or people you know?). If strangers, how/when/where are you going to ask them? You will be imposing on them to some extent, so you will have to think about an appropriate strategy. Rather than doing this unthinkingly, write down what you say (and also make a note of any changes you make – it will reveal something about your own communicative practices). Once you've decided on the participants and the setting, you need to think about recording the actual data. Are you intending that they write down their answers or would you prefer them to give their answer orally? In which case, are you going to record them? If so, what issues do you need to bear in mind? For example, do you need their permission? Might the fact that participants are being recorded have an effect on what they say? (See Unit A2.1.)

2   When you analyse your results, what do you need to consider? For example, Aijmer (1996) describes very many different ways of saying *thank you*. Can you categorize your data according to her description? Are there any aspects of how people say *thank you*, such as body language or tone of voice, which you cannot capture with your method of collecting the data?

3   Think of all the ways you could ask someone for a pen (e.g. *Give me a pen*; *Can you lend me a pen?*; *Can I borrow your pen for a minute please?*) In which situations would you expect to use the different forms? Use your ideas to design some discourse completion tasks like the one above, and test your assumptions by asking other people to complete them.

C1.3 TRANSCRIBING SPEECH

You saw in Unit A2.4 that transcribing spoken language is not a straightforward task. The amount of detail you include in your transcription depends very much on what the transcription is for. A record of parliamentary proceedings or court proceedings may wish to focus on the propositional content, i.e. what was said, and the transcriber might therefore 'clean' the text by leaving out repetitions and hesitations. If you are interested in how something is said, however, these features of spontaneous speech might be very important. This means that the notion of an 'accurate' transcription is not very helpful. To discover how the process of transcribing can vary, we suggest that you try it out for yourself.

1   Record:

   (a) about fifteen minutes of conversation between two or three people, and/or
   (b) about ten minutes of someone being interviewed on the radio, or someone telling an unscripted narrative.

   Choose between one and two minutes to transcribe from whichever set of data you have collected. If possible, ask someone else to transcribe the same data: then, working in pairs, compare your results. Did you find any differences in what you have written? If so, what are they? Are there points at which your transcriptions were the same? Again, what are they? Would your results have been different if you had discussed in advance what you were going to include?

2   If you have access to speech software (such as Praat), select a small clip from a part of the conversation that you found difficult to transcribe (or where there was disagreement between transcribers). Do you get a better idea of what is going on?

3   Focus on the pauses in your data – mark them in your transcription (if you have not already done so). If you have access to speech software that allows you to examine the sound wave, select a stretch of speech and identify pauses. Are they where you heard them when you transcribed the data? Note that this is not always straightforward because some words fade away and it is difficult to tell when the word has ended and the pause has begun. Some silences are the result of segmental effects (there is a short silence during the closure phase of plosives, for example) and researchers therefore choose a threshold below which they will ignore silences for the purpose of pause analysis. The threshold varies between around 250 and 500 msec.

4   Here is an example of a transcription (from ICE-GB) that has pauses marked (<,> and <,,>) and also contains filled pauses. Note that the filled pauses occur either side of a silent pause.

     The other thing is I suppose uhm <,> uh that we this extraordinary notion <,,> that adolescents <,> should have their family unit as their centre of their life which of course children who go to boarding school don't have
                             [ICE-GB:S1A-054 #64:1:A]

Can you identify filled pauses (*um*, *uh*, etc.) in your own data? What can you say about how and where they are used?

C1.4 ANNOTATING A CORPUS FOR PRAGMATIC INFORMATION

In Unit A2.5.3, we highlighted what is involved in pragmatically annotating a text. Such work is initially theory-driven – as you have to decide what constitutes a speech act like a compliment, for example. In other units you'll learn about using search strings to find compliments (see, e.g., Unit B11.4). Below, we've given you a concordance which has been produced for you (from the BNC) using the search string: *you look* nice*. This is because such a string 'sounds like' a compliment. However, we want you to go through the examples and identify any that do not function as a compliment in practice.

New suit. sing the hymns! You, oh yeah, **you look nice** in your suit. He's just gon na, he's just sing

Christmas cards. Mm? It's a Christmas card. Mm. **You look nice**. Yes. Who's that from your society? They always remember don't

us your box then and I'll put it. Totally bald. **You look nice**. I'm not. Don't think they've got any smell in them

its not for no its not for my husband cos my husband says **you look nice** whether I've got make up on or whether I haven't got make up

, her pretty pinned-up hair and her fancy black peep-toe shoes. "**You look nice**," said Dot. "Like a real star." Gloria was pleased

kitchen door behind him. It's worse than I thought. "**You look nice**," he said carefully. "Do I, George? I'm glad

on anything these days – and your mother tries so hard to make **you look nice**. I always thought that green a very pretty colour. It suited your mother

he would make sure that they got it! Chapter Seven 1966 "**You look nice**, Maws. Where you off to?" Sarah's voice was tight.

. "Wear your grey tweed," advised my mother. "**You look nice** in that." "Let me look," said Lili.

she felt panicky. She turned to wave to her mother. "**You look nice**," said David. He greeted her easily, with a small kiss on

---

> get. Some guy might walk past and say, "Hey, **you look nice** today", and leave it at that. That I think of as a
>
> man, Hey, I like your hair", or "**You look nice** today". They'd think: I know what you want, because girls
>
> , you lay the things out on the bed that you vaguely know **you look nice** in, you roughly know what make-up suits you..
>
> . well, that's the

Once you've identified those which function as compliments in context, consider how you might annotate them. Would you annotate the whole utterance of which the compliment was a part, for example? Would you annotate the search string only (i.e. *you look nice*). Provide reasons for adopting the approach that you take.

FURTHER READING

For an overview of methods used in historical pragmatics, you should read Fitzmaurice and Taavitsainen (2007). Rose and Kasper (2001) provide insights into the study of pragmatics in relation to language teaching. For methods used in Experimental Pragmatics, see the book of the same name, edited by Noveck and Sperber (2004). Cameron (2001) provides detailed discussion of the process of collecting and transcribing spoken language.

Unit C2
Exploring routinized speech acts using corpora

Compliments attribute something good to the addressee or evaluate something positively. A useful means of finding compliments, therefore, is to search corpora for a string of words containing a positive adjective or a verb – as Manes and Wolfson (1981) do in respect to modern (American English) compliments and Taavitsainen and Jucker (2008b) do in respect to (English) compliments of times past (see, e.g., Unit B11.4). A number of such strings are suggested by both Manes and Wolfson and Taavitsainen and Jucker. However, as we've learned in Units B4.2 and B11.4, the 'hits' received need to be checked carefully, because they may not function as compliments in context: it can be difficult to distinguish between flattery and complimenting, for example. In addition, compliments can be ironic in context. With this caveat in mind, this further exploration section has the ultimate aim of getting you using corpora to explore compliments – and other routinized speech acts such as thanking and requesting – for yourself.

C2.1 COMPARING COMPLIMENTS ACROSS VARIETIES OF ENGLISH

We'd like you to begin by exploring the extent to which the observations by Manes and Wolfson (1981) in regard to American English (Unit B4.2) also apply when we use corpus data representative of British English. The easiest way for you to do this is to use the online version of the BNC. Focus, in particular, on any differences – and then try to determine whether these apparent differences may be due to a more general difference in how complimenting is done in the two varieties of English. Effectively, you will be undertaking a similar study to that of Golato (2005), who has compared Manes and Wolfson's (American English) data with New Zealand data. The following table reproduced from Golato (ibid.: 87) and borrowed from Holmes and Brown (1987), shows the patterns typically found:

		USA	New Zealand
1	NP {be/look}(intensifier) Adj*e.g. *You look really lovely*	53.6	48.0
2	Pro *be* (intensifier) (a) Adj NP e.g. *That's a really nice coat*	14.9	12.0
3	I (intensifier) {like/love}** NP e.g. *I simply love that shirt*	16.1	18.0
Total		84.6	78.0

* Any semantically positive adjective
** Or any verb of liking (e.g. admire, enjoy)

Once you have retrieved data from the BNC, you might consider using it to compare the frequencies of compliments in British English with those found in the American or New Zealand data (see above).

C2.2 RESPONDING TO COMPLIMENTS

Manes and Wolfson's (1981) study deals with compliments only. However a compliment is not complete without a response in which the recipient of the compliment provides the 'complimenter' with information about how/that the compliment has been received. We can say 'Thank you' to respond to the compliment, for example. As you might imagine, there are considerable differences in this area depending on whether a compliment is given between friends or strangers, the topic of the compliment, etc. As a preliminary task, think about how you, yourself, might respond to a compliment:

1　Do you tend to automatically thank someone when they pay you a compliment?
2　Does it depend on who is doing the complimenting, and what you are being complimented on?
3　Have you ever rejected a compliment and, if so, can you remember how you did so?

You might check your intuitions by first using the patterns suggested by Manes and Wolfson (see Unit B4.2) to search for compliments in the BNC, and then looking particularly for response tokens to those compliments (you may also find it helpful to return to your answers for Task B11.4.1).

4　Where do your intuitions overlap with the findings from your corpus investigation?
5　Where do they differ?
6　Do any of the corpus results surprise you at all and, if so, why?

C2.3 REQUESTING PATTERNS

In Unit A4.4.1 we gave some examples of (more or less conventionalized) request forms. In order to describe them we need to consider a number of factors such as the weight of the imposition (the difficulty of the task), the social relationship between the participants (degree of social distance), power relations, etc. (cf. Unit A8). Use the BNC to search for the patterns *can I, could I, may I, could you, can you, will you, would you.* Once you have excluded examples where a request is not intended by S, seek to identify (where possible): (i) the relationship between the participants; (ii) the distance between them; (iii) the 'weightiness' of the request being made (i.e. the size of the imposition); and finally (iv) how the form of the request relates to these parameters (i.e. whether *could I* is used by more powerless speakers and *will you* by more powerful: but see also Unit A8).

C2.4 THANKING

Routinized speech acts such as apologies or thanking have to do with politeness. How they are expressed will depend on the type of favour, who the speaker is, etc. For example, depending on the situation the speaker may use a bald *thank you* or a more elaborate thanking formula. For the final task in this section, we'd like you to consider the social rules for the use of thanking and how they interact with the choice of a certain strategy: simply put, we want you to determine how speakers 'know' how to express thanking in a particular situation (i.e. what the contextual clues are). Do they consider the importance of the favour received, for example, and also the social relationship between the speakers? How much attention are they likely to give to the setting? Will an institutionalized setting and/or specific social roles affect the formality of this speech act, at all? What consequences (if any) may result from their choosing the wrong form? To what extent does this particular question bring in the notions of face and social etiquette (cf. Unit A8)?

Having considered the above questions, do you agree with us that it's impossible to predict (with 100% certainty) what S will say in a particular situation? Why/why not? Might it be more appropriate to suggest that, on the basis of particular examples, we can make certain observations about the interaction between the choice of thanking form and the type of favour, who the addressee is and the social event (for example, whether the situation is an informal conversation, a telephone conversation or a debate)? With this firmly in mind, study the following data from conversations in the ICE-GB and the BNC. There are examples of both the bald *thank you* and of *thank you* expressing a higher degree of gratitude. Once you have familiarized yourselves with the examples, answer the following:

■ What are the different ways of intensifying *thank you* in English (e.g. *thank you very much, thanks a million*, etc.)?
■ What are the situations in which the different forms are used?
■ What function in addition to thanking do some of these examples appear to fulfil?

C2.4.1 Examples of thanking

From a telephone call

A: OK
B: Right OK then. Thanks a lot.
A: All right. Let's hope it works
B: Yep. Thanks a lot.
A: OK. Bye now.
B: Cheers

A meeting

A: And thank you again Bob very very much for your year of office. It's all been so
efficiently organized and uh
B: Well the surface is what shows (unclear)
A: But uh .. it's been splendid and very many thanks. Uhm Denis can we have your
report?

Conversation at home about family photographs

A: I don't want big life-size photographs of relatives hanging on the wall thank you.
Especially not that side of the family. Any side of the family thank you from that
era.

A tribunal

A: Judith thanks very much indeed for coming in and giving evidence to us

A committee meeting

A: Mr Chairman, thank you very much for those extremely kind remarks

A conversation at work

A: You've done an absolutely splendid job . . .
B: Oh thank you

A business meeting

A: I'll leave you to Mike to take things further
B: Thank you very very much Norman that's great

In a chemist's shop

A: OK. Thanks very much. Here's your prescription
B: OK. Thanks very much

A: Keep you going OK (=that will keep you going OK)
B: OK thanks a lot. Bye
A: Bye
B: Bye bye

A Trades Union Association meeting

A: Er, minutes of the last meeting, can we take them as read? Yes. Thank you. Matters arising from that meeting which took place on the thirty first July.

A cinema board meeting

A: just wanted to let the board know about that and to say that erm er this is the route that I'm currently taking and erm I will be reporting to them when there are specific developments and that I hope that you approve of er me attempting to expand our provision in this area. Good. Thank you. Any questions? Any other business?

In a classroom while a student is writing on the board

A: While that's going on can everybody remind me who they are because I've forgotten everybody's name.
B: Vicky.
A: Yes. Vicky
A: Phil
B: Phil
A: Phil
A: Uh and you at the blackboard
B: Susan
A: Susan. Thank you

A teachers' conference: discussing assessment procedures

A: Lovely jubbly! Thank you very much, we've knocked that on the head. General skills and abilities we're down to now.

A student union induction speech

A: Er I shall let you get on to your lectures or what other pursuits you have and no doubt see you around. Any problem you've got do come and see me. Thank you very much indeed. Right then! Leading on from last week we were looking at menu planning and I actually asked you to bring in some menus.

An insurance firm: training session

A: Right thanks for that Maggie. Er I'd just like to move on now erm what future capital needs do you need?

A friend enters the room

A: Hello Ian. How are you
B: Oh fine thank you

Mothers' Union general discussion

A: If you do want to ask me anything about this I've got some little booklets or I'm
sure some other people here could talk to you about it. But that's the thought
that I would really like you to take with you today. Thank you.
B: That's very nice. Lovely. Thank you very much.

C2.5 WAYS OF SAYING *THANK YOU*

The following exercise focuses on intonation. Speech act routines tend to occur with
a fixed intonation pattern depending on the situation. In these examples (adapted
from ICE-GB), the intonation of the utterance has been transcribed to show both
stress and pitch movement: the symbol [\] means that the syllable is accented with
a falling contour, while the symbol [/] indicates a rising contour. The symbol [↑]
means that the pitch is higher than expected. Based on the following examples,
adapted from ICE GB, answer the following:

1   In what situations is the melody on *thank you* typically rising?
2   When do speakers appear to use the falling contour?
3   Emphatic thanking is expressed linguistically by means of adverbs such as *very
     much, indeed*. How is the emphatic meaning expressed with intonation?

   1   And thank you a\gain Rob | ↑very very \much.

   2   A: What's your \name?
        B: \Susan
        A: \Susan | \thank you

   3   A: How \are you?
        B: Oh \fine /thank you

   4   A: Here's your pres/cription
        B: Thanks very \much

   5   I don't want big lifesize photographs of relatives hanging on the wall /thank
        you.

   6   A: Here's your /ticket
        B: /Thank you

   7   A: Do you want a cuppa?
        B: \No /thanks

Unit C3
Testing for implicatures

In this unit, we focus on experimental pragmatic studies. Experimental pragmaticians – like clinical and developmental pragmaticians – study the relationship between theory and its practical application. As such, they provide theoreticians from linguistic pragmatics with useful methods with which to (in)validate theory (Archer 2011a): something which we'd like you to attempt too . . . albeit it on a much smaller scale!

Experimental pragmaticians are particularly interested in issues at the semantics-pragmatics interface (see Unit A3), but use methods of investigation (eye tracking, timed response to stimuli, the choice of a 'best' sentence to describe X from a set of candidates, etc.) which we more readily associate with psycholinguistics. For example, one of the best known GCI studies – undertaken by the pioneers of the experimental pragmatics movement, Raymond Gibbs and Jessica Moise (1997) – used a forced-judgement task, i.e. asked readers to choose the paraphrase (from a given list) that they believed most closely captured the meaning of statements such as 'Robert cut a finger.' Gibbs and Moise wanted to determine whether readers first accessed the semantically encoded meaning of such statements (i.e. Robert cut some finger or other), and then used context to infer the GCI (Robert cut *his* finger), or whether they bypassed the literal (encoded) meaning and accessed the GCI more directly. Their main finding was that readers rarely chose the 'minimal meanings' (i.e. the non-enrichment meanings semantically encoded in implicature-carrying – or explicature-carrying – words). Gibbs and Moise suggested that this pointed to enriched meanings being directly accessed by their readers. Nicolle and Clark (1999) undertook a similar experiment two years later, however, and found that their readers tended to favour the implicature paraphrases. They offered a relevance theoretic explanation for this, namely, that readers had based their choice(s) on what seemed to them to closely match the original in its degree of relevance. A different experimental pragmatic study which also corroborates the relevance theoretic perspective on implicature is that of Reboul (2004).

C3.1 GCIs – NONCE OR GENERALIZED?

Reboul (ibid.) poses the question, 'Conversational Implicatures: Nonce or Generalized?', and, by so doing, encapsulates an ongoing Neo-Gricean/Post-Gricean debate. The crux of the debate is whether all conversational implicatures are due to one-off inferences, as relevance theorists claim, or whether some conversational implicatures are triggered by lexical items belonging to a contrastive set, as Neo-Griceans such as Levinson have claimed (see, e.g., Levinson 2000).[1] Reboul undertook two forced-judgement experiments to determine whether the occurrence of lexical items belonging to the sets <*white wine, red wine*> and <*coffee, tea*> led 'to interpretive dead-ends' and concluded that they did not. She took this to mean that her 'experimental results . . . support[ed] global over local theories', at least in regard to 'this specific pragmatic phenomenon' (2004: 332) – that is, confirmed the relevance theoretic stance in regard to conversational implicature being due to one-off (*nonce*) inferences.

Reboul's experiments involved informing respondents of a scenario such as the following:

> A man arrives very late [for a] meeting. Everyone is having a hot drink but there isn't much left. Someone brings him a mug. The man says:

> *Better coffee than no tea.*
> *Better no coffee than tea.*
> *Better no coffee than no tea.*
> *Better coffee than tea.*

> (ibid.: 327)

The respondents then had to answer *coffee, tea* or *don't know* to the following: 'What was he given to drink?' and 'What does he prefer?' They were also asked to justify their answers.

➤ Undertake this experiment yourself by giving a group of your friends/colleagues the same scenario and asking them to answer the related questions. Do your findings concur with those of Reboul (ibid.: 331) – that the contrastive set <*coffee, tea*> does not lead 'to interpretative dead ends'?

➤ What problems can you see with the above test (if any)? For example, is there some argument for suggesting that GCI-carrying words belonging to contrastive sets may make inferencing more difficult – until respondents recognize that the context of utterance renders them defeasible?

➤ An issue that Reboul herself raises is that this kind of experiment 'only concern[s] the triggering of Q-implicatures through contrast[ive] sets. The experiment has nothing to say about Q-implicatures triggered by Horn scales' (ibid.: 331), for example. How might you adapt the above experiment so that it captures information in regard to the triggering of Horn scales (i.e. the special subclass of generalized implicature which we discussed in Unit A5)?

C3.2 SCALAR IMPLICATURES

As we explained in Unit A5.2.2, we use the term 'Horn scale', within the field of pragmatics, to explain a number of alternative sets. They include *<all, some>*, where *all* entails *some* but not vice versa, such that a speaker who utters 'Some S are P' is understood to scalar implicate that, as far as he/she knows, not all S are P (Bezuidenhout 2010: 149). Noveck's (2001) work respecting children's understanding of scalar implicature is particularly worthy of note, here, as it has proved influential for both experimental pragmaticians and also developmental pragmaticians.[2] Also important is the work of Katsos (2007). Katsos, like Noveck, used what have since come to be known as truth value judgement tasks to elicit child (and adult) listeners' judgements about utterances containing scalar implicature triggers. Specifically, he used a fictional character, Mr Caveman, who was struggling – and hence needed help with – the Horn scale *<all, some>*: adults and children (aged 5–11) were asked to help Mr Caveman to determine whether 'The elephant had pushed [some/all] of the trucks', when faced with describing various scenarios. Noveck's study involved an assessment of children's understanding of modal statements such as 'There must be a parrot in the box', using a puppet. Similar to Katsos, Noveck would manipulate various scenarios, so that the puppet was occasionally under-informative, i.e. stated that the parrot *might* be in the box even though the respondents knew the parrot was in the box. Noveck found that the younger the participants, the more likely they were to accept under-informative *might* statements – in spite of contradictory visual evidence. Indeed, between 69 and 80 per cent of 5- to 9-year-olds accepted such statements as compared to 35 per cent of adults. Katsos' findings were similar: that is, the younger children commonly accepted under-informative statements from Mr Caveman. As it's unlikely that you will be able to undertake such an experiment for yourself, we'd like you to think about truth value judgement experiments – from a 'design perspective' and also a 'results perspective'.

➤ You are responsible for designing a truth value judgement experiment. List any factors you need to bear in mind prior to beginning the experiment proper. For example, you will need to decide upon a 'venue' for your experiment. What would make the best venue, in your view, especially given the apparent difficulty of testing pragmatic phenomena in a laboratory setting? (see, e.g., Hamilton 1994; Schegloff 1999). You will need to ensure that you ask the participants the same questions, in which case, do you plan to use an interviewer script? Is it important to use age-appropriate language? Does this require your using different questions for each age group whilst keeping the content the same? Why might this be problematic? If you plan to use visual aids, how will you go about choosing them? Will they need to be age appropriate? What ethical considerations should you attend to, if any? (cf. Unit A2).

➤ Thirty-five per cent of adults in Noveck's experiment accepted under-informative *might* statements to be true (in spite of having contradictory visual evidence to the contrary). Is it possible that the adults who accepted under-informative *might* statements were taking the puppet's 'epistemic' situation into account (that is, seeing the situation from the puppet's perspective)? How might we test for this?

According to both Noveck and Katsos, pragmatic abilities such as being able to derive – and evaluate as false – scalar implicatures like 'Not all elephants have trunks' are a late development in children: Katsos suggests pragmatically intact children can (rapidly) access scalar implicatures by the age of 11, for example. Yet, subsequent work by Papafragou and Musolino (2003) and Feeney *et al.* (2004) has found that children as young as 6- and 7-years of age will reject under-informative statements when the context makes the pragmatically enriched response relevant (cf. Unit C3.1). Such a finding is interesting for at least two reasons. First, it (once again) supports a relevance-theoretic perspective in regard to implicature – consider, especially, the relevance-theoretic argument that semantic meanings of weak terms are readily accessible (to children as well as adults), and narrowed meanings are associated with extra effort (see Units A5.3 and B5.4). Second, it points to the possibility that Katsos' and Noveck's results reflect the unnaturalness of the experimental set up and the task demands rather than the children's (and adults') actual pragmatic abilities.

C3.3 REQUESTS ABOUT THE TIME

Not all experimental pragmatic studies are lab-based. Recall, for example, the three experiments undertaken by Van der Henst *et al.* (2002), as a means of determining whether a tendency to optimize relevance was a factor in rounding (or not rounding) the time (Unit B2.3). Van der Henst *et al.* found that 97 per cent of the people approached 14–0 minutes prior to the fictitious appointment in Experiment 3 – and asked *Hello, do you have the time please? I have an appointment at 1* – opted to give an accurate answer rather than rounding the time. Van der Henst and Sperber (2004: 168) have since claimed that this suggests 'not only were [they] willing to make the effort of reading their analogue watch more carefully and had enough confidence in its accuracy, but also made the extra effort of taking the perspective of the stranger who was addressing them'.

➤ Familiarize yourself with the three experiments and their stimulus questions – *Hello, do you have the time please?* (Experiment 1 and 2), *Hello! My watch isn't working properly. Do you have the time please?* (Experiment 2, alternative question), and *Hello, do you have the time please? I have an appointment at 1* (Experiment 3). You might find it helpful to draft a list of 'similarities' and 'differences'.

➤ Working in groups (where possible), undertake Experiment 3 at different times of the day in a given week – including during a 'rush hour' period (i.e. when people are trying to get into work or get home, having been at work all day) – and then compare your results with those of Van der Henst *et al.* (2002).

- ■ Do your results concur by and large?
- ■ Do your results suggest there are (age-related, cultural, social) factors which affect someone's willingness to take the perspective of the stranger?

➤ Van der Henst and Sperber (2004) conclude their paper by stating that these – and similar – experiments ably demonstrate 'how imagining, designing and carrying out experiments helps expand and sharpen pragmatic theory'. Having undertaken and/or imagined your own experiments, do you agree or disagree with Van der Henst and Sperber? Van der Henst and Sperber also claim that it's important to have 'a pragmatic theory that is precise enough to have testable consequences' (ibid.: 169). Do you think Relevance Theory (the approach used by Van der Henst and Sperber, and replicated by you) is 'precise enough to have testable consequences'? To what extent are the other pragmatic approaches you're familiar with 'testable'?

NOTES

1 According to Reboul, *nonce* implicatures exist at the *global* (sentential) level – we access them once we reach the end of a given utterance. *Generalized* implicatures, in contrast, exist at the *local* (subsentential) level – hence, we are thought to access them at the point we hear the GCI-carrying word.

2 Developmental pragmatics constitutes an umbrella term for research which has the primary goal of studying the way in which language-intact children develop their pragmatic skills and/or competence (Archer 2011a: 472).

Unit C4
The organization of discourse structure

Sections A and B have discussed some features which are characteristic of spoken interaction. The special discourse features discussed in Unit B6 included prefaces marking the transition to the following utterance. Prefaces are optional but are frequently used in more formal contexts to highlight what follows. Unit C4.1 gives some examples of prefaces and their functions. However it is important to also know how frequent they are and in what contexts they are used.

The description of the discourse organization must also take into account the listener. The listener uses backchannels or response items to show uptake or to evaluate what is said. It is clear that there is a large number of such items. We can also expect these items to be used differently in different varieties of English, in different text-types, by individual speakers, etc. In Unit C4.2 the focus will be on investigating differences between British and American English.

Much work on conversation has been carried out by sociologists and anthropologists within the framework of Conversation Analysis. Conversation analysts have been particularly interested in studying telephone conversation openings both in informal conversations between friends and in workplace settings. For example, much is happening at the beginning of the telephone conversation which requires special methods or techniques. In comparison with telephone openings the closings and preparations for closing have been less studied empirically. In Unit C4.3 you are asked to describe and compare two different telephone openings. Unit C4.4 is concerned with telephone closings and the methods used by the participants to end the call. Looking at more closings, as you will be asked to do, shows that there is considerable variation in the ways the closing is achieved.

Question-answer sequences are the backbone at least in some text-types. However, questions are used very differently depending on the activity and who the speakers are. This is apparent when we look at questions in court proceedings where the right to ask questions is constrained by special norms and regulations. In Unit C4.5 you will be asked to describe how the use of questions in the classroom is constrained by the structure of the lesson and the teacher role.

C4.1 PREFACES

Biber *et al.* (1999: 1075) refer to similar expressions as 'ouvertures'. They give the following examples.

I would have thought	Politely putting a point of disagreement
Like I say	Repeating a point the speaker made earlier
The question is	Presenting an issue in an explicit, forceful way
There again	Adding a contrastive point to an argument
What we can do is	Proposing a joint course of action
You mean to say	Asking for confirmation of a point the speaker finds difficult to believe
Going back to	Returning to an earlier topic

Use the BNC to check how frequently these expressions are used and describe in what types of context they occur (type of activity, speaker role).

C4.2 RESPONSE ITEMS

McCarthy (2003) gives examples of a large number of response items which can be used as responses either alone or together with other elements. His data include both British and American English but he is not interested in distinguishing between them. Compare the frequencies of the response item in Table 1 in British and American English using the BNC and COCA.

Table 1 Occurrences of relevant tokens in nonminimal responses[a]

Item	As response
Right	1,150
Wow	1,099
True	880
Exactly	872
Gosh	746
Absolutely	594
Great	493
Definitely	365
Sure	349
Fine	348
Good	313

Cool	229
Really	214
Excellent	200
Lovely	196
Wonderful	195
Certainly	101
Perfect	32

ª Turn-initial position or post-function word ('yes', 'no', etc.).

C4.3 TELEPHONE OPENINGS

Telephone openings have frequently been studied using Conversation Analysis methods and techniques. They are particularly interesting to study because the caller and answerer cannot see each other and therefore use the turn-taking systems and special techniques to identify themselves and to establish the social relationship with the other participant (e.g. if it is a friend). A business call on the other hand may have a completely different opening.

It is typical of the opening of the telephone call that we can distinguish a number of components such as the answering of the call (responding to the ringing tone), the exchange of greetings, the answerer's self-identification and questions about the other person's well-being. Notice especially how the answerer identifies him/herself. Is it only done explicitly? Other (optional) components are, for example, an apology for disturbing. How is it reflected in the opening that the caller (C) and answerer (A) are close friends?

(Telephone rings)
A: Hello
C: Hi Leo sorry sorry have I got you out of your bath or suchlike
A: Oh hi there hi uh<,> no I was just cleaning my teeth
C: Oh right
A: Cleaning my teeth
C: OK hi hi it's John then
    Did I say it was John did I
A: Hi hi how're you sorry no you didn't I recognized your voice
C: Oh right hi well how's it going
A: Oh well not too bad I've finished my exams so

(Adapted from the ICE-GB)

In the following telephone opening the answerer of the call is a member of the English department. Notice however that we can distinguish similar components such as the response to the ringing tone, a sequence of turns in which the caller identifies himself and the answerer signals his recognition, the exchange of greetings before the first topic is introduced. However, there is no exchange of 'How are you?s'.

(Telephone rings)
A: Hello English department <,,>
C: Hello <,,>
A: Hello <,> it's Jane here
C: Hello Jane Patrick
A: Hello Patrick <,>
C: uhm a business call Jane <,>

(Adapted from the London-Lund Corpus)

The examples show that telephone openings can have many different forms although there are similarities. The similarities can be explained by the fact that the caller and the answerer cannot see each other.

Collect and examine additional telephone openings from talk radio shows. How do they differ from the openings discussed in the extracts above? How can we explain the differences?

TASK C4.4 TELEPHONE CLOSINGS

In Conversation Analysis terms both opening and closing a conversation provide organizational problems requiring special solutions or techniques. The closing of a telephone conversation may take a long time to complete. In the example below the closing comprised 13 turns. The extract (from the London-Lund Corpus) starts where the answerer (R) has promised to do something and no more topic has been proposed by the caller (C).

1 R OK-right well I'll have a hunt around Jane and [əm] I'll be in touch with you
again about coming over to see you how's S\idney
2 C oh he's f/ine
3 R g/ood
4 C f/ine
5 R spl=endid #
O=K#
W=ELL#
nice to be in t\ouch with you ag/ain Jane #
and m#
6 C ((r\ight))#
7 R we'll be dropping you a c\ard#
or giving you a t\inkle#
8 C yes d\o ((please))
9 R /OK# b/ye
10 C please give my love to D/an
11 R yes I will
12 C bye b=ye
13 R b\ye

The closing of the conversation takes a long time to complete and it proceeds in several steps. The extract starts where the recipient has promised to do something and no more topic has been proposed. The participants show their willingness to prolong the conversation by polite questions about another person's health and making promises about future contact, etc.

➤ Give examples of 'polite' phrases and 'polite' exchanges in the extract which serve a pre-closing purpose.

➤ In an ordinary face-to-face conversation the closing sequence is normally shorter. Why do you think we find this difference?

➤ Collect additional examples of telephone closings and describe the different ways in which pre-closing and closing are achieved. Can the differences be explained in terms of factors such as the purpose of the telephone call or how well the caller and answerer know each other?

C4.5 QUESTIONS IN INSTITUTIONAL SETTINGS

Questions have a special role in asymmetrical settings such as the courtroom or the classroom. The right to ask questions is for instance distributed unequally. Unlike conversation, questions in the classroom are often the prerogative of the teacher who 'knows the answer' and uses the question to check whether the pupil knows the answer and to evaluate the answer. The importance of the question-answer-follow-up exchange is shown in the following example adapted from Sinclair and Coulthard's (1975: 63–5) pioneering work on the use of language in the classroom by teachers and by pupils:

1 Teacher: Well Today I thought we'd do three quizzes. We won't take the whole lesson to do a quiz because I want to talk to you some of the time. The first quiz is this. Can you fill in this sentence? See if you can do it in your books.
Finished Joan?
2 Pupil: —
3 Teacher: Good girl.
And Miri?
4 Pupil: Yes.
5 Teacher: Good
Finished?
6 Pupil: Yes.
7 Teacher: Right Read us what you've written, Joan
8 Pupil: The cat sat on the rug
9 Teacher: Yes that's right. I changed the last word.
. . .
10 Teacher: Why did I put 'rug' instead of 'mat'?

11 Pupil: Because nearly every sentence you see like that it's 'mat'.
12 Teacher: Yes. But why did I change mine to rug?
13 Pupil: 'cos there's too many 'a's'.
14 Teacher: He's near, isn't he. He's not quite there.

The extract above is from a classroom lesson with 8- to 9-year-olds. In it we find several examples of typical teacher-pupil exchanges: the teacher asks a question to check if the pupil has understood why (turn 10). The pupil's answer (turn 11) is acknowledged in a follow-up move in turn 12 (*Yes*). Questions are used by the teacher to control the turn-taking in the discourse and to establish who has power in the classroom. The pupils do not ask questions and their answers are short.

The assumption that power is institutionally invested in the teacher role has been questioned in recent work (Thornborrow 2002). We need to go beyond the description of classroom talk in structural terms and look at how power is brought about as a result of negotiation between the participants. For example, in some classrooms we can expect the interaction to be less controlled by the teacher and the patterns discussed by Sinclair and Coulthard to be less frequent. Collect your own classroom data to investigate if and how the use of language in the classroom differs from the extract above.

➤ To what extent is the classroom discourse directed by the teacher?

➤ Do the pupils ever self-select as next speaker?

➤ How well does speaker-allocation work in the classroom? Is there interruption, simultaneous speech?

➤ In the classroom we may also find discussion on a topic. How is that controlled by the teacher?

Unit C5
Pragmatic markers:
further explorations

There is no consensus about how pragmatic markers should be described, what elements belong to this category and what functions they have. It has been suggested in Unit A7 that pragmatic markers can be described as a category consisiting of a prototype and more peripheral members of the category. This approach makes it possible to capture the fuzziness of the category.

C5.1 PROTOTYPICAL FEATURES OF PRAGMATIC MARKERS

On the basis of the list of markers given by Brinton (1996: 32) – which we've replicated for you below – pick out markers corresponding to the prototype description or with as many as possible of the features discussed in Unit A7.3: phonological, syntactic, semantic, functional and sociolinguistic or stylistic.

Ah	If	Right
Actually	I mean/think	So
After all	Just	Say
Almost	Like	Sort of/kind of
And	Mind you	Then
And {stuff, things} like that	Moreover	Therefore
Anyway	Now	Uh huh
Basically	Oh	Well
Because	OK	Yes/no
But	Or	You know (y'know)
Go 'say'	Really	You see

1   Search for these markers in the BNC and compare the frequencies with which they occur. Do these frequencies differ when you compare spoken and written texts?

2   Some pragmatic markers also have propositional meaning (e.g. compare *well* in *well I think I'll be going*, where it acts as a pragmatic marker, with *well* in the

sentence *he speaks well*). Find some examples in the corpus that illustrate the propositional use of *sort of, kind of, I mean, you know*, and others that illustrate their use as pragmatic markers. Is there a difference in their position in the utterance (turn) depending on their use?

3   Pragmatic markers are multifunctional, i.e. they can for instance have both structural and interpersonal function. Find examples from the corpus that illustrate this. Are there markers which are most frequently (or only) either textual or interpersonal?

4   On the basis of this small study you can come to certain conclusions about the reliability of the criteria used to define pragmatic markers. Are there 'good' and 'bad' criteria? (Notice that the BNC does not provide information on some of the criteria, such as prosodic features.)

C5.2 *BE LIKE*

Be like is used especially in American English as a quotative introducing reported speech.

> And my mother, to cheer me up, was like, you know, don't worry.

You can look for more examples of the quotative *like* in COCA: http://www.americancorpus.org/. You can restrict your search to *was like* and to the spoken part of the corpus. Notice that a large number of examples of *was like* are not examples of the quotative *like*. By expanding the context of the example you can get some information about the speaker. Do you find any support for Buchstaller's claim that 'US respondents associate quotative *be like* . . .with younger speakers and women' (Buchstaller 2006: 363)?

C5.3 THE SOCIAL FUNCTION OF PRAGMATIC MARKERS

Pragmatic markers do not contribute to the propositional content (see, e.g., Unit A7.3). It may therefore be thought that they could easily be omitted. However, their omission will still effect the communication in some way. Try this for yourself, by omitting the pragmatic markers in the following two examples. The first is taken from an informal conversation and the second is from a legal cross-examination:

A: (I mean) <u>I mean</u> she's so little <u>I mean</u> you <u>you know sort of</u> one can imagine <u>a sort of</u> middle-aged woman with a coat that seemed <u>you know sort of just</u> slightly exaggerated her form <u>you know</u> (I mean) she could <u>sort of</u> slip things in inside pockets but

C: m m

B: no she <u>just</u> carried it all home in a carrier bag <u>didn't she</u>

(Simplified from the London-Lund Corpus)

A (= the prosecutor): <u>Well</u> did you hear his evidence yesterday
B (= the defendant): <u>Oh</u> I heard it yesterday yes
A: So he's wrong about that as well
B: and my mother was drunk
Several people in the house will have said that to you
A: <u>well</u> you say several people
who was in the house apart from your wife
(Simplified from the London-Lund Corpus)

1 (a) Categorize the pragmatic markers *I mean, you know, sort of, just, well* and *oh* according to whether they have a structural or interpersonal function.
   (b) What effect if any does it have on the communication when these pragmatic markers are omitted? Is this different for different markers?
   (c) Do pragmatic markers seem to be more necessary in some situational contexts than in others? Do any markers appear in some contexts and not others? Does the formality of the occasion play a part here? Is it to do with the activity type?
2 Find examples of your own, using short stretches of discourse, one from an everyday conversation and one from more formal discourse (e.g. political debate or interview), and carry out a similar analysis as in 1(a)–(c).

Unit C6
Facework and im/politeness

In Unit A8, we touched on the debate regarding what does and does not constitute impolite behaviour. There is also a similar debate with regard to what constitutes rude behaviour: Terkourafi (2008) for example has suggested that we should use *rudeness* when discussing behaviour that is intentionally face-attacking, and *impoliteness* when discussing behaviour that is unintentionally face-damaging (but see Culpeper (2008: 33), who argues the opposite, namely, that it is impoliteness and not rudeness which is *intentionally* face-damaging). In spite of such debates over terminology, Locher and Bousfield (2008: 4) contend that the terms *impoliteness* and *rudeness* occupy 'a very similar conceptual space' (see also our discussion of Jucker and Taavitsainen's (2000) 'fuzziness' approach to speech acts like insults and compliments in Unit A11.4 – such that the former represents the negative end and the latter the positive end of a scale of ['other'] evaluation).

C6.1 USING CORPORA TO STUDY FACEWORK AND IM/POLITENESS

One way of testing whether *impoliteness* and *rudeness* are conceptually similar is to do as Culpeper (2008) has done, i.e. explore the use of terms such as *impolite/impoliteness* and *rude/rudeness* in the BNC. According to Culpeper, this will reveal differences in terms of frequency: indeed, *rude/rudeness* are much more frequent than *impolite/impoliteness*, with 950 and 101 occurrences as opposed to 55 and 2 (see below). It will also reveal differences in terms of usage(s) (ibid.: 44), for *rude/rudeness* and *impolite/impoliteness* (i) are distributed differently across the BNC genres – spoken, fiction, magazine, newspaper, non-academic, academic, miscellaneous – as the graphs below reveal,[1] and (ii) have different collocates (for a selection of which also see below). *Rude*, in addition, occurs more frequently in adjectival or nominal position than do *impolite/impoliteness* (cf. *rude awakening; rude jokes*).

	Spoken	Fiction	Magazine	Newspaper	Non-academic	Academic	Miscellaneous	*Rude*	collocates =
Frequency	202	326	80	83	73	36	150	950 hits (= 9.66 instances per million words) (instances occur across 540 texts)	*being, awakening, words, downright, arrogant, a bit, extremely, jokes, shock, aggressive ... etc*

	Spoken	Fiction	Magazine	Newspaper	Non-academic	Academic	Miscellaneous	*Rudeness*	collocates =
Frequency	1	55	5	7	7	6	20	101 hits (= 1.03 instances per million words) (instances occur across 83 texts)	*man* [*blatant, point*]

	Spoken	Fiction	Magazine	Newspaper	Non-academic	Academic	Miscellaneous	*Impolite*	collocates =
Frequency	2	26	2	0	7	9	9	55 hits (= 0.56 instances per million words) (instances occur across 46 texts)	*would* [*thought, been, be, have, it*]

	Spoken	Fiction	Magazine	Newspaper	Non-academic	Academic	Miscellaneous	*Impoliteness*	collocates =
Frequency	0	1	0	0	0	1	0	2 hits (= 0.02 instances per million words) (instances occur across 2 texts)	[n/a]

Undertake your own investigation of facework and im/politeness using online corpora such as the BNC or COCA. You can replicate Culpeper's study exactly, for example, so that you can see for yourself when *rude/rudeness* is preferred to *impolite/ impoliteness* in the various genres, and also determine their different collocates. Alternatively, you can undertake a study that explores terms relating to facework more generally (as opposed to face damage specifically): begin by using the simple search string *sav* face*, which will retrieve *saving face*, *saved face* and *saves face*.[2] When applied to COCA, this will pull up instances such as the following:

---

1 . . . a compromise was reached . . . that **saved face** for everyone but left no one happy. Either Bush misled . . .

2 . . . the language that was worked out in this agreement **saved face** for the North Koreans . . .

3 I got into brief competitions, speeding up to pass the runner ahead of me, and then the one ahead of him . . . a minute later we'd been running hard . . . until one of us **saved face** by peeling off down a side street . . .

4 The . . . compromise . . . came on the last day . . . Both Arafat and Abbas **saved face**; Abbas got his choice for security minister . . . Arafat was assured he would be consulted on major security issues.

5 Archbishop Schrembs not only **saved face** in his urban diocese, but received a Vatican stamp of approval . . . for the 'tact [he] used in healing the situation' . . .

6 . . . A.C. was mortified to discover that his property on Sao Joao Avenue was occupied not only by . . . drug dealers, but by cockroaches which, too lazy to take the stairs, went up and down in the elevator. At least he'd **saved face** by leaving his secretary at the hotel.

7 Stephen Sondheim's Passion drew mixed reviews and is struggling to find an audience. But it's . . . the only serious new work and one that '**saved face**' for the Broadway season.

8 Lightweight Oscar De La Hoya **saved face** with his gold medal at 132 pounds; had he not won, this U.S. team would have been the first since the 48 London Games to fail to get at least one.

9 . . . Heydrich leaned forward, a spark of amusement in his cold pale eyes. '. . . The insurance may be granted, but as soon as it is paid to the Jews, it will be confiscated. That way we will have **saved face**.'

Notice that, although the above concordance list provides a minimal amount of context, we can nevertheless see that five of the nine examples (1, 2, 4, 5 and 9) relate to politics or religio-/political issues. To what extent can we therefore argue that the concept of face-saving is important within politics? And from where might we glean further evidence as a means of (in)validating such a hypothesis?

C6.2 FACEWORK, POLITICIANS AND THE MEDIA

One approach we might adopt is to collect news stories about particular members of parliament (MPs) and then determine those occasions when the MPs protect (i) their own face only, (ii) the reputation of their party only or (iii) their own and their party's reputation simultaneously. Such a study would require you to give some consideration to the difference(s) between 'public' face and 'private' face. Goffman's work will again be useful here, as he identified a division between the public and private spheres and further stressed that access to some public spheres was restricted to those who possessed the requisite power, role or status (Goffman 1963: 10). Goffman's emphasis, when it came to the public sphere, was that of managing behaviour appropriately. He also likened the public sphere to an open space and the private sphere to an enclosed space. Some researchers (see, e.g., Figueroa 2005: 82) have since found his ideas problematic, not least because (i) participants with access to the public sphere will occasionally contest or resist the regulations of the public sphere and (ii) participants without supposed access might seek to gain access to the public sphere by force.

Contesting and/or resisting the regulations of the public sphere is particularly evident in televised political interviews. We touched upon one such interview in Unit A8.9 – that between UK presenter Fred Emery and the then-president of the National Union of Mineworkers, Arthur Scargill. In particular, we highlighted how Scargill sought to frame Emery as someone who was acting in a way that was beyond the 'sanctioned' aggression which typifies 'this public form of social practice' in Britain (we discuss this particular interview in more detail in Unit A12.6, as part of our investigation in regard to pragmatics and power). As part of this unit, undertake your own study of a political interview from the perspective of facework and im/politeness. You can easily find such interviews using the BBC or similar media-related websites. To help you, we also include a link to one such (UK) interview here:

http://news.bbc.co.uk/1/hi/programmes/newsnight/2732979.stm: the interviewer is Jeremy Paxman, and the interviewee is Tony Blair.

C6.3 USING LEECH (1983) TO EXPLAIN IMPOLITENESS/ FACE DAMAGE IN POLITICAL INTERVIEWS

Analyse Jeremy Paxman's *Newsnight* interview of Tony Blair, using Leech's politeness model (see Unit A8.4). This will allow you to test Leech's claim that his model can account for impoliteness/face damage in addition to politeness/face enhancement. Begin by assessing the extent to which there is evidence of a violation of:

The approbation maxim   Focus in particular on the extent to which Paxman calls into question Blair's actions/ truthfulness, and on Blair's indirect assertion that Paxman is (being) ridiculous

The sympathy maxim   Look for evidence of antipathy between Paxman and Blair

The agreement maxim   Identify instances – implicit and explicit – of disagreement between the two

Once you have completed your analysis, consider the following:

1 How useful has Leech proved to be in this overtly 'conflictive' context?
2 Does the fact that Leech's approach is built on the premise of social cooperative-ness pose any problems, in your view? For example, is it problematic to see 'one pole of a given maxim . . . as more desirable than the other' such that 'the more modest [we are] the better' (cf. Spencer-Oatey and Jiang 2003: 1635)? Why might this position be difficult to sustain in conflictive contexts, in particular?
3 Are there ways of using (a revised) Leechian approach if we allow for 'politeness' violations in certain activity types or communities of practice? If yes, what might this revised approach look like?
4 Would one (or more) of the other approaches highlighted in Unit A8 better account for this dataset? If yes, which one(s) – and why? For example, do you agree with the view that if verbal aggression is a norm in a given context, behaviour should only be labelled impolite when it transgresses that norm (and hence becomes salient)? (See, e.g., Units A8.8–A8.9.)

When considering these questions, you might find it helpful to read Bousfield (2008) and Locher (2004). Bousfield, in particular, suggests that Leech's model will not be able to account for impoliteness because of his emphasis on *socially motivated cooperation*: Bousfield further argues that Leech is misapplying Grice (1975), for he (like several researchers) sees the CP as capturing *linguistic* cooperation primarily: imagine, if you will, a scenario whereby interlocutors are cooperating in the sense of being prepared to exchange information (hence, they do not withdraw from or refuse to take part in an interaction, for example), but are not cooperating *socially* (by, e.g., attending to each other's face needs). Does Bousfield's interpretation of Grice's CP better allow for impoliteness, in your view? What are its advantages and disadvantages?

NOTES

1   The graphs have been constructed using Mark Davies' CORPUS.BYU.EDU web
    interface.
2   'Save face' occurs ×30 in the BNC and ×185 in COCA; 'saving face', ×7 in the
    BNC and ×57 in COCA; 'saved face', ×2 in the BNC and ×10 in COCA; 'saves
    face', ×4 in COCA.

Unit C7
Prosody and non-verbal communication

Pragmatics is about understanding what people mean, rather than what words and sentences mean, and in spoken language an important part of that meaning is conveyed by our tone of voice – including variations in pitch and loudness, and by our body movements such as hand gestures, the direction of our gaze and the position of our body in relation to our interlocutor. In this section we will suggest tasks that help you explore both prosodic effects and some aspects of non-verbal communication.

C7.1 PARALINGUISTIC EFFECTS

The variations in pitch, loudness, timing and voice quality that consitute 'how' we speak are together known as prosodic features, and in Unit B9 we saw that some aspects of these features are thought of as linguistic, i.e. part of the prosodic system of a language, and some as paralinguistic. The linguistic features are usually categorical choices of, say, a rising or falling contour, whereas the paralinguistic features are more often a case of more or less, in other words gradient, rather than either or. Pitch movement, for example, can be part of the linguistic system of marking prominences, as in English: we hear a syllable as prominent when it is associated with a peak (or sometimes trough) in the pitch contour. However, that pitch peak can be made extra high or low to make it sound more emphatic – exactly how high or low is a gradient matter and typically paralinguistic. We should point out that the difference between linguistic and paralinguistic is still a matter for debate: relevance theorists avoid the terms, for example, and prefer instead to distinguish between non-verbal features that are involuntary and symptomatic, and those that are used to communicate something: i.e. are natural signs and natural signals (see, e.g., Wharton 2009).

It is often assumed that gradient variations, such as changes in pitch height, pitch range, timing and voice quality are used to express emotions and attitudes. We saw in Wichmann (2004) that this is not necessarily the case, and that some attitudinal meanings are in fact pragmatic inferences drawn from a certain linguistic choice (e.g., rising or falling contour) in a certain context. Nonetheless, many emotional and attitudinal meanings are expressed paralinguistically, and fictional texts are a good source of evidence for this, as we noted in the introduction to Unit A9. Some writers simply describe their characters' voices in terms that relate directly to prosodic features (*she said loudly*; *he growled*; *she squeaked*; *he whispered*; *she said slowly*), but others say more about the feelings of the character (*he said angrily*; *she implored*; *she snapped*; *he said gloomily*) and it is left to the reader to imagine what kind of voice might convey that meaning.

➤ Test this for yourselves: take a number of novels in English or in your own language and collect a list of examples of 'attitudinal' effects. Categorize them in terms of what they may convey to the reader. Then ask one or two friends to read them aloud. Are they consistent in their interpretations?

C7.2 POINTING

Pointing is one of the many gestures that are very intimately integrated with spoken communication. Typically we point with an extended index finger, but sometimes with the thumb, with the whole hand, or even with the head. As with other speech accompanying gestures, pointing can fulfil a variety of functions. According to Adam Kendon (2004: 84–107), there have been many attempts over the years – even centuries – to classify gestures according to their use and their shape. Cumulatively, that classification research suggests that, in addition to having a deictic function (typical of pointing), gestures may also be used to illustrate or depict what is being said, for structuring discourse and for expressing pragmatic meanings such as stance.

Choose a piece of recorded visual data, such as a television discussion or interview, and identify any pointing gestures used by the participants.

➤ Note down as much as you can about how they point: is it with one finger, with the whole hand or with the thumb? What is the orientation of the hand (palm down, palm upwards, palm inwards)? What are they pointing to? Is it a visible object, or a location? Or is someone pointing at their interlocutor?

➤ Attempt to identify the function or meaning of the pointing gestures in the context in which they occur.

C7.3 GREETINGS

A context in which non-verbal behaviour plays an important role is the moment when two people meet and greet each other. There is considerable variation in the non-verbal greeting behaviour depending on the situation, whether it is between men or women, and between different cultures. It can also be a source of misunderstanding or embarrassment. An early study of such behaviour, including the amount and type of bodily contact involved, was carried out by Greenbaum and

Rosenfeld (1980). They observed over 100 greetings at an American airport and categorized the behaviours they found. For example, they established that men generally shook hands while women usually kissed or embraced. The numbers below (cited in Argyle 1988: 222) indicate the different kinds of touch (please note that one greeting sequence could involve several gestures):

No touch	41
Kiss on mouth	41
Touch on head, arm or back	38
Kiss on cheek	30
Light hug	23
Solid hug	19
Arm round waist or back	15
Holding hands	12
Hand shake	10
Extended embrace	10
Extended kiss	3

➤ Which of these gestures would you expect to see most often in the culture in which you live? Are there any that would not be possible at all in your culture?

➤ Choose a situation where you are able to observe people greeting each other. This could be at an airport, as Greenbaum and Rosenfeld did, or at a station, or some other public place. Alternatively it could be a family gathering. If possible carry out your observations with a friend and note down the kind of greetings you observe. When you have counted a given number of meetings (depending on the time available 20, 50 or 100) count up the number of different gestures.

➤ Compare your results to your predictions and to those found by Greenbaum and Rosenfeld.

C7.4 REPORTED SPEECH AND MIMICRY

Sometimes we use paralinguistic features in order to report someone else's words, to make it quite clear that they are not our own words. It is in effect a prosodic strategy of 'othering' (see Unit C12). Couper-Kuhlen (1996: 389) relates this strategy to Goffman's notion of 'framing' discourse:

> This use of non-natural prosody can be seen to cue a shift in frame, if we understand 'frame' in the Goffmanian sense of interpretative schema (1974: 21). It signals that the words themselves are not the speaker's own and are not to be taken 'seriously' . . .

Couper-Kuhlen is referring to how we distance ourselves from the words of a third party, and she shows how this distancing can be indicated towards our interlocutor by means of mimicry. It is, of course, common in conversation for speakers to echo what the previous speaker has just said (see Walker *et al.* 2006), and in doing so they often imitate not just the words but also the intonation contour. Couper-Kuhlen (1996) examines this phenomenon, and shows that there are different degrees of imitation, with different results. If the imitation is relative to the speaker's own voice, it is perceived as unmarked, but if the imitation is too close it is perceived as parody or mimicry and has a negative effect. Culpeper (2005) describes the interaction in a British TV game show (the *Weakest Link*) in which part of the entertainment is the humiliation of participants by the host, and this often involves mimicry.

➤ In any recorded data that you have available, can you find examples of someone reporting someone else's words with a slightly different voice? You will find suitable datasets on the BBC website – see especially its repository of past programmes, interviews, etc., including the programme the *Weakest Link*.

C7.5 RESPONSE TOKENS AND VOCALIZATIONS

In Unit B6.4 you read about small response tokens in conversation: small words like *yes, no, really, right, good, great, true, sure, exactly, fine, wow* (McCarthy 2003). Sometimes minimal responses do not take the form of words at all but of vocalizations or 'pragmatic noise' (Culpeper and Kytö 2010) (such as *uh huh, uhm, mmm*).

➤ Investigate the equivalent response tokens and vocalizations in your own language. Using recorded conversational data, either making your own recordings or taking a clip from radio, television or the internet, gather a set of examples of small response tokens and categorize them according to their meanings. Identify the vocalizations used for backchannels.

➤ If you are native speaker of English, create a small corpus to make a comparative study of response tokens and vocalizations in two varieties of English.

Gunnel Tottie (1989), in a comparison of Swedish and American vocalizations, focuses specifically on those sounds that are used to mean *yes* and *no*. She cites American usage as *uh-huh* and *mm-hmm* for *yes*, and *uh-uh* or *mm-mm* for *no*.

➤ Collect a small corpus of American English in two different situations – an episode of an American TV comedy, for example, together with a political interview – and investigate the use of non-verbal alternatives to *yes* and *no*. You should consider their relative frequency of use, and their distribution in relation to the participants and the situation.

Unit C8
Cross-cultural and intercultural pragmatics

The focus of Units A10 and B10 has been the issue of acquiring or understanding pragmatic meaning in a foreign language – this is often a problem for people living in foreign countries, or when dealing with foreigners in their own country. The ways of creating pragmatic meaning are culture dependent, and ignorance of these can lead to misunderstandings. More seriously, the participants are not aware that there is a misunderstanding. On the contrary, they believe they have understood, but not necessarily what the other participant intended them to understand. In the case of Thomas' (1983) experience in the former Soviet Union (Unit B10. 3) the hosts believed that she had been very rude, when in fact she thought she was being honest. We saw in Unit A10 that court proceedings can fail to take into account the potential for pragmatic misunderstandings when the defendant is not a native speaker. Lack of awareness of cultural norms in such cases can have serious consequences.

C8.1 FORMS OF ADDRESS

Less serious, but nonetheless a common source of discomfort, is the inappropriate use of address forms. As we saw in Unit A10.3, the conventions governing forms of address vary according to the context of use and also according to culture. The following tasks show how to investigate for yourself some of the differences that can be found.

➤ Select informants of a similar age whose native languages are different. Find out how they address (or used to address) their teachers (e.g. title plus last name, first name, title only). If they speak a T/V language do/did they use T or V? Compare the results across languages.

➤ (The historical study reported in Unit A11.5.2 may be helpful here.) If you are a native speaker of English you may come from a culture (e.g. the United States or Britain) where the use of first names is quite common even between people who do not know each other well. However, it would be wrong to assume that this is always reciprocal. Conduct a survey of friends and/or family to find out where the use of first names is reciprocal for your informants, where it is asymmetrical and where it is not acceptable at all.

➤ The use of address forms is often particularly important in the talk between people at work or in an institutional environment (hospital, business, university etc.; see also Unit A12). Ask a number of people like doctors, shopkeepers, hairdressers and other professionals how they expect to address – and be addressed by – patients or clients. What conventions can you observe?

C8.2 DIRECTIVES (IN BRITISH AND AMERICAN ENGLISH)

In Unit A8 you read about the relationship between politeness and indirectness in English. While it is common to associate indirectness in English with being polite, the relationship is far from straightforward. It is not always the case that more direct equals less polite, for example.

We have constructed two scales for you with which to test the claim that modern (British) English directives can be located on a politeness–directness scale.

Replicate these scales on two sheets of blank paper – making sure there's a space between the two arrows for the second scale – and then construct a list of ten English directives which includes both commands and requests. The Kohnen extract in Unit B11 provides you with some example words (*Go!*) and phrases (*I order you to **, *I would like you to **, *Could you please *?*) as a starting point. You might also want to include examples such as *Shut up!*, *Stop it!*, *Come here!* and *Can you *?*

➤ Write down how many times each of your ten items occurs in the BNC and in what type of text, remembering to use the wild card symbol (*) if you are searching for a phrase:

  ▪ Which is the most popular? Which is the least popular? Does a common pattern seem to be emerging – i.e. that indirect items are more popular than direct ones or, alternatively, that direct items seem to be more popular in some text-types than others?
  ▪ Using your BNC concordance results as a guide, position as many of your 10 directives as you can on the first of your two scales: for example, if a directive seems to you to be particularly indirect and polite, given the context, position it closer to the left of the paper; if it seems particularly direct and less polite, however, position it closer to the right of the paper.

■ Are there any example words/phrases that you are struggling to position easily using the one-arrow scale – because, for example, they are direct without being less polite than you might expect given the context of utterance or the activity? To what extent does this suggest that a one-to-one mapping between indirectness/politeness and/or directness/less politeness may be problematic in modern British English?

■ Position the examples you have remaining (and which you identified in the point above) on your two-arrow scale: this will mean including each example twice, once in relation to the in/directness arrow and once in relation to the more polite/less polite arrow.

➤ Undertake a similar investigation to the one above, this time using COCA. Are your results for American English the same as those for British English? If not, how do they differ? Do any of your results suggest there is a cultural difference in either the level of politeness or the level of in/directness between these two modern English varieties?

➤ If you speak a language other than English, do you find that your other language is more or less direct than English (generally speaking)? Do you indicate politeness using indirectness at all? If the answer is yes, in what way(s) and when? If the answer is no, how is politeness most commonly signalled in this particular language?

➤ According to some researchers, the study of language of times past shares many similarities with the study of different languages of the same period or different varieties of the same language (see, e.g., Jucker and Taavitsainen 2000; Taavitsainen and Jucker 2008a). How might you use your experience of other varieties of English and/or your experience of other language varieties to make sense of the English of the past? You might find it useful to reread Units A11 and B11 before attempting this particular question.

C8.3 IMPLICATIONS FOR TEACHING AND LEARNING

Because pragmatic meanings are generated in ways that the speaker is not necessarily conscious of, it is important that pragmatics is included in the teaching of foreign languages. However, it is not easy to know how it can best be done. Halenko and Jones (2011) found that explicit instruction helped Chinese learners of English to improve their pragmatic abilities, but that the effect did not last. They suggest that regular explicit instruction would be beneficial.

➤ Examine two or three English language textbooks available to you and undertake a comparative study. Look for any guidance or exercises that have a specifically pragmatic focus. How much is there compared to, say, work on grammar or vocabulary?

Unit C9
Power

As part of our further exploration in Unit C6, we encouraged you to analyse a political interview from a facework and im/politeness perspective. In this unit, we continue with the political context and ask you to explore how pragmatic devices are used for persuasion and control. As you learned in Unit C3, pragmaticians are interested as much in what is 'unsaid or unwritten (yet communicated)' (Yule 2006: 84) as they are in what is said/written explicitly. One of the numerous ways in which meanings can be communicated powerfully despite being 'unsaid' is via words and expressions that have certain connotations and/or which immediately conjure up their opposite literal meaning. For example, when politicians in Britain refer to 'hard-working taxpayers' they implicitly create a comparison with those who do not work (and are therefore 'lazy'). Sometimes official terms are changed in order to bring about a change in perception: in order to change the public attitude towards the unemployed, for example, the term 'unemployment benefit' was changed to 'job-seekers' allowance' in Britain. The motivation was to change the focus from benefits as a right, to the idea of benefits as a temporary measure until employment was found. Some have argued that such changes (although seemingly trivial) also serve to encourage a societal mindset which perceives those on benefits as 'scroungers' and an unnecessary drain on (already) limited resources.

C9.1 INVESTIGATING *OTHERING* IN A POLITICAL CONTEXT

Creating a negative view of the 'other' is a common strategy in political discourse (as we learned in Unit A12: see, especially, the work of Wodak 2007). As Gerlinde Mautner reveals, corpus analysis can provide a useful means of uncovering *othering*: Mautner (2009: 127–8) has shown the negative evaluation of the word 'unemployed' by highlighting the words that regularly co-occur with it (i.e. its collocates). In one large corpus Mautner analysed, for example, 'unemployed' co-occurred with *angry, demoralized, disabled, dreary, drunk, excluded, poor, struggling* and *underprivileged*. Undertake your own study of the term 'unemployed' to see how it is used and in what contexts. If you undertake this study using COCA, you will notice that many of the most frequent collocates of 'unemployed' are not immediately negative. However, there are some interesting connections between unemployment and poverty or lack (see, e.g., *poor, homeless, hungry, penniless*). Go through the list of the top 100 collocates yourself and identify additional links between 'unemployed' and, for example, issues of gender, age, education, disability, etc. Once you have identified the associated 'semantic fields' of the term 'unemployed' in your corpus, explore the concordance results in more detail and look for any interesting metaphorical usage(s).

C9.2 WAR, METAPHORS, POLITICS AND THE MEDIA

According to Lakoff and Johnson (2006), much of our thought, language and action may be conceptualized – and hence governed – by metaphors. If true, then it is possible that politicians and media outlets can (knowingly and/or unknowingly) use metaphors to influence us – to the extent that they shape the way we think about things. Indeed, Lakoff (2006: 10–15) goes as far as to suggest that, as we are not as consciously introspective as we might imagine when engaged in thinking, the conceptual frames we use to make sense of the world can be manipulated relatively easily via, for example, repetition. In fact, the repetition of words/phrases is said to have the power to change our brains in addition to helping us to develop particular interpretative frames!

A common corpus linguistic technique, of course, is to investigate (the frequency of) word/phrasal patterns in a given text (written or spoken). Hence, it would seem profitable to use corpus linguistic techniques to study frequently occurring words/ phrases and any metaphorical associations they may have. Given the current prominence of war metaphors (e.g. 'war on drugs', 'war on crime', 'war on terror'), take as a starting point the phrase *war on terror* (especially given its frequency of use today). Indeed, a quick search, using COCA, reveals that *war* and *terror* co-occur very frequently in this particular corpus (i.e. 2,395 times; this equates to just under 6 occurrences per every million words). Moreover, most of these occurrences (2,092) relate to the specific phrase *war on terror*. A starting point for a study of *war on terror*, in turn, might be its collocates (which are numerous). Begin, as before, by trying to arrange the collocates into related semantic fields. You will find some words that are overtly American in orientation (e.g. *Bush, US-led, Kerry, Cheney*). You will also find that certain countries collocate strongly with *war on terror* (e.g. *Iraq, Afghanistan*). But what else do you find? Do any of the results surprise you?

As of 14 April 2011, there were 18 concordance entries for *war on terror* which had a 2011 publication date. We've reproduced them below for you:

1   . . . is a key ally of the U.S. in the **war on terror**. And in Egypt another important ally, protesters again called for the removal of . . .

2   . . . tested. And, you know, the most significant battle in the **war on terror** was left up to 70 U.S. Special Forces, some CIA guys, a handful . . .

3   . . . this is the most important battle in the **war on terror**. You still got the smoking ruins of the World Trade Center, 3,000 Americans . . .

4   . . . a new book, a history of the unfinished **war on terror** from both the perspective of the United States and its allies, and of al-Qaida . . .

5   . . . years did it get so wildly out of control? Was it the **war on terror** that did it? STEPHANOPOULOS: Well, I said, well, you're . . .

6   . . . I think it was the tax cuts passed in 2001 combined with the **war on terror**. And that's – that – that's what did it. And that . . .

7   . . . to push? Is it when Egypt stops being an ally in the **war on terror**? Is it when Egypt starts to threaten peace with Israel? At what point . . .

8   . . . democratic Egypt will not continue to cooperate in general on things like the **war on terror**. It may not participate in things like extraordinary rendition, which Mubarak's government . . .

9   . . . We had over 90 countries in the global **war on terror** that President Bush and Colin Powell put in place. We had dozens of countries . . .

10   . . . a crock. When was it normal these days, given the ever-expanding **war on terror**? The war on drugs? The war on wars? Hard choices call . . .

11   . . . will never achieve perfect security. But this is what success in the **war on terror** looks like: a steady degradation of terrorist capability to do harm. Presidents make . . .

12   . . . The Philippine mission is a rarity in the U.S. **war on terror**: a largely successful counterinsurgency at minimal cost in lives and dollars.

13   . . . are they too in Bahrain and Yemen, Western allies in "the **war on terror**." Isn't there a case for intervention in those places as well? . . .

14   . . . on the other hand, is a full-throated supporter of the "**war on terror**" and, as governor of Alaska, kept an Israeli flag in her office . . .

15   . . . order on a largely Wilsonian basis. Rather than embracing the "global **war on terror**" as an overarching strategic umbrella under which it could position a range of aid . . .

16   . . . Internationally, dualism is behind both jihad and the global **war on terror**. Americans who have accepted dualistic assumptions often find it unacceptable to accord those suspected . . .

> 17 . . . abuses of human rights by local officials, the Kremlin sees a "<u>war</u> <u>on</u> <u>terror</u>." Putin does not understand why the United Kingdom and the United States granted . . .
>
> 18 . . . set by George W. Bush, Uribe launched a Colombian version of the <u>War</u> <u>on</u> <u>Terror</u>, rounding up "subversives" under the rubric of his Democratic Security doctrine . . .

Summarize how *war on terror* is being used above. Now explore the COCA concordance results for *war on terror* which relate to previous years, and prepare summaries for 2010, 2009, 2008, etc. Given the sheer number of occurrences, you should undertake this with a colleague or as part of a team. Does the usage change at all (however, subtly)? Does the *othering* target change, for example?

According to Jackson (2005: 1):

> For a government to commit enormous amounts of public resources and risk the lives of its citizens in a military conflict, it has to persuade society that such an undertaking is necessary, desirable and achievable.

One of the ways it does this is to make the enemy – the *Other* – seem evil, barbarous and inhuman. This sometimes involves creating a 'new reality', according to Jackson, where 'diabolical and insane terrorists' are plotting to destroy 'our' cities, while 'heroic warriors of freedom risk their lives in foreign lands to save innocent and decent folk back home' (ibid.: 2). The effect? A justifiable war. Is this level of justification evident in any of your concordance results at all? If justification is evident, is it more explicit in some years than it is in others? Why might this be the case?

C9.3 EXPLORING ISSUES OF *FRAMING*

Framing techniques are discussed at great length by those interested in the *war on terror* (see, e.g., Entman 1993, 2003). By framing, researchers such as Entman mean the *purposeful* (i.e. motivated) selection/highlighting of 'aspects of a <u>perceived</u> reality' so as 'to promote a particular . . . definition, causal interpretation, moral evaluation . . . recommendation' and/or 'solution' (Entman 1993: 52, 2003: 5; cf. Tannen 1993). Is this feature in evidence in your concordance results for *war on terror*?

COCA is one of the few corpora whose content is not fixed but continually growing (unlike the BNC, which does not contain any data after the 1990s). COCA has a definite American bias, however. You may therefore like to extend your study of phrases such as *war on terror* (or metaphors more generally) by exploring one of the many newspaper databases available online. By extending your study in this way, you will also be able to determine the extent to which a different world-view becomes evident in data from different countries. A starting point might be the following archive, which provides users with access to the front pages of national and international newspapers across the world:

http://www.frontpagestoday.co.uk/?gclid=CJmdkdWTiKcCFYVjfAodFxUAfA

This allows you to compare what different newspapers consider to be the most important news of the day, and, in some cases, the broader frames and ideologies they reflect.

References

Adolphs, S. 2008. *Corpus and context. Investigating pragmatic functions in spoken discourse.* Amsterdam and New York: John Benjamins.

Adolphs, S. and R.A. Carter. 2003. '*And she's like it's terrible, like.* Spoken discourse, grammar, and corpus analysis'. *International Journal of English Studies* 3(1): 45–56.

Aijmer, K. 1996. *Conversational routines in English. Convention and creativity.* London and New York: Longman.

Aijmer, K. 2002. *English discourse particles. Evidence from a corpus.* Amsterdam and Philadelphia: John Benjamins.

Aijmer, K. and A.-M. Simon-Vandenbergen (eds). 2006. *Pragmatic markers in contrast.* Amsterdam: Elsevier.

Aijmer, K. and A.-M. Simon-Vandenbergen (eds). 2011. 'Pragmatic markers', in J. Zienkowski, J.-O. Östman and J. Verschueren (eds) *Discursive pragmatics*, pp. 223–47. Amsterdam and Philadelphia: John Benjamins.

Allwood, J. 2008. 'Multimodal corpora', in A. Lüdeling and M. Kytö (eds) *Corpus linguistics. An international handbook*, pp. 207–25. Berlin: Mouton de Gruyter.

Althusser, L. 1971. *Lenin and philosophy and other essays.* London: New Left Books.

Andersen, G. 2001. *Pragmatic markers and sociolinguistic variation. A relevance-theoretic approach to the language of adolescents.* Amsterdam and Philadelphia: John Benjamins.

Andersen, G. and T. Fretheim. 2000. *Pragmatic markers and propositional attitude.* Amsterdam and Philadelphia: John Benjamins.

Antaki, C. (ed.). 2011. *Applied conversation analysis intervention and change in institutional talk.* Basingstoke: Palgrave Macmillan.

Archer, D. 2005. *Questions and answers in the English courtroom (1640–1760).* Amsterdam and Philadelphia: John Benjamins.

Archer, D. 2008. 'Verbal aggression and impoliteness: related or synonymous?', in D. Bousfield and M. Locher (eds) *Impoliteness in language: studies in its interplay with power in theory and practice*, pp. 181–207. Berlin and New York: Mouton de Gruyter.

Archer, D. 2010. 'Speech acts', in A.H. Jucker and I. Taavitsainen (eds) *Historical pragmatics*, pp. 379–418. Berlin and New York: Mouton de Gruyter.

Archer, D. 2011a. 'Theory and practice in pragmatics', in D. Archer and P. Grundy (eds) *The pragmatics reader*, pp. 471–81. London and New York: Routledge.

Archer, D. 2011b. 'Libelling Oscar Wilde: the case of Regina vs. John Sholto Douglas'. *Journal of Politeness Research* 7(1): 73–99.

Archer, D. 2011c. 'Cross-examining lawyers, facework and the adversarial courtroom'. *Journal of Pragmatics* 43(13): 3216–30.

Archer, D. and J. Culpeper. 2003. 'Sociopragmatic annotation: new directions and possibilities in historical corpus linguistics', in A. Wilson, P. Rayson and T. McEnery (eds) *Corpus linguistics by the Lune: studies in honour of Geoffrey Leech*, pp. 37–58. Frankfurt: Peter Lang.

Archer, D. and P. Grundy (eds). 2011. *The pragmatics reader*. London and New York: Routledge.

Archer, D., J. Culpeper and M. Davies. 2008. 'Pragmatic annotation', in A. Lüdeling and M. Kytö (eds) *Corpus linguistics: an international handbook*, pp. 613–41. Berlin: Mouton de Gruyter.

Argyle, M. 1988 (2nd edition). *Bodily communication*. London: Routledge.

Arnovick, L. 2000. *Diachronic pragmatics: seven case studies in English illocutionary development*. Amsterdam and Philadelphia: John Benjamins.

Arundale, R.B. 1999. 'An alternative model and ideology of communication for an alternative to politeness theory'. *Pragmatics* 9: 119–53.

Arundale, R.B. 2008. 'Against (Gricean) intentions at the heart of human interaction'. *Intercultural Pragmatics* 5(2): 229–58.

Aston, G. 1993. 'Notes on the interlanguage of comity', in G. Kasper and S. Blum-Kulka (eds) *Interlanguage pragmatics*, pp. 224–50. New York: Oxford University Press.

Atkinson, J.M. and P. Drew. 1979. *Order in court. The organization of verbal interaction in judicial settings*. London: Macmillan.

Atkinson, J.M. and J. Heritage. 1985. 'Preference organisation', in J.M. Atkinson and J. Heritage (eds) *Structures of social action: studies in conversation analysis*, pp. 53–6. Cambridge: Cambridge University Press.

Atlas, J.D. 1977. 'Negation, ambiguity, and presupposition'. *Linguistics and Philosophy* 1: 321–36.

Atlas, J.D. 1979. 'How linguistics matters to philosophy: presupposition, truth, and meaning', in D. Dinneen and C.-K. Oh (eds) *Syntax and semantics 11: presupposition*, pp. 265–81. New York: Academic Press.

Atlas, J.D. 1989. *Philosophy without ambiguity: a logico-linguistic essay*. Oxford: Clarendon Press.

Atlas, J.D. 2004. 'Presupposition', in L.R. Horn and G. Ward (eds) *The handbook of pragmatics*, pp. 29–52. Oxford: Blackwell.

Atlas, J.D. 2005. *Logic, meaning and conversation: semantical underdeterminacy, implicature, and their interface*. Oxford: Oxford University Press.

Austin, J.L. 1962. *How to do things with words*. Ed. J.O. Urmson. London: Oxford University Press.

Bach, K. 1994. 'Semantic slack: what is said and more', in S.L. Tsohatzidis (ed.) *Foundations of speech act theory: philosophical and linguistic perspectives*, pp. 267–91. London: Routledge.

Bach, K. and R.M. Harnish. 1979. *Linguistic communication and speech acts*. Cambridge, MA: MIT Press.

Baker, P. 2006. *Using corpora in discourse analysis*. London and New York: Continuum.

Baker, P., C. Gabrielatos, M. Khosravinik, M. Krzyzanowski, T. McEnery and R. Wodak. 2008. 'A useful methodological synergy? Combining critical discourse analysis and corpus linguistics to examine discourses of refugees and asylum seekers in the UK press'. *Discourse and Society* 19(3): 273–306.

Bara, B.G. 2010. 'Cognitive pragmatics', in L. Cummings (ed.) *The pragmatics encyclopedia*, pp. 50–3. London and New York: Routledge.

Bargiela-Chiappini, F. 2003. 'Face and politeness: new (insights) for old (concepts)'. *Journal of Pragmatics* 35(10–11): 1453–69.

Bargiela-Chiappini, F. and S. Harris. 1996. 'Requests and status in business correspondence'. *Journal of Pragmatics* 28: 635–62.

Barron, A. and K. Schneider. 2009. 'Variational pragmatics: studying the impact of social factors on language use in interaction'. *Intercultural Pragmatics* 6(4): 425–42.

Barron, A. and M. Warga. 2007. 'Acquisitional pragmatics in foreign language learning'. Special Issue, *Intercultural Pragmatics* 4(2): 113–27.

Barth-Weingarten, D., N. Dehé and A. Wichmann (eds). 2009. *Where prosody meets pragmatics*. Bingley: Emerald.

Barth-Weingarten, D., E. Reber and M. Selting (eds). 2010. *Prosody in interaction*. Amsterdam: John Benjamins.

Bax, M. 2001. 'Historical frame analysis: hoaxing and make-believe in a seventeenth-century Dutch play'. *Journal of Historical Pragmatics* 2: 33–67.

Beattie, G. 1983. *Talk*. Milton Keynes: Open University Press.

Beattie, G. and R.J. Bradbury. 1979. 'An experimental investigation of the modifiability of the temporal structure of spontaneous speech'. *Journal of Psycholinguistic Research* 8: 225–48.

Beattie, G.W., A. Cutler and M. Pearson. 1982. 'Why is Mrs Thatcher interrupted so often?' *Nature* 300 (23 December): 744–7.

Beebe, L.M. and M.C. Cummings. 1996. 'Natural speech data versus written questionnaire data: how data collection method affects speech performance', in S.M. Gass and J. Neu (eds) *Speech acts across cultures*, pp. 65–86. Berlin: Mouton de Gruyter.

Berk-Seligson, S. 1990. *The bilingual courtroom*. Chicago: University of Chicago Press.

Berry, M. 1981. 'Systemic linguistics and discourse analysis: a multi-layered approach to discourse structure', in M. Coulthard and M. Montgomery (eds) *Studies in discourse analysis*, pp. 120–45. London: Routledge and Kegan Paul.

Berry, M. 1987. 'Is teacher an unanalyzed concept?', in M.A.K. Halliday and R.P. Fawcett (eds) *New developments in systemic linguistics*, Vol. 1, pp. 41–63. London: Frances Pinter.

Bertucelli Papi, M. 2000. 'Is a diachronic speech act theory possible?' *Journal of Historical Pragmatics* 1(1): 56–66.

Bezooijen, R. v. 1993. 'Verschillen in toonhoogte: Natuur of cultuur?' *Gramma/TTT* 2: 165–79.

Bezuidenhout, A.L. 2010. 'Experimental pragmatics', in L. Cummings (ed.) *The pragmatics encyclopedia*, pp. 148–53. London and New York: Routledge.

Biber, D., S. Johansson, G. Leech, S. Conrad and E. Finegan. 1999. *Longman grammar of spoken and written English*. London: Longman.

Biemans, M. 2000. *Gender variation and voice quality*. Utrecht: landelijke Onderzoekschool Taalwetenschap LOT, Utrecht University.

Blakemore, D. 2002. *Relevance and linguistic meaning. The semantics and pragmatics of discourse markers*. Cambridge: Cambridge University Press.

Blum-Kulka, S. 1982. 'Learning to say what you mean in a second language: a study of the speech act performance of learners of Hebrew as a second language'. *Applied Linguistics* III(1): 29–59.

Blum-Kulka, S., J. House and G. Kasper (eds). 1989a. *Cross-cultural pragmatics: requests and apologies*. Norwood, NJ: Ablex.

Blum-Kulka, S., J. House and G. Kasper. 1989b. 'Investigating cross-cultural pragmatics: an introductory overview', in S. Blum-Kulka, J. House and G. Kasper (eds) *Cross-cultural pragmatics: requests and apologies*, pp. 1–34. Norwood, NJ: Ablex.

Blum-Kulka, S., J. House and G. Kasper. 1989c. 'The CCSARP coding manual', in S. Blum-Kulka, J. House and G. Kasper (eds) *Cross-cultural pragmatics: requests and apologies*, pp. 273–94. Norwood, NJ: Ablex.

Boden, D. 1994. *The business of talk. Organizations in action*. London: Polity Press.

Boersma, P. 2001. 'Praat, a system for doing phonetics by computer'. *Glot International* 5(9/10): 341–5.

Bolden, G.B. 2006. 'Little words that matter: discourse markers "o" and "oh" and the doing of other-attentiveness in social interaction'. *Journal of Communication* 56: 661–88.

Bolinger, D. (ed). 1972. *Intonation: selected readings.* Harmondsworth: Penguin.

Bolinger, D. 1989. *Intonation and it uses: melody in grammar and discourse.* London: Edward Arnold.

Bourdieu, P. 1992. *Language and symbolic power.* Cambridge: Polity Press.

Bousfield, D. 2008. *Impoliteness in interaction.* Amsterdam and Philadelphia: John Benjamins.

Bousfield, D. and J. Culpeper (eds). 2008. 'Impoliteness'. Special issue, *Journal of Politeness Research* 4(2): 161–337.

Bousfield, D. and M.A. Locher (eds). 2008. *Impoliteness in language: studies on its interplay with power in theory and practice.* Berlin and New York: Mouton de Gruyter.

Bowles, H. and P. Seedhouse. 2007. *Conversation analysis and languages for specific purposes.* Bern and New York: Peter Lang.

Brenneis, D. and L. Lein. 1977. '"You fruithead": a sociolinguistic approach to children's dispute settlement', in S. Ervin-Tripp and C. Mitchell-Kernan (eds) *Child discourse,* pp. 49–65. New York: Academic Press.

Brinton, L.J. 1996. *Pragmatic markers in English. Grammaticalization and discourse functions.* Berlin and New York: Mouton de Gruyter.

Brinton, L.J. 2008. *The comment clause in English. Syntactic origins and pragmatic development.* Cambridge: Cambridge University Press.

Brown, G. 1977. *Listening to spoken English.* London: Longman.

Brown, G. and G. Yule. 1983. *Discourse analysis.* Cambridge: Cambridge University Press.

Brown, G., K. Currie and J. Kenworthy. 1980. *Questions of intonation.* London: Croom Helm.

Brown, P. and S. Levinson. 1978. 'Universals in language usage: politeness phenomena', in E.N. Goody (ed.) *Questions and politeness,* pp. 56–311. Cambridge: Cambridge University Press.

Brown, P. and S. Levinson. 1978/1987. *Politeness: some universals in language usage.* Cambridge: Cambridge University Press.

Brown, R. and A. Gilman. 1960. 'The pronouns of power and solidarity', in T. Sebeok (ed.) *Style in language,* pp. 253–76. London: Wiley.

Buchstaller, I. 2006. 'Diagnostics of age-graded linguistic behaviour: the case of the quotative system'. *Journal of Sociolinguistics* 10(1): 3–30.

Burton, D. 1981. 'Analyzing spoken discourse', in M. Coulthard and M. Montgomery (eds) *Studies in discourse analysis,* pp. 61–79. London: Routledge and Kegan Paul.

Cameron, D. 2001. *Working with spoken discourse.* London: Sage.

Carletta, J., A. Isard, S. Isard, J.C. Kowtko, G. Doherty-Sneddon and A.H. Anderson. 1997. 'The reliability of a dialogue structure coding scheme'. *Computational Linguistics,* 23(1): 13–31.

Carroll, L. 1871. *Through the Looking-Glass, and What Alice Found There.* London: Macmillan.

Carston, R. 1988. 'Implicature, explicature and truth-theoretic semantics', in R. Kempson (ed.) *Mental representations: the interface between language and reality,* pp. 155–81. Cambridge: Cambridge University Press.

Carston, R. 1998. 'Postscript (1995) to Carston 1988', in A. Kasher (ed.) *Pragmatics: critical concepts,* vol. 4, pp. 464–79. London: Routledge.

Carston, R. 2002. *Thoughts and utterances: the pragmatics of explicit communication.* Oxford: Blackwell.

Carston, R. 2010. 'Explicit/implicit distinction', in L. Cummings (ed.) *The pragmatics encyclopedia,* pp. 154–62. London and New York: Routledge.

Carter, R. and M. McCarthy. 2006. *Cambridge grammar of English. A comprehensive guide. Spoken and written English grammar and usage.* Cambridge: Cambridge University Press.

Chapman, S. 2005. *Paul Grice, philosopher and linguist.* Basingstoke: Palgrave Macmillan.

Chen, A., C. Gussenhoven and T. Rietveld. (2004). 'Language specificity in perception of paralinguistic intonational meaning'. *Language and Speech* 47(4): 311–49.

Clark, H.H. 1996. *Using language.* Cambridge: Cambridge University Press.

Clark, H.H. and A. Bangerter. 2004. 'Changing ideas about reference', in I. Noveck and D. Sperber (eds) *Experimental pragmatics*, pp. 25–49. Basingstoke: Palgrave Macmillan.

Clark, H.H. and J.E. Fox Tree. 2002. 'Using *uh* and *um* in spontaneous speaking'. *Cognition* 84: 73–111.

Claridge, C. and L. Arnovick. 2010. 'Pragmaticalisation and discursisation', in A.H. Jucker and I. Taavitsainen (eds) *Historical pragmatics*, pp. 165–92. Berlin and New York: Mouton de Gruyter.

Clayman, S. 1992. 'Footing in the achievement of neutrality: the case of news-interview discourse', in P. Drew and J. Heritage (eds) *Talk at work: interaction in institutional settings*, pp. 163–98. Cambridge: Cambridge University Press.

Clyne, M. 2009. 'Address in intercultural communication across languages'. *Intercultural Pragmatics* 6(3): 395–409.

Coates, J. 1989. 'Gossip revisited: language in all-female groups', in J. Coates and D. Cameron (eds) *Women in their speech communities: new perspectives on language and sex*, pp. 94–122. London and New York: Longman.

Coates, J. 1996. *Women talk.* Oxford: Blackwell.

Coates, J. 2004. *Women, men and language: a sociolinguistic account of gender differences in language.* Harlow: Pearson Education.

Cohen, A.D. and E. Olshtain. 1981. 'Developing a measure of sociocultural competence: the case of apology'. *Language Learning* 31(1): 113–34.

Cole, P. (ed.). 1981. *Radical pragmatics.* New York: Academic Press.

Coleman, L. and P. Kay. 1982. 'Prototype semantics: the English word *lie*'. *Language* 57(1): 26–44.

Cook, M. 1970. 'Experiments on orientation and proxemics'. *Human Relations* 23: 61–76.

Cotterill, J. 2003. *Language and power in court: a linguistic analysis of the O.J. Simpson trial.* Basingstoke: Palgrave Macmillan.

Coulthard, M. and M. Ashby. 1976. 'A linguistic description of doctor-patient interviews', in M. Wadsworth and D. Robinson (eds) *Studies in everyday medical life*, pp. 69–88. London: Martin Robertson.

Coulthard, M. and D. Brazil. 1981. 'Exchange structure', in M. Coulthard and M. Montgomery (eds) *Studies in discourse analysis*, pp. 82–106. London and Boston: Routledge and Kegan Paul.

Coulthard, M. and M. Montgomery (eds). 1981. *Studies in discourse analysis.* London: Routledge and Kegan Paul.

Couper-Kuhlen, E. 1996. 'The prosody of repetition: on quoting and mimicry', in E. Couper-Kuhlen and M. Selting (eds) *Prosody in conversation*, pp. 366–405. Cambridge: Cambridge University Press.

Couper-Kuhlen, E. and C.E. Ford. 2004. *Sound patterns in interaction.* Amsterdam: John Benjamins.

Couper-Kuhlen, E. and M. Selting (eds). 1996. *Prosody in conversation.* Cambridge: Cambridge University Press.

Cowie, R., E. Douglas-Cowie, S. Savvidou, E. McMahon, M. Sawey and M. Schröder. 2000. '"Feeltrace": an instrument for recording perceived emotion in real time', in R. Cowie,

E. Douglas-Cowie and M. Schröder (eds) *Speech and emotion: Proceedings of the ISCA workshop*, pp. 19–24. Belfast, NI: Textflow.

Croft, W. 1995. 'Intonation units and grammatical structure'. *Linguistics* 33: 839–82.

Cruttenden, A. [1986] 1997. *Intonation*. Cambridge: Cambridge University Press.

Crystal, D. 1969. *Prosodic systems and intonation in English*. Cambridge: Cambridge University Press.

Culpeper, J. 1996. 'Towards an anatomy of impoliteness'. *Journal of Pragmatics* 25: 349–67.

Culpeper, J. 2005. 'Impoliteness and entertainment in the television quiz show the *Weakest Link*'. *Journal of Politeness Research* 1(1): 35–72.

Culpeper, J. 2008. 'Reflections on impoliteness, relational work and power', in D. Bousfield and M.A. Locher (eds) *Impoliteness in language: studies on its interplay with power in theory and practice*, pp. 17–44. Berlin and New York: Mouton de Gruyter.

Culpeper, J. 2010. 'Historical pragmatics', in L. Cummings (eds) *The pragmatics encyclopedia*, pp. 188–92. London and New York: Routledge.

Culpeper, J. 2011. *Impoliteness: using language to cause offence*. Cambridge: Cambridge University Press.

Culpeper, J. and D. Archer. 2008. 'Requests and directness in Early Modern English trial proceedings and play texts, 1640–1760', in A.H. Jucker and I. Taavitsainen (eds) *Speech acts in the history of English*, pp. 45–84. Amsterdam and Philadelphia: John Benjamins.

Culpeper, J. and M. Kytö. 2000. 'Data in historical pragmatics: spoken discourse (re)cast as writing'. *Journal of Historical Pragmatics* 1: 175–99.

Culpeper, J. and M. Kytö. 2010. *Early Modern English dialogues: spoken interaction as writing*. Cambridge: Cambridge University Press.

Culpeper, J., D. Bousfield and A. Wichmann. 2003. 'Impoliteness revisited: with special reference to dynamic and prosodic aspects'. *Journal of Pragmatics* 35: 1545–79.

Culpeper, J., L. Marti, M. Mei, M. Nevala and G. Schauer. 2010. 'Cross-cultural variation in the perception of impoliteness: a study of impoliteness events reported by students in England, China, Finland, Germany and Turkey'. *Intercultural Pragmatics* 7(4): 597–624.

Cummings, L. 2005. *Pragmatics. A multidisciplinary perspective*. Edinburgh: Edinburgh University Press.

Cummings, L. (ed.). 2010. *The pragmatics encyclopedia*. London and New York: Routledge.

Curl, T., J. Local and G. Walker. 2006. 'Repetition and the prosody-pragmatics interface'. *Journal of Pragmatics* 38: 1721–51.

Cutting, J. 2002 (2nd edition). *Pragmatics and discourse: a resource book for students*. London and New York: Routledge.

Dehé, N. and A. Wichmann. 2010a. 'The multifunctionality of epistemic parentheticals in discourse: prosodic cues to the semantic-pragmatic boundary'. *Functions of Language* 17(1): 1–28.

Dehé, N. and A. Wichmann. 2010b. 'Sentence-initial *I think (that)* and *I believe (that)*: prosodic evidence for use as a main clause, comment clause and discourse marker'. *Studies in Language* 34(1): 36–74.

Deutschmann, M. 2003. *Apologising in British English*. Skrifter från moderna språk 10: Umeå University.

Deutschmann, M. 2006. 'Social variation in the use of apology formulae in the British National Corpus', in A. Renouf and A. Kehoe (eds) *The changing face of corpus linguistics*, pp. 205–21. Amsterdam and New York: Rodopi.

Diani, G. 2004. 'The discourse functions of *I don't know* in English conversation', in K. Aijmer and A.-B. Stenström (eds) *Discourse patterns in spoken and written corpora*, pp. 157–71. Amsterdam: John Benjamins.

Drew, P. and J. Heritage (eds). 1992. *Talk at work: interaction in institutional settings.* Cambridge: Cambridge University Press.

Eades, D. 2003. 'The politics of misunderstanding in the legal system: Aboriginal English speakers in Queensland', in J. House, G. Kasper and S. Ross (eds) *Misunderstandings in social life*, pp. 199–226. London: Longman.

Edelsky, C. 1981. 'Who's got the floor?' *Language and Society* 10: 383–421.

Eelen, G. 2001. *A critique of politeness theories.* Manchester: St Jerome Press.

Eemeren, Frans H. and R. Grootendorst. 1984. *Speech acts in argumentative discourse.* Dordrecht: Foris Publications.

Eggins, S. and D. Slade. 1997. *Analysing casual conversation.* London: Cassell.

Eisenstein, M. and J. Bodman. 1993. 'Expressing gratitude in American English', in G. Kasper and S. Blum-Kulka (eds) *Interlanguage pragmatics*, pp. 64–81. Oxford: Oxford University Press.

Enfield, N.J. 2000. 'The theory of cultural logic: how individuals combine social intelligence with semiotics to create and maintain cultural meaning'. *Cultural Dynamics* 12(1): 35–64.

Enfield, N.J. 2003. 'The definition of what-d'you-call-it: semantics and pragmatics of recognitional deixis'. *Journal of Pragmatics* 35: 101–17.

Entman, R.M. 1993. 'Framing: toward clarification of a fractured paradigm'. *Journal of Communication* 43(4): 51–8.

Entman, R.M. 2003. 'Cascading activation: contesting the White House's frame after 9/11'. *Political Communication* 20: 415–32.

Erickson, F. 1979. 'Talking down: some cultural sources of miscommunication in interracial interviews', in A. Wolfgang (ed.) *Nonverbal behaviour: applications and cultural implications*, pp. 99–126. New York: Academic Press.

Erickson, F. and J. Shultz. 1982. *The counselor as gatekeeper: social interaction in interviews.* New York: Academic Press.

Erman, B. and U.-B. Kotsinas. 1993. 'Pragmaticalization: the case of *ba* and *you know*', in J. Falk, K. Jonasson, G. Melchers and B. Nilsson (eds) *Stockholm studies in modern philology*, vol. 10, pp. 76–93. Stockholm: Almqvist and Wiksell International.

Fairclough, N. 1989. *Language and power* (2nd edition 2001). London: Longman.

Fairclough, N. 1992. *Discourse and social change.* Cambridge: Polity Press.

Fairclough, N. 2001. 'Critical discourse analysis', in. A. McHoul and M. Rapley (eds) *How to analyze talk in institutional settings*, pp. 25–41. London: Continuum.

Feeney, A., S. Scrafton, A. Duckworth and S. Handley. 2004. 'The story of some: everyday pragmatic inference by children and adults'. *Canadian Journal of Experimental Psychology* 58(2): 121–32.

Figueroa, E. 2005. 'Rude sounds: kiss teeth and negotiation of the public sphere', in S. Muehleisen and B. Migge (eds) *Politeness and face in Caribbean Creoles*, pp. 73–100. Amsterdam and Philadelphia: John Benjamins.

Finkenstaedt, T. 1963. *You and thou: Studien zur Anrede im Englischen.* Berlin: Walter de Gruyter.

Fischer, A. 1998. '*Marry*: from religious invocation to discourse marker', in R. Borgmeier, H. Grabes and A.H. Jucker (eds) *Proceedings Anglistentag 1997 Giessen*, pp. 35–46. Trier: Wissenschaftlicher Verlag.

Fischer, K. (ed.). 2006. *Approaches to discourse particles.* Amsterdam: Elsevier.

Fitzmaurice, S.M. and I. Taavitsainen (eds). 2007. *Methods in historical pragmatics.* Berlin: Mouton de Gruyter.

Fleischman, S. 1990. 'Philology, linguistics, and the discourse of the medieval text'. *Speculum* 65: 19–37.

Foucault, M. 1977. *Discipline and punish: the birth of the prison* (trans. A. Sheridan). London: Allen Lane.

Foucault, M. 1980. *Power/knowledge: selected interviews and other writings 1972–1977* (trans. C. Gordon). New York: Pantheon.

Fox Tree, J.E. 2010. 'Discourse markers across speakers and settings'. *Language and Linguistics Compass* 4(5): 269–81.

Francis, D.W. 1986. 'Some structures of negotiation talk'. *Language in Society* 15(1): 53–80.

Frankel, R.M. 1984. 'From sequence to sequence: understanding the medical encounter through interactional analysis'. *Discourse Processes* 7: 135–70.

Fraser, B. 1990. 'Perspectives on politeness'. *Journal of Pragmatics* 6: 167–90.

Fraser, B. 1996. 'Pragmatic markers'. *Pragmatics* 6(2): 167–90.

French, J.R.P. and B. Raven. 1959. 'The basis of social power', in D. Cartwright (ed.) *Studies in social power*, pp. 150–67. Ann Arbor: Institute for Social Research, University of Michigan.

Fukada, A. and N. Asato. 2004. 'Universal politeness theory: application to the use of Japanese honorifics'. *Journal of Pragmatics* 36: 1991–2002.

Gal, S. 1992. 'Language, gender and power: an anthropological view', in K. Hall, M. Bucholtz and B. Moonwomon (eds) *Locating power: proceedings of the second Berkeley Women and Language Conference, April 4 and 5, 1992*. Berkeley: Berkeley Women and Language Group, University of California.

Geertz, C. [1960] 1976. *The religion of Java*. Chicago: University of Chicago Press.

Gibbs, R.W. and J.F. Moise. 1997. 'Pragmatics in understanding what is said'. *Cognition* 62: 51–74.

Gilquin, G. 2008. 'Hesitation markers among EFL learners: pragmatic deficiency or difference?' In J. Romero-Trillo (ed.) *Pragmatics and corpus linguistics*, pp. 119–43. Berlin: Mouton de Gruyter.

Glover, K.D. 2000. 'Proximal and distal deixis in negotiation talk'. *Journal of Pragmatics* 32: 915–26.

Goddard, C. 1998. *Semantic analysis: a practical introduction*. Oxford: Oxford University Press.

Goddard, C. 2006. 'Ethnopragmatics: a new paradigm', in C. Goddard (ed.) *Ethnopragmatics: understanding discourse in cultural context*, pp. 1–30. Berlin: Mouton de Gruyter.

Goffman, E. 1963. *Behavior in public places*. New York: The Free Press.

Goffman, E. 1967. *Interaction ritual: essays on face-to-face behavior*. Garden City, NY: Anchor Books.

Goffman, E. 1971. *Relations in public: microstudies of the public order*. London: Allen Lane.

Goffman, E. 1974. *Frame analysis: an essay on the organisation of experience*. New York: Harper and Row.

Golato, A. 2005. *Compliments and compliment responses. Grammatical structure and sequential organization*. Amsterdam and Philadelphia: John Benjamins.

Goodwin, M. 1990. *He-said-she-said: talk as social organization among black children*. Bloomington and Indianapolis: Indiana University Press.

Gorisch, J., B. Wells and G.J. Brown. (2012). 'Pitch contour matching and interactional alignment across turns: an acoustic investigation'. *Language and Speech* 55(1): 57–76.

Gramsci, A. 1971. *Selections from the prison notebooks* (ed. and trans. Q. Hoare and G. Nowell-Smith). London: Lawrence and Wishart.

Greasley, P. 1994. 'An investigation into the use of the particle *well*: commentaries on a game of snooker'. *Journal of Pragmatics* 22: 477–94.

Green, G.M. 1996. *Pragmatics and natural language understanding*. Mahwah, NJ: Erlbaum.

Greenbaum, P.F. and H.M. Rosenfeld. 1980. 'Varieties of touching in greeting: sequential structure and sex-related differences'. *Journal of Nonverbal Behaviour* 5: 13–25.

Grice, H.P. 1957. 'Meaning'. *The Philosophical Review*, 66: 377–88. Reprinted in Grice 1989: 213–33.

Grice, H.P. 1969. 'Vacuous names', in D. Davidson and J. Hintikka (eds) *Words and objections: essays on the work of W.V. Quine*, pp. 118–145. Dordrecht: Reidel.

Grice, H.P. 1975. 'Logic and conversation', in P. Cole and J. Morgan (eds) *Syntax and semantics 3: speech acts*, pp. 41–58. New York: Academic Press. Reprinted in Grice 1989: 22–57.

Grice, H.P. 1978. 'Further notes on logic and conversation', in P. Cole (ed.) *Syntax and semantics*, vol. 9: New York: Academic Press. Reprinted in Grice 1989: 41–57.

Grice, H.P. 1989. *Studies in the way of words*. Cambridge, MA: Harvard University Press.

Grundy, P. 2008 (3rd edition). *Doing pragmatics*. London: Hodder Education.

Gu, Y. 1990. 'Politeness phenomena in modern Chinese'. *Journal of Pragmatics* 14(2): 237–57. Special Issue on 'Politeness'.

Gussenhoven, C. 2004. *The phonology of tone and intonation*. Cambridge: Cambridge University Press.

Haan, J., L. Heijmans, T. Rietveld and C. Gussenhoven. 2002. 'Explaining attitudinal ratings of Dutch rising contours: morphological structure vs. the Frequency Code'. *Phonetica* 59: 180–94.

Haberland, H. and J.L. Mey. 1977. 'Editorial: pragmatics and linguistics'. *Journal of Pragmatics* 1(1): 1–16.

Habermas, J. 1984. *The theory of communicative action, Vol. 1: reason and the rationalisation of society*. London: Heinemann.

Haddon, M. 2003. *The curious incident of the dog in the night-time*. London: Cape.

Hakulinen, A. and M. Selting (eds). 2005. *Syntax and lexicon in conversation. Studies on the use of linguistic resources in talk-in-interaction*. Amsterdam and Philadelphia: John Benjamins.

Halberstadt, A.G. 1985. 'Differences between blacks and whites in nonverbal communication', in A.W. Siegman and S. Feldstein (eds) *Multichannel integrations of nonverbal behaviour*, pp. 229–59. Hillsdale, NJ: Erlbaum.

Hale, S.B. 2004. *The discourse of court interpreting*. Amsterdam and Philadelphia: John Benjamins.

Halenko, N. and C. Jones. 2011. 'Teaching pragmatic awareness of spoken requests to Chinese EAP learners in the UK: is explicit instruction effective?' *System* 39: 240–50.

Hall, E.T. 1959. *The silent language*. Garden City, NY: Doubleday.

Halliday, M.A.K. 1961. 'Categories of the theory of grammar'. *Word* 17: 241–92.

Halliday, M.A.K. 1970. 'Language structure and language function', in J. Lyons (ed.) *New horizons in linguistics*, pp. 140–65. Harmondsworth: Penguin.

Halliday, M.A.K. 1973. *Explorations in the functions of language*. London: Edward Arnold.

Halliday, M.A.K. 1978. *Language as social semiotic: the social interpretation of language and meaning*. London: Edward Arnold.

Halliday, M.A.K. and W.S. Greaves. 2008. *Intonation and the grammar of English*. London: Equinox.

Halliday, M.A.K. and R. Hasan. 1976. *Cohesion in English*. London: Longman.

Hamilton, H.E. 1994. *Conversations with an Alzheimer's patient: an interactional sociolinguistic study*. Cambridge and New York: Cambridge University Press.

Hanna, J.L. 1984. 'Black/White nonverbal differences, dance and dissonance', in A.Wolfgang (ed.) *Nonverbal behaviour: perspectives, applications, intercultural insights*, pp. 373–409. Lewiston, NY: Hogrefe.

Hansen, M.-B.M. 1998. *The function of discourse particles, a study with special reference to spoken standard French.* Amsterdam and Philadelphia: John Benjamins.

Hansen, M.-B.M. and J. Visconti. 2009. *Grammaticalization and pragmatics: current trends in diachronic semantics and pragmatics.* Bingley: Emerald.

Harris, S. 1980. 'Language interaction in magistrates' courts'. Unpublished Ph.D. thesis. University of Nottingham.

Harris, S. 1984. 'Questions as a mode of control in a magistrate's court'. *International Journal of the Sociology of Language* 49: 5–27.

Harris, S. 1994. 'Ideological exchanges in British magistrates courts', in J. Gibbons (ed.) *Language and the law*, pp. 156–70. Harlow: Longman.

Harris, S. 1995. 'Pragmatics and power'. *Journal of Pragmatics* 23: 117–35.

Hartford, B.S. and K. Bardovi-Harlig. 1992. 'Experimental and observational data in the study of interlanguage pragmatics', in L.F. Bouton and Y. Kachru (eds) *Pragmatics and language learning monograph series*, Vol. 3, pp. 33–52.Urbana, IL: Division of English as an International Language, University of Illinois at Urbana-Champaign.

Hasselgren, A. 1994. 'Lexical teddy bears and advanced learners: a study into the ways Norwegian students cope with vocabulary'. *Applied Linguistics* 4(2): 237–60.

Hasselgren, A. 2002. 'Learner corpora and language testing. Smallwords as markers of learner fluency', in S. Granger, J. Hung and S. Petch-Tyson (eds) *Computer learner corpora, second language acquisition and foreign language teaching*, pp. 143–73. Amsterdam and Philadelphia: John Benjamins.

Haworth, K. 2006. 'The dynamics of power and resistance in police interview discourse'. *Discourse & Society* 17(6): 739–59.

Hayduk, L.A. 1983. 'The permeability of personal space'. *Canadian Journal of Behavioural Science* 13: 274–87.

Henton, C. 1995. 'Cross-language variation in the vowels of female and male speakers', in *Proceedings of the 13th International Congress of Phonetic Sciences* Vol. 4, pp. 420–3. Stockholm: Sweden.

Henton, C. 1999. 'Where is female synthetic speech?' *Journal of the International Phonetic Association* 29(1): 51–61.

Henton C. and A. Bladon. 1988. 'Creak as a sociophonetic marker', in L.M. Hyman and C.N. Li (eds) *Language, speech and mind: studies in honour of Victoria A. Fromkin*, pp. 3–29. London: Taylor and Francis.

Heritage, J. 1985. 'Analysing news interviews', in T. Van Dijk (ed.) *Handbook of discourse analysis*, Vol. 3, pp. 95–117. London: Academic Press.

Heritage, J. and J. Atkinson. 1984. 'Introduction', in J. Atkinson and J. Heritage (eds) *Structures of social action*, pp. 1–17. Cambridge: Cambridge University Press

Heritage, J. and D. Greatbatch. 1991. 'On the institutional character of institutional talk: the case of news interviews', in D. Boden and D. Zimmerman (eds) *Talk and social structure*, pp. 93–137. Cambridge: Polity Press.

Heritage, J. and D. Maynard. 2006. *Communication in medical care. Interaction between primary care physicians and patients.* Cambridge: Cambridge University Press.

Holmes, J. 1986. 'Functions of *you know* in women's and men's speech'. *Language in Society* 15(1): 1–22.

Holmes, J. 1988. 'Paying compliments: a sex-preference politeness strategy'. *Journal of Pragmatics* 12(4): 445–65.

Holmes, J. 1990. 'Politeness strategies in New Zealand women's speech', in A. Bell and J. Holmes (eds) *New Zealand ways of speaking English*, pp. 252–76. Clevedon: Multilingual Matters.

Holmes, J. 1995. *Women, men and politeness.* London: Longman.

Holmes, J. 2000. 'Doing collegiality and keeping control at work: small talk in government departments', in J. Coupland (ed.) *Small talk*, pp. 32–61. Amsterdam: John Benjamins.

Holmes, J. and D.E. Brown 1987. 'Teachers and students learning about compliments'. *TESOL Quarterly* 21(3): 523–46.

Holmes, J. and M. Marra. 2002. 'Over the edge? Subversive humour between colleagues and friends'. *Humor* 15(1): 1–23.

Holmes, J. and M. Marra. 2006. 'Humour and leadership style'. *Humor* 19(2): 119–38.

Holmes, J. and M. Stubbe. 2003. *Power and politeness in the workplace. A sociolinguistic analysis of talk at work.* London: Longman.

Hope, J. 1994. 'The use of "thou" and "you" in Early Modern spoken English: evidence from depositions in the Durham ecclesiastical court records', in D. Kastovsky (ed.) *Studies in Early Modern English*, pp. 141–51. Berlin: Mouton de Gruyter.

Hoppe-Graff, S., T. Herrman, P. Winterhoff-Spurk and R. Mangold. 1985. 'Speech and situation: a general model for the process of speech production', in J.P. Forgas (ed.) *Language and social situations*, pp. 81–95. New York: Springer-Verlag.

Hopper, P.J. 2010. 'Grammaticalization', in L. Cummings (ed.) *The pragmatics encyclopedia*, pp. 180–2. London and New York: Routledge.

Hopper, P.J. and E.C. Traugott. [1993] 2003. *Grammaticalization.* Cambridge: Cambridge University Press.

Horn, L.R. 1984. 'Towards a new taxonomy of pragmatic inference: Q- and R-based implicature', in D. Schiffrin (ed.) *Meaning, form, and use in context: linguistic applications*, pp. 11–42. Washington, DC: Georgetown University Press.

Horn, L.R. 2004. 'Implicature', in L.R. Horn and G. Ward (eds) *The handbook of pragmatics*, pp. 3–28. Oxford: Blackwell.

House, J. 1989. 'Politeness in English and German: the functions of please and bitte', in S. Blum-Kulka, J. House and G. Kasper (eds) *Cross-cultural pragmatics: requests and apologies*, pp. 96–122. Norwood, NJ: Ablex.

House, J. 1996. 'Contrastive discourse analysis and misunderstanding: the case of German and English', in M. Hellinger and U. Ammon (eds) *Contrastive sociolinguistics*, pp. 345–61. Berlin: Mouton de Gruyter.

Houtkoop-Steenstra, H. 1991. 'Opening sequences in Dutch telephone conversations', in D. Boden and D. Zimmerman (eds) *Talk and social structure*, pp. 232–50. Cambridge: Polity Press.

Huang, Y. 2007. *Pragmatics.* Oxford: Oxford University Press.

Huang, Y. 2010. 'Implicature', in L. Cummings (ed.) *The pragmatics encyclopedia*, pp. 205–10. London and New York: Routledge.

Hutchby, I. 1996a. 'Power in discourse: the case of arguments on a British talk radio show'. *Discourse and Society* 7(4): 481–97.

Hutchby, I. 1996b. *Confrontation talk: arguments, asymmetries, and power on talk radio.* Mahwah, NJ: Erlbaum.

Hutchby, I. 2010. 'Feelings-talk and therapeutic vision in child-counsellor interaction', in H. Gardner and M. Forrester (eds) *Analysing interactions in childhood*, pp. 146–62. London: Wiley.

Hutchby, I. and R. Wooffitt. 2008 (2nd edition). *Conversation analysis.* Cambridge: Polity Press.

Ishida, H. 2006. 'Learners' perception and interpretation of contextualization cues in spontaneous Japanese conversation: back-channel cue Uun'. *Journal of Pragmatics* 38(11): 1943–81.

Jackendoff, R. 1972. *Semantic interpretation in generative grammar.* Cambridge, MA: MIT Press.

Jackson, R. 2005. *Writing the war on terrorism: language, politics and counter-terrorism.* Manchester: Manchester University Press.

Jacobs, A. and A.H. Jucker. 1995. 'The historical perspective in pragmatics', in A.H. Jucker (ed.) *Historical pragmatics: pragmatic developments in the history of English*, pp. 3–33. Amsterdam and Philadelphia: John Benjamins.

James, D. and S. Clarke. 1993. 'Women, men and interruptions: a critical review', in D. Tannen (ed.) *Gender and conversational interaction*, pp. 231–74. Oxford: Oxford University Press.

Jaszczolt, K.M. 1999. *Discourse, beliefs, and intentions: semantic defaults and propositional attitude ascription.* Oxford: Elsevier Science.

Jaszczolt, K.M. 2010. 'Semantics-pragmatics interface', in L. Cummings (ed.) *The pragmatics encyclopedia*, pp. 428–32. London and New York: Routledge.

Jefferson, G. 1973. 'A case of precision timing in ordinary conversation'. *Semiotica* 9(1): 47–96.

Jeffries, L. 2010. *Critical stylistics: the power of English.* Basingstoke: Palgrave Macmillan.

Jordan, B. and N. Fuller. 1975. 'On the non-fatal nature of trouble: sense-making and trouble-managing in lingua franca', *Semiotica* 13(1): 11–31.

Jucker, A.H. (ed.). 1995. *Historical pragmatics: pragmatic developments in the history of English.* Amsterdam and Philadelphia: John Benjamins.

Jucker, A.H. 1997. 'The discourse marker "well" in the history of English'. *English Language and Linguistics* 1: 91–110.

Jucker, A.H. 2000a. *History of English and English historical linguistics.* Stuttgart: Klett-Lernen-und-Wissen.

Jucker, A.H. 2000b. 'English historical pragmatics: problems of data and methodology', in K. Lenz and R. Möhlig (eds) *Of dyuersitie & chaunge of language*, pp. 276–89. Heidelberg: C. Winter.

Jucker, A. 2009. 'Speech act research between armchair, field and laboratory. The case of compliments'. *Journal of Pragmatics* 41: 1621–5.

Jucker, A.H, and S. Smith. 1998. '*And people just you know like "wow"*: discourse markers as negotiating strategies', in A. Jucker and Y. Ziv (eds) *Discourse markers. Descriptions and theory*, pp. 171–201. Amsterdam and Philadelphia: John Benjamins.

Jucker, A.H. and I. Taavitsainen. 2000. 'Diachronic speech act analysis: insults from flyting to flaming'. *Journal of Historical Pragmatics* 1(1): 67–95.

Jucker, A.H. and I. Taavitsainen (eds). 2008. *Speech acts in the history of English.* (Pragmatics & Beyond New Series 176). Amsterdam and Philadelphia: John Benjamins.

Jucker, A.H. and I. Taavitsainen (eds). 2010. *Historical pragmatics.* Berlin and New York: Mouton de Gruyter.

Jucker, A.H. and Y. Ziv (eds). 1998. *Discourse markers. Descriptions and theory.* Amsterdam and Philadelphia: John Benjamins.

Jucker, A. H., G. Schneider, I. Taavitsainen and B. Breustedt. 2008. 'Fishing for compliments: precision and recall in corpus-linguistic compliment research', in A.H. Jucker and I. Taavitsainen (eds) *Speech acts in the history of English*, pp. 273–94. Amsterdam and Philadephia: John Benjamins.

Kasper, G. 1990. 'Linguistic politeness: current research issues', *Journal of Pragmatics* 14(2): 193–218.

Kasper, G. 2000. 'Data collection in pragmatics research', in H. Spencer-Oatey (ed.) *Culturally speaking – managing rapport through talk across cultures*, pp. 316–41. London and New York: Continuum.

Kasper, G. 2009. 'L2 Pragmatic development', in W.C. Ritchie and T.K. Bhatia (eds) (2nd edition) *The new handbook of second language acquisition*, pp. 259–93. Bingley: Emerald.

Kasper, G. and M. Dahl. 1991. 'Research methods in inter-language pragmatics'. *Studies in Second Language Acquisition* 13: 215–47.

Katsos, N. 2007. 'Pragmatic me, pragmatic you: the development of informativeness from a speaker's and a comprehender's perspective'. Paper presented at XPRAG, Berlin, December.

Katz, J.J. 1964. 'Analyticity and contradiction in natural language', in J.A. Fodor and J.J. Katz (eds) *The structure of language: readings in the philosophy of language*, pp. 519–43. Englewood Cliffs, NJ: Prentice-Hall.

Katz, J.J. and J.A. Fodor. 1963. 'The structure of a semantic theory', *Language* 39: 170–210.

Katz, J.J. and P. Postal. 1964. *An integrated theory of linguistic descriptions.* Cambridge, MA: MIT Press.

Kaur, J. 2011. 'Intercultural communciation in English as a lingua franca: some sources of misunderstanding'. *Intercultural Pragmatics* 8(1): 93–116.

Kecskes, I. 2011. 'Intercultural pragmatics', in D. Archer and P. Grundy (eds) *The pragmatics reader*, pp. 371–84. London and New York: Routledge.

Kempson, R.M. 1975. *Presupposition and the delimitation of semantics.* Cambridge: Cambridge University Press.

Kempson, R.M. 1979. 'Presupposition, opacity, and ambiguity', in C.-K. Oh and D.A. Dinneen (eds) *Syntax and semantics 11: presupposition,* pp. 283–97. New York: Academic Press.

Kempson, R.M. 1986. 'Ambiguity and the semantics-pragmatics distinction', in C. Travis (ed.) *Meaning and interpretation,* pp. 79–103. Oxford: Blackwell.

Kendon, A. 1967. 'Some functions of gaze-direction in social interaction'. *Acta Psychologica* 26: 22–63.

Kendon, A. 2001. 'Gesture as communication strategy'. *Semiotica* 135: 191–209.

Kendon, A. 2004. *Gesture: visible action as utterance.* Cambridge: Cambridge University Press.

Klos Sokol, L. 1997. *Shortcuts to Poland.* Warsaw: IPS Wydawnictwo.

Knowles, G. 1986. *Patterns of spoken English.* London: Longman.

Koch, P. and W. Oesterreicher. 1985. 'Sprache der Nähe – Sprache der Distanz: Mündlichkeit und Schriftlichkeit im Spannungsfeld von Sprachtheorie und Sprachgeschichte'. *Romanistisches Jahrbuch* 36: 15–43.

Kohnen, T. 2000a. 'Explicit performatives in Old English: a corpus-based study of directives'. *Journal of Historical Pragmatics* 1(2): 301–21.

Kohnen, T. 2000b. 'Corpora and speech acts: the study of performatives', in C. Mair and M. Hundt (eds) *Corpus linguistics and linguistic theory*, pp. 177–86. Amsterdam: Rodopi.

Kohnen, T. 2002. 'Towards a history of English directives', in A. Fischer, G. Tottie and H.M. Lehmann (eds) *Text types and corpora: studies in honour of Udo Fries*, pp. 165–75. Tübingen: Gunter Narr.

Kohnen, T. 2004. 'Methodological problems in corpus-based historical pragmatics. The case of English directives', in K. Aijmer and B. Altenberg (eds) *Advances in corpus linguistics.* Papers from the 23rd International Conference on English Language Research on Computerized Corpora (ICAME 23), pp. 237–47. Göteborg 22–26 May 2002. Amsterdam: Rodopi.

Kohnen, T. 2007. 'Text types and the methodology of diachronic speech act analysis', in S.M. Fitzmaurice and I. Taavitsainen (eds) *Methods in Historical Pragmatics*, pp. 139–66. Berlin: Mouton de Gruyter.

Kohnen, T. 2008. 'Tracing directives through text and time. Towards a methodology of a corpus-based diachronic speech act analysis', in A.H. Jucker and I. Taavitsainen (eds) *Speech acts in the history of English*, pp. 295–310. Amsterdam and Philadelphia: John Benjamins.

Kohnen, T. 2009. 'Historical corpus pragmatics', in A.H. Jucker, D. Schreier and M. Hundt (eds) *Corpora: pragmatics and discourse.* Papers from the 29th International Conference on English Language Research on Computerized Corpora (ICAME 29), pp. 13–36. Amsterdam: Rodopi.

Kopytko, R. 1995. 'Against rationalistic pragmatics'. *Journal of Pragmatics* 23: 475–91.

Kurtiç, E., G.J. Brown and B. Wells. 2010. 'Fundamental frequency height as a resource for the management of talk-in-interaction', in D. Barth-Weingarten, N. Dehé and A.Wichmann (eds) *Where prosody meets pragmatics,* pp. 183–203. Bingley: Emerald.

Kytö, M. 2010. 'Data in historical pragmatics', in A.H. Jucker and I. Taavitsainen (eds) *Historical pragmatics,* pp. 33–68. Berlin and New York: Mouton de Gruyter.

Labov, W. 1970. 'The study of language in its social context'. *Studium Generale* 23: 30–87.

Labov, W. 1972a. *Sociolinguistic patterns.* Philadelphia: University of Pennsylvania Press.

Labov, W. 1972b. *Language in the inner city: studies in the Black English vernacular.* Oxford: Blackwell.

Labov, W. and D. Fanshel. 1977. *Therapeutic discourse. Psychotherapy as conversation.* New York: Academic Press.

Ladd, D.R. 1996. *Intonational phonology.* Cambridge: Cambridge University Press.

Lakoff, G. 1971. 'On generative semantics', in D.D. Steinberg and L.A. Jakobovits (eds) *Semantics: an interdisciplinary reader in philosophy, linguistics and psychology,* pp. 232–96. Cambridge: Cambridge University Press.

Lakoff, G. 2004. *Don't think of an elephant: know your values and frame the debate.* White River Junction, VT: Chelsea Green Publishing.

Lakoff, G. 2006. *Whose freedom?: The battle over America's most important idea.* New York: Farrar, Straus and Giroux.

Lakoff, G. and M. Johnson. [1980, 1996] 2006. *Metaphors we live by.* Chicago: University of Chicago Press.

Lakoff, R. 1993. 'Lewis Carroll: subversive pragmaticist'. *Pragmatics* 3(4): 367–85.

L'Armand, K. 1984. 'Preferences in patterns of eye contact in India'. *Journal of Social Psychology* 122: 137–8.

Laver, J. 1975. 'Communicative functions of phatic communication', in A. Kendon, R. Harris and M.R. Key (eds) *The organization of behavior in face-to-face interaction,* pp. 215–38. The Hague: Mouton de Gruyter.

Laver, J. 1980. *The phonetic description of voice quality.* Cambridge: Cambridge University Press.

Leech, G. 1981 (2nd edition). *Semantics: the study of meaning.* Harmondsworth: Penguin Books.

Leech, G. 1983. *Principles of pragmatics.* London and New York: Longman.

Leech, G. 1997. 'Introducing corpus annotation', in R. Garside, G. Leech and A. McEnery (eds) *Corpus annotation: linguistic information from computer text corpora,* pp. 1–18. London: Longman.

Leech, G. 2007. 'Politeness: is there an East-West divide?' *Journal of Politeness Research* 3(2): 167–206.

Lein, L. and D. Brenneis. 1978. 'Children's disputes in three speech communities'. *Language in Society* 7: 299–323.

Lennon, P. 1990. 'Investigating fluency in EFL: a quantitative approach'. *Language Learning* 40(3): 387–417.

Levinson, S. 1983. *Pragmatics.* Cambridge: Cambridge University Press.

Levinson, S. 1995. 'Three levels of meaning', in F.R. Palmer (ed.) *Grammar and meaning. Essays in honour of Sir John Lyons,* pp. 90–115. Cambridge: Cambridge University Press.

Levinson, S. 2000. *Presumptive meanings: the theory of generalized conversational implicature.* Cambridge, MA: MIT Press.

Levinson, S. 2004. 'Deixis', in L.R. Horn and G. Ward (eds) *The handbook of pragmatics,* pp. 97–122. Oxford: Blackwell.

Lewis, D. 2003. 'Rhetorical motivations for the emergence of discourse particles, with special reference to English *of course*', in T. van der Wouden, A. Foolen and P. Van de Craen (eds) *Particles.* Special issue, *Belgian Journal of Linguistics* 16: 79–91. Amsterdam and Philadelphia: John Benjamins.

Limberg, H. 2008. 'Threats in conflict talk: impoliteness and manipulation', in D. Bousfield and M.A. Locher (eds) *Impoliteness in language: studies on its interplay with power in theory and practice,* pp. 155–80. Berlin and New York: Mouton de Gruyter.

Lindström, A. 1994. 'Identification and recognition in Swedish telephone conversation openings'. *Language in Society* 23: 231–52.

Local, J. 1996. 'Conversational phonetics: some aspects of news receipts in everyday talk', in E. Couper-Kuhlen and M. Selting (eds) *Prosody in conversation,* pp. 177–230. Cambridge: Cambridge University Press.

Local, J. and G. Walker. 2004. 'Abrupt-joins as a resource for the production of multi-unit, multi-action turns'. *Journal of Pragmatics* 36(8): 1375–403.

Locher, M.A. 2004. *Power and politeness in action: disagreements in oral communication.* Berlin: Mouton de Gruyter.

Locher, M.A. and D. Bousfield. 2008. 'Introduction: impoliteness and power and language', in D. Bousfield and M.A. Locher (eds) *Impoliteness in language: studies on its interplay with power in theory and practice,* pp. 1–8. Berlin and New York: Mouton de Gruyter.

Locher, M.A. and R. Watts. 2005. 'Politeness theory and relational work'. *Journal of Politeness Research* 1(1): 9–33.

Locher, M.A. and R. Watts. 2008. 'Relational work and impoliteness: negotiating norms of linguistic behaviour', in D. Bousfield and M.A. Locher (eds) *Impoliteness in language: studies on its interplay with power in theory and practice,* pp. 77–100. Berlin and New York: Mouton de Gruyter.

Louw, E. 2005. *The media and the political process.* London: Sage.

Lowndes, S. 2002. 'Barristers on trial', in S. Csabi and J. Zerkowitz (eds) *Textual secrets – the message of the medium,* pp. 150–61. Proceedings of the 21st PALA conference. Budapest: School of English and American Studies, Eötvös Loránd University.

Lycan, W.G. 1977. 'Conversation, politeness and interruption'. *Papers in Linguistics* 10(1/2): 23–53.

Lyons, J. 1977. *Semantics,* vols 1 and 2. Cambridge: Cambridge University Press.

Manes, J. and N. Wolfson. 1981. 'The compliment formula', in F. Coulmas (ed.) *Conversational routine. Explorations in standardized communication situations and prepatterned speech,* pp. 115–32. The Hague: Mouton de Gruyter.

Marmaridou, S.S.A. 2000. *Pragmatic meaning and cognition.* Amsterdam and Philadelphia: John Benjamins.

Marmaridou, S.S.A. 2010. 'Presupposition', in L. Cummings (ed.) *The pragmatics encyclopedia,* pp. 349–53. London and New York: Routledge.

Martinet, A. 1962. *A functional view of language.* Oxford: Clarendon Press.

Matsumoto, Y. 1988. 'Reexamination of the universality of face: politeness phenomena in Japanese'. *Journal of Pragmatics* 12(4): 403–26.

Mautner, G. 2009. 'Checks and balances: how corpus linguistics can contribute to CDA', in R. Wodak and M. Meyer (eds) *Methods of critical discourse analysis,* pp. 122–43. London: Sage.

Mazzon, G. 2010. 'Address terms', in A.H. Jucker and I. Taavitsainen (eds) *Historical pragmatics*, pp. 351–76. Berlin and New York: Mouton de Gruyter.

McCarthy, M. 2003. 'Talking back: "small" interactional response tokens in everyday conversation'. *Research on Language and Social Interaction* 36(1): 33–63.

McDonough, S.H. 1981. *Psychology in foreign language teaching.* London: George Allen & Unwin.

McHoul, A. 1978. 'The organization of turns at formal talk in the classroom'. *Language in Society* 7: 183–213.

Mehan, H. 1979. *Learning lessons – social organization in the classroom.* Cambridge, MA: Harvard University Press.

Meibauer, J. and M. Steinbach. 2011. *Experimental pragmatics/semantics.* Amsterdam and Philadelphia: John Benjamins.

Mennen, I. 2007. 'Phonological and phonetic influences in non-native intonation', in J. Trouvain and U. Gut (eds) *Non-native prosody: phonetic descriptions and teaching practice*, pp. 53–76. The Hague: Mouton de Gruyter.

Merritt, M. 1976. 'On questions following questions in service encounters'. *Language in Society* 5: 315–57.

Mey, J.L. 1979. 'Zur kritischen Sprachtheorie', in J.L. Mey (ed.) *Pragmalinguistics: theory and practice*, pp. 411–34. The Hague: Mouton de Gruyter.

Mey, J.L. 1985. *Whose language?: A study in linguistic pragmatics.* Amsterdam and Philadelphia: John Benjamins.

Mey, J.L. [1993] 2001. *Pragmatics: an introduction.* Oxford: Wiley-Blackwell.

Miller, J. and R. Weinert. 1998. *Spontaneous spoken language: syntax and discourse.* Oxford: Clarendon Press.

Mills, S. 2003. *Gender and politeness.* Cambridge: Cambridge University Press.

Mishler, E. 1975. 'Studies in dialogue and discourse: an exponential law of successive questioning'. *Language in Society* 4: 31–51.

Mishler, E. 1984. *The discourse of medicine: dialectics of medical interviews.* Norwood, NJ: Ablex.

Morris, C. 1938. *Foundations of the theory of signs.* Chicago: Chicago University Press.

Morton, E.W. 1977. 'On the occurrence and significance of motivation-structural rules in some bird and mammal sounds'. *The American Naturalist* 111: 855–69.

Mullany, L. 2004. 'Gender, politeness and institutional power roles: humour as a tactic to gain compliance in workplace business meetings'. *Multilingua* 23(1–2): 13–37.

Mullany, L. 2006. '"Girls on tour": politeness, small talk and gender in managerial business meetings'. *Journal of Politeness Research* 2(1): 55–77.

Müller, S. 2005. *Discourse markers in native and non-native English discourse.* Amsterdam and Philadelphia: John Benjamins.

Mushin, I. and R. Gardner 2009. 'Silence is talk: conversational silence in Australian Aboriginal talk-in-interaction'. *Journal of Pragmatics* 41: 2033–52.

Myers, G. 1999. 'Interactions in writing: principles and problems', in C.N. Candlin and K. Hyland (eds) *Writing: texts, processes and practices*, pp. 40–61. London: Longman.

Nakane, C. 1970. *Japanese society.* Berkeley: University of California Press.

Nelson, G., S. Wallis and B. Aarts. 2002. *Exploring natural language: working with the British component of the International Corpus of English.* Amsterdam and Philadelphia: John Benjamins.

Nerlich, B. 2010. 'History of pragmatics', in L. Cummings (ed.) *The pragmatics encyclopedia*, pp. 192–3. London and New York: Routledge.

Nerlich, B. and D. Clarke. 1996. *Language, action and context: the early history of pragmatics in Europe and America, 1780–1930.* Amsterdam and Philadelphia: John Benjamins.

Nevala, M. 2002. '*Youre moder send a letter to the*: pronouns of address in private correspondence from Late Middle to Late Modern English', in H. Raumolin-Brunberg, M. Nevala, A. Nurmi and M. Rissanen (eds) *Variation past and present: VARIENG studies on English for Terttu Nevalainen*, pp. 135–59. Helsinki: Société Néophilologique.

Nevala, M. 2003. 'Family first: address and subscription formulae in English family correspondence from the fifteenth to the seventeenth century', in I. Taavitsainen and A.H. Jucker (eds) *Diachronic perspectives on address term systems*, pp. 147–76. Amsterdam and Philadelphia: John Benjamins.

Nevala, M. 2004. *Address in Early English correspondence: its forms and sociopragmatic functions*. Helsinki: Société Néophilologique.

Nevala, M. 2010. 'Politeness', in A.H. Jucker and I. Taavitsainen (eds) *Historical pragmatics*, pp. 419–50. Berlin and New York: Mouton de Gruyter.

Nevalainen, T. and H. Raumolin-Brunberg. 1995. 'Constraints on politeness: the pragmatics of address formulae in Early English correspondence', in A.H. Jucker (ed.) *Historical pragmatics: pragmatic developments in the history of English*, pp. 541–601. Amsterdam and Philadelphia: John Benjamins.

Nicolle, S. and B. Clark. 1999. 'Experimental pragmatics and what is said: a response to Gibbs and Moise'. *Cognition* 69(3): 337–54.

Noesjirwan, J. 1978. 'A rule-based analysis of cultural differences in social behaviour: Indonesia and Australia'. *International Journal of Psychology* 13: 305–16.

Norrick, N.R. 2009. 'Interjections as pragmatic markers'. *Journal of Pragmatics* 41: 866–91.

Noveck, I.A. 2001. 'When children are more logical than adults: experimental investigations of scalar implicatures'. *Cognition* 78(2): 165–88.

Noveck, I.A. and D. Sperber (eds). 2004. *Experimental pragmatics*. Basingstoke: Palgrave Macmillan.

Ochs, E. 1996. 'Linguistic resources for socializing humanity', in J.J. Gumperz and S.C. Levinson (eds) *Rethinking linguistic relativity*, pp. 407–37. Cambridge: Cambridge University Press.

O'Driscoll, J. 2007. 'Brown and Levinson's face – how it can and can't help us to understand interaction across cultures'. *Intercultural Pragmatics* 4(4): 463–92.

Ohala, J.J. 1983. 'Cross-language use of pitch: an ethological view'. *Phonetica* 40: 1–18.

Ohala, J.J. 1984. 'An ethological perspective on common cross-language utilization of f_0 in voice'. *Phonetica* 41: 1–16.

Ohala J.J. 1996. 'The frequency code underlies the sound symbolic use of voice pitch', in L. Hinton, J. Nicols and J.J.Ohala (eds) *Sound symbolism*, pp. 325–47. Cambridge: Cambridge University Press.

Ohara, Y. 1992. 'Gender-dependent pitch levels in Japanese and English: a comparative study', in K. Hall, M. Bucholtz and B. Moonwomon (eds) *Locating power. Proceedings of the Second Berkeley Women and Language conference*, pp. 469–77. Berkeley: Berkeley Women and Language group.

O'Keeffe, A., S. Adolphus and B. Clancy. 2011. *Introducing pragmatics in use*. London: Routledge.

Östman, J.-O. 1982. 'The symbiotic relationship between pragmatic particles and impromptu speech', in N.E. Enkvist (ed.) *Impromptu speech: a symposium*, pp. 147–77. Åbo: The Research Institute of the Åbo Akademi Foundation.

Papafragou, A. and J. Musolino. 2003. 'Scalar implicatures: experiments at the semantics-pragmatics interface'. *Cognition* 86: 253–82.

Pearson, C.M., L.M. Andersson and J.W. Wenger. 2001. 'When workers flout convention: a study of workplace incivility'. *Human Relations* 54(11): 1387–420.

Peppé, S., J. McCann, F. Gibbon, A. O'Hare and M. Rutherford. 2006. 'Assessing prosodic and pragmatic ability in children with high-functioning autism'. *Journal of Pragmatics* 38(10): 1776–91.

Pierrehumbert, J.B. 1980. *The phonetics and phonology of English intonation*. Ph.D. thesis, MIT. [Published by Garland Press, NY, 1990.]

Pierrehumbert, J.B. and M.E. Beckman. 1988. *Japanese tone structure*. Cambridge, MA: MIT Press.

Pizziconi, B. 2003. 'Re-examining politeness, face and the Japanese language'. *Journal of Pragmatics* 35: 1471–506.

Pomerantz, A. 1978. 'Compliment responses: notes on the co-operation of multiple constraints', in J. Schenkein (ed.) *Studies in the organization of conversational interaction*, pp. 79–112. New York: Academic Press.

Pomerantz, A. 1984. 'Agreeing and disagreeing with assessment: some features of preferred/ dispreferred turn shapes', in J.M. Atkinson and J. Heritage (eds) *Structure of social action: studies in conversation analysis*, pp. 57–101. Cambridge: Cambridge University Press.

Quaglio, P. 2009. *Television dialogue: the sitcom Friends vs. natural conversation*. Amsterdam: John Benjamins.

Raumolin-Brunberg, H. 1996. 'Forms of address in early English correspondence', in T. Nevalainen and H. Raumolin-Brunberg (eds) *Sociolinguistics and language history*, pp. 167–81. Amsterdam: Rodopi.

Reboul, A. 2004. 'Conversational implicatures: nonce or generalized?', in I.A. Noveck and D. Sperber (eds) *Experimental pragmatics*, pp. 322–33. Basingstoke: Palgrave Macmillan.

Recanati, F. 1989. 'The pragmatics of what is said'. *Mind and Language* 4: 295–329.

Recanati, F. 2004. *Literal meaning*. Cambridge: Cambridge University Press.

Recanati, F. 2005. 'Literalism and contextualism: some varieties', in G. Preyer and G. Peter (eds) *Contextualism in philosophy: knowledge, meaning, and truth*, pp. 171–96. Oxford and New York: Oxford University Press.

Rietveld, T., J. Haan, L. Heijmans and C. Gussenhoven. 2002. 'Explaining attitudinal ratings of Dutch rising contours: morphological structure vs. The Frequency Code'. *Phonetica* 59: 180–94.

Rintell, E. and C.J. Mitchell. 1989. 'Studying requests and apologies: an inquiry into method', in S. Blum-Kulka, J. House and G. Kasper (eds) *Cross-cultural pragmatics*, pp. 248–72. Norwood, NJ: Ablex.

Romaine, S. and D. Lange. 1991. 'The use of *like* as a marker of reported speech and thought: a case of ongoing grammaticalization in progress'. *American Speech* 66(3): 227–79.

Rose, K.R. and G. Kasper (eds). 2001. *Pragmatics in language teaching*. Cambridge: Cambridge University Press.

Rossari, C. 2009. *Grammaticalization and pragmatics: facts, approaches, theoretical issues*. Bingley: Emerald.

Rühlemann, C. 2007. *Conversation in context. A corpus-driven approach*. London: Continuum.

Sacks, H. 1972. 'On the analysability of stories by children', in J.J. Gumperz and D. Hymes (eds) *Directions in sociolinguistics: the ethnography of communication*, pp. 329–45. New York: Holt, Rinehart and Winston. [Reprinted in R. Turner (ed.). 1974. *Ethnomethodology: selected readings*, pp. 216–32. Harmondsworth: Penguin.]

Sacks, H. 1975. 'Everyone has to lie', in M. Sanches and B.G. Blount (eds) *Sociocultural dimensions of language use*, pp. 57–79. New York: Academic Press.

Sacks, H. 1992. *Lectures on conversation*. Volumes I and II. Ed. G. Jefferson, with an introduction by E.A. Schegloff. Oxford: Blackwell.

Sacks, H., E.A. Schegloff and G. Jefferson. 1974. 'A simplest systematics for the organization of turn-taking for conversation'. *Language* 50: 696–735.

Saeed, J.I. 1997. *Semantics*. Oxford: Blackwell.

Sajavaara, K. and J. Lehtonen. 1997. 'The silent Finn revisited', in A. Jaworski (ed.) *Silence: interdisciplinary perspectives*, pp. 263–83. Berlin and New York: Walter de Gruyter.

Schegloff, E.A. 1972. 'Notes on a conversational practice. Formulating place', in D. Sudnow (ed.) *Studies in social interaction*, pp. 75–119. New York: Free Press.

Schegloff, E.A. 1979. 'The relevance of repair to syntax-for-conversation', in T. Givon (ed.) *Syntax and semantics 12: discourse and syntax*, pp. 261–88. New York: Academic Press.

Schegloff, E.A. 1986. 'The routine as achievement'. *Human Studies* 9: 111–51.

Schegloff, E.A. 1996. 'Turn organization: one intersection of grammar and interaction', in E. Ochs, E.A. Schegloff and S.A. Thompson (eds) *Interaction and grammar*, pp. 52–133. Cambridge: Cambridge University Press.

Schegloff, E.A. 1999. 'Discourse, pragmatics, conversation analysis'. *Discourse Studies* 1(4): 405–35.

Schegloff, E.A. and H. Sacks. 1973. 'Opening up closings'. *Semiotica* 7: 289–327.

Scherer, K. 1979. 'Personality markers in speech', in K. Scherer and H. Giles (eds) *Social markers in speech*, pp. 147–201. Cambridge: Cambridge University Press.

Scherer, K.R. 2000. 'A cross-cultural investigation of emotion inferences from voice and speech: implications for speech technology', in *ICSLP-2000*, vol. 2, pp. 379–82.

Schiffrin, D. 1987. *Discourse markers*. Cambridge: Cambridge University Press.

Schneider, K. and A. Barron (eds). 2008. *Variational pragmatics: a focus on regional variation in pluricentric languages*. Amsterdam and Philadelphia: John Benjamins.

Schnurr, S. 2010. 'Humour', in M.A. Locher and S.L. Graham (eds) *Interpersonal pragmatics*, pp. 307–26. Berlin and New York: Walter de Gruyter.

Schnurr, S. and C. Rowe. 2008. 'The "dark side" of humour. An analysis of subversive humour in workplace emails'. *Lodz Papers in Pragmatics* 4(1): 109–30.

Schourup, L. 1985. *Common discourse particles in English conversation*. New York and London: Garland Publishing.

Scollon, R. and S.W. Scollon. 2001 (2nd edition [1st edition 1995]). *Intercultural communication: a discourse approach*. Oxford: Blackwell.

Searle, J.R. 1969. *Speech acts*. Cambridge: Cambridge University Press.

Searle, J.R. 1975. 'Indirect speech acts', in P. Cole and J.L. Morgan (eds) *Syntax and semantics: speech acts*, vol. 3, pp. 59–82. New York: Academic Press.

Searle, J.R. 1976. 'A classification of illocutionary acts'. *Language in Society* 5: 1–23.

Searle, J.R. 1978. 'Literal meaning'. *Erkenntnis* 13: 207–24.

Seedhouse, P. 2005. *The interactional architecture of the language classroom: a conversation analysis perspective*. Oxford: Blackwell.

Seidlhofer, B. 2001. 'Closing a conceptual gap: the case for a description of English as a lingua franca'. *International Journal of Applied Linguistics* 11(2): 133–58.

Seidlhofer, B. 2005. 'English as a lingua franca'. *ELT Journal* 59(4): 339–41.

Semino, E. 2008. *Metaphor in discourse*. Cambridge: Cambridge University Press.

Seuren, P.A.M. 1995. *Western linguistics: an historical introduction*. Oxford: Blackwell.

Shoemaker, R. 1998. *Gender in English society, 1650–1850*. London and New York: Longman.

Shriberg, E., A. Stolcke, D. Jurafsky, N. Coccaro, M. Meteer, R. Bates, P. Taylor, K. Ries, R. Martin and C. van Ess-Dykema. 1998. 'Can prosody aid the automatic classification of dialog acts?' *Language and Speech* 41(3–4): 443–92.

Shuter, R. 1976. 'Proxemics and tactility in Latin America'. *Journal of Communication* 26: 46–52.

Siewierska, A. 2004. *Person*. Cambridge: Cambridge University Press.

Sifianou. M. 2002. 'On the telephone again! Telephone conversation openings in Greek', in K.K. Luke and T.-S. Pavlidou (eds) *Telephone calls: unity and diversity in conversational structure across languages and cultures*, pp. 49–85. Amsterdam and Philadelphia: John Benjamins.

Simmons-Mackie, N.N. and J.S. Damico. 1996. 'The contribution of discourse markers to communicative competence in aphasia'. *American Journal of Speech-Language Pathology* 5: 37–43.

Simpson, P. and A. Mayr. 2010. *Language and power: a resource book for students*. London and New York: Routledge.

Sinclair, J. McH. 1991. *Corpus, concordance, collocation*. Oxford: Oxford University Press.

Sinclair, J. McH. and M. Coulthard. 1975. *Towards an analysis of discourse. The English used by teachers and pupils*. Oxford: Oxford University Press.

Spencer-Oatey, H. 2000. *Culturally speaking – managing rapport through talk across cultures*. London: Continuum.

Spencer-Oatey, H. 2002. 'Managing rapport in talk: using rapport sensitive incidents to explore the motivational concerns underlying the management of relations'. *Journal of Pragmatics* 34: 529–45.

Spencer-Oatey, H. and W. Jiang. 2003. 'Explaining cross-cultural pragmatic findings: moving from politeness maxims to sociopragmatic interactional principles (SIPs)'. *Journal of Pragmatics* 35: 1633–50.

Sperber, D. and Wilson, D. [1986] 1995. *Relevance: communication and cognition*. Oxford: Blackwell.

Sperber, D. and Wilson, D. 2002. 'Pragmatics, modularity and mindreading'. *Mind and Language* 17: 3–23.

Stalnaker, R. 1974. 'Pragmatic presuppositions', in M.K. Monitz and P.K. Unger (eds) *Semantics and philosophy*, pp. 197–214. New York: New York University Press.

Stein, D. 1992. *Cooperating with written texts: the pragmatics and comprehension of written texts*. Berlin and New York: Mouton de Gruyter.

Stenström, A.-B. 1984. *Questions and responses in English conversation*. Malmö: Gleerup.

Stenström, A.-B. 1994. *An introduction to spoken interaction*. London and New York: Longman.

Stetter, C. 1991. 'Text und Struktur: hat die Sprechakttheorie eine historische Dimension?', in D. Busse (ed.) *Diachrone Semantik und Pragmatik: Untersuchungen zur Erklärung und Beschreibung des Sprachwandels*, pp. 67–81. Tübingen: Max Niemeyer Verlag.

Stubbs, M. 1983. *Discourse analysis*. Oxford: Blackwell.

Suchman, L. 1987. *Plans and situated actions*. Cambridge: Cambridge University Press.

Surtees Society. 1845. *Depositions and other ecclesiastical proceedings from the courts of Durham extending from 1311 to the reign of Elizabeth*. Ed. J. Raine. Publications of the Surtees Society, vol. 21. London and Edinburgh.

Svartvik, J. (ed.). 1990. *The London Lund Corpus of spoken English: description and research*. Lund: Lund University Press.

Taavitsainen, I. and A.H. Jucker. 2007. *Methods in historical pragmatics*. Berlin: Mouton de Gruyter.

Taavitsainen, I. and A.H. Jucker. 2008a. 'Speech acts now and then: towards a pragmatic history of English', in A.H. Jucker and I. Taavitsainen (eds) *Speech acts in the history of English*, pp. 1–23. Amsterdam and Philadelphia: John Benjamins.

Taavitsainen, I. and A.H. Jucker. 2008b. '"Methinks you seem more beautiful than ever." Compliments and gender in the history of English', in A.H. Jucker and I. Taavitsainen (eds) *Speech acts in the history of English*, pp. 195–228. Amsterdam and Philadelphia: John Benjamins.

Taavitsainen, I. and A.H. Jucker. 2010. 'Trends and developments in historical pragmatics', in A.H. Jucker and I. Taavitsainen (eds) *Historical pragmatics*, pp. 3–30. Berlin and New York: Mouton de Gruyter.

Tannen, D. 1981. 'New York Jewish conversational style'. *International Journal of Sociology of Language* 30: 133–49.

Tannen, D. 1984. *Conversational style: analyzing talk among friends.* Norwood, NJ: Ablex.

Tannen, D. 1986. *That's not what I meant: how conversational style makes or breaks relations with others.* London: Virago Press.

Tannen, D. 1990. *You just don't understand. Women and men in conversation.* New York: Ballatine Books.

Tannen, D. (ed.). 1993. *Framing in discourse.* Oxford: Oxford University Press.

Tannen, D. 1994. *Talking from 9 to 5: how women's and men's conversational styles affect who gets heard, who gets credit, and what gets done at work.* London: W. Morrow.

Tannen, D. 1999. 'New York Jewish conversational style', in A. Jaworski and N. Coupland (eds) *The discourse reader*, pp. 459–73. London: Routledge.

Taylor, K. 2010. 'Contextualism', in L. Cummings (ed.) *The pragmatics encyclopedia*, pp. 75–9, London and New York: Routledge.

Taylor, P. and P. Bain. 2003. '"Subterranean worksick blues": humour as subversion in two call centres'. *Organization Studies* 24(9): 1487–509.

Terkourafi, M. 2008. 'Toward a unified theory of politeness, impoliteness, and rudeness', in D. Bousfield and M.A. Locher (eds) *Impoliteness in language: studies on its interplay with power in theory and practice*, pp. 45–75. Berlin and New York: Mouton de Gruyter.

Thomas, J. 1983. 'Cross-cultural pragmatic failure'. *Applied Linguistics* 4: 91–112.

Thomas, J. 1995. *Meaning in interaction: an introduction to pragmatics.* London: Longman.

Thornborrow, J. 2002. *Power talk: language and interaction in institutional discourse.* London: Longman.

Tottie, G. 1989. 'What does *uh-(h)uh* mean? American English vocalisations and the Swedish learner', in B. Odenstedt and G. Persson (eds) *Instead of flowers*, pp. 269–81. Festschrift for Mats Ryden. University of Umeå.

Tiersma, P.M. 2000. *Legal language.* London: University of Chicago Press.

Traugott, E.C. 1982. 'From propositional to textual and expressive meanings: some semantic-pragmatic aspects of grammaticalization', in W.P. Lehmann and Y. Malkiel (eds) *Perspectives on historical linguistics*, pp. 245–71. Amsterdam: John Benjamins.

Traugott, E.C. 1989. 'On the rise of epistemic meanings in English: an example of sub-jectification in semantic change'. *Language* 57: 33–65.

Traugott, E.C. 1995. 'Subjectification in grammaticalization', in D. Stein and S. Wright (eds) *Subjectivity and subjectivisation: linguistic perspectives*, pp. 31–54. Cambridge: Cambridge University Press.

Traugott, E.C. 1999. 'The role of pragmatics in semantic change', in J. Verschueren (ed.) *Pragmatics in 1998: selected papers from the sixth International Pragmatics Conference*, vol. 2. Antwerp, Belgium: International Pragmatics Association (IPrA).

Traugott, E.C. 2003. 'From subjectification to inter-subjectification', in R. Hickey (ed.) *Motives for language change*, pp. 124–39. Cambridge: Cambridge University Press.

Traugott, E.C. 2010. 'Grammaticalization', in A.H. Jucker and I. Taavitsainen (eds) *Historical pragmatics*, pp. 97–126. Berlin and New York: Mouton de Gruyter.

Traugott, E.C. and R.B. Dasher. 2002. *Regularity in semantic change.* Cambridge: Cambridge University Press.

Trosborg, A. 1995. *Interlanguage pragmatics. Requests, complaints and apologies.* The Hague: Mouton de Gruyter.

Tsui, A.B.M. 1991. 'The pragmatic functions of "I don't know"'. *TEXT* 11(4): 607–22.

Tsui, A.B.M. 1994. *English conversation.* Oxford: Oxford University Press.

Uldall E. 1964. 'Dimensions of meaning in intonation', in D. Abercrombie, D.B. Fry, P.A. MacCarthy, N. Scott and J.L. Trim (eds) *In honour of Daniel Jones: papers contributed on the occasion of his eightieth birthday*, pp. 271–79. London: Longman. Reprinted in Bolinger 1972: 250–9.

Valkonen, P. 2008. 'Showing a little promise: identifying and retrieving explicit illocutionary acts from a corpus of written prose', in A.H. Jucker and I. Taavitsainen (eds) *Speech acts and the history of English*, pp. 247–72. Amsterdam and Philadelphia: John Benjamins.

Van Bezooijen, R. 1993. 'Verschillen in toonhoogte: Natuur of cultuur?' *Gramma/TTT* 2: 165–79.

Van Bezooijen, R. 1995. 'Sociocultural aspects of pitch differences between Japanese and Dutch women'. *Language and Speech* 38(3): 253–65.

Van der Henst, J.-B. and D. Sperber. 2004. 'Testing the cognitive and communicative principles of relevance', in I.A. Noveck and D. Sperber (eds) *Experimental pragmatics*, pp. 141–71. Basingstoke: Palgrave Macmillan.

Van der Henst, J.-B., L. Carles and D. Sperber. 2002. 'Truthfulness and relevance in telling the time'. *Mind and Language* 17: 457–66.

Van Dijk, T. 1972. *Some aspects of text grammars*. The Hague: Mouton de Gruyter.

Van Dijk, T. 1992a. 'Analyzing racism through discourse analysis. Some methodological reflections', in J.H. Stanfield and R.M. Dennis (eds) *Race and ethnicity in research methods*, pp. 92–134. Newbury Park, CA: Sage, 1993.

Van Dijk, T. 1992b. 'Discourse and the denial of racism'. *Discourse and Society* 3(1): 87–118.

Van Dijk, T. 2006. 'Discourse, context and cognition'. *Discourse Studies* 8(1): 159–77.

Verschueren, J. 1999. *Understanding pragmatics*. London: Edward Arnold.

Vine, B. 2004. *Getting things done at work: the discourse of power in workplace interaction*. Amsterdam and Philadelphia: John Benjamins.

Vine, B. 2010. 'International issues in the workplace', in M.A. Locher and S.L. Graham (eds) *Interpersonal pragmatics*, pp. 329–52. Berlin and New York: Walter de Gruyter.

Vine, B., S. Kell, M. Marra and J. Holmes. 2009. 'Institutional, gender and ethnic demarcation in the workplace', in N.R. Norrick and D. Chiaro (eds) *Humor in interaction*, pp. 94–139. Amsterdam and Philadelphia: John Benjamins.

Vuchinich, S. 1990. 'The sequential organization of closing in verbal family conflict', in A.D. Grimshaw (ed.) *Conflict talk: sociolinguistic investigations of arguments and conversations*, pp. 118–38. Cambridge: Cambridge University Press.

Walker, T., J. Local and G. Walker. 2006. 'Repetition and the prosody-pragmatics interface'. *Journal of Pragmatics* 38: 1721–51.

Watson, O.M. 1970. *Proxemic behaviour: a cross-cultural study*. The Hague: Mouton de Gruyter.

Watts, R. 2003. *Politeness*. Cambridge: Cambridge University Press.

Wells, J. 2006. *English intonation*. Cambridge: Cambridge University Press.

Wharton, T. 2009. *Pragmatics and non-verbal communication*. Cambridge: Cambridge University Press.

Wharton, T. 2010. 'H.P. Grice', in L. Cummings (ed.) *The pragmatics encyclopedia*, pp. 182–3. London and New York: Routledge.

Wichmann, A. 2000. *Intonation in text and discourse*. London: Longman.

Wichmann, A. 2004. 'The intonation of *please*-requests: a corpus-based study'. *Journal of Pragmatics* 36: 1521–49.

Wichmann, A. 2005. '*Please* – from courtesy to appeal: the role of intonation in the expression of attitudinal meaning'. *English Language and Linguistics* 9(2): 229–53.

Wichmann, A. and J. Caspers. 2001. 'Melodic cues to turntaking in English: evidence from perception', in J. van Kuppevelt and R. Smith (eds) *Proceedings, 2nd SIGdial Workshop on discourse and dialogue*. Aalborg, Denmark, 1–2 September.

Wichmann, A., A.-M. Simon-Vandenbergen and K. Aijmer. 2010. 'How prosody reflects semantic change: a synchronic case study of *of course*', in H. Cuyckens, K. Davidse and L. Vandelanotte (eds) *Subjectification, intersubjectification and grammaticalization*, pp. 103–54. Berlin: Mouton de Gruyter.

Wierzbicka, A. [1991] 2003. *Cross-cultural pragmatics. The semantics of human interaction.* Berlin: Mouton de Gruyter.

Wilcox, J.M. and A.G. Davis. 2005. 'Speech act analysis of aphasic communication in individual and group settings'. *Aphasiology* 19(7): 683–90.

Wilkinson, R. 1995. 'Aphasia: conversation analysis of a non-fluent aphasic person', in M. Perkins and S. Howard (eds) *Case studies in clinical linguistics*, pp. 271–92. London: Whurr.

Willing, K. 1992. *Talking it through: clarification and problem-solving in professional work.* Sydney: Macquaire University.

Wilson, D. 1975. *Presuppositions and non-truth-conditional semantics.* London: Academic Press.

Wilson, D. 2010. 'Relevance Theory', in L. Cummings (ed.) *The pragmatics encyclopedia*, pp. 393–7. London and New York: Routledge.

Wilson, D. and D. Sperber. 1981. 'On Grice's theory of conversation', in P. Werth (ed.) *Conversation and discourse*, pp. 155–78. London: Croom Helm. [Reprinted in A. Kasher (ed.). 1998. *Pragmatics: critical concepts*, vol. II, pp. 347–67. London: Routledge.]

Wilson, D. and D. Sperber. 2002. 'Truthfulness and relevance'. *Mind and Language* 111: 583–632.

Wilson, D. and T. Wharton. 2006. 'Relevance and prosody'. *Journal of Pragmatics* 38(10): 1559–79.

Wodak, R. 2007. 'Pragmatics and Critical Discourse Analysis: a cross-disciplinary enquiry'. *Pragmatics and Cognition* 15(1): 203–25.

Wolfson, N. 1989. 'The social dynamics of native and non-native variation in complimenting behavior', in M. Eisenstein (ed.) *The dynamic interlanguage: empirical studies in second language variation*, pp. 219–36. New York: Plenum Press.

Wooffitt, R. 2005. *Conversation analysis and discourse analysis. A comparative and critical introduction.* London: Sage.

Wright, L.A. 1999. 'Aspects of turn-taking in deaf-hearing conversation'. Unpublished MA dissertation. University of Central Lancashire, UK.

Yohena, S.-O. 2003. 'Ellipsis in Japanese couples' conversations', in L. Thiesmeyer (ed.) *Discourse and silencing*, pp. 79–111. Amsterdam and Philadelphia: John Benjamins.

Yuan, Y. 2001. 'An enquiry into empirical pragmatics data-gathering methods: written DCTs, oral DCTs, field notes, and natural conversations'. *Journal of Pragmatics* 33: 271–92.

Yule, G. [1996] 2006. *Pragmatics.* Oxford: Oxford University Press.

Zamborlin, C. 2007. 'Going beyond pragmatic failure: dissonance in intercultural communication'. *Intercultural Pragmatics* 4(1): 21–50.

Zipf, G.K. 1949. *Human behavior and the Principle of Least Effort: an introduction to human ecology.* New York: Hafner.

Zwicky, A. and J. Sadock. 1975. 'Ambiguity tests and how to fail them', in J.P. Kimball (ed.) *Syntax and semantics*, vol. 4, pp. 1–36. New York: Academic Press.

Index

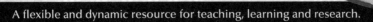